The Science of Social Influence

Advances and Future Progress

Edited by
Anthony R. Pratkanis

Ψ Psychology Press
Taylor & Francis Group

NEW YORK AND HOVE

Published in 2007
by Psychology Press
270 Madison Avenue
New York, NY 10016
www.psypress.com

Published in Great Britain
by Psychology Press
27 Church Road
Hove, East Sussex BN3 2FA
www.psypress.com

Psychology Press is an imprint of the Taylor & Francis Group, an informa business

Typeset by RefineCatch Limited, Bungay, Suffolk, UK
Printed in the USA by Edwards Brothers, Inc. on acid-free paper
Cover design by Lisa Dynan

10 9 8 7 6 5 4 3 2 1

Library of Congress Cataloging in Publication Data
The science of social influence : advances and future progress / edited by Anthony R. Pratkanis.
    p. cm. – (Frontiers of social psychology)
   Includes bibliographical references and index.
   ISBN 978-1-84169-426-9 (hardcover : alk. paper)   1. Social influence—Research.
I. Pratkanis, Anthony R.
  HM1176.S35 2007
  302'.13—dc22

                                               2007008423

ISBN: 978-1-84169-426-9 (hbk)

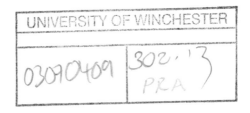

The Science of Social Influence

FRONTIERS OF SOCIAL PSYCHOLOGY

Series Editors:
Arie W. Kruglanski, *University of Maryland at College Park*
Joseph P. Forgas, *University of New South Wales*

Frontiers of Social Psychology is a series of domain-specific handbooks. The purpose of each volume is to provide readers with a cutting-edge overview of the most recent theoretical, methodological, and practical developments in a substantive area of social psychology, in greater depth than is possible in general social psychology handbooks. The editors and contributors are all internationally renowned scholars, whose work is at the cutting edge of research.

Scholarly, yet accessible, the volumes in the *Frontiers* series are an essential resource for senior undergraduates, postgraduates, researchers, and practitioners, and are suitable as texts in advanced courses in specific sub-areas of social psychology.

Published titles

Negotiation Theory and Research, Thompson
Close Relationships, Noller & Feeney
Evolution and Social Psychology, Schaller, Simpson, & Kenrick
Affect in Social Thinking and Behavior, Forgas
Social Psychology and the Unconscious, Bargh
Social Communication, Fiedler

Forthcoming titles

The Self, Sedikides & Spencer
Personality and Social Behavior, Rhodewalt
Explorations in Political Psychology, Krosnick & Chiang
Culture and Social Psychology, Chiu & Mallorie
Social Cognition, Strack & Förster

For continually updated information about published and forthcoming titles in the *Frontiers of Social Psychology* series, please visit: **www.psypress.com/frontiers**

Contents

About the Editor

Anthony R. Pratkanis earned his Ph.D. in 1984 from the famed social psychology program at the Ohio State University. His research program has investigated such topics as the delayed effects of persuasion, attitudes and memory, groupthink, affirmative action, subliminal persuasion, mass communications, source credibility, persuasion and democracy, economic fraud, the use of influence in international conflicts, and a variety of influence tactics such as the pique technique, phantoms, the projection tactic, the 1-in-5 prize tactic, and altercasting.

He has appeared in the mass media over 500 times as an expert on social influence processes, has been called as an expert witness in numerous advertising deceptiveness cases, and served as a consultant to AARP, NASD, and other law enforcement and civic groups on countering the undue influence used in fraud crimes and to the United States military on countering the propaganda of terrorists and dictators.

He is the co-author (with Elliot Aronson) of *Age of Propaganda: The Everyday Use and Abuse of Persuasion* and (with Doug Shadel) of *Weapons of Fraud: A Source Book for Fraud Fighters*.

Anthony Pratkanis is the founding editor of *Social Influence*, a new scientific journal from Psychology Press.

Contributors

Elliot Aronson
Emeritus Professor of Psychology
University of California in Santa Cruz
Santa Cruz, CA, USA

Prashant Bordia
School of Management
University of South Australia
Adelaide, South Australia, Australia

Jerry M. Burger
Department of Psychology
Santa Clara University
Santa Clara, CA, USA

Robert B. Cialdini
Regent's Professor of Psychology
Arizona State University
Tempe, AZ, USA

Carsten K. W. De Dreu
Professor of Work and Organizational
    Psychology
Department of Psychology
University of Amsterdam
Amsterdam, The Netherlands

Nicholas DiFonzo
Department of Psychology
Rochester Institute of Technology
Rochester, NY, USA

Dariusz Dolinski
Professor and Dean of Wrocław
    Campus
Warsaw School of Social Psychology
Wrocław, Poland

Noah J. Goldstein
Department of Psychology
Arizona State University
Tempe, AZ, USA

Eric S. Knowles
Department of Psychology
University of Arkansas
Fayetteville, AR, USA

Roderick M. Kramer
William R. Kimball Professor of
    Organizational Behavior
Stanford Graduate School of Business
Stanford, CA, USA

Geoff MacDonald
Department of Psychology
University of Toronto
Toronto, ON, Canada

Paul R. Nail
Department of Psychology and
    Counseling
University of Central Arkansas
Conway, AR, USA

Anthony R. Pratkanis
Department of Psychology
University of California
Santa Cruz, CA, USA

Dan D Riner
Department of Psychology
University of Arkansas
Fayetteville, AR, USA

Brad J. Sagarin
Department of Psychology
Northern Illinois University
DeKalb, IL, USA

Christina K. Struckman
University of San Francisco
San Francisco, CA, USA

Marlene E. Turner
Department of Organization and
    Management
San Jose State University
San Jose, CA, USA

Sarah E. Wood
Department of Psychology
University of Wisconsin-Stout
Menomonie, WI, USA

1

An Invitation to Social Influence Research

ANTHONY R. PRATKANIS

*D*o you ever wonder why people do things? For example, why, all of a sudden, is everyone wearing the same purple shirt or the same hairstyle or using the same cool, groovy, or is it spot-on jargon to describe what they like and agree with? How can a group of people watch someone else commit acts of violence on another human being and not intervene? How can a person be urged on to commit such acts of violence in the first place? Why does a seemingly normal person give his or her money to a con criminal? What happens to get us to purchase things on the used car lot or the cosmetic counter or the infomercial, among other places? How can a leader of a nation move us to accomplish great things? What social forces cause groups and leaders to make brilliant decisions one minute, and bad choices with disastrous consequences the next? How does a small group (and sometimes just one person) come to change the behavior and folkways of an entire community, nation, or world? And, perhaps most importantly, how can we resist unwanted and undesirable social influence attempts?

If you find yourself pondering such things, then you have come to the right place. You wonder about the same things as the authors of the chapters of this book. The purpose of this book is to introduce you to the science of social influence – a science that addresses the issue of how and why people change the thoughts, feelings, and behavior of other people through such processes as conformity, persuasion and attitude change, compliance, and yielding to social forces. Our goal is to have you join us in this science of social influence and conduct your own research into the question of why and how we humans do what we do.

In this book, you will find chapters designed to introduce you to the literature of social influence. In each chapter, you will discover what sorts of research scientists have conducted on a social influence topic along with current theorizing and the next set of questions that remain to be answered. The book begins with two chapters that present a review of social influence tactics that scientists have studied to date. In Chapter 2, I review 107 different experimentally tested social influence tactics along with 18 techniques for increasing credibility and attraction.

In Chapter 3, Eric Knowles and Dan Riner present their Omega approaches for overcoming resistance to influence. The next chapter (by Elliot Aronson) switches gears and looks at perhaps the single most important theory for generating novel predictions about social influence and for understanding its more counterintuitive nature – cognitive dissonance theory.

The next set of three chapters looks at specific social influence tactics in detail, including the emotional see-saw (in Chapter 5 by Dariusz Dolinski), fleeting attraction (in Chapter 6 by Jerry Burger), and norms (in Chapter 7 by Noah Goldstein and Robert Cialdini). These chapters provide a tutorial on how to conduct a program of research to investigate social influence techniques. In Chapter 8, Paul Nail and Geoff MacDonald take a closer look at conformity pro-cesses by presenting their model for understanding social responses to group pressure. Chapter 9 continues the theme of group pressure as Marlene Turner, Christina Struckman, and I look at a classic conformity effect – Janis's groupthink – through a new lens of social identity maintenance. In Chapter 10, Carsten De Dreu reverses our perspective and addresses the issue of when the few (minority dissent) will change the beliefs and performance of the many. The process by which influence spreads in a community is the topic of Nicholas DiFonzo and Prashant Bordia's Chapter 11 as they develop a dynamic social impact theory of rumor. In Chapter 12, Rod Kramer addresses a novel area of social influence research – how do leaders think about influence and, more importantly, why do they fail to use power in an effective manner? Finally, Brad Sagarin and Sarah Wood close out the volume by reviewing the literature on when and how people resist influence.

The chapters in this volume provide a great introduction to recent research on social influence. The goal of the present chapter is to complete this introduction by providing a broad overview of the tools you need to get started as a social influence researcher. Specifically, I will review the history of research on social influence, look at the nature of explanation in social influence research along with research methods and strategies, and then describe how you can find out more about this topic.

A BRIEF HISTORY OF SOCIAL INFLUENCE RESEARCH, 1895–1984

Although humans have always pondered why they do things, we can date the birth of the scientific exploration of social influence to two events in the late 19th century. In 1895 Gustave Le Bon published *Psychologie des foules*, which is often translated as *The crowd*. In this book, Le Bon provides a theory of behavior in groups based on the concept of a group mind – that individuals placed within the anonymity and invincibility of a crowd would display their unconscious per-sonality and merge with the group to perform savage behaviors. The metaphor for Le Bon's theory was hypnosis – the notion that the crowd took over the will of the person much like the suggestions of a hypnotist command the unconscious of the hypnotized. Le Bon wasn't the first to promote these ideas (indeed, he "borrowed" heavily from the Italian Scipio Sighele), but his popularization of the concept of group mind provided a theoretical framework used before the First World War for elucidating social influence as well as serving as a foil for later research (see van Ginneken, 1992; McPhail, 1991 for excellent histories of this idea).

The second major event of this period was the first experiment to investigate social influence processes. In 1898 Norman Triplett published an article looking at archival data on the performance of bicyclists in groups and alone. He then conducted an experiment manipulating the presence of others, and showed that when other people were watching an individual would turn a fishing crank faster. Triplett's work opened up a line of research on social facilitation but perhaps more importantly introduced the experimental method as a viable means to study influence.

The First World War changed the trajectory of social influence research. In the United States and Britain, the war was marked by a period of patriotism; after the war, many citizens became disillusioned by the results and came to feel that they had been duped by propaganda. The *Zeitgeist* of the times encouraged the belief that social influence and mass propaganda was all-powerful (based on either suggestion theories from psychoanalysis or behaviorism's belief in malleable human behavior). Researchers and scholars began documenting this belief as well as attempting to find ways to inoculate citizens from propaganda. Social influence research during the interwar period featured (a) case and descriptive analyses of propaganda, particularly war propaganda (e.g., Lasswell, 1927) and the influence of demagogues (e.g., Lee, 1939), (b) use of the experimental method to document that "persuasion" happens, (c) the development of survey research procedures and techniques to measure attitudes by L. L. Thurstone and others (to assess the state of society as it responds to propaganda), and (d) field studies of the effects of mass media such as the Payne Studies. In the 1930s, a group of scholars formed the Institute for Propaganda Analysis with the expressed goal of teaching Americans about propaganda (see Chapter 13 of this volume for a modern equivalent). Running counter to this trend was the investigation of the use of influence among those who needed to be able to persuade others. Specifically, research on advertising during this time was marked by the use of learning theory to understand how to improve the effectiveness of an ad, and research on influence in organizations saw the rise of self-help books providing leaders with tips on how to persuade (e.g., Webb & Morgan, 1930).

Two experiments conducted during the interwar period would later have enormous impact on the course of social influence research. In 1935, Muzafer Sherif published the results of his doctoral dissertation in which groups of people judged the autokinetic effect (an illusion that a light moves when placed against a dark background). His results showed that groups quickly developed norms for making these judgments and that these norms would guide subsequent judgments. His research was significant because it (a) provided one of the two major alternative theories to the group mind in terms of emergent norms (the other major alternative was Floyd Allport's response amplification theory) and (b) created major lines of research on norms (such as Newcomb's 1943 Bennington studies; see Chapter 7 of this volume) and on the power of the situation (see Chapter 8 of this volume).

In 1939, Kurt Lewin – a recent immigrant to the United States as a result of fleeing the Nazi regime – along with his students Lippitt and White began publishing their work on the effects of democracy and autocracy (summarized in White & Lippitt, 1960). The results showed that democratic leadership resulted in more creative productivity than autocratic regimes, among other findings. The experiments are significant for a number of reasons, including demonstrating (a) that the experimental method can be applied to complex social influence phenomena, and (b) the fruitfulness of field theory (how people construe their social world and the resulting tension states) as a meta-theory for producing research hypotheses. Perhaps more significantly, Kurt Lewin would go on to train the first generation of experimentalists looking directly at social influence processes.

Like the First World War, the Second World War changed the trajectory of social influence research. As part of the war effort many scholars became deeply involved in social influence research, including Carl Hovland's work on mass communications, Kurt Lewin's research on changing food habits, Irving Janis's study of the stress effects of air bombing (Janis would later introduce the term "groupthink"), Leonard Doob's study of Nazi propaganda, and Gordon Allport and Leo Postman's research on controlling rumors. After the war, these researchers returned to their universities and began (along with their students) to study social influence phenomena such as conformity, mass communications, prejudice, power, and obedience to authority that had been at the heart of the war. The result was a flourishing of exciting social influence research from a variety of perspectives and on a range of topics. I shall briefly summarize six areas of research that capture the nature of research during the post-war period.

1. *Mass communications.* After the Second World War, two lines of research converged to challenge the view of "all-powerful propaganda of the mass media" popular during the interwar period (see Pratkanis, 1997 for more details). At Yale University, Carl Hovland conducted a program of experimental research (known as the Yale School) investigating the effects of various variables (e.g., source credibility, individual differences, organization of the message) on persuasion. The results, published in a series of monographs, showed weak effects of these variables on social influence. Survey researchers were finding similar minimum effects. For example, in *The people's choice*, Lazarsfeld, Berelson, and Gaudet (1948) found that during the 1940 Presidential campaign few voters changed their voting preferences as a result of mass media content. The resulting model of influence was termed "minimum effects" and posited that persuasion was the result of a series of steps (attention to the message, comprehension, learning, yielding, and behavior), each with a decreasing probability of occurring. A summary of this research can be found in McGuire's (1969) seminal *Handbook* chapter.

In 1968, Tony Greenwald amended the learning model of persuasion and replaced the intervening steps with one core process – cognitive response. The resulting approach to persuasion – known as the Ohio State School – states that influence is the result of the thoughts running through a person's head as he or she processes a persuasive communication. In this case, the power of the mass media is dependent on its ability to change cognitive responses, resulting in a model in which the mass media is capable of producing a range of effects depending on the reception of its content. Subsequent research has focused on the question "What determines a person's cognitive response to the message?", with one of the most comprehensive answers provided by the elaboration likelihood model (ELM) of Petty and Cacioppo (1986). The cognitive response approach along with the ELM have become the dominant model for understanding advertising and mass media effects.

2. *Cognitive dissonance.* In 1957, Leon Festinger published a book that followed up on Kurt Lewin's (Festinger's Ph.D. advisor) notion that tension states motivate behavior. In *A theory of cognitive dissonance*, Festinger puts forth a deceptively simple thesis (that two conflicting thoughts create a tension state that needs to be reduced), which stimulated a wealth of interesting research hypotheses and experiments. In Chapter 4 of this volume, Elliot Aronson describes the fundamentals of this research.

3. *Power.* In the late 1950s and early 1960s, a new theory of power based on dependencies and interdependencies in exchange relationships was put forward (see Emerson, 1962; Thibaut & Kelley, 1959). According to this approach, power is determined by the control of critical resources that another person needs or desires. This approach to power has been very successful in elucidating the nature of influence in and between organizations (see Pfeffer, 1981; Pfeffer & Salancik, 1978).

4. *Research strategy.* In 1966, Freedman and Fraser published an experiment looking at the foot-in-the-door technique for inducing compliance – an initial small request increases compliance with a subsequent large request. While the findings of this experiment are important in their own right (resulting in many follow-up studies), Freedman and Fraser's most important contribution was to provide a model for studying a specific social influence tactic. In this work, a single tactic is identified (foot-in-the-door) and then subsequent research uses experimental techniques to elucidate its underlying causes and the conditions under which it is most and least effective. Chapters 5, 6, and 7 of this volume all follow this paradigmatic model.

5. *Power of the situation.* Perhaps the single most important discovery in the discipline of psychology began by questioning the results of Sherif's (1935) dissertation. In the late 1940s, Solomon Asch believed that the conformity results obtained by Sherif were dependent on the nature of the ambiguous "autokinetic" stimuli employed in the research. Asch reasoned that surely conformity would not occur if a group of people made obviously incorrect judgments of an unambiguous stimulus. In the true spirit of science, Asch promptly designed a set of experiments to prove himself wrong (Asch, 1951). In his studies, Asch had a group of confederates judge the length of lines and clearly provide a wrong answer. Surprisingly, he found that a majority of subjects went along with the group in at least one of the twelve trials. Asch's research resulted in a stream of research looking at when and how people conform to the group (see Blake & Mouton, 1961; Crutchfield, 1955).

In the early 1960s, Stanley Milgram was interested in explaining obedience to authority in terms of personality and culture-based character traits (i.e. "Germans are most obedient" as an explanation for the Holocaust). He believed that Asch's line judgment task had no personal consequences for the subjects and thus was not a full test of conformity. Milgram designed his famed "obedience to authority" procedures to take account of these hypotheses (Milgram, 1974). The results showed that a majority of people were willing to give another person painful shocks when commanded to do so by an authority, and that character and personality did not explain these results. Instead, Milgram demonstrated the power of social situations to control behavior – a finding that has been repeatedly demonstrated in studies such as Latané and Darley's bystander apathy research and Zimbardo's Stanford prison study.

6. *Cialdini (1984)*. In 1984, Bob Cialdini published *Influence*. This seminal work summarized past social influence research in terms of six core influence principles. More importantly, it served as an inspiration for a new generation of social influence researchers. In no uncertain terms, Cialdini showed that complex influence processes can be understood in terms of basic principles and that these principles can be powerful in understanding and changing the social world. In his empirical work, Cialdini has shown that seemingly intractable social influence processes can be untangled and made sense of through the careful application of the experimental method. I end my brief history of social influence research with the publication of Cialdini's book, as many of the chapters in this book pick up on the themes and approaches popularized in his volume.

Major milestones in social influence research are set out in Table 1.1.

WHAT IS AN EXPLANATION OF INFLUENCE?

One of the most important findings to come out of research on social influence is that situations are more powerful in controlling our behavior than we normally think (Ross & Nisbett, 1991). To account for this state of affairs, Lee Ross (1977) coined the term "fundamental attribution error" for the tendency to over-emphasize dispositional explanations for behaviors observed in others while underemphasizing the role and power of situational influences. Knowledge of the fundamental attribution error and the power of the situation has led social influence researchers to appreciate two important dictums of research, which in turn results in important applied benefits.

First, social influence researchers tend to be wary of explanations that rely heavily on dispositional causes such as "people conform because they are gullible" or "the person obeyed because just the necessary mental thoughts were primed (suggested)." This class of explanation is at least doubly wrongheaded because it (a) is a classic example of the fundamental attribution error that often fails to elucidate the true underlying causes of behavior (see for example, Pratkanis' (2006) description of the failure to find a "gullibility" or "persuasibility" factor to explain influence) and (b) merely names the thing to be explained without explaining it. The use of such explanation is what Gilbert Ryle and B. F. Skinner term a *homunculus* (Latin for "the little man") that supposedly resides inside each person to act in just the way needed to explain the behavior of the person. Without independent verification that the *homunculus* is actually controlling behavior (such as through an experimental analysis), such explanations are tautologies.

TABLE 1.1   Important events in the history of social influence research, 1895–1984

1895	Le Bon borrows extensively from Sighele to author *The crowd* – a treatise that views collective action as a result of a group mind and suggestion.
1898	Triplett conducts the first experimental investigation of social influence, showing that the speed of crank turning is a function of the presence of others.
1925	Lund publishes an experimental analysis of the primacy–recency effect in persuasion – the first experimental manipulation of a persuasive communication.
1935	Sherif demonstrates how norms can impact social judgment.
1939	After fleeing the Nazi regime, Lewin and his students conduct research on the nature of democracy (summarized in 1960 by White & Lippitt); the Lewinian experimental approach comes to dominate social influence research in the postwar period.
1943	Newcomb investigates the influence processes involved in the development of political attitudes at Bennington College.
1947	Allport and Postman report a series of studies on rumors to launch this field of investigation.
1951	Asch publishes the first report of his "line" experiment showing conformity to the group even in the face of objective reality.
1953	Hovland and colleagues publish the first of a series of monographs representing the Yale learning approach to persuasion.
1954	Sherif *et al.* report on the Robbers Cave experiment showing how group identities can create competition and conflict.
1955	Deutsch and Gerard review past conformity research in terms of two fundamental processes: informational and normative.
1957	Festinger publishes *A theory of cognitive dissonance* – perhaps the single most important theory for understanding social influence.
1958	Pettigrew demonstrates the role of norms in prejudice.
1959	Thibaut & Kelley develop a theory of power in groups based on interdependencies.
1962	Emerson present a theory of power based on dependency.
1963	Milgram publishes the first report on his experiments on obedience to authority.
1966	Freedman & Fraser conduct the first foot-in-the-door experiment; this becomes an exemplar of how to do research on influence tactics.
1969	McGuire publishes his *Handbook of social psychology* chapter on attitude change, providing an extended summary of research in the Yale school. Greenwald advances the cognitive response approach of the Ohio State school to account for empirical shortcomings in a learning model.
1970	Latané & Darley publish their monograph on bystander apathy.
1971	Zimbardo conducts the Stanford Prison Experiment (see Zimbardo, 2007).
1972	Janis publishes *Groupthink*.
1978	Aronson and colleagues complete experiments on the jigsaw classroom.
1979	Petty & Cacioppo publish the first of many experiments demonstrating the elaboration likelihood model of persuasion.
1984	Cialdini publishes *Influence* to usher in a new era of social influence research.

Second, social influence researchers are particularly attentive to the *level* at which they explain a given phenomenon. A useful approach is to think in terms of three levels of analysis or explanation (see Pettigrew, 1996, particularly Chapter 6): the *micro* (the individual including personality, biology, cognitions, and emotions), the *meso* (situation, with an emphasis on social relationships; Lewin's field), and the *macro* (social structure including institutions and organizations) levels. Each level has its own processes and properties, and together they add up to more than the sum of the parts (which is one reason why micro explanations either fail or tell an incomplete story). In explaining social influence phenomena, it is helpful to remember that causes can be within levels (e.g., at the micro level fear reduces cognitive capacity; at the meso level see DiFonzo & Bordia's network analysis of rumor) and can span levels (e.g., macro level changes in mass media result in the use of different types of influence tactics at the meso level; a micro level queasiness in the stomach insures norm compliance at the meso level). Thus, a full understanding of a social influence phenomenon requires a clear specification of the causes within and across levels of explanation.

Social influence researchers generally work at the meso level since their phenomenon of interest (how people influence each other) is defined at that level. This results in an enormous practical benefit of social influence research – it is particularly useful for interventions that actually change human behavior. For example, consider a cognitivistic explanation of prejudice as based on the priming of (often unconscious) stereotypes (see for example, Devine, 1989). In such an analysis, there is little that can be done to reduce prejudices other than to hope that the person can control their stereotypes (which is a difficult thing to do given the assumed unconscious nature of cognition). In contrast, a social influence analysis looks at not only micro causes (for example, a person's beliefs), but also such things as the pattern of social relationships at the meso level and economic forces at the macro level that maintain prejudice. Armed with such an analysis, the person seeking to reduce prejudice has a number of options (at all possible levels) for addressing the issue including changing the pattern of social relationships at the meso level. Indeed, one of the most effective means of prejudice reduction – the jigsaw classroom – does exactly that (Aronson, Blaney, Stephan, Sikes, & Snapp, 1978; see Chapter 2 for a brief description).

RESEARCH METHODS

How does a researcher go about clearly specifying the causes of a social influence phenomenon within and across levels of explanation? As can be seen in the chapters in this volume, social influence researchers employ a variety of methods to uncover how and when social influence appeals are effective. Some of these methods are: case studies or the in-depth analysis of a specific influence event (e.g., Turner, Pratkanis, & Struckman on groupthink; DiFonzo & Bordia's rumor cases), use of archival records (e.g., Kramer's exploration of leaders' use of influence), descriptive field studies looking at how influence is used in a particular situation or setting (e.g., Pratkanis & Shadel's (2005) analysis of the influence tactics used by con criminals), participant observation, where a researcher joins a group and reports on the influence patterns (e.g., Festinger, Riecken, & Schachter's 1956 analysis of a doomsday cult), content analysis of influence appeals (e.g., Lasswell, 1927; Schreiber et al., 2006), surveys and questionnaires (e.g., Lazarsfeld, Berelson, & Gaudet, 1948), computer simulations (e.g., DiFonzo & Bordia; Nowak, Szamrej, & Latané, 1990), and correlational studies and quasi-experiments (e.g., Lieberman, 1956). Excellent references on research methods include Campbell and Stanley (1966), Festinger and Katz (1953), Lindzey and Aronson (1968), Rosenthal and Rosnow (1984), Rossi, Wright, and Anderson (1983), Shadish, Cook, & Campbell (2002), Webb, Campbell, Schwartz, and Sechrest (1966), and excellent sources on statistics include Cohen, Cohen, West and Aiken (2002), Pedhazur (1982), Rosenthal and Rosnow (1985), Siegel (1956), and Winer (1971).

You may notice that both lab and field experiments make up the bulk of the research findings presented in this volume. This is for good reason – the experiment is the Cadillac of research methods. In an experiment, subjects are randomly assigned to one of multiple groups in which an experimenter holds everything constant while manipulating one or more independent variables to observe their effects on a dependent variable. Social influence researchers have a particular fondness for experiments that manipulate high-impact variables in experimentally realistic situations (that is, the experimental situation is realistic to the subject as in the Asch, Milgram, and other experiments; see Aronson's chapter for a discussion of the value of this approach). Social influence researchers prefer this sort of research method because they have learned that people are often unable to report on the sources that influence them and the only way to find out about social influence is to actually try to influence someone. More importantly, the experimental method is the only method for teasing apart causal relationships underlying an effect (Sigall & Mills, 1998; see Aronson, Ellsworth, Carlsmith, & Gonzales, 1990 for an excellent tutorial on the experimental method). In instances where an independent variable cannot be manipulated, social influence researchers still apply the logic of the experiment by using a hypothetical–deductive approach in which the researcher raises hypotheses and then looks for naturally occurring cases to support or refute these (see Znaniecki, 1934).

STRATEGIES OF SOCIAL INFLUENCE RESEARCH

Armed with the knowledge gained from this book and with research methods, the next questions become: What should I research and what questions should I ask? Two complementary strategies of research are useful for addressing these questions. Cialdini (1980) describes a full-cycle approach to designing research. In this research strategy, the researcher scouts out the real world looking for interesting social influence phenomena – for example, the conformity of Nazi Germany, the failure of bystanders to help, the low-balling at the sales lot, or even a little child ending her plea for a donation with "even a penny will help." The next step is to bottle that effect in an experiment and to tease it apart to find out if and how it works. Armed with the theoretical knowledge gained from such an exercise, the researcher is then in a better position to make successful applications to real-world problems.

Greenwald, Pratkanis, Leippe, and Baumgardner (1986) recommend a result-centered research strategy designed to identify the conditions under which an effect will occur. They suggest two ways to accomplish this goal. In the *design* approach, a given effect is engineered in the lab or field. This effect could be one identified via Cialdini's scouting procedure or it could be a worthy goal that doesn't occur (often) in the real world (say, prejudice reduction). In engineering the effect, the researcher learns the conditions needed to obtain the results. In a *condition-seeking* approach, the research's goal is to find out when a known effect will and will not occur. The end result of both approaches is a detailed knowledge of how to produce a given effect. Such knowledge can then be used to build strong theories capable of suggesting applications and solutions to real-world problems.

LITERATURE ON THE SCIENCE OF SOCIAL INFLUENCE

After you have read this book, you may be wondering: "How do I find out more about the science of social influence?" One approach, of course, is to identify areas that you find particularly interesting and pursue those topics through the extensive bibliographies associated with each chapter (and then pursuing the bibliographies in each of the new articles you read). However, you may also be interested in getting a broad overview of the field and staying current on recent findings. The literature on social influence is vast and thus can be daunting for a new researcher. In this regard, I can recommend two approaches.

First, to gain an overview of past research on social influence, it is useful to read the major works in the area. Table 1.2 presents a list of a dozen books to get you started in mastering this literature. These books, which are on the shelves of most social influence researchers, run the gamut from major theoretical treatises to empirical monographs to popular books for a general audience.

Second, you will want to stay up on the literature by reading scientific journals. The year 2006 represented a banner year for the science of social influence with the publication of the first scientific journal devoted to this topic – aptly named *Social Influence*. The purpose of this journal is to publish empirical and theoretical articles on all topics related to social influence (for more details, go to http://www.tandf.co.uk/journals/titles/15534510.asp). The significance of this journal is made clear by looking over the reference sections of the chapters in this book. If you do so, you will find that the references are scattered across journals and disciplines, making it difficult for a researcher to stay abreast of the issues. Hopefully, *Social Influence* will address this need.

Historically, social psychology was the primary discipline interested in the topic of social influence and much of the basic research on this topic was published

TABLE 1.2   A dozen books to get you started in social influence research

Author(s)	Title
Robert Cialdini	*Influence*
Leon Festinger, Henry W. Riecken, and Stanley Schachter	*When prophecy fails*
Leon Festinger	*A theory of cognitive dissonance*
Anthony Greenwald, Timothy Brock, and Thomas Ostrom	*Psychological foundations of attitudes*
Carl Hovland, Irving Janis, and Harold Kelley	*Communication and persuasion*
Irving Janis	*Groupthink* (2nd ed.)
Stanley Milgram	*Obedience to authority*
Richard Petty and John Cacioppo	*Communication and persuasion*
Jeffrey Pfeffer	*Power in organizations*
Anthony Pratkanis and Elliot Aronson	*Age of propaganda: The everyday use and abuse of persuasion*
Muzafer Sherif, O. J. Harvey, Jack White, William Hood, and Carolyn Sherif	*Intergroup conflict and cooperation: The Robbers Cave experiment*
Ralph K. White and Ronald Lippitt	*Autocracy and democracy*

in its flagship journals (*Journal of Personality and Social Psychology, Journal of Experimental Social Psychology*, and *Personality and Social Psychology Bulletin*). The discipline of social psychology has given us the core findings of Sherif, Asch, Milgram, and others. However, in recent years, social psychology has pursued a more cognitivistic agenda, with the result that some of the best social influence research in social psychology often appears on the fringes (in places such as *Journal of Applied Social Psychology*). The flagship journals of social psychology remain an excellent archival source of research.

Fortunately, other research disciplines have stepped up to the plate and are taking social influence research away from its parent discipline. These disciplines include marketing and consumer psychology (see particularly *Journal of Consumer Research* and *Journal of Consumer Psychology*), communications (*Human Communication Research, Journal of Communication*, among others), organization science (see *Administrative Science Quarterly, Journal of Applied Psychology*, and *Organizational Behavior and Human Decision Processes*), advertising (*Journal of Advertising* and *Journal of Advertising Research*), negotiation (*Negotiation and Conflict Management Research* and *Negotiation Journal*), and political science (*Political Communication, Political Psychology*, and *Public Opinion Quarterly*). Two recent areas of growth in social influence research have been economics (e.g., Henrich, Boyd, Bowles, Camerer, Fehr, & Gintis, 2004) and animal behavior (e.g., de Waal & Tyack, 2003). In each of these disciplines, the understanding of social influence is pursued within the context of the discipline's core mission, resulting in a tapestry of findings and theories that provide the social influence researcher with an in-depth understanding of the phenomena and a rich source of research hypotheses.

FUTURE ADVANCES IN SOCIAL INFLUENCE RESEARCH

The authors of the chapters of this book take a variety of approaches and perspectives on the issues raised by the scientific study of influence. However, collectively, we endorse three propositions about the future of scientific research in this area.

First, as the chapters in this book make clear, the past 60 years of research on social influence and persuasion has seen some major advances in our understanding of how and why people do things. As in any science, these discoveries raise new and even more interesting questions to pursue and answer with programs of research. The time is ripe for new discoveries and advances.

Second, humans, due in part to the complexity and flexibility of our social influence processes, are one of the most successful species on the planet earth. However, our success as a species has also brought problems. In a speech he was about to give just before his death, Franklin D. Roosevelt was planning to make this point: "If civilization is to survive, we must cultivate the science of human relationships – the ability of all peoples, of all kinds, to live together, in the same world at peace." Roosevelt's words are truer now than ever before as our world faces international conflict with increasingly deadly weapons, ethnic tension and strife, the advent of global climate change, population growth and the subsequent pressures on natural resources, to name just a few concerns. These problems will be solved only by changing human behavior, and that will occur only if we understand how we humans influence each other and then use that knowledge for best results.

Finally, the authors of the chapters of this book believe that the next set of advances in the science of social influence will come, in part, from those individuals who are holding this book in their hands right now.

REFERENCES

Allport, G. W., & Postman, L. J. (1947). *The psychology of rumor*. New York: Holt, Rinehart & Winston.

Aronson, E., Blaney, N., Stephan, C., Sikes, J., & Snapp, M. (1978). *The jigsaw classroom*. Beverly Hills, CA: Sage.

Aronson, E., Ellsworth, P. C., Carlsmith, J. M., & Gonzales, M. H. (1990). *Methods of research in social psychology*. New York: McGraw-Hill.

Asch, S. E. (1951). Effects of group pressure upon modification and distortion of judgment. In H. Guetzkow (Ed.), *Groups, leadership and men* (pp. 177–190). Pittsburgh, PA: Carnegie Press.

Blake, R. R., & Mouton, J. S. (1961). The experimental investigation of interpersonal influence. In A. D. Biderman & H. Zimmer (Eds.), *The manipulation of human behavior* (pp. 216–276). New York: Wiley.

Campbell, D. T., & Stanley, J. C. (1966). *Experimental and quasi-experimental designs for research*. Chicago: Rand McNally.

Cialdini, R. B. (1980). Full-cycle social psychology. In L. Bickman (Ed.), *Applied social psychology* (Vol. 1, pp. 21–47). Beverly Hills, CA: Sage.

Cialdini, R. B. (1984). *Influence: The new psychology of modern persuasion*. New York: Quill.

Cohen, J., Cohen, P., West, S. G., & Aiken, L. S. (2002). *Applied multiple regression correlation analysis for the behavioral sciences* (3rd ed.). Mahwah, NJ: Lawrence Erlbaum Associates, Inc.

Crutchfield, R. S. (1955). Conformity and character. *American Psychologist, 10*, 191–198.

Deutsch, M., & Gerard, H. B. (1955). A study of the normative and informational social influences upon individual judgment. *Journal of Abnormal and Social Psychology, 51*, 629–636.

Devine, P. G. (1989). Stereotypes and prejudice: Their automatic and controlled components. *Journal of Personality and Social Psychology, 56*, 5–18.

de Waal, F. B. M., & Tyack, P. L. (Eds.). (2003). *Animal social complexity*. Cambridge, MA: Harvard University Press.

Emerson, R. M. (1962). Power–dependence relations. *American Sociological Review, 27*, 31–41.

Festinger, L. (1957). *A theory of cognitive dissonance*. Stanford, CA: Stanford University Press.

Festinger, L., & Katz, D. (1953). *Research methods in the behavioral sciences*. New York: Holt, Rinehart, & Winston.

Festinger, L., Riecken, H. W., & Schachter, S. (1956). *When prophecy fails*. Minneapolis: University of Minnesota Press.

Freedman, J., & Fraser, S. (1966). Compliance without pressure: The foot-in-the-door technique. *Journal of Personality and Social Psychology, 4*, 195–202.

Greenwald, A. G. (1968). Cognitive learning, cognitive response in persuasion, and attitude change. In A. G. Greenwald, T. C. Brock, & T. M. Ostrom (Eds.), *Psychological foundations of attitudes* (pp. 147–170). New York: Academic Press.

Greenwald, A. G., Brock, T. C., & Ostrom, T. M. (Eds.). (1968). *Psychological foundations of attitudes*. New York: Academic Press.

Greenwald, A. G., Pratkanis, A. R., Leippe, M. R., & Baumgardner, M. H. (1986). Under what conditions does theory obstruct research progress? *Psychological Review, 93*, 216–229.

Henrich, J., Boyd, R., Bowles, S., Camerer, C., Fehr, E., & Gintis, H. (Eds.). (2004). *Foundations of human sociality*. Oxford: Oxford University Press.

Hovland, C. I., Janis, I. L., & Kelley, H. H. (1953). *Communication and persuasion*. New Haven, CT: Yale University Press.

Janis, I. L. (1972). *Victims of groupthink*. Boston: Houghton-Mifflin.

Janis, I. L. (1983). *Groupthink*. Boston: Houghton-Mifflin.

Lasswell, H. D. (1927). *Propaganda technique in the world war*. New York: Knopf.

Latané, B., & Darley, J. M. (1970). *The unresponsive bystander: Why doesn't he help?* New York: Appleton-Century Crofts.

Lazarsfeld, P., Berelson, B., & Gaudet, H. (1948). *The people's choice*. New York: Columbia University Press.

LeBon, G. (1895/1960). *The crowd [Psychologie des foules]*. New York: Viking Press.

Lee, A. M. (1939). *The fine art of propaganda: A study of Father Coughlin's speeches*. New York: Harcourt, Brace & Co.

Lieberman, S. (1956). The effects of changes in role on the attitudes of role occupants. *Human Relations, 9*, 385–402.

Lindzey, G., & Aronson, E. (Eds.). (1968). *Handbook of social psychology: Research methods* (Vol. 2). Reading, MA: Addison-Wesley.

Lund, F. H. (1925). The psychology of belief. *Journal of Abnormal and Social Psychology, 20*, 68–81; 174–196.

McGuire, W. J. (1969). The nature of attitudes and attitude change. In G. Lindzey & E. Aronson (Eds.), *Handbook of social psychology* (2nd ed., Vol. 3, pp. 136–314). Reading, MA: Addison-Wesley.

McPhail, C. (1991). *The myth of the madding crowd*. New York: Aldine de Gruyter.

Milgram, S. (1974). *Obedience to authority*. New York: Harper & Row.

Newcomb, T. M. (1943). *Personality and social change*. New York: Holt, Rinehart, and Winston.

Nowak, A., Szamrej, J., & Latané, B. (1990). From private attitude to public opinion: A dynamic theory of social impact. *Psychological Review, 97*, 362–376.

Pedhazur, E. J. (1982). *Multiple regression in behavioral research*. New York: Holt, Rinehart, & Winston.

Pettigrew, T. F. (1958). Personality and sociocultural factors and intergroup attitudes: A cross-national comparison. *Journal of Conflict Resolution, 2*, 29–42.

Pettigrew, T. F. (1996). *How to think like a social scientist*. New York: HarperCollins.

Petty, R. E., & Cacioppo, J. T. (1986). *Communication and persuasion: Central and peripheral routes to attitude change*. New York: Springer-Verlag.

Pfeffer, J. (1981). *Power in organizations*. Cambridge, MA: Ballinger.

Pfeffer, J., & Salancik, G. R. (1978). *The external control of organizations*. New York: Harper & Row.

Pratkanis, A. R. (1997). The social psychology of mass communications: An American perspective. In D. F. Halpern & A. Voiskounsky (Eds.), *States of mind: American and post-Soviet perspectives on contemporary issues in psychology* (pp. 126–159). New York: Oxford University Press.

Pratkanis, A. R. (2006). Why would anyone do or believe such a thing? A social influence analysis. In R. J. Sternberg, H. Roediger, III, & D. Halpern (Eds.), *Critical thinking in psychology* (pp. 232–250). Cambridge: Cambridge University Press.

Pratkanis, A. & Aronson, E. (2001). *Age of propaganda: The everyday use and abuse of persuasion*. New York: W. H. Freeman.

Pratkanis, A. R., & Shadel, D. (2005). *Weapons of fraud: A source book for fraud fighters*. Seattle, WA: AARP Washington.

Rosenthal, R., & Rosnow, R. L. (1984). *Essentials of behavioral research*. New York: McGraw-Hill.

Rosenthal, R., & Rosnow, R. L. (1985). *Contrast analysis*. Cambridge: Cambridge University Press.

Ross, L. (1977). The intuitive psychologist and his shortcomings: Distortions in the attribution process. In L. Berkowitz (Ed.), *Advances in experimental social psychology* (vol. 10, pp. 173–220). New York: Academic Press.

Ross, L., & Nisbett, R. E. (1991). *The person and the situation: Perspectives of social psychology*. New York: McGraw-Hill.

Rossi, P. H., Wright, J. D., & Anderson, A. B. (Eds.). (1983). *Handbook of survey research*. San Diego, CA: Academic Press.

Ryle, G. (1949). *The concept of mind*. New York: Barnes and Noble.

Schreiber, N., Bellah, L. D., Martinez, Y., McLaurin, K. A., Strok, R., Garven, S., & Wood, J. M. (2006). Suggestive interviewing in the McMartin and Kelly Michaels daycare abuse cases: A case study. *Social Influence, 1*, 16–47.

Shadish, W. R., Cook, T. D., & Campbell, D. T. (2002). *Experimental and quasi-experimental designs for generalized causal inference*. Boston: Houghton-Mifflin.

Sherif, M. (1935). A study of some social factors in perception. *Archives of Psychology*, No. 187.

Sherif, M., Harvey, O. J., White, J., Hood, W., & Sherif, C. (1954). *Intergroup conflict and cooperation: The Robbers Cave experiment*. Norman: University of Oklahoma Press.

Siegel, S. (1956). *Nonparametric statistics for the behavioral sciences*. New York: McGraw-Hill.

Sigall, H., & Mills, J. (1998). Measures of independent variables and mediators are useful in social psychology experiments: But are they necessary? *Personality and Social Psychology Review, 2*, 218–226.

Skinner, B. F. (1974). *About behaviorism*. New York: Knopf.

Thibaut, J. W., & Kelley, H. H. (1959). *The social psychology of groups*. New York: Wiley.

Triplett, N. (1898). The dynamogenic factors in pacemaking and competition. *American Journal of Psychology, 9*, 507–533.

van Ginneken, J. (1992). *Crowds, psychology, and politics, 1871–1899*. Cambridge: Cambridge University Press.

Webb, E. J., Campbell, D. T., Schwartz, R. D., & Sechrest, L. (1966). *Unobtrusive measures: Nonreactive research in the social sciences*. Chicago: Rand McNally.

Webb, E. T., & Morgan, J. B. (1930). *Strategy in handling people*. Garden City, NY: Garden City Publishing.

White, R. K., & Lippitt, R. (1960). *Autocracy and democracy: Experimental inquiry*. New York: Harper & Brothers.

Winer, B. J. (1971). *Statistical principles in experimental design*. New York: McGraw-Hill.

Zimbardo P. (2007). *The Lucifer effect: Understanding how good people turn evil*. New York: Random House.

Znaniecki, F. (1934). *The method of sociology*. New York: Farrar & Rinehart.

2

Social Influence Analysis: An Index of Tactics

ANTHONY R. PRATKANIS

*O*ne of the defining attributes of all species of eusocial insects and social animals is a distinct means of social influence – a way for one or more members of the species to direct, coordinate, and influence other members of the species. Such social influence tactics determine the allocation of resources within a community of the species and also provide an evolutionary advantage to eusocial and social species in their quest to gain the resources needed for survival. To understand a eusocial or social species and to predict the behavior of its members, it is essential to analyze the nature of social influence within that species. Such a *social influence analysis* consists of a description of the social influence tactics used by species members, principles or psychological processes underlying those tactics (e.g., dissonance, social cognition principles), how influence is exchanged within a community (e.g., likely tactics employed, profiling of influence agents), patterning of influence within a species and its communities (e.g., communication networks, channels of influence, social institutions), and theories and models of the operation of influence.

In this chapter, I will look explicitly at the social influence tactics used by a species of social organisms known as *Homo sapiens*. By a *social influence tactic* I mean any noncoercive technique, device, procedure, or manipulation capable of creating or changing the belief or behavior of a target of the influence attempt, whether this attempt is based on the specific actions of an influence agent or the result of the self-organizing nature of social systems. By *noncoercive* I mean those tactics that do not rely on (a) outright deception or (b) the control of critical resources or what is often called power (Emerson, 1962; Pfeffer & Salancik, 1978) but instead have as their basis the social psychological nature of a member of the species. Social influence can refer to such processes as conformity (creating or changing behavior or belief to match the response of others), persuasion or attitude change (change in response to a message, discourse, or communication), compliance (change in response to an explicit request), yielding to social forces (change in response to the structure of the social situation), or helping (change in response to someone's need).

Social influence tactics are present in all eusocial and social species. For example, *Pogonomyrmex barbatus* (red harvester ants) use pheromones to signal such things as alarms and food trails. Tasks within the colony (e.g., forging, patrolling, midden work) are dynamically allocated by having each ant follow a social consensus rule of "the more contact with another ant succeeding at a task, the more likely I should switch to that task" (Gordon, 1999). *Apis mellifera* (honey bees) also use pheromones to convey alarm and to recruit others. A successful forager will use either a round or a waggle dance to convince other bees to harvest from her source. She will perform a dance if unloader bees take her food quickly, indicating it is in scarce supply (Gould & Gould, 1998). *Canis lupus* (grey wolves) develop a hierarchical structure within the pack with decisions (regarding hunting, travel, food allocation, etc.) based on the authority of the alpha (highest ranking) pair. Subordinates attempt to wheedle food from the alphas by taking a submissive, dependent role and begging like a pup in need (Mech, 1991). *Stenella longirostris* (spinner dolphins) form highly cohesive schools; this collective group is maintained and influenced by such influence tactics as social modeling, coalition formation, identity-whistles to convey emotional meaning to others, friendship development through touch, and mimicry of signals from others to create a chorusing of social consensus (Norris, Würsig, Wells, & Würsig, 1994). *Pan troglodytes* (chimpanzees) use a number of influence tactics to establish social relationships and to allocate resources including coalition formation, reciprocity, submissive greetings to establish a dependency relationship, empathy, and the establishment of norms (de Waal, 1996, 1998). A social influence tactic that appears to be common to all social species is the development of ingroup and outgroup boundaries and the use of this social group, be it a colony, hive, school, pack, troop, or granfalloon of *Homo sapiens*, to make decisions and choices.

As the only known self-conscious species with a writing system, *Homo sapiens* have attempted to describe and classify the means of persuasion and influence that they use. Some of these attempts have sought to categorize power tactics (control of resources), including those used in the most extreme exercise of power known as war (see for example, the writings of Sun Tzu, Machiavelli, and Clausewitz; Handel, 2001 for an exposition). Probably the first attempt to classify social influence tactics was conducted by the Sophists (including Protagoras, Isocrates, and Gorgias) of 5th century BCE Greece. These itinerant teachers of persuasion created handbooks of "commonplaces" – general arguments and techniques that could be adapted for a variety of persuasive purposes. Sometime around 333 BCE, Aristotle began compiling a list of influence techniques in his book *Rhetoric*. Aristotle claimed that there were three facets to effective communication: *ethos* (good character), *logos* (an effective message), and *pathos* (control of the emotions). Many of the tactics described by Aristotle (such as scarcity, source credibility, and vividness) would be recognized by readers of today's books on influence. The Romans Cicero and Quintilian followed in Aristotle's footsteps and wrote similar treatises. As the centuries passed, although the topic of rhetoric was taught in nearly every European university, it lost its emphasis as "the art of persuasion" and instead focused on the style and beauty of speech. A recent attempt to revive the persuasive element of rhetoric is Perelman and Olbrechts-Tyteca's (1958/ 1969) *The New Rhetoric*, which attempts to develop a classification scheme for argumentation.

With the rise of the industrial revolution, commercial (and later political) interests sought new and improved manners of influence. In response, at the turn of the 20th century, academics began preparing lists of influence tactics to be used in sales and advertising (see Adams, 1916; Poffenberger, 1932) and later international affairs (Harter & Sullivan, 1953). These volumes described tactics for holding the audience's attention, associating the product with a positive image, and appealing to desires and emotions. However, the wholesale use of influence to sell things (be they products, war, or political candidates) resulted in a backlash. In the late 1930s, a group of scholars funded by Edward A. Filene created the Institute for Propaganda Analysis of 33 Morningside Drive in New York City (Lee, 1952; Werkmeister, 1948). The Institute created a list of nine common influence devices used in propaganda (including name calling, glittering generalities, tabloid thinking, testimonials, bifurcation, association, just-plain folks, band wagon, and cardstacking). It also distributed a monthly newsletter to schools and other organizations describing how these propaganda devices were used in current communications, and thus became the first organized attempt in human history to teach how to resist influence.

TACTICAL ANALYSIS OF SOCIAL INFLUENCE

Previous attempts to classify and describe the influence tactics of *Homo sapiens* have one thing in common – they are based on speculation and not empirical evidence as to what works and why. In the early 1920s, the experimental method began to be used to identify and analyze social influence tactics. This effort has resulted in a plethora of knowledge about the social influence process. In one of the most important books in social psychology, Bob Cialdini (2001) summarized this literature in terms of six principles or weapons of influence: reciprocity, commitment and consistency, social proof, liking, authority, and scarcity. (Social scientists have also taken the approach of asking people about the influence tactics they use, resulting in various classification schemes; see Falbo, 1977; Marwell & Schmitt, 1967).

In this chapter, I attempt to compile a list of influence tactics (a level below Cialdini's principles) that have been studied experimentally by researchers. The result is a collection of 107 social influence tactics (plus 18 techniques for gaining credibility). For convenience, the tactics are divided into four categories corresponding to the four main tasks of a communicator according to classical rhetoric theory: (a) establish a favorable climate for the influence attempt (landscaping or pre-persuasion), (b) create a relationship with the audience (source credibility), (c) present the message in a convincing fashion, and (d) use the emotions to persuade. (Obviously, some tactics may serve more than one goal; in such cases, each is listed with its primary goal.) Underlying all of these tactics is the cognitive response law of influence (Greenwald, 1968; Pratkanis & Aronson, 2001): The successful persuasion tactic is one that directs and channels thoughts so that the target thinks in a manner agreeable to the communicator's point of view; the successful tactic disrupts negative thoughts and promotes positive thoughts about the proposed course of action.

Landscaping (Pre-persuasion) Tactics

Suppose I wished to move a marble across a table. In general, there are two ways to do this. I could apply force to the marble (say, striking it with my finger) or I could gently lift one end of the table so that the marble rolled to the other end. The first can be thought of as persuasion or influence proper; the second can be termed landscaping (or pre-persuasion) – structuring the situation in such a way that the target is likely to be receptive to a given course of action and respond in a desired manner.

In rhetoric, the concept of landscaping can be traced back to Aristotle, who referred to it as *atechnoi* (without technique) or facts and events immediately outside the control of the speaker. Aristotle provides some advice for dealing with such "facts" (e.g., discredit a law or witness), but considered it outside the normal course of rhetoric. However, Cicero, the great Roman lawyer, brought such matters into the fold of rhetoric with his theory of the *statis* (status of the issue) – the orator should define the issue in a way that is to best advantage. He even gave advice on just how to do this when defending murderers in a court of law (e.g., deny the facts, change the quality of the deed, suggest extenuating circumstances).

More recently, the concept of landscaping has re-emerged in a number of dispersed lines of scholarship. Asch (1952) argued that a person's response to an object is often a function of how the object is defined and construed as opposed to any long-held attitudes or beliefs. Researchers in the field of decision analysis have found that how a decision is structured (e.g., how the problem is represented, which alternatives are included, what is the decision criterion) can ultimately impact the outcome of decision-making (Farquhar and Pratkanis, 1993; Keeney, 1982; von Winterfeldt & Edwards, 1986). In his analysis of propaganda, Jacques Ellul (1973) developed the concept of pre-propaganda – the preconditioning of the masses to accept propaganda through the creation of images, myths, and stereotypes. In the area of political science, William Riker (1986) coined the term *heresthetics* to describe political tactics and strategy designed to "set up the situation in such a way that other people will want to join [a cause] . . . even without any persuasion at all" (p. ix). Riker provides as examples of heresthetics the use of coalitions and alliances, wedge issues to divide majorities, vote ordering, and committee stacking, among other devices. Pratkanis and Aronson (2001) used the term "pre-persuasion" to refer to the process of taking control of a situation to establish a favorable climate for influence. (The terms "pre-persuasion" and "landscaping" can be used interchangeably, although landscaping has the advantage in connoting a process that can be continuous as opposed to just before influence.) In common parlance, landscaping tactics are referred to as spin (Maltese, 1992), brand positioning (Ries & Trout, 1981), and turf battles (Cuming, 1985).

To clarify the concept of landscaping, consider Figure 2.1, where two options,

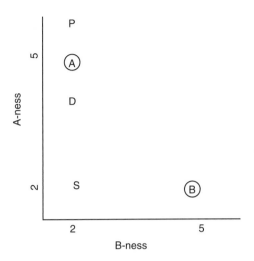

FIGURE 2.1   A choice set containing two options, A and B, where Option A is superior on A-ness and B is best on B-ness (and the more of A-ness and B-ness, the better). Option D is a decoy, Option P is an unavailable phantom, and Option S is a stinker no one wants. The choice of A or B is dependent, in part, on how the choice set is landscaped (or the nature and number of the options present in the set).

A and B, are being considered (ignore the other options for the moment). Option A is superior on A-ness whereas B is best on B-ness (and the more of A-ness and B-ness, the better). Suppose you are leaning to Option B, but I want you to take A. How can I get you to select A without arguing for the advantages of A over B, putting on social pressure to select A (e.g., "9 out of 10 influence professionals choose A"), or playing on your emotions (e.g., "B causes cancer, you know")? Answer: I could landscape the situation so that you naturally selected A without much further ado. I could do such things as change the names of the options to make A look better, add options to the set to change perceptions so that A is favored, make it essential for you to decide on A-ness, or present biasing information. Given that much decision-making is social (involves other people), I could declare a favorable voting rule (e.g., need a supermajority to obtain B), assign the decision to someone who is favorable to my cause, or form a coalition with your significant other to outnumber you in your desire for B. In other words, with landscaping tactics, I control the cognitive (e.g., perceptions of issues, options, etc.) and social (e.g., the process of decision making) structures used to reach your opinion or decision. The following are some tactics that have been identified for accomplishing this goal.

Define and Label an Issue in a Favorable Manner   How an issue is labeled and represented (e.g., pro-choice vs. pro-abortion) structures and directs thought that then impacts persuasion. For example, the use of the generic "he" in job announcements lowered the number of women applying for a job (Bem &

Bem, 1973; see Henley, 1989). Similarly, support for political issues such as affirmative action varies as a function of how it is labeled in opinion polls (Kravitz & Platania, 1993). Thaler (1992) provides evidence that how people treat money (spend or save) depends on how the money is labeled and categorized; for example, people are much less likely to spend a cash windfall if it comes from an investment account than, say, from winning the office football pool. In a clever demonstration of the power of descriptive language, Eiser and Pancer (1979) required schoolchildren to write an essay on adult authority using words that were either pro- or anti-adult authority. After writing the essays, the children's attitudes towards adult authority changed consistent with the bias of the words they used in the essay. Recently, Lord, Paulson, Sia, Lepper, and Thomas (2004) showed that when people do not possess stable exemplars representing a category, attitudes related to that category are highly susceptible to change. Although there is agreement that how an object is labeled can influence judgment and evaluations, there continues to be debate on how extensive is the impact of language on thought (e.g., Young, 1991).

Association   Another way to change the meaning of a concept is through association – the linking of an issue, idea, or cause to another positive or negative concept in order to transfer the meaning from the second to the first. For example, Staats and Staats (1958) paired national names and masculine names with either positive or negative words and found that the positive or negative meaning tended to transfer to the original names. In a similar vein, Lott and Lott (1960) found that receiving a reward in the presence of a previously neutral person was sufficient to increase the probability of liking that person – the positive aspects of the reward became associated with the person. One particularly effective means of association is to make the object similar to another object on irrelevant attributes (Warlop & Alba, 2004; see Farquhar & Herr, 1993 for a discussion of associations and brand equity).

Change the Meaning of an Object Category   Objects (say, people) typically belong to one or more categories (say, ideal job candidate). By changing the meaning (or range) of a category, any given object can be made to look better or worse. For example, Rothbart, Davis-Stitt, and Hill (1997) presented subjects with numerical ratings of job candidates along with an arbitrary categorization of those scores as representing ideal, acceptable, or marginal applicants. Subjects' ratings of the similarity of job candidates increased when the job candidates were in the same category as opposed to when they appeared on opposite sides of the category boundary. Salancik and Conway (1975) demonstrated another way of changing the perceptions of an object (in this case, the self) by changing the meaning of a category (in this case, religiosity). In their experiment, students endorsed pro- and anti-religious survey questions that used either the word "frequently" or "occasionally" in the stem. Those subjects who rated themselves using the "occasionally" questions perceived themselves as more religious (because they endorsed more items) compared to those who responded to stems with the word "frequently."

Set Expectations   An expectation is a belief about the future. As such, expectations can sculpt the influence landscape in at least one of two ways. First, expectations serve as a reference point by which options are judged. For example, much research shows that customer satisfaction with a product is a function of whether the product met or failed to meet expectations (e.g., Ross & Kraft, 1983). Second, expectations guide interpretations and perceptions to create a picture of reality that is congruent with expectations (Kirsch, 1999). For example, Pratkanis, Eskenazi, and Greenwald (1994) had subjects listen to subliminal self-help tapes designed either to improve memory or to build self-esteem. Half of the tapes were mislabeled so that the subject received a memory tape labeled as self-esteem or vice versa. The results showed no therapeutic effects of the subliminal messages but that subjects thought there was an improvement based on the tape label. In other words, expectations had created a reality that didn't really exist. In some cases, when expectation-driven perceptions are acted on, a placebo effect (Shapiro & Shapiro, 1997) or a self-fulfilling prophecy (Darley & Fazio, 1980) can result.

Limit and Control the Number of Choices and Options   One simple way to induce someone to select Option A in Figure 2.1 is to offer a choice of only Option A and Option S (an unwanted stinker). Lee (1952) terms this approach the "least-of-evils" tactic, whereby a person selects from a limited number of options so that the person is "free" to select the lesser of evils. Vidmar (1972) provides a legal example of this tactic as used by defense and prosecution lawyers. In his experiment, mock jurors were more likely to render guilty verdicts when potential penalty options contained at least one moderate penalty as opposed to all severe choices. Conversely, too many options can result in decision avoidance (Iyengar & Lepper, 2000). Weaver and Conlon (2003) remind us that it is important to maintain at least a façade of choice to lend a sense of legitimacy and procedural justice to the decision.

Control the Range and Meaning of a Response   Expanding and contracting the range of a response scale can change the meaning of that scale and thus become a determining factor in response. For example, Ostrom (1970) asked subjects to recommend sentences for a criminal found guilty of a felony. Those who were told that the typical sentence ranged from 1 to 5 years gave less of a penalty than those who were told a typical sentence ranged from 1 to 30 years. In a similar experiment, Steele and Ostrom (1974) found that the effects of manipulating the range of possible sentences for a given felony case extended to an unrelated but similar case (see Eiser, 1975 for additional examples).

Valence Framing   Critical information concerning a decision can be cast in a positive (gain) or negative (loss) way. In general, people seek to avoid losses; it is more painful to lose $20 than it is pleasurable to gain $20. Issues framed in terms of losses (as opposed to gains) will thus generate motivation to avoid the loss. Tversky and Kahneman (1981) developed a classic demonstration of this phenomenon using what has become known as the Asian disease problem. In these problems, subjects are asked to imagine preparation for an outbreak of a disease and to decide on which course of action to take. In one set of actions, Program A is framed as a gain:

> Which program do you favor to solve the disease epidemic?
> If Program A is adopted, 200 people will be saved.
> If Program B is adopted, there is a $\frac{1}{3}$ probability that 600 people will be saved, and a $\frac{2}{3}$ probability that no people will be saved.

When the problem is framed in this manner, most subjects (78%) select Program A. However, consider this framing of the same actions but with Program A framed as a loss:

> If Program A is adopted, 400 people will die.
> If Program B is adopted, there is a $\frac{1}{3}$ probability that nobody will die and a $\frac{2}{3}$ probability that 600 will die.

In this frame, most subjects (78%) select Program B.

Tversky and Kahneman's findings generated considerable subsequent research, which found mixed results for their type of *risky choice frames* (see Levin, Schneider, & Gaeth, 1998 for a review). However, consistent support has been obtained for *attribute framing*, as in research by Levin and Gaeth (1988) showing that consumers prefer beef that is 75% lean to beef that is 25% fat, and for *goal framing*, as in research by Meyerowitz and Chaiken (1987) showing that women who read pamphlets about breast self-examinations emphasizing the negative consequences of not performing the exam were more likely to later do the exam than those receiving messages about the positive consequences of performing the exam.

Set the Decision Criterion   In Figure 2.1, Option A would be readily selected if A-ness were seen as the primary criterion that needs to be maximized. Eiser, Eiser, Patterson, and Harding (1984) provide a straightforward example of setting the decision criterion. In their experiment, five groups of subjects were asked to memorize how 21 common foods rated on one of five possible nutrients (such as iron, fat, or protein). A subsequent evaluation of each food revealed that the nutritional quality of the food was determined by how the food was rated on the previously memorized attribute. In organizations, the decision criteria are set by the rules and policy of the organization and, perhaps more importantly, by asserting criteria on an as-needed basis (Pfeffer, 1981; Uhlmann & Cohen, 2005). One devious means for setting a decision criterion is the hot potato – the creation of a sensational event, incident, or situation that must be dealt with and in the process determines the decisive factors to be used in making a decision (Lee, 1952).

Agenda Setting: Determining What Issues Will Be Discussed   Issues placed on an agenda appear important and serve to define the criteria used in subsequent decisions. For example, Iyengar and Kinder (1987) found that repeated discussions of an issue in the mass media led viewers to think that issue was important and, most interestingly, to support candidates who took strong positions on that issue. Agenda setting limits discussion to those items on the agenda, thereby limiting the available information for discussion and formally excluding some options from being considered (Plott & Levine, 1978; see also Baumgartner & Jones, 1993; Dearing & Rogers, 1996).

Decoys   A decoy is an inferior option that no one would choose. Including a decoy in a choice set makes other options appear superior in comparison and thus more likely to be chosen. For example, in Figure 2.1, a decoy shadowing Object A would be represented by Object D, located at the same level of B-ness as Object A but slightly less A-ness. The inclusion of Object D in the choice set would increase the probability of A being selected over B. The impact of decoys on choice was first identified by Tadeusz Tyszka in 1977 (see Tyszka, 1983) and has been replicated subsequently in a variety of manners (see Huber, Payne, & Puto, 1982; Pratkanis & Aronson, 2001).

Phantoms   A phantom alternative is an option that looks real, is typically superior to other options, but is unavailable at the time a decision is made (see Farquhar & Pratkanis, 1993; Pratkanis & Farquhar, 1992). For example, in Figure 2.1, a phantom is represented by an unavailable option (Object P), which is slightly better than Object A on A-ness and the same on B-ness. The inclusion of a phantom in a choice set (a) decreases the positive evaluation of other options, (b) alters the relative importance of decision criteria so that attributes on which the phantom is strong are seen as more important, and (c) serves as a reference point in decision-making. The impact of a phantom on choice depends on the exact magnitude of these processes. For example, Object P would increase the probability of selecting A in this choice set since it produces a mild contrast effect and a strong change in attribute weights such that A-ness is now of increased importance in decision-making.

In addition to these landscaping effects, a phantom also has the ability to create strong emotional effects. When the denial of a phantom implicates the self, it can produce such emotions as frustration, relative deprivation, and self-threat. These emotions can be used for propaganda purposes such as motivating a person to attempt to obtain the phantom (phantom fixation; see 1-in-5 prize tactic below) or blaming others for the denial of a phantom (scapegoating).

Establish a Favorable Comparison Point or Set   People evaluate options and choices by comparing them to salient alternatives. By making certain comparisons more salient than others, an agent can gain an influence advantage. For example, Thaler (1992) marshals evidence for an endowment effect – the use of the status quo as a reference point serves to make salient the disadvantages of any new option, resulting in a bias favoring the status quo. Other common points of comparison include: expectations (see above), goals, social comparisons (upward or downward comparisons to others), group standards (e.g., Blake, Rosenbaum, & Duryea, 1955), salient exemplars, counterfactuals (i.e. comparisons to what might have been), foregone options (lost opportunities), temporal reframing (e.g., the pennies-a-day effect; Gourville, 1998), temporal construal (Trope & Liberman, 2003), anchors, asking price, BATNA (best alternative to a negotiated agreement), reservation price, aspiration level, and a distribution of possible comparison objects (Mellers & Birnbaum, 1983; see Kahneman, 1992 for a discussion of reference points in general).

Control the Flow of Information   The selective presentation of information (facts or falsehoods) can bias decision-making. For example, in 1934, Annis and Meier found that planting biased information in college newspapers changed opinions about a political event (see also Becker's 1949 discussion of black propaganda). There are a number of ways to control the flow of information including censorship, self-censorship (e.g., avoiding thought about controversial issues, limited motivation to obtain information, and biased information search), disinformation campaigns, jamming enemy communications in war, selected leaks and plants of information, biased sequencing and timing of the presentation of information (for additional examples see Crosby, Iyer, Clayton, & Downing, 2003, pp. 104–105; Pratkanis & Aronson, 2001, pp. 98–99), and control of the communication network, especially gatekeepers (Friedkin, 1998; Goldberg, 1955). One caveat: When people realize that information is being kept secret and that this censorship is not justified, there may be an increased desire for information (via reactance) and a two-sided message may be more impactful (see discussion of reactance and two-sided messages below).

Metaphor   The use of metaphor can constrain and focus thought about an issue, thereby impacting how that issue will be decided. For example, Gilovich (1981) found that comparing a military crisis to Nazi Germany invites thoughts about intervention whereas a comparison to Vietnam elicits thoughts about avoiding involvement. Metaphors are effective influence devices because metaphors guide information processing (selective attention to details) and suggest solutions for resolving the issue (Mio, 1996; Sopory & Dillard, 2002).

Storytelling   A story is a narrative that provides a causal structure to facts and evidence. Plausible stories serve to guide thought, determine the credibility of information, and ultimately direct evaluation and choice about story-related decisions (Hastie & Pennington, 2000). For example, Pennington and Hastie (1992) presented mock jurors with either a murder or a hit-and-run case in which the preponderance of evidence argued for either the guilt or innocence of the defendant. When information was organized in a story format (a sequence of events), the mock jurors were more likely to render verdicts consistent with the preponderance of evidence compared to a mere listing of that evidence. Similarly, Slusher and Anderson (1996) were much more effective in arguing that the AIDS virus is not spread by casual contact when they used facts embedded in a causal structure on how the disease is transmitted compared to when they used statistical facts. Such causal stories or social theories tend to persist even in the face of strong, discrediting information (Anderson, Lepper, & Ross, 1980).

(Mis)Leading Questions   Question asking is a way to structure information and to imply certain answers or solutions. How a question is asked can determine the range of thought about an issue. For example, Loftus and Palmer (1974) found higher estimates of vehicle speed when people were asked, "How fast were the cars going when they *smashed*?" as opposed to *hit*. Ginzel (1994) found that interviewers who asked biased questions (designed to promote a positive or negative view of a speech) tended to bias their impressions consistent with the questions (see also Snyder & Swann, 1978). Questioning is a powerful influence device because it is capable of directing attention and inferences about the situation.

Innuendo   An innuendo is an insinuation (often subtle or hidden) of a fact, especially concerning reputation and character. As such, innuendoes set up expectations, which serve to filter future information. For example, in courtroom settings, inadmissible evidence, pretrial publicity, and accusatory questioning can all impact jury verdicts (e.g., Kassin, Williams, & Saunders, 1990; Sue, Smith, & Caldwell, 1973). In the political domain, Wegner, Wenzlaff, Kerker, and Beattie (1981) found that merely asking about the possible wrongdoing of a political candidate can result in negative perceptions of that politician. Of course, intensive lies and character attacks can be quite coercive for the victim.

Projection Tactic   A more specific form of innuendo is based on projection – accusing another person of the negative traits and behaviors that one possesses and exhibits with the goal of deflecting attention from one's own misdeeds and towards the accused. In four experiments, Rucker and Pratkanis (2001) found that projection was effective in increasing the blame placed on the target of projection and decreasing the culpability of the accuser. In addition, the effects of projection persisted despite attempts to raise suspicions about the motives of the accuser and providing evidence that the accuser was indeed guilty of the deeds.

Perspective and Point of View   In a now classic experiment, Storms (1973) reversed the typical actor–observer attribution bias (i.e. explaining others' behavior in terms of dispositional factors in a manner consistent with the fundamental attribution error and explaining one's own behavior in terms of the situation) merely by changing perspective with a reversed camera angle (i.e. showing the actor as others see him or her). Any given point of view (frame or interpretative schema) makes available and accessible specific information that then impacts judgment and evaluation. For example, Iyengar (1991) showed viewers news stories from either an episodic (depicting a single concrete event such as a murder or drug abuse) or thematic (an abstract report about a topic such as crime or drug addiction) perspective. The results showed that those who were exposed to an episodic perspective located responsibility for problems in terms of the individual wrongdoer whereas those who saw a thematic perspective were more likely to hold society and government responsible.

Debias Techniques   We have seen how landscaping tactics such as decoys, phantoms, storytelling, and comparison points can influence judgment and choice.

Suppose you don't want that choice. What can be done to disrupt landscaping tactics? In 1897, Chamberlin suggested the "method of multiple working hypotheses" or to bring up all rational explanations, perspectives, and alternatives for consideration as a means of avoiding premature closure on a suggested option. Anderson and Sechler (1986) demonstrated the wisdom of this advice in their research showing that subjects asked to provide a counter-explanation of a relationship evidenced less bias based on initial theories. Mussweiler, Strack, and Pfeiffer (2000) found that inducing a "consideration of the opposite" reduced the impact of a comparison point. Similarly, Maier's problem-solving discussion techniques such as the risk technique, structured discussion guidelines, developmental discussion, two-column method, and second-solution are all designed to generate multiple hypotheses and perspectives to overcome landscaping biases (Maier, 1952; Maier & Hoffman, 1960a, 1960b).

Control the Procedures for Making a Decision   Whether you are reaching into your pocket for some spare change for a panhandler, negotiating with a loved one concerning the purchase of a new car, or working legislation through Congress, every decision involves a set of procedures for making that decision. Control of the procedures translates into control of the outcomes. The specific procedures differ for any given decision, making it difficult to draw blanket conclusions about the given effectiveness of controlling any given aspect of the process. However, researchers (especially those working in the area of negotiations) have identified common procedures that appear in a number of decision domains (Raiffa, 1982; Thompson, 2001). Some of these procedural aspects are decision rule (e.g., majority, consensus, unanimity); ability to gerrymander; allocation norms and rules (e.g., equity, equality, despotism); sequencing of decision (e.g., prescreening, committee assignments, sequencing multiple issues); one time or multiple negotiations; opportunity to make linkages between issues; time constraints (e.g., time pressure, deadlines, stalling); decision task (e.g., selecting versus eliminating options; optimizing versus satisficing); need to reach an agreement and to ratify an agreement; organizational rules, norms, and constraints bearing on the decision; and physical environment (e.g., public versus private negotiation). Lewin's (1947) marketing of sweetbreads during the Second World War provides a practical illustration of how to specify the procedures for making a decision and how to target those procedures for social change. Effective control of the procedures for making a decision also involves making the process appear fair and legitimate (procedural justice) or else the manipulation of those procedures will appear coercive (Lind & Tyler, 1988).

Committee-Packing   Determining who will make the decision will often determine the outcome. The tactic gets its name from attempts to obtain a desired outcome by putting supporters on the appropriate committee (as in Franklin Roosevelt's attempt to pack the Supreme Court), although it can also refer to any attempt to control who will make a decision. One's desired outcome can be obtained by assigning decision-making to friends and supporters, denied by assigning the decision to enemies, and never voted upon by assigning the responsibility to incompetents. In negotiations and mediation, the selection of a third-party intervener and the characteristics of that intervention can impact the ultimate results (Rubin, 1981). In organizations, assigning a task to a committee has the effects of legitimizing the outcome (i.e., procedural justice) as well as distancing an administrator from a potentially adverse result (Pfeffer, 1981).

Coalition Formation   Whenever a decision involves more than two partici-pants, there is the strong possibility that the matter will not be decided by prin-ciple, reason, or the self-interest of the whole, but by coalition formation. Whether we are discussing outcomes in the US House of Representatives, balance of power in 19th-century Europe, or the winner in a game of Parcheesi in a laboratory setting, the combination of one group of actors against another will determine the allocation of resources and the resolution of conflicting interests (Groennings, Kelley, & Leiserson, 1970; for discussion of theories on how coalitions form see Kahan & Rapoport, 1984; Komorita & Chertkoff, 1973).

Jigsawing (or Creating Mutual Interdependence)   On occasion, it may be useful to landscape the situation in such as way as to promote intergroup harmony and positive social relations (in contrast to the often divisive nature of coalition politics). Aronson, Blaney, Stephan, Sikes, and Snapp (1978) developed a jigsaw technique for creating mutual interdependence that results in positive rela-tions in the classroom. In this technique, students from different backgrounds are each given a part of a topic to be studied and then must work together to learn the material; jigsaw classrooms have been shown to produce dramatic reductions in prejudice as well as improving academic performance. Jigsawing is one way of establishing the conditions underlying Allport's (1954) equal-status contact hypothesis. According to this principle, positive intergroup relations are most likely to occur when members from two groups (a) possess equal status, (b) seek common goals, (c) are cooperatively dependent on each other, and (d) interact with the support of authorities, customs, and laws (see Pettigrew, 1998 for an update). Another example of the use of these principles can be found in Sherif, Harvey, White, Hood, and Sherif's (1954) famous Robbers Cave research. In this study, intergroup conflict between two groups of youths (Rattlers vs. Eagles) was ameliorated by having the groups work together on common goals.

Social Traps (Sometimes Called Social Dilemmas)   A social trap is a situation in which the behavior of an individual produces a small, immediate positive outcome but results in a larger negative outcome after a delay. The classic example of a social trap is the tragedy of the commons: each person brings a cow to graze at a common grassland (small positive outcome), but the combined effect is that the commons is destroyed through overgrazing (long-term negative outcome). Cross and Guyer (1980) discuss a number of such social traps, which structure action and ultimately direct behavior (see also Komorita & Parks, 1994; Platt, 1973).

Fait Accompli: Creating a Psychology of the Inevitable   Fait accompli is a French phrase meaning "accomplished fact" or, in other words, "it is a done deal." Creating a sense that a certain course of action is inevitable and there is nothing to be done to prevent it induces people to reconcile themselves to their fate and to come to accept it and even like it. For example, Brehm (1959) led children to eat a disliked vegetable with some of the children believing that it was inevitable that they would eat more of the vegetable in the future. Those children who expected to eat more of the vegetable convinced themselves that it wasn't all that bad a foodstuff (see Comer & Laird, 1975 for additional examples; Pratkanis & Turner, 1994 for a discussion of the use of the psychology of the inevitable in social change).

Tactics That Rely on Social Relationships: Source Credibility and Social Roles

As early as the 4th century BCE, Aristotle argued that an essential ingredient of influence is that the communicator must be of good character. For Aristotle, a good character (or *ethos*) meant someone who possesses good sense, good morals, and goodwill. Much research has found support for Aristotle's observations but has also found that in some circumstances a communicator of weak character or possessing irrelevant characteristics can still persuade and prevail. Additional research finds that the mere presence of others, even when the nature of their character is unclear, can influence a target through conformity or what Cialdini (2001) terms *social proof*. In contrast to Aristotle's "good character," research has shown that what is important for influence is the establishment of a social relationship that facilitates influence between the source and target of influence. The following tactics describe how this can be accomplished and in the process explores the nature of relationships that promote and deter persuasion.

Be a Credible Source   One of the most prominent demonstrations of Aristotle's "good character" rule of influence was conducted by Hovland and Weiss (1951; Hovland, Janis, & Kelley, 1953). In this experiment, expert and trustworthy sources (e.g., Robert J. Oppenheimer, *New England Journal of Biology and Medicine*) were more effective in securing persuasion to various issues (e.g., future of atomic submarines, sale of antihistamine drugs) compared to communicators lacking in expertise and trust (e.g., *Pravda*, a pictorial magazine). The explanation for this effect given by Hovland et al. (1953) assumed that people desire to hold a correct attitude (see also Petty & Cacioppo, 1986) and that relying on an expert and trustworthy source is rewarding in terms of meeting this goal.

In addition to communicators who are expert and trustworthy, researchers have identified a number of other attributes of credible (or effective) communicators. These include sources that are physically attractive (Chaiken, 1979), similar to the target (Brock, 1965), likeable (Cialdini, 2001), an authority (Bickman, 1974), and of high social status (Lefkowitz, Blake, & Mouton, 1955), and members of ingroups (Abrams, Wetherell, Cochrane, Hogg, & Turner, 1990). Some divide the nature of credibility into two general types: the hard (expert, authority, high social status) and the soft (attractive, likeable, similar) sell. For example, Cialdini (2001) describes the two influence principles of liking (the friendly thief) and authority (directed deference). Additional source-related principles might be added, such as a warm or benefic sell (taking the role of someone who is dependent and needs help to induce compliance with a request for aid). Nevertheless, some of these attributes strain the Hovland et al. (1953) explanation of source credibility. For example, the desire to hold a correct attitude toward shaving would suggest that the independent assessment of a barber or dermatologist would be a more effective source than a high-status pro football player paid for his endorsement. An alternative explanation of credibility is that the credible communicator is one that holds a prominent, positive status in the web of relationships in a social system – the prestige hypothesis of research conducted in the 1930s and 1940s (Lorge, 1936; Wegrocki, 1934).

Much research has been devoted to identifying techniques for manufacturing source credibility. Some of these techniques are: (a) put on the trappings (ornamentation) of authority and attractiveness (make-up, clothing, symbols, stories and narratives, etc.; Cialdini, 2001; Pratkanis & Aronson, 2001); (b) do a favor for the target (Lott & Lott, 1960); (c) get the target to do a favor for you (Jecker & Landy, 1969); (d) agree (attitude similarity) with the target (Byrne, 1971); (e) show or demonstrate liking for the target (Curtis & Miller, 1986); (f) personalize or individuate the source (Garrity & Degelman, 1990); (g) be critical and then praise the target (Sigall & Aronson, 1967); (h) commit a blunder or pratfall (to appear human) if you are a competent source (Aronson, Willerman, & Floyd, 1966); (i) be confident in tone and manner (Leippe, Manion, & Romanczyk, 1992); (j) create a sense that future anticipated interaction is inevitable or a *fait accompli* (Darley & Berscheid, 1967); (k) increase familiarity and proximity (Segal, 1974); (l) admit a small flaw to establish overall credibility (Settle & Golden, 1974); (m) surround yourself with beautiful people (Sigall & Landy, 1973); (n) punish a target's enemy or reward a target's friend (Aronson & Cope, 1968); (o) imitate the target (Thelen & Kirkland, 1976); (p) share a secret (Wegner, Lane, & Dimitri, 1994); (q) reciprocate self-disclosures (Derlega, Harris, & Chaikin, 1973); and (r) be perceived as empathetic, warm, and genuine (Girard, 1977; Rogers, 1942).

In general, the advice to "be credible" should be heeded by all who seek to persuade. However, there are cases when low-credible sources are more effective. For example, Walster, Aronson, and Abrahams (1966) found that a low-credible source (a hardened criminal) was more effective than a high-credible source (a judge) when arguing for tougher judicial sentencing. Aronson and Golden (1962) found that an outgroup member (an African-American for whites) was more effective under certain conditions in arguing for the value of arithmetic than a more prestigious ingroup member (see also White & Harkins, 1994). In addition, there are a number of cases where sources with differing basis of credibility (say, expert versus attractiveness) produce differential persuasion under varying treatments (see Pratkanis, 2000).

To account for these cases, I have proposed an altercasting theory of source credibility as an extension of the hypothesis (from prestige research) that credibility is a function of the nature of the social relationship between source and recipient (Pratkanis, 2000; Weinstein & Deutschberger, 1963). According to an altercasting theory, source credibility (effectiveness) is a function of the roles taken by the source and recipient of a message. Altercasting describes a social interaction in which an ego (e.g., source of the message) adopts certain lines of action (e.g., self-descriptions, mannerisms, impression management) to place alter (e.g., message recipient) into a social role that specifies an interpersonal task (e.g., message acceptance or rejection). A *role* is "a set of mutual (but not necessarily harmonious) expectations of behavior between two or more actors, with reference to a particular type of situation" (Goode, 1968, p. 249). In other words, a set of roles provides the occupants of those roles with certain responsibilities and privileges that then structure and shape future interaction. Once a person accepts a role, a number of social pressures are brought to bear to insure the role is enacted, including the expectations of self and others, the possibility of sanctions for role violations, selective exposure and processing of information consistent with role constraints, and the formation of an identity that provides the actors with a stake in a given social system. Any influence attempt is more or less effective depending on what roles are invoked and how it makes use of the responsibilities and privileges inherent in each role. The next seventeen tactics illustrate some of the more common uses of altercasting to secure influence.

Tact Altercast   In tact altercasting, alter (the target of an influence attempt) is placed in a role through mere contact with others in the social world. (The term is based on the Skinnerian term "tact," which is derived from con*tact*.) In other words, the agent of influence takes a social role to place the target in a complementary role. Pratkanis and Gliner (2004–2005) conducted simple experiments to illustrate tact altercasting. In one of their experiments, a child or an expert argued in favor of either nuclear disarmament or the presence of a tenth planet in the solar system. Traditional theories of source credibility (Hovland et al., 1953; Petty & Cacioppo, 1986) would predict that the expert should always be more effective than the child in terms of holding a correct belief. However, Pratkanis and Gliner found differential persuasion based on the social roles invoked. Specifically, a child was more effective than the expert when arguing for nuclear disarmament whereas the expert was more effective than the child when arguing for a tenth planet. A child places the message recipient in the role of "protector" and thus gains an advantage when arguing for protection-themed messages such as nuclear disarmament. An expert places the message recipient in the role of "unknowing public" and thus is most effective when advocating for technical issues such as a tenth planet. Pratkanis (2000) lists a number of role-pairs and role sets frequently used in influence attempts. The next ten tactics describe common tact altercasts.

Authority–Agent Altercast   An authority is a person who is perceived to have a legitimate right to command others to be her or his agent. Whether the role is obtained rightfully or merely faked, authority induces obedience, as illustrated in the classic Milgram (1974) experiments in which an authority was able to induce subjects ostensibly to give a series of painful shocks to others. In a similar vein, Bickman (1974) found that a man dressed as a guard (an authority) could successfully order passersby to pick up a paper bag, give a dime to a stranger, and move away from a bus stop (compared to when the man was dressed as a civilian or milkman; see Bushman, 1984 for a replication).

Expert–Unknowing Public Altercast

An expert is an individual with specialized knowledge in a given domain (e.g., lawyer, doctor, nuclear engineer). An expert casts the target into the role of someone who is "not in the know;" in other words, the message recipient feels as if he or she does not know enough to evaluate the issues and thus is required to rely on the expert. In general, linking a message with a source that appears to be high in expertise increases persuasion (Hovland et al., 1953; Maddux & Rogers, 1980; Moore, 1921). Nevertheless, the message recipient's inferior status of "unknowing" and ignorant is to be avoided, if possible, and thus the ability of an expert to persuade can be limited in certain cases (see Pratkanis, 2000; Pratkanis & Gliner, 2004–2005). An expert's persuasiveness is typically strongest when limited to the domain of expertise and instances when the target has little motivation or ability to process the information.

High Status–Admirer Altercast

The celebrity, the popular kid in class, the movie star, the famous person, and the star athlete all occupy a prominent and prestigious position in the status hierarchy; as such others tend to admire and seek to be like the high-status person or win their approval, and thus accord the high-status person preferential treatment that can serve as the basis of influence. For example, Lefkowitz et al. (1955) found that people were more likely to jaywalk as a result of observing a person dressed in a suit and tie compared to when the person was dressed in denim. Bickman (1971) found that people were more likely to return a dime lost in a phone booth when the request was made by males in suits and females in nice dresses compared to those same males and females wearing work and casual clothing. Weick, Gilfillan, and Keith (1973) found that orchestras made fewer errors playing the same music attributed to a high- as opposed to low-status composer. Interestingly, Bushman (1984) found that a person dressed in a business suit was not much more effective than a bum in getting a passerby to put a dime in a parking meter, suggesting that the effects of high status are different than those produced by an authority.

Physically Attractive–Admirer Altercast

The physically attractive person, just like other high-status persons, occupies a prestigious position in the status hierarchy; others tend to admire physically attractive persons and desire to be part of their world. This desire to identify with the beautiful can result in an increased persuasive effectiveness for attractive communicators. For example, attractive communicators tend to be more effective in personal selling (Reingen & Kernan, 1993), in soliciting participation in surveys (Guéguen, Legoherel, & Jacob, 2003), and as an attitude change agent (Chaiken, 1979). Pratkanis (2000) lists some limitations of the attractive source as an influence agent.

Just Plain Folks: Similarity Altercast

In the 1930s, the Institute of Propaganda Analysis identified an influence device it termed "just plain folks" – the attempts by politicians, leaders, and others to take the role of being similar to the common folk (Werkmeister, 1948). Considerable research demonstrates that source–recipient similarity increases influence and persuasion, although the exact mechanism or mechanisms have not yet been pinned down. For example, Brock (1965) found that a paint salesman was more influential when he had performed a job similar to the one facing the target compared to when the salesman was highly experienced. Berscheid (1966) found that similarity was effective in promoting influence if the shared similarity was directly relevant to the issue. Berscheid's research indicates that the similarity altercast works via Festinger's (1954) social comparison process; people have a tendency to turn to similar others as referents for their opinions on specific issues. However, other research has shown that irrelevant and even trivial similarity can impact social influence processes. For example, Stotland, Zander, and Natsoulas (1961) found that sharing music preferences increased agreement with a confederate in rating nonsense syllables. Baron (1971) observed that shared attitudes increased compliance with a request, especially when the request was large in magnitude (see also Baron, 1970; Burger, Messian, Patel, del Prado, & Anderson, 2004). In these cases, similarity appears to create a unit bond between source and target that then increases compliance (see discussion of granfalloon below).

Associative Casting and Avoidant Miscasting

A person can have the aspiration to be linked with desirable others (associative casting) and to shun a connection with undesirables (avoidant miscasting). Associative casting can result in social influence as the person attempts to conform, adopt attitudes, or engage in other behavior to been seen as similar to the desired associate (see Cialdini, Borden, Thorne, Walker, Freeman, & Sloan's (1976) BIRGing or basking in reflected glory). For example, Siegel and Siegel (1957) found that that those who aspired to be part of an elusive group (but were randomly denied this opportunity) adopted beliefs similar to the elusive group but not as strongly as those who became members of the group. Cocanougher and Bruce (1971) found that students who aspired to be business executives were more likely to adopt product preferences consistent with their aspirations. Avoidant miscasting results when a person is linked to an undesirable association and produces negative influence or adopting behavior to dissociate from the potentially socially damaging other. For example, Cooper and Jones (1969) had subjects interact with an obnoxious discussion partner who was either similar or dissimilar to the subject in terms of beliefs. When interacting with an obnoxious but similar partner, subjects changed their previously held attitudes to avoid any linkage with this loathsome other (see also Snyder, Lassegard, & Ford, 1986).

Intimates (Friends and Lovers) Altercast

Close relationships such as friendships and lovers create obligations to place the needs of others before our own (Roloff, Janiszewski, McGrath, Burns, & Manrai, 1988); failure to meet these obligations generates guilt which in turn produces more motivation to comply with the request of an intimate (Vangelisti, Daly, & Rudnick, 1991). Thus, establishing an intimate relation can serve as a basis for securing requests for help. Friends are also a major social influence when adopting cultural practices such as smoking

(Goodrow, Seier, & Stewart, 2003), smokeless tobacco (Boyle, Claxton, & Forster, 1997), and underage drinking (Reifman, Barnes, Dintcheff, Farrell, & Uhteg, 1998). However, friends may not induce more conformity in laboratory situations where the obligations of the friendship may not be engaged (Ex, 1960; Harper & Tuddenham, 1964).

Dependency–Responsibility Altercast   One effective method for obtaining compliance with a request is to feign or exhibit dependency on another person, thereby placing that person in the role of responsible agent. For example, Berkowitz and Daniels (1963) created work relationships in which workers (the subjects in the experiment) believed they were responsible (or not) for the content of an evaluation of a supervisor; the workers were more productive when they were responsible for the supervisor's evaluation. Doob and Ecker (1970) found that subjects were more likely to comply with a request to complete a questionnaire when asked by someone who wore an eye patch compared to a requester without a patch. The eye patch suggested a stigma and that the person was dependent on the target for getting the task done. Ross and Braband (1973) had subjects wait alone, with a blind confederate, or with a sighted one and then staged an emergency, which threatened the subject and confederate. Those subjects waiting with a blind confederate responded more frequently and rapidly than those waiting with a sighted one. As I noted above, a child also creates a dependency relationship and is thus more effective (than an expert) in arguing for protection-themed issues (Pratkanis & Gliner, 2004–2005). Berkowitz (1969) describes some of the limitations of using this altercast role.

Defector–Confidant Altercast   A defector is someone who takes a position opposite to the apparent self-interest of his or her social role. In general, arguing against one's self-interest increases the overall effectiveness of the communication. For example, research has demonstrated the effectiveness of these communicators: a criminal arguing for tougher sentencing (compared to a judge; Walster et al., 1966), a politician arguing against a position taken previously (Eagly, Wood, & Chaiken, 1978), an ex-alcoholic opposing alcohol use (Levine & Valle, 1975), a US general claiming the Vietnam war was going badly, and an African-American stating that African-Americans lack initiative (Koeske & Crano, 1968). The defector casts the target of the communication into the role of an attentive confidant – someone who is surprised by what is said and feels the defector is speaking out to set the record straight and thus can be trusted on the issue.

Opinion Deviant–Majority Altercast (Minority Influence)   The opinion deviant advocates a position opposite to the majority and thus casts others into the role of protecting the status quo. The typical response of majority members is to direct frequent communications to the opinion deviant (which gives the opinion deviant the opportunity to set the agenda), followed by shunning, avoiding, and ignoring the now disliked deviant (Schachter, 1951). An opinion deviant can be a more effective communicator by adopting Moscovici's (1976) behavioral style of successful minority influence, including consistency of response, flexibility in

negotiation, self-confidence, and linking position to an objective standard (see De Dreu, Chapter 10, this volume for more details).

Manded Altercast   A manded altercast is a verbal expression that specifies the role to be taken by the alter or target of the influence attempt. (It is based on the Skinnerian term "mand," which is derived from com*mand*, de*mand*, and counter-*mand*.) A manded altercast is an effective influence tactic to the extent that the target is placed in a social role favorable to the influence attempt. The manded altercast can be accomplished in a number of manners. One method is to make salient already existing social roles and identities. For example, Piliavin and Callero (1991) observed that among those who gave blood, those who developed a salient identity as "blood donors" were more likely to continue to donate blood. Another technique of manded altercast is to place alter in a pre-existing role. For example, Lieberman (1956) found that workers who were promoted to a super-visory position became more pro-management whereas those that were promoted to union stewards became more pro-union; these changes in attitude diminished when the supervisors and union stewards reverted to their old worker role. Finally, manded altercasting can be accomplished by attributing to alter a new identity or role. For example, Miller, Brickman, and Bolen (1975) told school children that they were neat and tidy or great at math and found that the children subsequently littered less and did better at math. A variant of this technique is the *hidden-self* procedure, where the target is told that some hidden aspect of their selves just happens to coincide with the target request (Spanos, Radtke, & Bertrand, 1985). The effectiveness of manded altercasting further underscores the significance of social relationships for inducing influence. The credibility of an appeal depends just as much on the social position of the recipient as on the social status of the source. Given that the nature of social roles varies as a function of social systems, there are as many ways of executing the manded altercast as there are social roles. Nevertheless, some social roles are common to a variety of settings; the next five tactics look at influence devices based on manded altercasting into common roles.

Role-Play of Advocacy (Manded Altercast)   Asking a person to play (pretend) the role of advocating a given course of action increases the likelihood that the person will accept that position. For example, Janis and King (1954) asked students to pretend to be sincere advocates for a position that they normally oppose; the results showed considerably more acceptance of that position (com-pared to controls who merely heard the message). Subsequent research has shown that the tactic is most effective when the advocate improvises the content of the speech (King & Janis, 1956; see self-generated persuasion below) and the pro-cedure induces a biased scanning of arguments to complete the role-play (Elms & Janis, 1965), increases the openmindedness of the role player (Greenwald, 1969), and promotes consideration of opposing information not previously rejected (Greenwald, 1970).

Cooptation (Manded Altercast)   Cooptation is the process of absorbing opponents into the leadership of an organization, thereby reducing the likelihood of opposition and increasing the likelihood that opponents will conform to the interests of the organization – for example, a leader of a dissenting group may be given a position (role) in the ruling group. In one of a series of experimental demonstrations of cooptation, Lawler (1983) found that group members will put up with inequitable pay and be less likely to revolt if there is the potential to be coopted into leadership. In his classic analysis of the Tennessee Valley Authority, Selznick (1949) observed that cooptation that involves power-sharing could result in democratic participation among citizens whereas cooptation that is symbolic or involves sharing only the burdens of power can be a tool for implementing the mandates of group leaders (for another example of the use of cooptations see Pratkanis & Turner, 1994).

The Helping Label (Manded Altercast)

One tactic for increasing helping and compliance with requests to give to charitable causes is to label the target as a prosocial person. For example, Strenta and DeJong (1981) gave subjects a bogus personality test and then declared the subject to be either kind or intelligent. (Control subjects were either told nothing or told the upcoming task would depend on kindness.) Subjects who had been labeled kind (compared to the other treatments) were more likely to help a confederate who dropped a large number of cards. Similarly, Kraut (1973) found that telling someone that he or she was "a generous person" (relative to a control) increased the likelihood that that person would make a larger contribution on a subsequent request to give to prevent multiple sclerosis.

Granfalloon (Social Identity) Tactic (Manded Altercast)

According to the novelist Kurt Vonnegut, a granfalloon is "a proud and meaningless association of human beings" such as Hoosiers, Buckeyes, devotees of Klee or Kandinsky, or Nazis. Once an individual is altercast into a social identity, social influence follows in at least two ways (see Abrams et al., 1990; Burger et al., 2004; Cadinu & Cerchioni, 2001; Kelley & Volkart, 1952). First, influence can be based on the unit relationship established between the target and the social identity (Sole, Marton, & Hornstein, 1975). The social identity provides a simple rule to tell the individual what to believe; in other words, "I am a _____ [fill in the blank with an identity] and we do and believe _____ [fill in the blank with identity-related behavior and belief]." Second, in specialized cases, some identities become important as a source of self-esteem and locate a person in a system of social statuses. In such cases, influence is based on a desire to stay in the good graces of a positive group and avoid the pain of associating with a derogated identity (Pool, Wood, & Leck, 1998) or exclusion from a desired group (Williams, 2001). A skilled propagandist can link an advocated course of action with a target's social identity and thus the target must perform the desired behavior as a way of maintaining a social identity (and any related self-esteem and status).

Expert Snare (Manded Altercast)

The expert snare is a reversal of the typical use of an expert as the source of a communication. In the expert snare, the recipient or alter is cast into the role of "expert." In that role, alter attempts to maintain status by putting on the trappings of expertise, avoiding embarrassing disclosures, and accepting absurd proposals deemed necessary to uphold the role. In two experiments, Pratkanis and Uriel (2005) altercast surfers, Frisbee players, and recreational dancers as experts in their respective domains. Relative to controls, such "experts" were more likely to support absurd proposals within their domain of expertise such as requiring surfboard bellies to be painted yellow with purple polka dots and students to take an orientation on the nonexistent activities of Tanzimat Frisbee or root dancing (see Pratkanis & Shadel, 2005 for additional examples).

Social Consensus (Bandwagon)

The more it appears that everyone is doing "it" or supports a given position, the more likely others will join in and agree. For example, Milgram, Bickman, and Berkowitz (1969) positioned confederates on a busy city street and had them look up at a building. Passersby readily copied the "looking up" response with overall conformity described by a negatively accelerating curve as a function of number of those looking up (that is, each additional person looking up increased conformity, but at a lower rate; Latané, 1981). Social consensus engages two psychological processes that promote conformity (Deutsch & Gerard, 1955). First, social consensus provides *information* or social proof about what to do and think via a simple rule: "If other people are doing it, it must be correct." The informational value of social agreement can be seen in experiments that expose subjects to the knowledge that others support a given cause or action. For example, Reingen (1982) conducted five field experiments in which a target is first shown a list of other compliers and then asked to comply with a request; the results showed that such a procedure increases both money and blood donations (see Moore, 1921 for a variation). Similarly, Nosanchuk and Lightstone (1974) and Axsom, Yates, and Chaiken (1987) showed that the presence of canned laughter and other audience responses could serve as a cue to elicit agreement. Second, social consensus provides *normative* influences or social pressure to agree or go along with the group. We saw previously that an opinion deviant receives much negative attention and sanctions. Although such attention can result in influence in certain conditions (De Dreu, Chapter 10, this volume), it is for the most part a painful psychological state as the target attempts to fulfill a need to belong (Baumeister & Leary, 1995) and conversely to avoid ostracism or exclusion from others (Williams, 2001). Such social pressure can be a powerful force to induce agreement with others. Consider the classic experiments of Asch (1951, 1952) in which six confederates select a clearly incorrect line in an ostensible perceptual task. In this research, subjects are confronted with two conflicting goals – to be correct or to maintain a positive relationship with the group. Although few subjects actually come to believe that the incorrect line is of a different length (informational influence), over half of the subjects in the Asch studies conformed at least once and swung to the majority on over 35% of the trials. The social pressure of the Asch procedure can readily be observed in the replication of the study I conducted for *Dateline NBC* (Pratkanis, 1997). As one subject put it after conforming to the group: "I didn't want to be different anymore."

Social Norms   A norm is a rule that states expectations about the appropriate and correct behavior in a situation – for example, tip 15%, don't urinate in public, and African-Americans shouldn't be CEO. As Goldstein and Cialdini (Chapter 7, this volume) point out, norms can be either descriptive (a summary of what most people do) or injunctive (an expectation of what ought to be done). As such, a norm represents an implied social consensus and thus carries both informational influence (especially descriptive norms) and social pressures (especially in ought norms) useful for influencing behavior. For example, Sherif (1936) found that groups quickly developed norms that would in turn guide judgment and perceptions of the autokinetic effect. Pettigrew (1991) has repeatedly observed the power of norms in the regulation of interracial beliefs and behavior. Perkins (2003) describes a number of studies showing that informing college students about the actual norm in regard to substance abuse (fewer students engage in substance abuse than most students think) may result in a decrease in such abuse. Goldstein and Cialdini (this volume) review a number of experiments illustrating the use of norms in social influence.

Social Modeling   The presence of a person (either live or on film) demonstrating a given behavior generally increases the probability of the emission of that behavior by observers. In other words, social models are a source of social proof on what to do in any given situation. For example, Bryan and Test (1967) found that passersby were more likely to contribute to the Salvation Army or help a distressed motorist with the presence of a helping model. Bandura and Menlove (1968) found that children who were afraid of dogs reduced their avoidance of dogs after watching models interacting nonanxiously with dogs. Phillips (1986) observed that watching highly publicized prizefights increased the homicide rate in the viewing area. The tendency to follow and imitate social models is especially likely for models who are high in prestige, power, and status, are rewarded for performing a behavior to be imitated, provide information on how to perform the behavior, and are attractive and competent (Pratkanis & Aronson, 2001).

Social Reinforcement   Insko (1965) demonstrated the power of a verbal reinforcer to influence attitudes. In his experiment, students were contacted via phone to take a survey of campus attitudes. On this survey, students were asked if they agreed or disagreed with fourteen statements concerning a campus Aloha week. The survey-taker then positively reinforced with the word "good" for agreement (or disagreement) with each statement. A week later, Insko surveyed the students in an unrelated class and found that those who were reinforced for agreeing with Aloha week statements evaluated it more favorably than those reinforced for disagreeing with such statements. Insko and Cialdini (1969; Cialdini & Insko, 1969) advanced a two-factor theory of verbal reinforcement: Verbal reinforcement (a) provides information about the survey-taker's opinion (or social proof) and (b) indicates that the survey-taker likes or approves of the respondent (social pressure).

Multiple Sources   An increase in the number of sources for a communication can, under certain conditions, result in an increase in persuasion. For example,

Harkins and Petty (1981a; see also Harkins & Petty, 1981b) found that three different speakers delivering three different cogent arguments were more effective than one source delivering the same three arguments (see Lee & Nass, 2004 for a replication using synthetic voices). Through experimental analysis, Harkins and Petty showed that increasing the number of sources of a communication increases thinking about each argument. This leads to more persuasion when the arguments are strong and compelling, but less persuasion when the arguments are weak.

Public Audience   The presence of an audience can increase concerns for maintaining a positive public image; this can result in increased compliance when the request is one that is socially approved. For example, Rind and Benjamin (1994) asked male shoppers to purchase raffle tickets to support the United Way; male shoppers with a female companion purchased almost twice as many tickets compared to lone male shoppers. Similarly, Froming, Walker, and Lopyan (1982) found that subjects were more or less willing to use shocks as punishment in an experiment depending on the perceived beliefs of an evaluative audience. In contrast, when compliance is not socially approved (say, when the person would look wish-washy or weak), the presence of a public audience may hinder persuasion. (As an aside, the presence of an audience can also facilitate or hinder performance on a task; see Guerin, 1993; Zajonc, 1965.)

Fleeting Interactions   A number of studies demonstrate that having a fleeting, brief social interaction with the target of a request increases compliance with a request. Such fleeting interactions have included introducing yourself (Garrity & Degelman, 1990), a gentle touch (Guéguen & Fisher-Lokou, 2002; Segrin, 1993 for a review), asking about how a person feels (Howard, 1990), engaging in a short dialogue before asking the request (Dolinski, Nawrat, & Rudak, 2001), personalizing a message (Howard & Kerin, 2004), and just sitting in a room with someone (Burger, Soroka, Gonzago, Murphy, & Somervell, 2001). There are a number of explanations for these effects, including the invoking of a liking heuristic (Burger et al., 2001), mimicking friendship (Dolinski et al., 2001), inducing positive mood, desire to maintain a social relationship, reciprocity, and individuating the requester and thus making her or him seem more human. Sorting out these explanations will be a fruitful research endeavor (see Burger, Chapter 6, this volume for an introduction to the issues).

Effective Message Tactics

The next set of tactics are ones in which the influence agent organizes, provides and/or induces the target to generate arguments and reasons for a given course of action. For Aristotle an effective communication appeared to follow the rules of logic. He also gave his students advice for creating effective messages, such as the use of vivid historical and imaginary examples to prove a point and tailor the message to fit the pre-existing beliefs of the audience. Recent research has shown that an effective persuasive message is one that focuses the targets' attention and cognitive activity on exactly what the communicator wants them to think about. This may involve such processes as inducing the target to think of reasons for a given action, making it appear that there are good reasons for an action, disrupting a person's ability to counterargue, focusing attention on certain reasons, selecting the most powerful arguments, and delivering the message for best effect. The following are some ways to increase the effectiveness of a message.

Self-Generated Persuasion   One of the most effective means of influence is to design the situation subtly so that the target generates arguments in support of a position and thereby persuades herself or himself. Lewin's (1947) work during the Second World War provides a classic demonstration of the effectiveness of self-generated persuasion. In this research, Lewin attempted to get housewives to serve sweetbreads (organ meats) by either giving a lecture on the value of serving sweetbreads or having the housewives generate their own reasons for serving sweetbreads. The results showed that those housewives who generated their own arguments were nearly eleven times more likely to serve sweetbreads than those who received the lecture. Miller and Wozniak (2001) provide a contemporary example. In their experiment, after listening to a lecture on the ineffectiveness of subliminal influence, students either summarized the points made in the lecture or generated the arguments they thought were most effective. The results showed that those students who self-generated arguments were least likely to believe in the effectiveness of subliminal influence. Self-generated persuasion typically results in persistence of attitude change (Boninger, Brock, Cook, Gruder, & Romer, 1990; Miller & Wozniak, 2001; Watts, 1967).

Imagery Sells   Imaging the adoption of an advocated course of action increases the probability that that course of action will indeed be adopted. For example, Gregory, Cialdini, and Carpenter (1982) sent salespersons door-to-door to sell cable TV subscriptions. Some potential customers were merely informed of the advantages of cable TV. Others were asked to "take a moment and imagine how cable television will provide *you* with broader entertainment" followed by inducing the potential customer to imagine how he or she would enjoy each benefit of cable TV. The results showed that those customers who were asked to imagine the benefits of cable TV were 2.5 times more likely to purchase a subscription compared to those who were merely given the information (see also Anderson, 1983; Taylor, Pham, Rivkin, & Armor, 1998).

Omitting an Explicit Message Conclusion   Should a persuasive message draw or omit an explicit conclusion? Based on what is known about the effectiveness of self-generated persuasion, it would be reasonable to conclude that open-ended communications that let a target draw her or his conclusion would be most effective. Although there is some research consistent with this proposition (Linder & Worchel, 1970), many experiments find that it is better to state an explicit conclusion (cf. Fine, 1957; Hovland & Mandell, 1952). Sawyer & Howard (1991) provide a simple solution to account for these conflicting results. In two experiments, Sawyer and Howard found that omitting the conclusion of a message resulted in more persuasion when the target was motivated to process the message (for example, when it was personally relevant). For communications that are low in personal relevance (low involvement), an influence advantage can be gained by explicitly stating the main conclusion of the message.

Rhetorical Questions   Don't you think you should be using rhetorical questions in your communications? A rhetorical question is one that is asked for effect and for which an answer is not expected. In general, rhetorical questions motivate more intensive processing of message content (Burnkrant & Howard, 1984). This increased message attention results in an increase in persuasion when the message is strong, but a decrease in persuasion when the message is weak. (However, when message recipients are already highly motivated to process a message, rhetorical questions can disrupt thinking, resulting in less persuasion for a strong message; Petty, Cacioppo, & Heesacker, 1981.) Recently, Ahluwalia and Burnkrant (2004) developed a model of rhetorical question effects. In their model, rhetorical questions can also draw attention to the source of the message, resulting in an increase in persuasion for positive sources and a decrease for negative ones.

Pique Technique   According to Santos, Leve, and Pratkanis (1994), the pique technique consists of the disruption of a mindless refusal script by making a strange or unusual request so that the target's interest is piqued, the refusal script is disrupted, and the target is induced to think positively about compliance. To test this tactic, Santos et al. had panhandlers ask for money in either a strange (e.g., "Can you spare 17 cents?") or typical (e.g., "Can you spare a quarter?") manner. Subjects receiving the strange request were almost 60% more likely to give money than those receiving the typical plea. Davis and Knowles (1999) have also found evidence that a strange request can promote compliance, but hypothesized that such requests operate through a different process and gave the technique a different name (disrupt-then-reframe). According to Davis and Knowles, an odd request disrupts resistance and creates confusion that makes the target more susceptible to a reframe that leads to influence; this process is similar to the role of distraction in persuasion (see below). In contrast, Santos et al. argue that an odd request disrupts a refusal script and then induces the target to wonder why the strange request was made. Compliance is then dependent on the nature of cognitive responses (e.g. disruption of counterarguments and promotion of support arguments) that result from this attempt to understand the strange request; this process is similar to that invoked by rhetorical questions (see above). Cognitive responses can be internally generated (in the Santos et al. study the strange request prompted targets to like the panhandler) or supplied externally (as in the Davis and Knowles reframe). Santos et al. provide process data in support of their hypothesized mechanism. They find that the pique technique results in more question asking and that these questions are specifically addressed to understanding the nature of the strange request. More recently, Fennis, Das, and Pruyn (2004) have provided experimental data to elucidate the process involved when one makes a strange request. In three experiments, they found that odd requests increased compliance. In their third experiment, they coupled an odd request

designed to promote a college fee increase with either a weak goal-incongruent or a strong goal-congruent message. Davis and Knowles would predict either that both messages would produce the same results or that the weak message would gain an advantage over the strong (as in distraction research). Santos et al. would predict the opposite. The results showed that the odd request produced significantly more compliance when paired with the strong as opposed to the weak argument, as predicted by Santos et al.

Message Fit: Link the Content of a Message to the Pre-Existing Beliefs, Experiences, and Knowledge of the Recipient   Both Plato (in *Gorgias*) and Aristotle advised would-be influence agents to link their arguments and appeals to the beliefs and experiences of their audiences. The Institute of Propaganda Analysis referred to this as tabloid thinking – reducing complex issues to one simple, widely-accepted slogan, commonplace, or truism (Werkmeister, 1948). Similarly, Pratkanis and Shadel (2005) find that fraud criminals often tailor a scam or pitch to the psychological and other characteristics of their target of victimization. Considerable research in a variety of domains demonstrates the effectiveness of this technique. For example, Cacioppo, Petty, and Sidera (1982) presented messages based on religious and legalistic arguments to religious- and legalistic-oriented subjects and found that message arguments were rated as more convincing when they fit the subject's orientation. Snyder and DeBono (1989) demonstrated that high self-monitors found ads emphasizing image and appearance to be more appealing and convincing whereas low self-monitors found ads emphasizing argument quality to be most persuasive. Howard (1997) obtained increased persuasion for messages that used familiar phrases or slogans (compared to unfamiliar phrases conveying the same meaning), especially in limited-thinking situations. In implementing this tactic, the message can be tailored to fit a variety of pre-existing beliefs, experiences, and knowledge including the attitude heuristic (Pratkanis, 1988), balancing processes (Heider, 1958), ideal and ought self (Evans & Petty, 2003), experimentally induced needs (Julka & Marsh, 2000), slogans (Bellak, 1942; Sherif, 1937), commonplaces (or widely accepted arguments; Pratkanis, 1995), prejudice and stereotypes (Ruscher, 2001), wishful thinking (Lund, 1925), natural heuristic (Rozin et al., 2004), tendency for egocentric thought (e.g., Barnum statements; Petty & Brock, 1979), laws of sympathetic magic such as physical contagion (Rozin & Nemeroff, 2002) and a host of cognitive biases such as representativeness, availability, accessibility, fundamental attribution error, illusory correlation, naïve realism, and hindsight (Gilovich, Griffin, & Kahneman, 2002; Kahneman, Slovic, & Tversky, 1982; Nisbett & Ross, 1980).

Placebic Reasons   A placebic argument is a reason that appears to make sense but is really vacuous and without information. Langer, Blank, and Chanowitz (1978) attempted to cut in line to make photocopies of either a small or large number of papers. The request was made with no information (e.g., "Excuse me . . . May I use the Xerox machine?"), with a real reason added ("because I am in a rush?"), or with a placebic reason ("because I have to make copies?"). Langer et al.

found that real reasons increased compliance with both small and large requests (compared to controls), whereas placebic arguments increased compliance for a small but not a large request. However, it should be noted that Folkes's (1985) attempted replication of the Langer et al. findings yielded inconsistent results, and thus additional research is required before we fully understand the effectiveness of placebic arguments.

Misleading Inference

Another way to increase the effectiveness of an argument is to induce a misleading inference – in other words, "say what you don't mean, and mean what you don't say" while giving the appearance of "saying what you mean, and meaning what you say." For example, Harris (1977) found that consumers would falsely assume that juxtaposing two imperative statements in an ad would imply a causal relationship, and Shimp (1978) found that incomplete comparatives in an ad are often used by consumers to incorrectly infer that a product is superior to competitors. Such misleading inferences can result in inflated product beliefs, evaluations, and purchase intentions (Burke, DeSarbo, Oliver, & Robertson, 1988; Olson & Dover, 1978). Preston (1994) presents a scheme for classifying misleading inferences and deception in advertising (see also Geis, 1982).

One-Sided versus Two-Sided Refutation Messages

A two-sided message that states the opposing position and then refutes it is most effective when the audience is well-informed, can process a complex message, and the target is mildly opposed to the message. A one-sided message is effective with partisans and the uninformed. A two-sided message without refutations is rarely effective (Hovland, Lumsdaine, & Sheffield, 1949; McGinnies, 1966). Two-sided messages gain an advantage in persuasion because such messages tend to reduce counterarguing and increase the perceived credibility of the source (Bohner, Einwiller, Erb, & Siebler, 2003; Kamins, Brand, Hoeke, & Moe, 1989).

The Defusing Objections Technique

A request to perform a behavior often induces the target to counterargue and raise objections. The defusing objections technique developed by Pardini and Katzev (1986) seeks to remove these excuses by acknowledging the objections and then refuting them before the target can raise them. For example, Pardini and Katzev (1986) found increased support for energy conservation in appeals that defused common objections (i.e., it is too much trouble; doesn't save much money) relative to controls. More recently, Werner, Stoll, Birch, and White (2002) were able to increase recycling rates by posting signs that acknowledged common excuses for not recycling (e.g., "it may be inconvenient but it is important").

Legitimizing Paltry Contributions (Even a Penny Will Help)

Another technique for removing objections to comply with a request is to legitimize a minimal level of compliance. For example, in collecting for the American Cancer Society, Cialdini and Schroeder (1976) added the phrase "even a penny will help" to the standard pitch for a contribution. Such a phrase increased the percentage of those who gave to the American Cancer Society without decreasing the size of the average gift (see Reingen, 1978 for a replication). The technique works because it eliminates many excuses for not giving (such as "I don't have enough money") and at the same time makes the target appear cheap and heartless if they don't give.

Dilution: Mild Arguments Weaken an Appeal   Adding weak arguments or neutral information to a persuasive communication can diminish the impact of a message, making a strongly positive message less positive and a strongly negative message less negative. For example, Lewan and Stotland (1961) gave subjects neutral information about a fictitious country and found that it weakened the impact of a negative, emotional appeal about that country (see Zukier, 1982 for a similar effect with person impressions). Friedrich, Fetherstonhaugh, Casey, and Gallagher (1996) gave messages that varied in length and in the mixture of strong and weak arguments and found that weak arguments diluted the appeal. (They also found that message length equals message strength; see below.) These patterns of data can be described by Anderson's (1981) average model of information integration.

Negativity Effect   In general, negative information receives more attention and weight than positive information when one is making judgments about persons, issues, and things (Kanouse & Hanson, 1972). For example, Hodges (1974) gave subjects personality descriptors varying in the amount of positive and negative information and found that negative information had a greater impact on evaluation. Lau (1982) found that negative information was more influential than positive information about US Presidential candidates in the 1968, 1972, and 1980 elections. Rozin and Royzman (2001) review evidence to conclude that this negativity bias is manifested in both animals and humans and may be innate.

Discrepancy of a Message   Should a message ask the target for a small or a big change in belief? The answer is that it depends on how easy it is to disparage the communication. When the source of the message is of high credibility (and thus difficult to disparage), asking for a large opinion change is most effective (cf., Zimbardo, 1960). On the other hand, when the communicator is of low credibility or the issue is involving (or any other factor that makes the extreme request appear incredulous), asking for a large opinion change is not as effective as asking for a smaller change (a curvilinear result) and may backfire (Hovland, Harvey, & Sherif, 1957; for an illustration of both processes see Aronson, Turner, & Carlsmith, 1963; Brewer & Crano, 1968).

Message Length = Message Strength   A simple rule of thumb for accepting the conclusion of a message is "the longer the message (larger the number of arguments), the more it appears that the message has something to say." Petty and Cacioppo (1984) varied the number of arguments (three or nine), the cogency of those arguments (weak or strong), and the level of involvement of the message recipient. When involvement was low (and the recipient was not carefully processing the message), a long message increased persuasion, whereas when involvement

was high (and the recipient was motivated to scrutinize the message), persuasion was dependent on the cogency of the arguments (see also Friedrich et al., 1996).

Vivid Appeals   A vivid appeal is a message that is (a) emotionally interesting, (b) concrete and image-provoking, and (c) immediate (Nisbett & Ross, 1980). Such messages can be compelling. For example, Gonzales, Aronson, and Costanzo (1988) taught energy auditors to speak in a vivid language (e.g., instead of saying, "the attic needs insulation," they said such things as, "you have a naked attic that is facing winter without any clothes on") and found an increase in compliance with recommendations for making homes more energy-efficient. Similarly, Borgida and Nisbett (1977) found that students' selection of courses was much more dependent on receiving a vivid comment from another person than on average ratings of the course by previous students (see also Hamill, Wilson, & Nisbett, 1980). Although it is an effective tactic, there are conditions when vividness is ineffective or may boomerang, such as when it is paired with a weak argument (Pratkanis & Aronson, 2001) or when vividness becomes distracting (Frey & Eagly, 1993; see Taylor & Thompson, 1982 for a review).

Distraction   A mild distraction such as keeping track of lights on a display while processing a persuasion message disrupts dominant cognitive responses (see Festinger & Maccoby, 1964 for the original finding). Thus, it can result in more persuasion when the message is weak or counterattitudinal (and likely to provoke counterarguments) and less persuasion when the message is strong (and likely to elicit supporting arguments; see Petty, Wells, & Brock, 1970 for the definitive experiments on this topic). In other words, distraction can be viewed as a response deamplification.

Overt Behavior Movements   Overt behavior movements such as smiles, frowns, body positions, and head movement can result in social influence consistent with the meaning of those movements. For example, in a test of the facial feedback hypothesis, Strack, Martin, and Stepper (1988) had subjects hold a pen in their mouths (under the guise of testing procedures for use with paraplegics) in a manner that inhibited or facilitated muscles used in smiling. The results showed that cartoons were rated as more humorous when a smile was facilitated as opposed to inhibited. Recently, Briñol and Petty (2003) identified what may be the nature of the feedback in the feedback hypothesis: Overt behavior movements serve to self-validate (increase or decrease confidence in one's thoughts). In the first of a series of experiments, Briñol and Petty had subjects engage in head nodding or shaking (under the guise of testing the quality of equipment) as they listened to a strong or weak message. For a strong message, nodding produced more attitude change than shaking; for a weak message the results were reversed, indicated that the head movement served to validate what the target was thinking during message processing.

Overheard Communication   In a series of clever experiments, Walster and Festinger (1962) invited subjects to tour the psychology labs and especially the one-way mirror room. As part of this tour, the subjects listened in on a conversation about smoking, living in dorms, or student husbands spending more time with their wives. Some of the subjects thought they just overheard (eavesdropped) on a conversation (the participants didn't know they were there) whereas others thought the conversationalists knew that the subject was listening. The results showed that the overheard communication produced more opinion change for subjects who found the topic to be important and involving. Brock and Becker (1965) replicated these results and added a limiting condition to the findings: The overheard message must be agreeable to the subject and not counterattitudinal. The principal reason advanced for the overheard communication effect is that listeners will not infer self-serving motives on the part of the communicator, although there is disagreement on whether or not this is the mechanism (Brock & Becker, 1965).

Hostile Audience Effect   The knowledge that a communicator previously delivered a message to an audience that opposed and was hostile to the message conclusion increases the acceptance of that message. For example, Mills and Jellison (1967) gave subjects a message arguing for the tripling of tractor trailer license fees and told the subjects that the message was given at a meeting of either a union of railroad workers or long-haul truck drivers (a hostile audience). The subjects were much more likely to endorse the tripling of license fees when they thought the message was given to truck drivers as opposed to railroaders (see Eagly, Wood, & Chaiken, 1978 for a replication).

Heckling   Heckling refers to attempts by an audience member or members to disrupt a speech and to make it clear to others that the speaker is wrong and not to be listened to. Four research efforts have all converged on the finding that heckling, in general, is an effective means for countering a speaker. For example, Sloan, Love, and Ostrom (1974) found that heckling caused listeners who were neutral to a speaker to disagree with the speaker's views (relative to no-heckling controls; partisans showed a complex relationship to heckling). Similarly, Silverthorne and Mazmanian (1975) found that booing a speaker resulted in less persuasion (compared to controls), regardless of whether the speech was given live, on audiotape, or on videotape (see also Ware & Tucker, 1974). The best way to respond to a heckler is with a calm and relevant reply (Petty & Brock, 1976). Although heckling seems to produce consistent results, there is yet no agreed upon theory to account for these findings with distraction, variation in response range, identification with the heckler, and negative associations proposed as mediators of the effect.

Repetition of a Message   Repeating a message over and over generally increases believability and acceptance of the communication. Message repetition works by increasing liking for the object through the mere exposure effect (Zajonc, 1968) and by increasing the perceived validity of "facts" stated in the message (Boehm, 1994). However, when a target carefully attends to a message, repetition can result in no increase and sometimes a decrease in persuasion as tedium sets in and as the target becomes motivated to counterargue the message. Such "wear-out" effects can be reduced by using repetition with variation (Schumann, Petty, & Clemons, 1990).

Primacy Effect (in the Order of Presentation)

In general, when a series of information is presented on a given topic (say, a list of trait words or product attributes), the first information given will have more weight in the overall attitude or impression developed about the topic (Anderson, 1965). The results have been less clear when two opposing messages on the same topic are presented in sequence. In an experiment varying the order of presentation of pro and con messages on the topic of protective tariffs, Lund (1925) found evidence for a "law of primacy," in which the first message given had disproportionate impact on final attitudes. However, subsequent research has sometimes found evidence for a primacy effect, a recency effect, or no effect at all (see reviews by Lana, 1964; Rosnow, 1966). Two sets of research have begun to clarify the conditions under which a primacy or recency effect will be obtained. First, Miller and Campbell (1959) found a recency effect when the presentation of the two messages was separated by a week and opinions were assessed immediately after the presentation of the second message. A primacy effect was obtained at longer measurement delays. Pratkanis, Greenwald, Leippe, and Baumgardner (1988) used this principle of "differential decay of impact" to specify the conditions under which a sleeper effect (delayed increase in the impact of a message) would obtain. Second, Haugtvedt and Wegener (1994) have an attitude strength model of the primacy effect; primacy effects will obtain when the first message produces a strong attitude. In two experiments, Haugtvedt and Wegener found that primacy effects occurred under conditions when the message was of high personal relevance (inducing message elaboration resulting in a strong attitude on the first message) and that recency effects occur when message relevance is low.

Forewarning of Persuasive Intent

In this chapter, I have presented a number of ways to increase compliance and influence. This tactic and the next three tactics are designed to decrease the impact of an influence attempt. Forewarning of persuasive intent means providing the target of an influence attempt with a warning that what will happen next is designed to persuade. Such an appeal can be effective in increasing resistance to influence (but not always; for reviews see Cialdini & Petty, 1979; Sagarin & Wood, Chapter 13, this volume; Wood & Quinn, 2003). For example, Milgram and Sabini (1978) asked subway riders in New York City for their seat and found that over 68% of the riders would yield their seat. However, if these subway riders overheard a conversation warning them that they were about to be asked to give up their seats, only 36.5% of the riders would do so. There are two factors that limit the effectiveness of forewarning for increasing influence resistance. First, the forewarning should induce the target to prepare to counterargue the persuasive appeal; without such preparation, forewarning does not increase resistance. As such, forewarning is most effective in increasing resistance when the topic is involving, the target has time to marshal defenses and is motivated to counterargue a discrepant message. Second, a forewarning can result in attitudinal politics – moderating one's position to a neutral stance or midpoint of a scale when faced with having to discuss the issue with another person (Cialdini, Levy, Herman, & Evenbeck, 1973).

Inoculation
Another tactic for preventing persuasion is inoculation – a target receives a brief, opposing message that can be easily refuted and thus immunizes against a subsequent attack. This technique was pioneered by McGuire (1964) in a series of research investigations. In these experiments, McGuire created effective messages capable of changing attitudes about various cultural truisms (e.g., one should brush after every meal and get a routine chest x-ray). He then developed effective inoculation messages in which he taught possible responses (counter-arguments) to these attack messages, with the result that the target of the com-munication could resist a later, stronger influence attempt (see An & Pfau, 2004 for a recent application to political communications).

Stealing Thunder
Another tactic for mitigating or reducing the impact of an opponent's persuasive message is the technique of stealing thunder or revealing potentially damaging information before it can be stated by an opponent. The effectiveness of this tactic was demonstrated in two experiments by Williams, Bourgeois, and Croyle (1993). In these experiments, mock jurors received trial transcripts in which negative information was presented by the opposing side about the defendant (Experiment 1) or a witness (Experiment 2). This information had strong, negative effects on the target. However, for some of the mock jurors the "thunder was stolen" by having the negative information presented by the defendant's attorney or the witness himself (before it was given by the opposing side). In such cases, the negative effects of the information was mitigated (Experiment 1) and eliminated (Experiment 2; for a summary of stealing thunder research see Williams & Dolnik, 2001).

Damn It, Refute It, Damn It, Replace It
Once a belief is established or an innuendo spread, it is often difficult to counter and refute. For example, Tybout, Calder, and Sternthal (1981) attempted to counter the rumor that McDonald's hamburgers contain worms and found that simple refutation was ineffective (see also attempts at corrective advertising; Wilkie, McNeill, & Mazis, 1984). Thus, it is best to use the previous three tactics in counterinfluence. However, a number of lines of research including rumor control during the Second World War (Allport & Postman, 1947), replies to ethnic slurs (Citron, Chein, & Harding, 1950), responses to dirty campaigning (Jamieson, 1992), and recent research on rumor transmission (DiFonzo, Bordia, & Rosnow, 1994; DiFonso & Bordia, Chapter 11, this volume) have all converged on some guideline for dealing with rumor and innuendo summarized by the phrase "damn it, refute it, damn it, replace it." Specifically, begin and end any refutation with a clear message that the innuendo is false and negated (damn it). Don't repeat the false information in a memorable manner. The refutation should be logical, short, factual, consistent, conclusive, and presented calmly. If at all possible, replace the false information with positive information about the target of the innuendo (see Tybout et al., 1981) or otherwise change the topic of conversation.

Emotional Tactics

An emotional appeal is one that uses the message recipient's subjective feelings, affect, arousal, emotions, and tension-states as the basis for securing influence (see Lewis, 1993 for a discussion of the definition of emotion). Aristotle urged communicators who want to be effective to control the emotions (or *pathos*) of the audience and to use emotions such as pity, pleasure, fear, and anger, to bring about the desired effects. In order to be able to effectively use an emotion in persuasion, Aristotle believed that one must know the names of the emotions and understand what produces them, who is most likely to experience each emotion, and the way each emotion is excited (its course and effects). Since Aristotle, those who seek to persuade have advocated the use of emotions while those concerned about misguided influence have warned us of the power of emotions to propagandize. There are two general reasons why emotions are effective as an influence device.

First, emotions are relatively easy to create and marshal in any given influence situation. Emotions can be aroused directly by appeals to fear, laying on a "guilt trip," piling on the flattery, and similar techniques. Emotions can also be aroused indirectly by placing a target in a situation that is likely to invoke emotions – for example, providing a gift to invoke a sense of obligation, inducing the person to behave in a counterattitudinal manner without a clear, apparent reason for the behavior in order to create a need for self-justification, or attacking the target's self-esteem.

Second, when an emotion is aroused and experienced, it can involve a number of psychological processes that can then be used as a platform for promoting and securing influence and compliance. For example, emotions have been shown to (a) provide valenced information that can be used to interpret the situation and guide behavior (Clore, 1992; Schwartz, 1990), (b) supply emotion-specified influences that impact judgment and choice (Lerner & Keltner, 2000), (c) change information processing priorities in the sense that dealing with the emotion becomes paramount (Simon, 1967), (d) reduce attentional capacity and narrow attention to goal-relevant information, especially when strong emotions are involved (Baron, 2000; Easterbrook, 1959; Kahneman, 1973), (e) motivate behavior to avoid or reduce negative feelings, especially in the case of negative tension-states or dissonance (Aronson, Chapter 4, this volume; Festinger, 1957), and (f) regulate behavior for the survival and adaptation of a social structure (Kemper, 1984).

The following tactics are designed to allow a communicator to control the emotions of the target for desired effects. These tactics follow a simple rule: Arouse an emotion and then offer the target a way of responding to that emotion that just happens to be the desired course of action. The emotion comes to color the target's world. The target becomes preoccupied with dealing with the emotion, is unable to critically analyze the issue, and thus complies with the request in hopes of escaping a negative emotion or maintaining a positive one.

Fear Appeals   A fear appeal is one that creates fear by linking an undesired action (e.g., smoking) with negative consequences, or a desired action (e.g., brushing teeth) with the avoidance of a negative outcome. Fear as an emotion creates an avoidance tendency – a desire to shun the danger. As an influence device, fear has proved to be effective in changing attitudes and behavior when the appeal (a) arouses intense fear, (b) offers a specific recommendation for overcoming the fear and (c) the target believes he or she can perform the recommendation (Leventhal, 1970, Maddux & Rogers, 1983). In other words, the arousal of fear creates an aversive state that must be escaped. If the message includes specific, doable recommendations for overcoming the fear, then it will be effective in encouraging the adoption of that course of action. Without a specific, doable recommendation, the target of the communication may find other ways of dealing with the fear such as avoidance of the issue and message, resulting in an ineffective appeal. Propagandists find fear to be a particularly useful influence device because it is easy to create "things that go bump in the night" along with a ready, doable solution – namely supporting the propagandist.

Guilt Sells   Guilt is the feeling of responsibility for some wrongdoing or transgression. Guilt induces a desire to make restitution and to repair a self-image. It can be used as an influence tactic by turning the act of restitution and image-repair into an act of compliance. For example, Carlsmith and Gross (1969) induced students to perceive that they had given a series of painful shocks to another person as part of a learning experiment. These guilty students were more likely to comply (relative to controls) to a subsequent request to make phone calls to "Save the Redwoods" when asked either by the person they supposed shocked or another person who knew nothing about the shocks (see Kassin & Kiechel, 1996 for an example of how guilt can induce false confessions). In cases where restitution is not possible, guilt for a transgression can result in self-justification for the wrongdoing (Glass, 1964).

Embarrass the Target of Influence   Embarrassment is a function of public self-consciousness and is typically produced when someone finds herself or himself in a predicament or committing an act that may result in a poor social evaluation. Embarrassment promotes a response of striving to avoid it or escape it once it has occurred (Miller, 1996). It is this aspect that gives embarrassment its power to influence. For example, out of embarrassment, males are less likely to help a female who dropped a box of tampons compared to a box of envelopes (Foss & Crenshaw, 1978), and everyone is less likely to help someone who has dropped a condom as opposed to a mitten (McDonald & McKelvie, 1992). As with guilt, embarrassment creates a need to restore a self-image, and this can lead to compliance. Apsler (1975) had students perform a set of four embarrassing acts (e.g., sing "The Star Spangled Banner," imitate a 5-year-old throwing a temper tantrum) in front of another student. Compared to controls, embarrassed students were more likely to consent to help another student with a class project regardless of whether the requester was the person who observed the embarrassing acts or someone who knew nothing about the incident.

Jeer Pressure   Ridicule and insults can increase compliance with a request. Steele (1975) found that insulting (name-calling) the target of a request increased the rate of completing a survey regardless of whether the insult was relevant (the target was uncooperative and selfish) or irrelevant (the target wasn't a safe driver) to the request. More recently, Janes and Olson (2000) found that merely having a target observe another person being ridiculed increased the target's rate of conformity. Such jeer pressure increases compliance because the target seeks to repair a self tarnished by the attack and hopes to avoid future ridicule by going along with the request. Abelson and Miller (1967) have identified one limiting factor for jeer pressure: An insult on a specific, previously held belief (especially in a public setting) can result in a boomerang effect (an increase in the original opinion).

Flattery (Ingratiation)   It is a widely held belief that flattery is a powerful influence device (see Pratkanis & Abbott, 2004 for a review). There is a considerable amount of research showing that we like those that flatter us, as illustrated by Gordon's (1996) meta-analysis of 106 effect sizes. However, only two experiments have looked explicitly at the effects of flattery on compliance with a direct request. Hendrick, Borden, Giesen, Murray, and Seyfried (1972) found that flattery (compliments on the goodness and kindness of the target) increased compliance with a request to complete a seven-page questionnaire relative to a control condition. Pratkanis and Abbott (2004) asked passersby on a city street to participate in a "stop junk mail" crusade after they were flattered about an article of clothing or asked the time of day (control treatment). We found that flattery increased compliance by ten percentage points over control. Interestingly, these effects were obtained regardless of whether the "stop junk mail" request was made by the flatterer or a different person (immediately after the flattery was given), indicating that in this experiment flattery was working primarily through intrapersonal (e.g., mood and disposition of the target) as opposed to interpersonal (e.g., liking of the flatterer) processes.

Empathy   Empathy consists of two aspects: a cognitive awareness of another person's internal states (thoughts, feelings, perceptions, intentions) and a vicarious affective response of concern and distress for another person. Empathy can be induced by instructions to "put yourself in another's shoes" or assessed using standard measures (Davis, 1996). In general, empathetic concern for another person increases the likelihood of agreeing to requests to help that person (e.g., Batson, Duncan, Ackerman, Buckley, & Birch, 1981). For example, Archer, Foushee, Davis, and Aderman (1979) found that increased empathy with a defendant in a legal trial (e.g., imagine how you would feel if you were on trial) resulted in more favorable decisions for the defendant.

Norm of Reciprocity   Every human society (as well as chimpanzee ones too) has a simple rule of reciprocity: If I do something for you, then you should do something for me in return. Invoking this rule triggers a feeling of indebtedness or obligation to the person who has given a gift or performed a favor. A tension state is thus created: Do I live up to my social obligation or not? The norm of reciprocity is one of the glues of primate society. It can be employed for influence purposes when the compliance agent supplies a desired course of action for resolving the indebtedness tension state. For example, Regan (1971) staged an experiment where a confederate of the experimenter gave a subject a soft drink as a favor or provided no favor. The subject was more likely to purchase raffle tickets when a favor was rendered than when no drink was provided.

Door-in-the-Face (Rejection-then-Retreat) The door-in-the-face (DITF) tactic involves a requester first asking for a large favor (which is refused) and then for a smaller favor, which is typically granted at a rate higher than just asking for the small favor to begin with. For example, Cialdini, Vincent, Lewis, Catalan, Wheeler, and Darby (1975) asked passersby on a university campus to volunteer two hours a week for a minimum of 2 years working with juvenile delinquents. When the passerby rejected this request, the solicitors followed-up with the real request – to work 2 hours with juvenile delinquents. The results showed three times as much compliance with the request to work 2 hours when preceded by the large request as opposed to a control that merely made the smaller request. The DITF has created a vast literature with multiple meta-analytic reviews. The explanation most consistent with this literature is one based on the norm of reciprocity – when the requester retreats from the large request, it obligates the target to also make a concession (in this case, acquiesce to the smaller request) or feel the pangs of unrequited indebtedness. In addition, the unattractive first request serves as a comparison point to make the second request appear more attractive via contrast effects (Miller, 1974; see Cialdini & Goldstein, 2004 for a discussion of the cogency of other possible explanations). One limiting condition of the DITF tactic is that the first request cannot be extreme and outside the bounds of a legitimate request (Schwarzwald, Raz, & Zvibel, 1979).

The That's-Not-All Technique Another tactic that employs the norm of reciprocity is the "that's-not-all technique." This effective tactic (and staple of TV infomercials) consists of offering a product at a high price, not allowing the customer to respond for a few seconds, and then offering a better deal by adding another product or lowering the price. The sweetening of the deal invokes a feeling of indebtedness that increases compliance. For example, Burger (1986) sponsored a bake sale offering unpriced cupcakes. When a passerby asked about the price of the cupcakes, he or she was told the price was 75 cents and then, after a pause, that they would also get some cookies. In the control treatment, passersby were merely told that the cupcake and cookies were 75 cents. Burger found nearly double the sale of cupcakes using the that's-not-all technique (see also Burger, Reed, DeCesare, Rauner, & Rozolios, 1999). The that's-not-all technique bears similarity to the DITF tactic in that (a) both involve an initial less attractive request followed by a more attractive second request, (b) both invoke the processes of norm of reciprocity and contrast, and (c) the effectiveness of both tactics is reduced if the initial offer is large and lacks legitimacy. The two tactics differ in two important ways: (a) in DITF the initial offer is rejected whereas no response is elicited in the that's-not-all tactic, and (b) in DITF the initial offer is made less sour whereas in the that's-not-all tactic the initial offer is made sweeter.

Commitment Trap   Commitment is defined as the binding of an individual to a behavior or course of action. In other words, the person becomes identified with a certain behavior; commitments are strongest when that behavior is visible, irreversible, and perceived to be freely chosen (Salancik, 1977). Breaking this binding produces a negative tension of not living up to one's promises and a concern that one will look inconsistent and untrustworthy (e.g., a need to save face). As such, securing a commitment increases the likelihood that the target will comply and perform that behavior. A commitment can be secured through a number of devices including a public verbal commitment (Wang & Katzev, 1990), investment in a course of action (Brockner & Rubin, 1985), sunk costs, self-selection of goals, and the pretense that a commitment has been made (e.g., presumptive close in sales). Commitment can lead to disastrous results when negative setbacks result in escalating commitment to a failing course of action (Staw, 1976).

Foot-in-the-Door   In the foot-in-the-door (FITD) tactic, a target is first asked to do a small request (which most people readily perform) and then is asked to comply with a related and larger request (that was the goal of influence all along). For example, Freedman and Fraser (1966) asked suburbanites to put a big, ugly sign stating "Drive Carefully" in their yard. Less than 17% of the homeowners did so. However, 76% of the homeowners agreed to place the sign in their yards if, two weeks earlier, they had agreed to post in their homes a small, unobtrusive 3-inch sign urging safe driving. Burger (1999) has conducted a thoughtful analysis of over 55 published research reports on the FITD and concludes that it has the potential to invoke a number of psychological processes that may increase (self-perceptions that one is the type of person to perform an action, commitment, and desire for consistency) or decrease (reactance, norm of reciprocity, and other social pressures) the magnitude of compliance.

Low-Balling   A common sales tactic is low-balling or throwing the low-ball. In this tactic, the target first makes a commitment to perform a course of action (say, purchase a car for $20,000) and then this action is switched for a more costly behavior (oops, the car really costs $20,859). The target is more likely to perform this costlier task as a result of the earlier commitment. For example, Cialdini, Cacioppo, Bassett, and Miller (1978) found that securing students' agreement to sign up for a psychology experiment before telling them that the experiment was at 7 a.m. (a high-cost behavior for most students) resulted in more compliance compared to asking them to sign up for a 7 a.m. experiment. Burger and Petty (1981) have replicated the low-balling effect and argue that it is based on commitment, not necessarily to the task, but to the requester. Low-balling bears a similarity to the FITD in that both involve a commitment to an initial request or requester followed by a less attractive second request. In addition, the effectiveness of both tactics is reduced if there is no commitment to the first task (Burger, 1999; Burger & Cornelius, 2003). Low-balling differs from FITD in that the first request is the actual target behavior (only later made less attractive by adding costs) whereas in FITD the first request may be related to the second request but it is not the target behavior.

Bait-and-Switch   Joule, Gouilloux, and Weber (1989) demonstrated a tactic they called "the lure" that is similar to what is called bait-and-switch in sales. In their experiment, subjects volunteered to participate in an exciting study on film clips. This experiment was then cancelled and subjects were asked to switch to a boring experiment involving word memorization. These subjects were three times more likely to continue with the boring experiment relative to a control treatment. Bait and switch is based on commitment processes. It differs from low-balling in that the bait or lure is not available in bait-and-switch, as opposed to merely made less desirable in low-balling.

Counterattitudinal Advocacy with Insufficient Justification   In this dissonance-based tactic (Aronson, Chapter 4, this volume; Festinger, 1957), a person is induced to try to convince others of the rightness of a position that differs from her or his own privately held belief. When given minimum justification for doing so, the person must find additional justification for the advocacy and in the process is more likely to accept the original counterattitudinal position. Some examples of the implementation of this tactic are (a) Festinger and Carlsmith's (1959) experiment in which subjects falsely told others about the value of a boring experimental task, (b) Cohen's (1962) counterattitudinal role-play in which students wrote essays discrepant from their beliefs for minimum reward, and (c) Aronson and Carlsmith's (1963) forbidden toy research in which children failed to play with a desirable toy with minimum punishment.

Overjustification of an Intrinsic Activity   Providing too much justification (e.g., extrinsic rewards) for an activity can serve to reduce the intrinsic value of that task. For example, Deci (1971) found that providing monetary incentives to perform a task reduced intrinsic motivation. Similarly, Lepper, Greene, and Nisbett (1973) found that children who expected to receive a reward for performing an enjoyable task subsequently showed less interest in the task than children who did not receive a reward or received an unexpected reward (see Deci, Koestner, & Ryan, 1999 for a review). Benware and Deci (1975) also found that paying someone to make a proattitudinal communication reduces support for that position.

Effort Justification   In general, requiring a person to expend large amounts of effort to obtain an object leads to a justification of this expenditure by increased liking of the object. For example, Aronson and Mills (1959) required students to engage in a severe initiation (reciting obscene words to an opposite sex experimenter) in order to join what turned out to be a very boring discussion of sex. Compared to those students who engaged in a mild or no initiation, those who expended effort in the form of a severe initiation liked the boring discussion and found it interesting and worthwhile (see Axsom & Cooper, 1985 for an application of this technique to weight loss). In addition, the mere expectation of expending effort can lead to attitude change (Wicklund, Cooper, & Linder, 1967). Recent research also shows that humans possess an effort heuristic – the more effort it takes to produce an object, the higher that object is rated in terms of quality and liking (Kruger, Wirtz, Van Boven, & Altermatt, 2004).

Hypocrisy Reduction   Hypocrisy is aroused by having a person make a public commitment (say, tell teenagers to practice safe sex) and then make that person mindful of past failures to meet the commitment (say, complete a questionnaire on past sexual practices). To reduce the negative feelings of hypocrisy, the person is more likely to adopt the advocated behavior (in this case, practice safe sex; see Stone, Aronson, Crain, Winslow, & Fried, 1994 who conducted this experiment). In addition to increasing the use of condoms, the induction of hypocrisy has been shown to encourage water conservation (Dickerson, Thibodeau, Aronson, & Miller, 1992) and increase recycling (Fried & Aronson, 1995).

Question-Behavior Effect   The tactic of question-behavior entails asking a person to make a self-prediction about their intention to perform a certain behavior; the result is an increase in the likelihood of performing that action. For example, Greenwald, Carnot, Beach, and Young (1987) asked potential voters before an election, "What do you expect to do between now and the time the polls close tomorrow? Do you expect that you will vote or not?" Those voters who answered this question (relative to a no-question control) voted at a 20% higher rate. The technique has been applied to a wide variety of issues including recycling, fund-raising, and nutrition (Spangenberg & Greenwald, 2001). The self-prophecy appears to work through one of two mechanisms: (a) cognitive dissonance arousal – the respondent seeks to reduce the discrepancy between what was predicted and his or her behavior (Spangenberg, Sprott, Grohmann, & Smith, 2003) and (b) evoking a cognitive script for the behavior that then increases performance through imaging processes (Williams, Block, & Fitzgerald, 2006).

Self-affirmation   When a person receives a threatening message, say one that presents a disturbing conclusion or contains counterattitudinal information, a common response is to act defensively – to ignore, reject, or otherwise resist the message. One technique for overcoming this defensiveness is to have the target affirm the value of her or his self by engaging in such tasks as endorsing important values or writing an essay about one's values. For example, Sherman, Nelson, and Steele (2000) found that self-affirmations increased the likelihood that a person would accept threatening health information about the causes of breast cancer and about the practice of safe sex. Similarly, Cohen, Aronson, and Steele (2000) found that self-affirmations increased acceptance of counterattitudinal information concerning capital punishment and abortion. Blanton, Cooper, Skurnik, and Aronson (1997) have identified an important limiting condition of this technique: The self-affirmation should be unrelated to the content of the message since topic-relevant self-affirmations may increase defensiveness.

Self-efficacy   Another approach for changing high-risk, defensive, and anxiety-producing behavior is to increase the target's perceived self-efficacy or the beliefs about one's capability to organize and execute the courses of action required to reach given goals (Bandura, 1997). Perceived self-efficacy can be increased by such procedures as teaching skills, guided mastery, vicarious learning, and verbal persuasion (Maddux & Gosselin, 2003). The development of self-efficacy has been instrumental in inducing at-risk targets to accept a persuasive communication and change behavior in such areas as exercise, diet, smoking cessation, HIV prevention, and alcohol abuse (see Bandura, 1997; Maddux & Gosselin, 2003 for reviews).

Scarcity   As long ago as Aristotle, people realized that making an alternative appear scarce or rare increases its perceived value. Scarcity invokes a number of psychological processes. Consider an experiment conducted by Worchel, Lee, and Adewole (1975). In their experiment, subjects were asked to rate the attractiveness of cookies. They found that the cookies were deemed more attractive when there were only two cookies in a jar as opposed to ten cookies. This finding illustrates one of the reasons that scarcity is an effective influence device: We humans possess a rule in our head, "if it is rare, it must be valuable." Worchel et al. included another treatment in their experiment in which the subject began with a jar of ten cookies but an experimenter replaced that jar with one containing only two cookies under the pretense that he needed the cookies because subjects in his experiment had eaten more cookies than expected. In this case, subjects rated the cookies as even more attractive than the constant two cookies in a jar, illustrating the ability of scarcity to create a sense of urgency and panic that increases its effectiveness as an influence device. Scarcity also has the power to implicate the self for better or worse. The failure to possess or obtain a scarce object can create frustration and imply that the self is lacking in some regard (see summary by Pratkanis & Farquhar, 1992 of early work on barriers conducted in the Lewin tradition) as well as inducing reactance (see next tactic). In contrast, possessing a rare item may result in increased feelings of uniqueness and self-worth (Fromkin, 1970) that can serve as the basis for conspicuous consumption (Braun & Wicklund, 1989).

Psychological Reactance   Reactance occurs when an individual perceives that his or her freedom of behavior is restricted; it is an aversive tension state that motivates behavior to restore the threatened freedom (Brehm, 1966; Brehm & Brehm, 1981). Reactance can be aroused by a number of threats to freedom including the elimination of an alternative, social pressure to take a course of action, physical barriers, censorship, requiring everyone in a group to agree with another's decision, and authorities overstepping their mandates. The exact response to reactance may vary with the situation; however, two common responses designed to restore threatened freedoms are increased attractiveness and desire for an eliminated or threatened alternative and an oppositional response (boomerang) of attempting to do the reverse of the reactance-arousing social pressure. Once reactance is created, it can be used as an influence device by directing responses to restore freedom in a manner consistent with the goals of the influence agent. Brehm's (1966) theory of psychological reactance is important for understanding social influence in that it places a limiting condition (the production of reactance) on the effectiveness of many tactics listed in this chapter.

Evocation of Freedom (But you are Free to . . . Technique)   In contrast to reactance, reminding the target of her or his freedom to choose with a simple statement such as "But you are free to accept or refuse" can increase compliance. For example, Guéguen and Pascual (2000) solicited money for a bus in a shopping mall. When they included the statement "But you are free to accept or to refuse" at the end of the request, compliance increased almost 5-fold (see also Guéguen & Pascual, 2002; Horowitz, 1968).

Anticipatory Regret   Regret is a negative feeling or emotion that a decision or choice may not work out as you want it to, and you will not be able to reverse it later. Anticipating such regret can lead to attempts to minimize the chances of self-blame (e.g., "I blew that decision") and experiencing regret (Bell, 1982; Festinger, 1964). For example, Hetts, Boninger, Armor, Gleicher, and Nathanson (2000) staked subjects with $10 and then had them play a game with a 50% chance of losing this stake. Before playing the game, subjects could purchase insurance against loss. The critical manipulation consisted of emphasizing the regret that might be experienced if a disaster occurred and there was no insurance versus regret over purchasing insurance followed by no disaster. Subjects purchased insurance consistent with their anticipated regrets (see also Crawford, McConnell, Lewis, & Sherman, 2002; Wicklund, 1970).

1-in-5 Prize Tactic   The 1-in-5 prize tactic is commonly used in telemarketing scams and other swindles. The con criminal will tell a mark that he or she has won one of five prizes (such as an automobile, a vacation, a Van Gogh lithograph, a beachfront home, or $50,000 in cash). In order to claim the prize, all the target needs to do is to send in a fee – ostensibly to pay for shipping, taxes, or for some other seemingly plausible reason. The prize is a phantom and is rarely won; on those occasions when an award is given it is usually a "gimme" prize (such as the Van Gogh lithograph which sounds good in the context of the other prizes but is in reality a cheap reproduction). Surveys reveal that over 90% of Americans have been targeted by this pitch, with over 30% responding to the appeal. Horovitz and Pratkanis (2002) conducted an experimental analog of the 1-in-5 prize tactic by telling subjects at the end of another experiment that they had won one of these five prizes: a TV, a CD player, a university mug (the gimme prize), a VCR, or a $50 mall gift certificate. In order to claim the prize, the subject had to agree to write essays for about 2 hours. In a control condition in which subjects were merely asked to write essays, 20% of the subjects complied with the request. In the 1-in-5 prize treatment, 100% of the subjects across two experiments agreed to write essays. Horvitz and Pratkanis suggest that phantom fixation (Pratkanis & Farquhar, 1992) along with other psychological processes is the reason that the 1-in–5 prize tactic is so effective.

Self-threat   Students of the history of propaganda repeatedly observe that when many members of a society feel their selves to be threatened (e.g., experience relative deprivation, fear devaluation of self), fertile ground is established for the seeds of propaganda to grow and flourish (Pratkanis & Aronson, 2001). A similar relationship has been found in numerous experiments. For example, van Duüren and di Giacomo (1996) showed that failure on a test increased the chances of complying with a request to commit a theft. Kaplan and Krueger (1999) observed that giving subjects a negative personality profile generally increased compliance with participation in a charity food drive. Zeff and Iverson (1966) demonstrated that subjects faced with downward mobility were more likely to privately conform to a group. A self-threat appears to induce a state of social dependency and a desire to re-establish the positive aspects of the self, thus making the individual vulnerable to influence that appeals to these goals.

Emotional See-saw   What happens when a person experiences an emotion that is then rapidly withdrawn? Dolinski and his colleagues (Chapter 5, this volume; Dolinski & Nawrat, 1998; Dolinski, Ciszek, Godlewski, & Zawadzki, 2002) have conducted a program of research to show that when people experience an emotion that is then removed, they are more likely to comply with a request. For example, in one set of experiments, subjects experienced a fear that was then immediately removed – the subjects thought they had received a parking ticket or were caught jaywalking but it turned out to be a false alarm. In such cases, subjects were more likely to comply with a request to fill out a burdensome questionnaire or help out an orphanage. Similarly, in another set of experiments, subjects experienced happiness and delight that was quickly eliminated – the subjects thought they had found some money or received a high grade on a test only to find that the money was really an advertisement and the grade was only average. In such cases, subjects were more likely to comply with a request to watch a bag or help their school. Dolinski explains his findings by noting that emotions invoke specific plans of action and that when the emotion is removed the plan is no longer operative but the person has not yet invoked a new plan. In this state of confusion and disorientation, the person is more likely to comply with a request.

Sensory Deprivation   In sensory deprivation experiments, mostly conducted in the 1950s and 1960s, an individual is placed for 24 to 96 hours in a room designed to eliminate as much as possible such sensations as light, sound, and touch. The research showed that individuals in such environments experienced decrements in cognitive performance, hallucinations (after an extended period), and a desire for stimulation (Zubek, 1969). In addition, individuals experiencing sensory deprivation also showed an increase in susceptibility to influence as evidenced by increased (a) suggestibility as measured by the Hull body-sway test and responses to the autokinetic effect, (b) desire to listen to counterattitudinal propaganda, (c) attitude change in response to propaganda, and (d) conformity (although (c) and (d) may be lessened for those high in cognitive complexity and intelligence; see Suedfeld, 1969 for a review). Sensory deprivation results in a "cocktail" of cognitive (e.g., performance decrements), and emotional (e.g., boredom, tedium, anxiety, arousal) effects, making it difficult to identify the causal nexus of influence. Nevertheless, the research is significant in that it was originally motivated by reports of brainwashing of American soldiers by Red Chinese during the Korean conflict and confession extraction during the Stalinist purges in the Soviet Union. (Interestingly, preliminary research is emerging to show that increased cognitive stimulation or interest may also result in higher influence rates; Rind, 1997.)

Positive Happy Mood Isen and her colleagues have found that people placed in a positive mood (e.g., by the discovery of a dime in a coin return or a gift of cookies) are more likely to comply with a request to render help and assistance (e.g., volunteering to meet a request, picking up papers, mailing a letter; see Isen & Levin, 1972; Levin & Isen, 1975). In a review of positive mood and helping research, Carlson, Charlin, and Miller (1988) found consistent results that happy mood leads to helpfulness and identified a variety of mechanism for why this is so. Positive mood also impacts the processing of a persuasive message. For example, Petty, Schumann, Richman, and Strathman (1993) found that positive mood results in persuasion through one of two routes: (a) when a target is not motivated to think about an issue, a positive mood directly impacts the positivity of the attitude and (b) when a target is motivated to think about an issue, a positive mood results in more positive thoughts about the issue, resulting in positive attitude. In addition, Wegener, Petty, and Smith (1995) found that happiness can produce more message scrutiny when message processing is useful for maintaining a positive mood and less scrutiny when processing might mean the reduction of a positive mood, with persuasion dependent on how well the message stands up to this scrutiny. Thus, we end our tour of influence tactics on a happy note.

CONCLUDING REMARKS

Research Applications: A Periodic Table of Influence?

Recently, I had the opportunity to sit in on a series of lectures on chemistry and the periodic table of elements. The periodic table is a remarkable poetic and scientific achievement. Each element in the known universe is assigned an atomic number and weight and placed in a column and a row. Based on this table, chemists have been able to predict the characteristics of previously unknown elements as well as summarize how a known element will react to other elements. Is such a table possible for social influence?

Before the advent of the periodic table, chemists debated how best to categorize the vast array of specimens of elements and minerals stored in museum drawers. (A similar story can be told about understanding biological species before the development of DNA analysis.) My approach in this chapter has been to metaphorically dump out onto the table (with minimum organization) all the influence tactics I could find in psychology's museum drawers (journal archives) with the hope of stimulating research on the nature of these tactics. To develop a classification system of influence, we will need to identify the underlying social psychological process or processes employed by each tactic. In doing so, it is useful to remember that while some tactics and underlying processes may be isomorphic (one tactic and one process), most will likely be polygenetic (a given tactic involves multiple processes such as door-in-the-face and its underlying processes of reciprocity and contrast) and pleiotropic (one process will be involved in many tactics, such as the use of reciprocity in multiple tactics).

Unlike chemical elements, whose properties have remained fixed from the Big Bang, social influence tactics evolve and are modified and even created over time and place. (In this regard, the task of the social influence researcher is more similar to that of the biologist classifying species than that of the chemist.) In other words, classification (identifying the social psychological basis of a tactic) does not equal phylogeny (the history of the development of a given tactic). For example, tactics such as altercasting and reciprocity appear in every human culture (including the first communities), although how these tactics are implemented (e.g. the characteristics of role-sets and norms governing gifts) can vary with time and place. Some tactics may be found in only one location, such as the 1-in-5 prize tactic, which is a creation of late 20th-century North American telemarketing fraud (although it may have its roots in 19th-century scams). In order to be effective, an influence tactic must appeal to social psychological processes and form and evolve as a function of task (what influence goal needs to be accomplished) and ecology (relationship between the organism and its natural resource and social environment).

Thus, the full exploration of influence tactics will require the use of both experiments and comparative (e.g., case, survey, historical review) analysis based on the hypothetical–deductive method. Some of the scientific tasks involved in this exploration are: (a) identify new tactics through real-world observation (e.g., 1-in-5 prize), through theory (e.g., dissonance and effort justification), or in response to real-world problems (e.g., jigsaw); (b) specify the conditions under which a tactic is more or less effective; (c) identify the social psychological process underlying a tactic; (d) prune tactics that may not be as robust as first thought; (e) combine tactics that rely on the same processes; (e) elucidate the effects of tactics when they are used in combination; (f) identify variables or factors that may affect multiple tactics (such as involvement, ambiguity of the situation, cognitive load, pre-existing beliefs, and dissonance); (g) state the factors that increase (and decrease) the susceptibility of a person to a given tactic; (h) delineate the effects of a given tactic on different influence responses (e.g., attitude change, compliance, helping); (i) discover the age-related effectiveness (developmental basis) of a given influence tactic; (j) describe the effects on the influence agent of the use of a given tactic; (k) elucidate how people perceive the effectiveness of a tactic and select tactics in influence attempts; (l) explicate how tactics are learned (e.g., informal and formal cultural transmission, individual learning in response to similar tasks and ecology); (m) describe when people are capable of identifying influence attempts; (n) state the conditions under which influence is resisted; (o) develop counterinfluence techniques; (p) compare the use of tactics across species, history, cultures, and influence tasks; and (q) specify how tasks and ecology shape the implementation of tactics. Addressing these issues will result in a pool of empirical information to be used in theory development and synthesis.

Applications of Influence Tactics

Although there is considerable research to be done, this should not cause us to miss the scientific accomplishments that have already occurred and the value of these contributions for elucidating and changing social behavior. The index of social influence tactics described in this chapter can be used to conduct a social influence analysis – to analyze a given social situation in terms of the influence processes that are occurring along with suggesting interventions for bringing about desired changes in that situation. Specifically, this index can be used to (a) understand the power of situations; (b) devise social change campaigns and interventions; (c) increase tactical effectiveness by stating the conditions under which a tactic is most impactful; (d) identify poor or backfiring campaigns; (e) provide an estimation of the effectiveness of a tactic (in the absence of empirical data); (f) profile how an influence agent uses persuasion and conduct a propaganda analysis (e.g., understanding the goals, motives, and operational codes of an influence agent); (g) develop a counterpropaganda campaign to defuse unwanted influence; (h) teach the ethical use of influence and the resistance of undue influence; (i) shape social policies concerning issues involving social influence; (j) generate discussion about the ethical use of influence; and (k) describe how influence is best used in, and to create, a democracy.

The application of social influence tactics to elucidate and change behavior is certainly a valuable activity in its own right. However, such applied pursuits also yield information about new influence tactics and when such tactics are most effective – information that can stimulate new research and theory development, which in turn stimulates new applications (Cialdini, 1980; Greenwald, Pratkanis, Leippe, & Baumgardner, 1986). By engaging in basic and applied research on social influence, we can gain a deeper understanding of how we *Homo sapiens* direct, coordinate, and influence each other along with insights into the core social psychological processes that characterize our species.

REFERENCES

Abelson, R. P., & Miller, J. C. (1967). Negative persuasion via personal insult. *Journal of Experimental Social Psychology*, 3, 321–333.

Abrams, D., Wetherell, M., Cochrane, S., Hogg, M. A., & Turner, J. C. (1990). Knowing what to think by knowing who you are: Self-categorization and the nature of norm formation, conformity, and group polarization. *British Journal of Social Psychology*, 29, 97–119.

Adams, H. F. (1916). *Advertising and its mental laws*. New York: Macmillan.

Ahluwalia, R., & Burnkrant, R. E. (2004). Answering questions about questions: A persuasion knowledge perspective for understanding the effects of rhetorical questions. *Journal of Consumer Research*, 31, 26–42.

Allport, G. W. (1954). *The nature of prejudice*. Reading, MA: Addison-Wesley.

Allport, G. W., & Postman, L. (1947). *The psychology of rumor*. New York: Henry Holt.

An, C., & Pfau, M. (2004). The efficacy of inoculation in televised political debates. *Journal of Communication*, 54, 421–436.

Anderson, C. A. (1983). Imagination and expectation: The effects of imagining behavioral scripts on personal influences. *Journal of Personality and Social Psychology, 45,* 293–305.

Anderson, C. A., Lepper, M. R., & Ross, L. (1980). Perseverance of social theories: The role of explanation in the persistence of discredited information. *Journal of Personality and Social Psychology, 39,* 1037–1049.

Anderson, C. A., & Sechler, E. S. (1986). Effects of explanation and counterexplanation on the development and use of social theories. *Journal of Personality and Social Psychology, 50,* 24–34.

Anderson, N. H. (1965). Primacy effect in personality impression formation using a generalized order effect paradigm. *Journal of Personality and Social Psychology, 2,* 1–9.

Anderson, N. H. (1981). *Foundations of information integration theory.* New York: Academic Press.

Annis, A. D., & Meier, N. C. (1934). The induction of opinion through suggestion by means of "planted content." *Journal of Social Psychology, 5,* 65–81.

Apsler, R. (1975). Effects of embarrassment on behavior toward others. *Journal of Personality and Social Psychology, 32,* 145–153.

Archer, R. L., Foushee, H. C., Davis, M. H., & Aderman, D. (1979). Emotional empathy in a courtroom simulation: A person–situation interaction. *Journal of Applied Social Psychology, 9,* 275–291.

Aristotle (circa 350 B.C.E./1954). *Rhetoric.* New York: Modern Library.

Aronson, E., Blaney, N., Stephan, C., Sikes, J., & Snapp, M. (1978). *The jigsaw classroom.* Beverly Hills, CA: Sage.

Aronson, E., & Carlsmith, J. M. (1963). Effect of severity of threat on the devaluation of forbidden behavior. *Journal of Abnormal and Social Psychology, 66,* 584–588.

Aronson, E., & Cope, V. (1968). My enemy's enemy is my friend. *Journal of Personality and Social Psychology, 8,* 8–12.

Aronson, E., & Golden, B. W. (1962). The effects of relevant and irrelevant aspects of communicator credibility on opinion change. *Journal of Personality, 30,* 135–146.

Aronson, E., & Mills, J. (1959). The effect of severity of initiation on liking for a group. *Journal of Abnormal and Social Psychology, 59,* 177–181.

Aronson, E., Turner, J., & Carlsmith, J. M. (1963). Communication credibility and communication discrepancy as determinants of opinion change. *Journal of Abnormal and Social Psychology, 67,* 31–36.

Aronson, E., Willerman, B., & Floyd, J. (1966). The effect of a pratfall on increasing interpersonal attractiveness. *Psychonomic Science, 4,* 227–228.

Asch, S. E. (1951). Effects of group pressure upon modification and distortion of judgment. In H. Guetzkow (Ed.), *Groups, leadership and men* (pp. 177–190). Pittsburgh, PA: Carnegie Press.

Asch, S. E. (1952). *Social psychology.* Englewood Cliffs, NJ: Prentice Hall.

Axsom, D., & Cooper, J. (1985). Cognitive dissonance and psychotherapy: The role of effort justification. *Journal of Experimental and Social Psychology, 21,* 149–160.

Axsom, D., Yates, S., & Chaiken, S. (1987). Audience response as a heuristic cue in persuasion. *Journal of Personality and Social Psychology, 53,* 30–40.

Bandura, A. (1997). *Self-efficacy.* New York: W. H. Freeman.

Bandura, A., & Menlove, F. L. (1968). Factors determining vicarious extinction of avoidance behavior through symbolic modeling. *Journal of Personality and Social Psychology, 8,* 99–108.

Baron, R. A. (1970). Attraction toward the model and model's competence as determinants of adult imitative behavior. *Journal of Personality and Social Psychology, 14,* 345–351.

Baron, R. A. (1971). Behavioral effects of interpersonal attraction: Compliance with requests from liked and disliked others. *Psychonomic Science, 25*, 325–326.

Baron, R. S. (2000). Arousal, capacity, and intense indoctrination. *Personality and Social Psychology Review, 4*, 238–254.

Batson, C. D., Duncan, B. D., Ackerman, D., Buckley, T., & Birch, K. (1981). Is empathic emotion a source of altruistic motivation? *Journal of Personality and Social Psychology, 40*, 290–302.

Baumeister, R. F., & Leary, M. R. (1995). The need to belong: Desire for interpersonal attachments as fundamental human motivation. *Psychological Bulletin, 117*, 497–529.

Baumgartner, F. R., & Jones, B. D. (1993). *Agendas and instability in American politics.* Chicago: University of Chicago Press.

Becker, H. (1949). The nature and consequences of black propaganda. *American Sociological Review, 14*, 221–235.

Bell, D. E. (1982). Regret in decision making under uncertainty. *Operations Research, 30*, 961–981.

Bellak, L. (1942). The nature of slogans. *Journal of Abnormal and Social Psychology, 37*, 496–510.

Bem, S. L., & Bem, D. J. (1973). Does sex-biased job advertising "aid and abet" sex discrimination? *Journal of Applied Social Psychology, 3*, 6–18.

Benware, C., & Deci, E. L. (1975). Attitude change as a function of the inducement for espousing a proattitudinal communication. *Journal of Experimental Social Psychology, 11*, 271–278.

Berkowitz, L. (1969). Resistance to improper dependency relationships. *Journal of Experimental Social Psychology, 5*, 283–294.

Berkowitz, L., & Daniels, L. R. (1963). Responsibility and dependency. *Journal of Abnormal and Social Psychology, 66*, 429–436.

Berscheid, E. (1966). Opinion change and communicator–communicatee similarity and dissimilarity. *Journal of Personality and Social Psychology, 4*, 670–680.

Bickman, L. (1971). The effect of social status on the honesty of others. *Journal of Social Psychology, 85*, 87–92.

Bickman, L. (1974). The social power of a uniform. *Journal of Applied Social Psychology, 4*, 47–61.

Blake, R. R., Rosenbaum, M., & Duryea, R. A. (1955). Gift-giving as a function of group standards. *Human Relations, 8*, 61–73.

Blanton, H., Cooper, J., Skurnik, I., & Aronson, J. (1997). When bad things happen to good feedback: Exacerbating the need for self-justification with self-affirmations. *Personality and Social Psychology Bulletin, 23*, 684–692.

Boehm, L. E. (1994). The validity effect: A search for mediating variables. *Personality and Social Psychology Bulletin, 20*, 285–293.

Bohner, G., Einwiller, S., Erb, H. P., & Siebler, F. (2003). When small means comfortable: Relations between product attributes in two-sided advertising. *Journal of Consumer Psychology, 13*, 454–463.

Boninger, D. S., Brock, T. C., Cook, T. D., Gruder, C. L., & Romer, D. (1990). Discovery of reliable attitude change persistence resulting from a transmitter tuning set. *Psychological Science, 1*, 268–271.

Borgida, E., & Nisbett, R. E. (1977). The differential impact of abstract vs. concrete information on decisions. *Journal of Applied Social Psychology, 7*, 258–271.

Boyle, R. G., Claxton, A. J., & Forster, J. L. (1997). The role of social influences and tobacco availability on adolescent smokeless tobacco use. *Journal of Adolescent Health, 20,* 279–285.

Braun, O. L., & Wicklund, R. A. (1989). Psychological antecedents of conspicuous consumption. *Journal of Economic Psychology, 10,* 161–187.

Brehm, J. W. (1959). Increasing cognitive dissonance by a *fait accompli. Journal of Abnormal and Social Psychology, 58,* 379–382.

Brehm, J. W. (1966). *A theory of psychological reactance.* New York: Academic Press.

Brehm, S. S., & Brehm, J. W. (1981). *Psychological reactance.* New York: Academic Press.

Brewer, M. B., & Crano, W. D. (1968). Attitude change as a function of discrepancy and source of influence. *Journal of Social Psychology, 76,* 13–18.

Briñol, P., & Petty, R. E. (2003). Overt head movements and persuasion: A self-validation analysis. *Journal of Personality and Social Psychology, 84,* 1123–1139.

Brock, T. C. (1965). Communicator–recipient similarity and decision change. *Journal of Personality and Social Psychology, 1,* 650–654.

Brock, T. C., & Becker, L. A. (1965). Ineffectiveness of "overheard" counterpropaganda. *Journal of Personality and Social Psychology, 2,* 654–660.

Brockner, J., & Rubin, J. Z. (1985). *Entrapment in escalating conflicts.* New York: Springer-Verlag.

Bryan, J. H., & Test, M. A. (1967). Models and helping: Naturalistic studies in aiding behavior. *Journal of Personality and Social Psychology, 6,* 400–407.

Burger, J. M. (1986). Increasing compliance by improving the deal: The that's-not-all technique. *Journal of Personality and Social Psychology, 51,* 277–283.

Burger, J. M. (1999). The foot-in-the-door compliance procedure: A multiple-process analysis and review. *Personality and Social Psychology Review, 3,* 303–325.

Burger, J. M., & Cornelius, T. (2003). Raising the price of agreement: Public commitment and the lowball compliance procedure. *Journal of Applied Social Psychology, 33,* 923–934.

Burger, J. M., Messian, N., Patel, S., del Prado, A., & Anderson, C. (2004). What a coincidence! The effects of incidental similarity on compliance. *Personality and Social Psychology Bulletin, 30,* 35–43.

Burger, J. M., & Petty, R. E. (1981). The low-ball compliance technique: Task or person commitment? *Journal of Personality and Social Psychology, 40,* 492–500.

Burger, J. M., Reed, M., DeCesare, K., Rauner, S., & Rozolios, J. (1999). The effect of initial request size on compliance: More about the that's-not-all technique. *Basic and Applied Social Psychology, 21,* 243–249.

Burger, J. M., Soroka, S., Gonzago, K., Murphy, E., & Somervell, E. (2001). The effect of fleeting attraction on compliance to requests. *Personality and Social Psychology Bulletin, 27,* 1578–1586.

Burke, R. R., DeSarbo, W. S., Oliver, R. L., & Robertson, T. S. (1988). Deception by implication: An experimental investigation. *Journal of Consumer Research, 14,* 483–494.

Burnkrant, R. E., & Howard, D. J. (1984). Effects of the use of introductory rhetorical questions versus statements on information processing. *Journal of Personality and Social Psychology, 47,* 1218–1230.

Bushman, B. J. (1984). Perceived symbols of authority and their influence on compliance. *Journal of Applied Social Psychology, 14,* 501–508.

Byrne, D. E. (1971). *The attraction paradigm.* San Diego, CA: Academic Press.

Cacioppo, J. T., Petty, R. E., & Sidera, J. (1982). The effects of a salient self-schema on the evaluation of proattitudinal editorials: Top-down versus bottom-up message processing. *Journal of Experimental Social Psychology, 18,* 324–338.

Cadinu, M. R., & Cerchioni, M. (2001). Compensatory biases after ingroup threat: "Yeah, but we have a good personality." *European Journal of Social Psychology, 31,* 353–367.

Carlsmith, J. M., & Gross, A. E. (1969). Some effects of guilt on compliance. *Journal of Personality and Social Psychology, 11,* 232–239.

Carlson, M., Charlin, V., & Miller, N. (1988). Positive mood and helping behavior: A test of six hypotheses. *Journal of Personality and Social Psychology, 55,* 211–229.

Chaiken, S. (1979). Communicator physical attractiveness and persuasion. *Journal of Personality and Social Psychology, 37,* 1387–1397.

Chamberlin, T. C. (1897). The method of multiple working hypotheses. *Journal of Geology, 5,* 837–848.

Cialdini, R. B. (1980). Full-cycle social psychology. In L. Bickman (Ed.), *Applied social psychology annual* (Vol. 1, pp. 21–47). Beverly Hills, CA: Sage.

Cialdini, R. B. (2001). *Influence.* Boston: Allyn & Bacon.

Cialdini, R. B., Borden, R. J., Thorne, A., Walker, M. R., Freeman, S., & Sloan, L. R. (1976). Basking in reflected glory: Three (football) field studies. *Journal of Personality and Social Psychology, 34,* 366–375.

Cialdini, R. B., Cacioppo, J. T., Bassett, R., & Miller, J. A. (1978). Low-ball procedure for producing compliance: Commitment then cost. *Journal of Personality and Social Psychology, 36,* 463–476.

Cialdini, R. B., & Goldstein, N. J. (2004). Social influence: Compliance and conformity. *Annual Review of Psychology, 55,* 591–621.

Cialdini, R. B., & Insko, C. A. (1969). Attitudinal verbal reinforcement as a function of informational consistency: A further test of the two-factor theory. *Journal of Personality and Social Psychology, 12,* 342–350.

Cialdini, R. B., Levy, A., Herman, C. P., & Evenbeck, S. (1973). Attitudinal politics: The strategy of moderation. *Journal of Personality and Social Psychology, 25,* 100–108.

Cialdini, R. B., & Petty, R. E. (1979). Anticipatory opinion effects. In R. E. Petty, T. M. Ostrom, & T. C. Brock (Eds.), *Cognitive response in persuasion* (pp. 217–235). Hillsdale, NJ: Lawrence Erlbaum Associates, Inc.

Cialdini, R. B., & Schroeder, D. A. (1976). Increasing compliance by legitimizing paltry contributions: When even a penny helps. *Journal of Personality and Social Psychology, 34,* 599–604.

Cialdini, R. B., Vincent, J. E., Lewis, S. K., Catalan, T., Wheeler, D., & Darby, B. L. (1975). Reciprocal concessions procedure for inducing compliance: The door-in-the-face technique. *Journal of Personality and Social Psychology, 31,* 206–215.

Citron, A. F., Chein, I., & Harding, J. (1950). Anti-minority remarks: A problem for action research. *Journal of Abnormal and Social Psychology, 45,* 99–126.

Clore, G. L. (1992). Cognitive phenomenology: Feelings and the construction of judgment. In L. L. Martin & A. Tesser (Eds.), *The construction of social judgments* (pp. 133–163). Hillsdale, NJ: Lawrence Erlbaum Associates, Inc.

Cocanougher, A. B., & Bruce, G. D. (1971). Socially distant reference groups and consumer aspirations. *Journal of Marketing Research, 8,* 379–381.

Cohen, A. R. (1962). An experiment on small rewards for discrepant compliance and attitude change. In J. W. Brehm & A. R. Cohen, *Explorations in cognitive dissonance* (pp. 73–78). New York: Wiley.

Cohen, G. L., Aronson, J., & Steele, C. M. (2000). When beliefs yield to evidence: Reducing biased evaluation affirming the self. *Personality and Social Psychology Bulletin, 26,* 1151–1164.

Comer, R., & Laird, J. D. (1975). Choosing to suffer as a consequence of expecting to suffer: Why do people do it? *Journal of Personality and Social Psychology, 32,* 92–101.

Cooper, J., & Jones, E. E. (1969). Opinion divergence as a strategy to avoid being miscast. *Journal of Personality and Social Psychology, 13,* 23–30.

Crawford, M. T., McConnell, A. R., Lewis, A. C., & Sherman, S. J. (2002). Reactance, compliance, and anticipated regret. *Journal of Experimental Social Psychology, 38,* 56–63.

Crosby, F. J., Iyer, A., Clayton, S., & Downing, R. A. (2003). Affirmative action: Psychological data and the policy debates. *American Psychologist, 58,* 93–115.

Cross, J. G., & Guyer, M. J. (1980). *Social traps.* Ann Arbor: University of Michigan Press.

Cuming, P. (1985). *Turf and other corporate power plays.* Englewood Cliffs, NJ: Prentice Hall.

Curtis, R. C., & Miller, K. (1986). Believing another likes or dislikes you: Behaviors making the beliefs come true. *Journal of Personality and Social Psychology, 51,* 284–290.

Darley, J. M., & Berscheid, E. (1967). Increased liking as a result of the anticipation of personal contact. *Human Relations, 20,* 29–40.

Darley, J. M., & Fazio, R. H. (1980). Expectancy confirmation processes arising in the social interaction sequence. *American Psychologist, 35,* 867–881.

Davis, B. P., & Knowles, E. S. (1999). A disrupt-then-reframe technique of social influence. *Journal of Personality and Social Psychology, 76,* 192–199.

Davis, M. H. (1996). *Empathy.* Boulder, CO: Westview.

Dearing, J. W., & Rogers, E. M. (1996). *Agenda-setting.* Thousand Oaks, CA: Sage.

Deci, E. L. (1971). Effects of externally mediated rewards on intrinsic motivation. *Journal of Personality and Social Psychology, 18,* 105–115.

Deci, E. L., Koestner, R., & Ryan, R. M. (1999). A meta-analytic review of experiments examining the effects of extrinsic rewards on intrinsic motivation. *Psychological Bulletin, 125,* 627–668.

Derlega, V. J., Harris, M. S., & Chaikin, A. L. (1973). Self-disclosure reciprocity, liking, and the deviant. *Journal of Experimental Social Psychology, 9,* 277–284.

Deutsch, M., & Gerard, H. B. (1955). A study of the normative and informational social influences upon individual judgment. *Journal of Abnormal and Social Psychology, 51,* 629–636.

de Waal, F. (1996). *Good natured.* Cambridge, MA: Harvard University Press.

de Waal, F. (1998). *Chimpanzee politics* (Rev. Ed.). Baltimore: Johns Hopkins University Press.

Dickerson, C. A., Thibodeau, R., Aronson, E., & Miller, D. (1992). Using cognitive dissonance to encourage water conservation. *Journal of Applied Social Psychology, 22,* 841–854.

DiFonzo, N., Bordia, P., & Rosnow, R. L. (1994). Reining in rumors. *Organizational Dynamics, 23*(1), 47–62.

Dolinski, D., Ciszek, M., Godlewski, K., & Zawadzki, M. (2002). Fear-then-relief, mindlessness, and cognitive deficits. *European Journal of Social Psychology, 32,* 435–447.

Dolinski, D., & Nawrat, R. (1998). "Fear-then-relief" procedure for inducing compliance. Beware when the danger is over. *Journal of Experimental Social Psychology, 34,* 27–50.

Dolinski, D., Nawrat, M., & Rudak, I. (2001). Dialogue involvement as a social influence technique. *Personality and Social Psychology Bulletin, 27,* 1395–1406.

Doob, A. N., & Ecker, B. P. (1970). Stigma and compliance. *Journal of Personality and Social Psychology, 14,* 302–304.

Eagly, A. H., Wood, W., & Chaiken, S. (1978). Causal inferences about communicators and their effect on opinion change. *Journal of Personality and Social Psychology*, 36, 424–435.

Easterbrook, J. A. (1959). The effect of emotion on cue utilization and the organization of behavior. *Psychological Review*, 66, 183–201.

Eiser, J. R. (1975). Attitudes and the use of evaluative language: A two-way process. *Journal for the Theory of Social Behavior*, 5, 235–248.

Eiser, J. R., Eiser, C., Patterson, D. J., & Harding, C. M. (1984). Effects of information about specific nutrient content on ratings of "goodness" and "pleasantness" of common foods. *Appetite*, 5, 349–359.

Eiser, J. R., & Pancer, S. M. (1979). Attitudinal effects of the use of evaluatively biased language. *European Journal of Social Psychology*, 9, 39–47.

Ellul, J. (1973). *Propaganda*. New York: Vintage Books.

Elms, A., & Janis, I. L. (1965). Counter-norm attitudes induced by consonant versus dissonant conditions in role playing. *Journal of Experimental Research in Personality*, 1, 50–60.

Emerson, R. M. (1962). Power–dependence relations. *American Sociological Review*, 27, 31–41.

Evans, L. M., & Petty, R. E. (2003). Self-guide frame and persuasion: Responsibly increasing message processing to ideal levels. *Personality and Social Psychology Bulletin*, 29, 313–324.

Ex, J. (1960). The nature of the relationship between two persons and the degree of their influence on each other. *Acta Psychologica*, 17, 39–54.

Falbo, T. (1977). Multidimensional scaling of power strategies. *Journal of Personality and Social Psychology*, 35, 537–547.

Farquhar, P. H., & Herr, P. M. (1993). The dual structure of brand associations. In D. A. Aaker & A. L. Biel (Eds.), *Brand equity and advertising: Advertising's role in building strong brands* (pp. 263–277). Hillsdale, NJ: Lawrence Erlbaum Associates, Inc.

Farquhar, P. H., & Pratkanis, A. R. (1993). Decision structuring with phantom alternatives. *Management Science*, 39, 1214–1226.

Fennis, B. M., Das, E. H. H. J., & Pruyn. A. T. H. (2004). "If you can't dazzle them with brilliance, baffle them with nonsense": Extending the impact of the disrupt-then-reframe technique of social influence. *Journal of Consumer Psychology*, 14, 280–290.

Festinger, L. (1954). A theory of social comparison processes. *Human Relations*, 7, 117–140.

Festinger, L. (1957). *A theory of cognitive dissonance*. Stanford, CA: Stanford University Press.

Festinger, L. (1964). *Conflict, decision, and dissonance*. Stanford, CA: Stanford University Press.

Festinger, L., & Carlsmith, J. M. (1959). Cognitive consequences of forced compliance. *Journal of Abnormal and Social Psychology*, 58, 203–210.

Festinger, L., & Maccoby, N. (1964). On resistance to persuasive communications. *Journal of Abnormal and Social Psychology*, 68, 359–366.

Fine, B. J. (1957). Conclusion-drawing, communicator credibility, and anxiety as factors in opinion change. *Journal of Abnormal and Social Psychology*, 54, 369–374.

Folkes, V. S. (1985). Mindlessness or mindfulness: A partial replication and extension of Langer, Blank, and Chanowitz. *Journal of Personality and Social Psychology*, 48, 600–604.

Foss, R. D., & Crenshaw, N. C. (1978). Risk of embarrassment and helping. *Social Behavior and Personality*, 6, 243–245.

Freedman, J., & Fraser, S. (1966). Compliance without pressure: The foot-in-the-door technique. *Journal of Personality and Social Psychology, 4*, 195–202.

Frey, K. P., & Eagly, A. H. (1993). Vividness can undermine the persuasiveness of messages. *Journal of Personality and Social Psychology, 65*, 32–44.

Fried, C. B., & Aronson, E. (1995). Hypocrisy, misattribution, and dissonance reduction. *Personality and Social Psychology Bulletin, 21*, 925–933.

Friedkin, N. E. (1998). *A structural theory of social influence.* Cambridge: Cambridge University Press.

Friedrich, J., Fetherstonhaugh, D., Casey, S., & Gallagher, D. (1996). Argument integration and attitude change: Suppression effects in the integration of one-sided arguments that vary in persuasiveness. *Personality and Social Psychology Bulletin, 22*, 179–191.

Froming, W. J., Walker, G. R., & Lopyan, K. J. (1982). Public and private self-awareness: When personal attitudes conflict with societal expectations. *Journal of Experimental Social Psychology, 18*, 476–487.

Fromkin, H. L. (1970). Effects of experimentally aroused feelings of undistinctiveness upon valuation of scarce and novel experiences. *Journal of Personality and Social Psychology, 16*, 321–329.

Garrity, K., & Degelman, D. (1990). Effect of server introduction on restaurant tipping. *Journal of Applied Social Psychology, 20*, 168–172.

Geis, M. L. (1982). *The language of television advertising.* New York: Academic Press.

Gilovich, T. (1981). Seeing the past in the present: The effects of associations to familiar events on judgments and decisions. *Journal of Personality and Social Psychology, 40*, 797–808.

Gilovich, T., Griffin, D., & Kahneman, D. (Eds.). (2002). *Heuristics and biases.* Cambridge: Cambridge University Press.

Ginzel, L. E. (1994). The impact of biased inquiry strategies on performance judgments. *Organizational Behavior and Human Decision Processes, 57*, 411–429.

Girard, J. (1977). *How to sell anything to anybody.* New York: Warner Books.

Glass, D. (1964). Changes in liking as a means of reducing cognitive discrepancies between self-esteem and aggression. *Journal of Personality, 32*, 531–549.

Goldberg, S. C. (1955). Influence and leadership as a function of group structure. *Journal of Abnormal and Social Psychology, 51*, 119–122.

Gonzales, M. H., Aronson, E., & Costanzo, M. (1988). Increasing the effectiveness of energy auditors: A field experiment. *Journal of Applied Social Psychology, 18*, 1049–1066.

Goode, W. J. (1968). Norm commitment and conformity to role-status obligations. *American Sociological Review, 33*, 246–258.

Goodrow, B., Seier, E., & Stewart, K. (2003). Social influences and adolescent attitudes on smoking: Analysis of the 2000 Tennessee Youth Tobacco Survey. *Adolescent and Family Health, 3*, 89–94.

Gordon, D. (1999). *Ants at work.* New York: Norton.

Gordon, R. A. (1996). Impact of ingratiation on judgments and evaluations: A meta-analytic investigation. *Journal of Personality and Social Psychology, 71*, 54–70.

Gould, J. L., & Gould, C. G. (1998). *The honey bee.* New York: Scientific American Library.

Gourville, J. T. (1998). Pennies-a-day: The effect of temporal reframing on transaction evaluation. *Journal of Consumer Research, 24*, 395–408.

Greenwald, A. G. (1968). Cognitive learning, cognitive response in persuasion, and attitude change. In A. G. Greenwald, T. C. Brock, & T. M. Ostrom (Eds.), *Psychological foundations of attitudes* (pp. 147–170). New York: Academic Press.

Greenwald, A. G. (1969). The open-mindedness of the counterattitudinal role player. *Journal of Experimental Social Psychology*, 5, 375–388.

Greenwald, A. G. (1970). When does role playing produce attitude change? Toward an answer. *Journal of Personality and Social Psychology*, 16, 214–219.

Greenwald, A. G., Carnot, C. G., Beach, R., & Young, B. (1987). Increasing voting behavior by asking people if they expect to vote. *Journal of Applied Psychology*, 72, 315–318.

Greenwald, A. G., Pratkanis, A. R., Leippe, M. R., & Baumgardner, M. H. (1986). Under what conditions does theory obstruct research progress? *Psychological Review*, 93, 216–229.

Gregory, W. L., Cialdini, R. B., & Carpenter, K. M. (1982). Self-relevant scenarios as mediators of likelihood estimates and compliance: Does imagining make it so? *Journal of Personality and Social Psychology*, 43, 89–99.

Groennings, S., Kelley, E. W., & Leiserson, M. (Eds.). (1970). *The study of coalition behavior*. New York: Holt, Rinehart, & Winston.

Guéguen, N., & Fisher-Lokou, J. (2002). An evaluation of touch on a large request: A field setting. *Psychological Reports*, 90, 267–269.

Guéguen, N., Legoherel, P., & Jacob, C. (2003). Solicitation of participation in an investigation by e-mail: Effects of the social presence of the physical attraction of the petitioner on the response rate. *Canadian Journal of Behavioural Science*, 35, 84–96.

Guéguen, N., & Pascual, A. (2000). Evocation of freedom and compliance: The "but you are free of . . ." technique. *Current Research in Social Psychology*, 5, 264–270.

Guéguen, N., & Pascual, A. (2002). Request solicitation and semantic evocation of freedom: An evaluation in a computer-mediated communication context. *Perceptual & Motor Skills*, 95, 208–212.

Guerin, B. (1993). *Social facilitation*. Cambridge: Cambridge University Press.

Hamill, R., Wilson, T. D., & Nisbett, R. E. (1980). Insensitivity to sample bias: Generalizing from atypical cases. *Journal of Personality and Social Psychology*, 39, 578–589.

Handel, M. I. (2001). *Masters of war*. London: Frank Cass.

Harkins, S. G., & Petty, R. E. (1981a). Effects of source magnification of cognitive effort on attitudes: An information-processing view. *Journal of Personality and Social Psychology*, 40, 401–413.

Harkins, S. G., & Petty, R. E. (1981b). The multiple source effect in persuasion: The effects of distraction. *Personality and Social Psychology Bulletin*, 7, 627–635.

Harper, F. B. W., & Tuddenham, R. D. (1964). The sociometric composition of the group as a determinant of yielding to a distorted norm. *Journal of Psychology*, 58, 307–311.

Harris, R. J. (1977). Comprehension of pragmatic implications in advertising. *Journal of Applied Psychology*, 62, 603–608.

Harter, D. L., & Sullivan, J. (1953). *Propaganda handbook*. Media, PA: 20th Century Publishing.

Hastie, R., & Pennington, N. (2000). Explanation-based decision making. In T. Connolly, H. R. Arkes, & K. R. Hammond (Eds.), *Judgment and decision making* (2nd ed., pp. 212–228). Cambridge: Cambridge University Press.

Haugtvedt, C. P., & Wegener, D. T. (1994). Message order effects in persuasion: An attitude strength perspective. *Journal of Consumer Research*, 21, 205–218.

Heider, F. (1958). *The psychology of interpersonal relations*. New York: Wiley.

Hendrick, C., Borden, R., Giesen, M., Murray, E. J., & Seyfried, B. A. (1972). Effectiveness of ingratiation tactics in a cover letter on mail questionnaire response. *Psychonomic Science*, 26, 349–351.

Henley, N. (1989). Molehill or mountain? What we know and don't know about sex bias in language. In M. Crawford & M. Gentry (Eds.), *Gender and thought* (pp. 59–78). New York: Springer-Verlag.

Hetts, J. J., Boninger, D. S., Armor, D. A., Gleicher, F., & Nathanson, A. (2000). The influence of anticipated counterfactual regret on behavior. *Psychology & Marketing, 17*, 345–368.

Hodges, B. H. (1974). Effect of valence on relative weighting in impression formation. *Journal of Personality and Social Psychology, 30*, 378–381.

Horowitz, I. A. (1968). Effect of choice and locus of dependence on helping behavior. *Journal of Personality and Social Psychology, 8*, 373–376.

Horvitz, T., & Pratkanis, A. R. (2002). A laboratory demonstration of the fraudulent telemarketers' 1-in-5 prize tactic. *Journal of Applied Social Psychology, 32*, 310–317.

Hovland, C. I., Harvey, O. J., & Sherif, M. (1957). Assimilation and contrast effects in reaction to communication and attitude change. *Journal of Abnormal and Social Psychology, 55*, 244–252.

Hovland, C. I., Janis, I. L., & Kelley, H. H. (1953). *Communication and persuasion*. New Haven, CT: Yale University Press.

Hovland, C. I., Lumsdaine, A. A., & Sheffield, F. D. (1949). *Experiments on mass communication*. Princeton, NJ: Princeton University Press.

Hovland, C. I., & Mandell, W. (1952). An experimental comparison of conclusion-drawing by the communicator and by the audience. *Journal of Abnormal and Social Psychology, 47*, 581–588.

Hovland, C. I., & Weiss, W. (1951). The influence of source credibility on communication effectiveness. *Public Opinion Quarterly, 15*, 635–650.

Howard, D. J. (1990). The influence of verbal responses to common greetings on compliance behavior: The foot-in-the-mouth effect. *Journal of Applied Social Psychology, 20*, 1185–1196.

Howard, D. J. (1997). Familiar phrases as peripheral persuasion cues. *Journal of Experimental Social Psychology, 33*, 231–243.

Howard, D. J., & Kerin, R. A. (2004). The effects of personalized product recommendations on advertisement response rates: The "try this it works!" technique. *Journal of Consumer Psychology, 14*, 271–279.

Huber, J., Payne, J. W., & Puto, C. (1982). Adding asymmetrically dominated alternatives: Violations of regularity and the similarity hypothesis. *Journal of Consumer Research, 9*, 90–98.

Insko, C. A. (1965). Verbal reinforcement of attitude. *Journal of Personality and Social Psychology, 2*, 621–623.

Insko, C. A., & Cialdini, R. B. (1969). A test of three interpretations of attitudinal verbal reinforcement. *Journal of Personality and Social Psychology, 12*, 333–341.

Isen, A. M., & Levin, P. F. (1972). Effect of feeling good on helping: Cookies and kindness. *Journal of Personality and Social Psychology, 21*, 384–388.

Iyengar, S. (1991). *Is anyone responsible? How television frames political issues*. Chicago: University of Chicago Press.

Iyengar, S., & Kinder, D. R. (1987). *News that matters*. Chicago: University of Chicago Press.

Iyengar, S. S., & Lepper, M. R. (2000). When choice is demotivating: Can one desire too much of a good thing? *Journal of Personality and Social Psychology, 79*, 995–1006.

Jamieson, K. H. (1992). *Dirty politics*. New York: Oxford.

Janes, L. M., & Olson, J. M. (2000). Jeer pressure: The behavioral effects of observing ridicule of others. *Personality and Social Psychology Bulletin, 26*, 474–485.

Janis, I. L., & King, B. T. (1954). The influence of role playing on opinion change. *Journal of Abnormal and Social Psychology, 49*, 211–218.

Jecker, J., & Landy, D. (1969). Liking a person as a function of doing him a favor. *Human Relations, 22*, 371–378.

Joule, R. V., Gouilloux, F., & Weber, F. (1989). The lure: A new compliance procedure. *Journal of Social Psychology, 128*, 741–749.

Julka, D. L., & Marsh, K. L. (2000). Matching persuasive messages to experimentally induced needs. *Current Research in Social Psychology, 5*(21), 299–319.

Kahan, J. P., & Rapoport, A. (1984). *Theories of coalition formation.* Hillsdale, NJ: Lawrence Erlbaum Associates, Inc.

Kahneman, D. (1973). *Attention and effort.* Englewood Cliffs, NJ: Prentice Hall.

Kahneman, D. (1992). Reference points, anchors, norms, and mixed feelings. *Organizational Behavior and Human Decision Processes, 51*, 296–312.

Kahneman, D., Slovic, P., & Tversky, A. (Eds.). (1982). *Judgment under uncertainty: Heuristics and biases.* Cambridge: Cambridge University Press.

Kamins, M. A., Brand, M. J., Hoeke, S. A., & Moe, J. C. (1989). Two-sided versus one-sided celebrity endorsements: The impact on advertising effectiveness and credibility. *Journal of Advertising, 18*(2), 4–10.

Kanouse, D. E., & Hanson, L. R. (1972). Negativity in evaluations. In E. E. Jones, D. E. Kanouse, H. H. Kelley, R. E. Nisbett, S. Valins, & B. Weiner (Eds.), *Attribution: Perceiving the causes of behavior* (pp. 47–62). Morristown, NJ: General Learning Press.

Kaplan, A., & Krueger, J. (1999). Compliance after threat: Self-affirmation or self-presentation? *Current Research in Social Psychology, 4*, 178–197.

Kassin, S. M., & Kiechel, K. L. (1996). The social psychology of false confessions: Compliance, internalization and confabulation. *Psychological Science, 7*, 125–128.

Kassin, S. M., Williams, L. N., & Saunders, C. L. (1990). Dirty tricks of cross-examination: The influence of conjectural evidence on the jury. *Law and Human Behavior, 14*, 373–384.

Keeney, R. L. (1982). Decision analysis: An overview. *Operations Research, 30*, 803–838.

Kelley, H. H., & Volkart, E. H. (1952). The resistance to change of group-anchored attitudes. *American Sociological Review, 17*, 453–465.

Kemper, T. D. (1984). Power, status, and emotions: A sociological contribution to a psycho-physiological domain. In K. R. Scherer & P. Ekman (Eds.), *Approaches to emotion* (pp. 369–383). Hillsdale, NJ: Lawrence Erlbaum Associates, Inc.

King, B. T., & Janis, I. L. (1956). Comparison of the effectiveness of improvised versus non-improvised role-playing in producing opinion changes. *Human Relations, 9*, 177–186.

Kirsch, I. (Ed.). (1999). *How expectancies shape experience.* Washington, DC: American Psychological Association.

Koeske, G. F., & Crano, W. D. (1968). The effect of congruous and incongruous source–statement combinations upon the judged credibility of a communication. *Journal of Experimental and Social Psychology, 4*, 384–399.

Komorita, S. S., & Chertkoff, J. M. (1973). A bargaining theory of coalition formation. *Psychological Review, 80*, 149–162.

Komorita, S. S., & Parks, C. D. (1994). *Social dilemmas.* Madison, WI: WCB Brown & Benchmark.

Kraut, R. E. (1973). Effects of social labeling on giving to charity. *Journal of Experimental Social Psychology, 9*, 551–562.

Kravitz, D. A., & Platania, J. (1993). Attitudes and beliefs about affirmative action: Effects of target and respondent sex and ethnicity. *Journal of Applied Psychology, 78,* 928–938.

Kruger, J., Wirtz, D., Van Boven, L., & Altermatt, T. W. (2004). The effort heuristic. *Journal of Experimental Social Psychology, 40,* 91–98.

Lana, R. E. (1964). Three theoretical interpretations of order effects in persuasive communications. *Psychological Bulletin, 61,* 314–320.

Langer, E., Blank, A., & Chanowitz, B. (1978). The mindlessness of ostensibly thoughtful action: The role of "placebic" information in interpersonal interaction. *Journal of Personality and Social Psychology, 36,* 635–642.

Latané, B. (1981). The psychology of social impact. *American Psychologist, 36,* 343–356.

Lau, R. (1982). Negativity in political perception. *Political Behavior, 4,* 353–377.

Lawler, E. J. (1983). Cooptation and threats as "divide and rule" tactics. *Social Psychology Quarterly, 46,* 89–98.

Lee, A. M. (1952). *How to understand propaganda.* New York: Rinehart.

Lee, K. M., & Nass, C. (2004). The multiple source effect and synthesized speech: Doubly-disembodied language as a conceptual framework. *Human Communication Research, 30,* 182–207.

Lefkowitz, M., Blake, R. R., & Mouton, J. S. (1955). Status factors in pedestrian violation of traffic signals. *Journal of Abnormal and Social Psychology, 51,* 704–706.

Leippe, M. R., Manion, A. P., & Romanczyk, A. (1992). Eyewitness persuasion: How and how well do fact finders judge the accuracy of adults' and children's memory reports? *Journal of Personality and Social Psychology, 63,* 181–197.

Lepper, M. R., Greene, D., & Nisbett, R. E. (1973). Undermining children's intrinsic interest with extrinsic reward: A test of the "overjustification" hypothesis. *Journal of Personality and Social Psychology, 28,* 129–137.

Lerner, J. S., & Keltner, D. (2000). Beyond valence: Toward a model of emotion-specific influence on judgement and choice. *Cognition and Emotion, 14,* 473–493.

Leventhal, H. (1970). Findings and theory in the study of fear communications. In L. Berkowitz (Ed.), *Advances in experimental social psychology* (Vol. 5, pp. 119–186). New York: Academic Press.

Levin, I. P., & Gaeth, G. J. (1988). How consumers are affected by the framing of attribute information before and after consuming the product. *Journal of Consumer Research, 15,* 374–378.

Levin, I. P., Schneider, S. L., & Gaeth, G. J. (1998). All frames are not created equal: A topology and critical analysis of framing effects. *Organizational Behavior and Human Decision Processes, 76,* 148–188.

Levin, P. F., & Isen, A. M. (1975). Further studies on the effect of feeling good on helping. *Sociometry, 38,* 141–147.

Levine, J. M., & Valle, R. S. (1975). The convert as a credible communicator. *Social Behaviour and Personality, 3,* 81–90.

Lewan, P. C., & Stotland, E. (1961). The effects of prior information on susceptibility to an emotional appeal. *Journal of Abnormal and Social Psychology, 62,* 450–453.

Lewin, K. (1947). Group decision and social change. In T. M. Newcomb & E. L. Hartley (Eds.), *Readings in social psychology* (pp. 330–344). New York: Holt.

Lewis, M. (1993). The emergence of human emotions. In M. Lewis & J. M. Haviland (Eds.), *Handbook of emotions* (pp. 223–235). New York: Guilford Press.

Lieberman, S. (1956). The effects of changes in role on the attitudes of role occupants. *Human Relations, 9,* 385–402.

Lind, E. A., & Tyler, T. R. (1988). *The social psychology of procedural justice.* New York: Plenum Press.

Linder, D. E., & Worchel, S. (1970). Opinion change as a result of effortfully drawing a counterattitudinal conclusion. *Journal of Experimental Social Psychology, 6,* 432–448.

Loftus, E. F., & Palmer, J. C. (1974). Reconstruction of automobile destruction: An example of the interaction between language and memory. *Journal of Verbal Learning and Verbal Memory, 13,* 585–589.

Lord, C. G., Paulson, R. M., Sia, T. L., Lepper, M. R., & Thomas, J. C. (2004). Houses built on sand: Effects of exemplar stability on susceptibility to attitude change. *Journal of Personality and Social Psychology, 87,* 733–749.

Lorge, I. (1936). Prestige, suggestion, and attitudes. *Journal of Social Psychology, 7,* 386–402.

Lott, B., & Lott, A. (1960). The formation of positive attitudes towards group members. *Journal of Abnormal and Social Psychology, 61,* 297–300.

Lund, F. (1925). The psychology of belief: IV. The law of primacy in persuasion. *Journal of Abnormal and Social Psychology, 20,* 183–191.

McDonald, J., & McKelvie, S. J. (1992). Playing it safe: Helping rates for a dropped mitten and a box of condoms. *Psychological Reports, 71,* 113–114.

McGinnies, E. (1966). Cross-cultural studies in persuasion: III. Reactions of Japanese students to one-sided and two-sided communications. *Journal of Social Psychology, 70,* 87–93.

McGuire, W. J. (1964). Inducing resistance to persuasion: Some contemporary approaches. In L. Berkowitz (Ed.), *Advances in experimental social psychology* (Vol. 1, pp. 191–229). New York: Academic Press.

Maddux, J. E., & Gosselin, J. T. (2003). Self-efficacy. In M. R. Leary & J. P. Tangney (Eds.), *Handbook of self and identity* (pp. 218–238). New York: Guilford.

Maddux, J. E., & Rogers, R. W. (1980). Effects of source expertise, physical attractiveness, and supporting arguments on persuasion: A case of brains over beauty. *Journal of Personality and Social Psychology, 39,* 235–244.

Maddux, J. E., & Rogers, R. W. (1983). Protection motivation and self-efficacy: A revised theory of fear appeals and attitude change. *Journal of Experimental Social Psychology, 19,* 469–479.

Maier, N. R. F. (1952). *Principles of human relations.* New York: Wiley.

Maier, N. R. F., & Hoffman, L. R. (1960a). Using trained "developmental" discussion leaders to improve further the quality of group decisions. *Journal of Applied Psychology, 44,* 247–251.

Maier, N. R. F., & Hoffman, L. R. (1960b). Quality of the first and second solution in group problem solving. *Journal of Applied Psychology, 44,* 278–283.

Maltese, J. A. (1992). *Spin control.* Chapel Hill: University of North Carolina Press.

Marwell, G., & Schmitt, D. R. (1967). Dimensions of compliance-gaining behavior: An empirical analysis. *Sociometry, 30,* 350–364.

Mech, L. D. (1991). *The way of the wolf.* Stillwater, MN: Voyageur Press.

Mellers, B. A., & Birnbaum, M. H. (1983). Contextual effects in social judgment. *Journal of Experimental Social Psychology, 19,* 157–171.

Meyerowitz, B. E., & Chaiken, S. (1987). The effect of message framing on breast self-examination attitudes, intentions, and behavior. *Journal of Personality and Social Psychology, 52,* 500–510.

Milgram, S. (1974). *Obedience to authority.* New York: Harper & Row.

Milgram, S., Bickman, L., & Berkowitz, L. (1969). Note on the drawing power of crowds of different size. *Journal of Personality and Social Psychology, 13,* 79–82.

Milgram, S., & Sabini, J. (1978). On maintaining social norms: A field experiment in the subway. In A. Baum, J. E. Singer, & S. Valins (Eds.), *Advances in environmental psychology* (Vol. 1, pp. 31–40). Hillsdale, NJ: Lawrence Erlbaum Associates, Inc.

Miller, N., & Campbell, D. T. (1959). Recency and primacy in persuasion as a function of the timing of speeches and measurements. *Journal of Abnormal and Social Psychology*, 59, 1–9.

Miller, R. (1996). *Embarrassment: Poise and peril in everyday life*. New York: Guilford Press.

Miller, R. L. (1974). Facilitating compliance by manipulating the nature of the comparison: Relative cost vs. reciprocal concession. *Personality and Social Psychology Bulletin*, 1, 160–162.

Miller, R. L., Brickman, P., & Bolen, D. (1975). Attribution versus persuasion as a means of modifying behavior. *Journal of Personality and Social Psychology*, 31, 430–441.

Miller, R. L., & Wozniak, W. (2001). Counter-attitudinal advocacy: Effort vs. self-generation of arguments. *Current Research in Social Psychology*, 6(4), 46–57.

Mills, J., & Jellison, J. M. (1967). Effect on opinion change of how desirable the communication is to the audience the communicator addressed. *Journal of Personality and Social Psychology*, 6, 98–101.

Mio, J. S. (1996). Metaphor, politics, and persuasion. In J. S. Mio & A. N. Katz (Eds.), *Metaphor: Implications and applications* (pp. 127–146). Mahwah, NJ: Lawrence Erlbaum Associates, Inc.

Moore, H. T. (1921). The comparative influence of majority and expert opinion. *American Journal of Psychology*, 32, 16–20.

Moscovici, S. (1976). *Social influence and social change*. London: Academic Press.

Mussweiler, T., Strack, F., & Pfeiffer, T. (2000). Overcoming the inevitable anchoring effect: Considering the opposite compensates for selective accessibility. *Personality and Social Psychology Bulletin*, 26, 1142–1150.

Nisbett, R. E., & Ross, L. (1980). *Human inference: Strategies and shortcomings of social judgment*. Englewood Cliffs, NJ: Prentice Hall.

Norris, K. S., Würsig, B., Wells, R. S., & Würsig, M. (1994). *The Hawaiian spinner dolphin*. Berkeley: University of California Press.

Nosanchuk, T. A., & Lightstone, J. (1974). Canned laughter and public and private conformity. *Journal of Personality and Social Psychology*, 29, 153–156.

Olson, J. C., & Dover, P. A. (1978). Cognitive effects of deceptive advertising. *Journal of Marketing Research*, 15(1), 29–38

Ostrom, T. M. (1970). Perspective as a determinant of attitude change. *Journal of Experimental Social Psychology*, 6, 280–292.

Pardini, A. U., & Katzev, R. D. (1986). Applying full-cycle social psychology to consumer marketing: The defusing objections technique. *Journal of Economic Psychology*, 7, 87–94.

Pennington, N., & Hastie, R. (1992). Explaining the evidence: Tests of the story model for juror decision making. *Journal of Personality and Social Psychology*, 62, 189–206.

Perelman, Ch., & Olbrechts-Tyteca, L. (1958/1969). *The new rhetoric*. Notre Dame, IN: University of Notre Dame Press.

Perkins, H. W. (Ed.). (2003). *The social norms approach to preventing school and college substance abuse*. San Francisco: Jossey-Bass.

Pettigrew, T. F. (1991). Normative theory in intergroup relations: Explaining both harmony and conflict. *Psychology and Developing Societies*, 3, 3–16.

Pettigrew, T. F. (1998). Intergroup contact theory. *Annual Review of Psychology*, 49, 65–85.

Petty, R. E., & Brock, T. C. (1976). Effects of responding or not responding to hecklers on audience agreement with a speaker. *Journal of Applied Social Psychology*, 6, 1–17.

Petty, R. E., & Brock, T. C. (1979). Effects of Barnum personality assessments on cognitive behavior. *Journal of Consulting and Clinical Psychology, 47*, 201–203.

Petty, R. E., & Cacioppo, J. T. (1984). The effects of involvement on responses to argument quantity and quality: Central and peripheral routes to persuasion. *Journal of Personality and Social Psychology, 46*, 69–81.

Petty, R. E., & Cacioppo, J. T. (1986). *Communication and persuasion: Central and peripheral routes to attitude change.* New York: Springer-Verlag.

Petty, R. E., Cacioppo, J. T., & Heesacker, M. (1981). Effects of rhetorical questions on persuasion: A cognitive responses analysis. *Journal of Personality and Social Psychology, 40*, 432–440.

Petty, R. E., Schumann, D. W., Richman, S. A., & Strathman, A. (1993). Positive mood and persuasion: Different roles for affect under high- and low-elaboration conditions. *Journal of Personality and Social Psychology, 64*, 5–20.

Petty, R. E., Wells, G. L., & Brock, T. C. (1970). Distraction can enhance and reduce yielding to propaganda: Thought disruption versus effort justification. *Journal of Personality and Social Psychology, 34*, 874–884.

Pfeffer, J. (1981). *Power in organizations.* Cambridge, MA: Ballinger.

Pfeffer, J., & Salancik, G. R. (1978). *The external control of organizations.* New York: Harper & Row.

Phillips, D. P. (1986). Natural experiments on the effects of mass media violence and fatal aggression: Strengths and weaknesses of a new approach. In L. Berkowitz (Ed.), *Advances in experimental social psychology* (Vol. 19, pp. 207–250). New York: Academic Press.

Piliavin, J. A., & Callero, P. L. (1991). *Giving blood.* Baltimore: Johns Hopkins University Press.

Platt, J. (1973). Social traps. *American Psychologist, 28*, 641–651.

Plott, C. R., & Levine, M. E. (1978). A model of agenda influence on committee decisions. *American Economic Review, 68*, 146–160.

Poffenberger, A. T. (1932). *Psychology in advertising.* New York: McGraw-Hill.

Pool, G. J., Wood, W., & Leck, K. (1998). The self-esteem motive in social influence: Agreement with valued majorities and disagreement with derogated minorities. *Journal of Personality and Social Psychology, 75*, 967–975.

Pratkanis, A. R. (1988). The attitude heuristic and selective fact identification. *British Journal of Social Psychology, 27*, 257–263.

Pratkanis, A. R. (1995). How to sell a pseudoscience. *Skeptical Inquirer, 19*, 19–25.

Pratkanis, A. R. (1997). *Unpublished replication of Asch's line experiment.* On A. Gitow & F. Rothenberg (Producers). (1997, August 10). *NBC Dateline: Follow the leader.* Distributed by NBC News.

Pratkanis, A. R. (2000). Altercasting as an influence tactic. In D. J. Terry & M. A. Hogg (Eds.), *Attitudes, behavior, and social context* (pp. 201–226). Mahwah, NJ: Lawrence Erlbaum Associates, Inc.

Pratkanis, A. R., & Abbott, C. J. (2004). *Flattery and compliance with a direct request: Towards a theory of toady influence.* Unpublished manuscript, University of California, Santa Cruz.

Pratkanis, A.R., & Aronson, E. (2001). *Age of propaganda: The everyday use and abuse of persuasion.* New York: W. H. Freeman.

Pratkanis, A. R., Eskenazi, J., & Greenwald, A. G. (1994). What you expect is what you believe (but not necessarily what you get): A test of the effectiveness of subliminal self-help audiotapes. *Basic and Applied Social Psychology, 15*, 251–276.

Pratkanis, A. R., & Farquhar, P. H. (1992). A brief history of research on phantom alternatives: Evidence for seven empirical generalizations about phantoms. *Basic and Applied Social Psychology, 13*, 103–122.

Pratkanis, A. R., & Gliner, M. D. (2004–2005). And when shall a little child lead them? Evidence for an altercasting theory of source credibility. *Current Psychology, 23*, 279–304.

Pratkanis, A. R., Greenwald, A. G., Leippe, M. R., & Baumgardner, M. H. (1988). In search of reliable persuasion effects: III. The sleeper effect is dead. Long live the sleeper effect. *Journal of Personality and Social Psychology, 54*, 203–218.

Pratkanis, A. R., & Shadel, D. (2005). *Weapons of fraud*. Seattle, WA: AARP Washington.

Pratkanis, A. R., & Turner, M. E. (1994). Nine principles of successful affirmative action: Mr. Branch Rickey, Mr. Jackie Robinson, and the integration of baseball. *Nine, 3*, 36–65.

Pratkanis, A. R. & Uriel, Y. (2005). *The expert snare as an influence tactic: Surf, turf, and ballroom demonstrations of the compliance consequences of being altercast as an expert*. Unpublished manuscript, University of California, Santa Cruz.

Preston, I. L. (1994). *The tangled web they weave*. Madison: University of Wisconsin Press.

Raiffa, H. (1982). *The art and science of negotiation*. Cambridge, MA: Harvard University Press.

Regan, D. T. (1971). Effects of a favor on liking and compliance. *Journal of Experimental Social Psychology, 7*, 627–639.

Reifman, A., Barnes, G. M., Dintcheff, B. A., Farrell, M. P., & Uhteg, L. (1998). Parental and peer influences on the onset of heavier drinking among adolescents. *Journal of Studies of Alcohol, 59*, 311–317.

Reingen, P. H. (1978). On inducing compliance with requests. *Journal of Consumer Research, 5*, 96–102.

Reingen, P. H. (1982). Test of a list procedure for inducing compliance with a request to donate money. *Journal of Applied Psychology, 67*, 110–118.

Reingen, P. H., & Kernan, J. B. (1993). Social perception and interpersonal influence: Some consequences of the physical attractiveness stereotype in a personal selling setting. *Journal of Consumer Psychology, 2*, 25–38.

Ries, A., & Trout, J. (1981). *Positioning: The battle for your mind*. New York: Warner.

Riker, W. H. (1986). *The art of political manipulation*. New Haven, CT: Yale University Press.

Rind, B. (1997). Effects of interest arousal on compliance with a request for help. *Basic and Applied Social Psychology, 19*, 49–59.

Rind, B., & Benjamin, D. (1994). Effects of public image concerns and self-image on compliance. *Journal of Social Psychology, 134*, 19–25.

Rogers, C. R. (1942). *Counseling and psychotherapy*. Boston: Houghton-Mifflin.

Roloff, M. E., Janiszewski, C. A., McGrath, M. A., Burns, C. S., & Manrai, L. A. (1988). Acquiring resources from intimates: When obligation substitutes for persuasion. *Human Communication Research, 14*, 364–396.

Rosnow, R. L. (1966). Whatever happened to the "law of primacy?" *Journal of Communication, 16*, 10–31.

Ross, A. S., & Braband, J. (1973). Effect of increased responsibility on bystander intervention: II. The cue value of a blind person. *Journal of Personality and Social Psychology, 25*, 254–258.

Ross, R. H., & Kraft, F. B. (1983). Creating low consumer product expectations. *Journal of Business Research, 11*, 1–9.

Rothbart, M., Davis-Stitt, C., & Hill, J. (1997). Effects of arbitrarily placed category boundaries on similarity judgments. *Journal of Experimental Social Psychology*, *33*, 122–145.

Rozin, P., & Nemeroff, C. (2002). Sympathetic magical thinking: The contagion and similarity "heuristics." In T. Gilovich, D. Griffin, & D. Kahneman (Eds.), *Heuristics and biases* (pp. 201–216). Cambridge: Cambridge University Press.

Rozin, P., & Royzman, E. B. (2001). Negativity bias, negativity dominance, and contagion. *Personality and Social Psychology Review*, *5*, 296–320.

Rozin, P., Spranca, M., Krieger, Z., Neuhaus, R., Surillo, D., Swerdlin, A., & Woos, K. (2004). Preference for natural: Instrumental and ideational/moral motivations, and the contrast between foods and medicines. *Appetite*, *43*, 147–154.

Rubin, J. Z. (Ed.). (1981). *Dynamics of third party intervention*. New York: Praeger.

Rucker, D. D., & Pratkanis, A. R. (2001). Projection as an interpersonal influence tactic: The effects of the pot calling the kettle black. *Personality and Social Psychology Bulletin*, *27*, 1494–1507.

Ruscher, J. B. (2001). *Prejudiced communication*. New York: Guilford Press.

Salancik, G. R. (1977). Commitment is too easy! *Organizational Dynamics*, *6*(1), 62–80.

Salancik, G. R., & Conway, M. (1975). Attitude inferences from salient and relevant cognitive content about behavior. *Journal of Personality and Social Psychology*, *32*, 829–840.

Santos M. D., Leve, C., & Pratkanis, A. R. (1994). Hey buddy, can you spare seventeen cents? Mindful persuasion and the pique technique. *Journal of Applied Social Psychology*, *24*, 755–764.

Sawyer, A. G., & Howard, D. J. (1991). Effects of omitting conclusions in advertisements to involved and uninvolved audiences. *Journal of Marketing Research*, *28*, 467–474.

Schachter, S. (1951). Deviation, rejection, and communication. *Journal of Abnormal and Social Psychology*, *46*, 190–207.

Schumann, D. W., Petty, R. E., & Clemons, D. S. (1990). Predicting the effectiveness of different strategies of advertising variation: A test of the repetition–variation hypothesis. *Journal of Consumer Research*, *17*, 192–202.

Schwartz, N. (1990). Feelings as information: Informational and motivational functions of affective states. In E. T. Higgins & R. M. Sorrentino (Eds.), *Handbook of motivation and cognition: Foundations of social behavior* (Vol. 2, pp. 527–561). New York: Guilford Press.

Schwarzwald, J., Raz, M., & Zvibel, M. (1979). The application of the door-in-the-face technique when established behavioral customs exist. *Journal of Applied Social Psychology*, *9*, 576–586.

Segal, M. W. (1974). Alphabet and attraction: An unobtrusive measure of the effect of propinquity in a field setting. *Journal of Personality and Social Psychology*, *30*, 654–657.

Segrin, C. (1993). The effects of nonverbal behavior on outcomes of compliance gaining attempts. *Communication Studies*, *44*, 169–187.

Selznick, P. (1949). *TVA and the grass roots*. Berkeley: University of California Publications in Culture and Society.

Settle, R. B., & Golden, L. L. (1974). Attribution theory and advertiser credibility. *Journal of Marketing Research*, *11*, 181–185.

Shapiro, A. K., & Shapiro, E. (1997). *The powerful placebo*. Baltimore: Johns Hopkins University Press.

Sherif, M. (1936). *The psychology of social norms*. New York: Harper & Row.

Sherif, M. (1937). The psychology of slogans. *Journal of Abnormal and Social Psychology*, *32*, 450–461.

Sherif, M., Harvey, O. J., White, J., Hood, W., & Sherif, C. (1954). *Intergroup conflict and cooperation: The Robbers Cave experiment.* Norman: University of Oklahoma Press.

Sherman, D. A. K., Nelson, L. D., & Steele, C. M. (2000). Do messages about health risks threaten the self? Increasing the acceptance of threatening health messages via self-affirmations. *Personality and Social Psychology Bulletin, 26,* 1046–1058.

Shimp, T. A. (1978). Do incomplete comparisons mislead? *Journal of Advertising Research, 18*(6), 21–27.

Siegel, A. E., & Siegel, S. (1957). Reference groups, membership groups, and attitude change. *Journal of Abnormal and Social Psychology, 55,* 360–364.

Sigall, H., & Aronson, E. (1967). Opinion change and the gain–loss model of interpersonal attraction. *Journal of Experimental Social Psychology, 3,* 178–188.

Sigall, H., & Landy, D. (1973). Radiating beauty: Effects of having a physically attractive partner on person perception. *Journal of Personality and Social Psychology, 28,* 218–224.

Silverthorne, C. P., & Mazmanian, L. (1975). The effects of heckling and media of presentation on the impact of a persuasive communication. *Journal of Social Psychology, 96,* 229–236.

Simon, H. A. (1967). Motivational and emotional controls of cognition. *Psychological Review, 74,* 29–39.

Sloan, L. R., Love, R. E., & Ostrom, T. M. (1974). Political heckling: Who really loses? *Journal of Personality and Social Psychology, 30,* 518–525.

Slusher, M. P., & Anderson, C. A. (1996). Using causal persuasive arguments to change beliefs and teach new information: The mediating role of explanation availability and evaluation bias in the acceptance of knowledge. *Journal of Educational Psychology, 88,* 110–122.

Snyder, C. R., Lassegard, M., & Ford, C. E. (1986). Distancing after group success and failure: Basking in reflected glory and cutting off reflected failure. *Journal of Personality and Social Psychology, 51,* 382–388.

Snyder, M., & DeBono, K. G. (1989). Understanding the functions of attitudes: Lessons from personality and social behavior. In A. R. Pratkanis, S. J. Breckler, & A. G. Greenwald (Eds.), *Attitude structure and function* (pp. 339–359). Hillsdale, NJ: Lawrence Erlbaum Associates, Inc.

Snyder, M., & Swann, W. B. (1978). Hypothesis testing processes in social interaction. *Journal of Personality and Social Psychology, 36,* 1202–1212.

Sole, K., Marton, J., & Hornstein, H. A. (1975). Opinion similarity and helping: Three field experiments investigating the bases of promotive tension. *Journal of Experimental Social Psychology, 11,* 1–13.

Sopory, P., & Dillard, J. P. (2002). The persuasive effects of metaphor: A meta-analysis. *Human Communication Research, 28,* 382–419.

Spangenberg, E. R., & Greenwald, A. G. (2001). Self-prophecy as a behavior modification technique in the United States. In W. Wosinska, R. B. Cialdini, J. Reykowski, & D. W. Barrett (Eds.), *The practice of social influence in multiple cultures* (pp. 51–62). Mahwah, NJ: Lawrence Erlbaum Associates, Inc.

Spangenberg, E. R., Sprott, D. E., Grohmann, B., & Smith, R. J. (2003). Mass-communicated prediction requests: Practical application and a cognitive dissonance explanation of self-prophecy. *Journal of Marketing, 67,* 47–62.

Spanos, N. P., Radtke, H. L., & Bertrand, L. D. (1985). Hypnotic amnesia as a strategic enactment: Breaching amnesia in highly susceptible subjects. *Journal of Personality and Social Psychology, 47,* 1155–1169.

Staats, A. W., & Staats, C. K. (1958). Attitudes established by classical conditioning. *Journal of Abnormal and Social Psychology, 57*, 37–40.

Staw, B. M. (1976). Knee-deep in the Big Muddy: A study of escalating commitment to a chosen course of action. *Organizational Behavior and Human Decision Process, 16*, 27–44.

Steele, C. M. (1975). Name-calling and compliance. *Journal of Personality and Social Psychology, 31*, 361–369.

Steele, C. M., & Ostrom, T. M. (1974). Perspective-mediated attitude change: When is indirect persuasion more effective than direct persuasion? *Journal of Personality and Social Psychology, 29*, 737–741.

Stone, J., Aronson, E., Crain, A. L., Winslow, M. P., & Fried, C. (1994). Inducing hypocrisy as a means of encouraging young adults to use condoms. *Personality and Social Psychology Bulletin, 20*, 116–128.

Storms, M. D. (1973). Videotape and the attribution process: Reversing actors' and observers' points of view. *Journal of Personality and Social Psychology, 27*, 165–175.

Stotland, E., Zander, A., & Natsoulas, T. (1961). Generalization of interpersonal similarity. *Journal of Abnormal and Social Psychology, 62*, 250–256.

Strack, F., Martin, L. L., & Stepper, S. (1988). Inhibiting and facilitating conditions of the human smile: A nonobtrusive test of the facial feedback hypothesis. *Journal of Personality and Social Psychology, 54*, 768–777.

Strenta, A., & DeJong, W. (1981). The effect of a prosocial label on helping behavior. *Social Psychology Quarterly, 44*, 142–147.

Sue, S., Smith, R. E., & Caldwell, C. (1973). Effects of inadmissible evidence on the decisions of simulated jurors. *Journal of Applied Social Psychology, 3*, 345–353.

Suedfeld, P. (1969). Changes in intellectual performance and in susceptibility to influence. In J. P. Zubek (Ed.), *Sensory deprivation: Fifteen years of research* (pp. 126–166). New York: Appleton-Century-Crofts.

Taylor, S. E., Pham, L. B., Rivkin, I. D., & Armor, D. A. (1998). Harnessing the imagination: Mental stimulation, self-regulation, and coping. *American Psychologist, 53*, 429–439.

Taylor, S. E., & Thompson, S. C. (1982). Stalking the elusive "vividness" effect. *Psychological Review, 89*, 155–181.

Thaler, R. H. (1992). *Winner's curse: Paradoxes and anomalies of economic life*. Princeton, NJ: Princeton University Press.

Thelen, M. H., & Kirkland, K. D. (1976). On status and being imitated: Effects on reciprocal imitation and attraction. *Journal of Personality and Social Psychology, 35*, 691–697.

Thompson, L. (2001). *The mind and heart of the negotiator*. Upper Saddle River, NJ: Prentice Hall.

Trope, Y., & Liberman, N. (2003). Temporal construal. *Psychological Review, 110*, 403–421.

Tversky, A., & Kahneman, D. (1981). The framing of decisions and the psychology of choice. *Science, 211*, 453–458.

Tybout, A. M., Calder, B. J., & Sternthal, B. (1981). Using information processing theory to design marketing strategies. *Journal of Marketing Research, 18*, 73–79.

Tyszka, T. (1983). Contextual multiattribute decision rules. In L. Sjöberg, T. Tyszka, & J. Wise (Eds.), *Human decision making* (pp. 243–256). Lund, Sweden: Doxa.

Uhlmann, E. L., & Cohen, G. L. (2005). Constructed criteria: Redefining merit to justify discrimination. *Psychological Science, 16*, 474–480.

van Duüren, F., & di Giacomo, J. P. (1996). Degrading situations and antisocial behavior:

An experimental approach to delinquency. *European Journal of Social Psychology, 26*, 763–776.

Vangelisti, A. L., Daly, J. A., & Rudnick, J. R. (1991). Making people feel guilty in conversations: Techniques and correlates. *Human Communication Research, 18*, 3–39.

Vidmar, N. (1972). Effects of decision alternatives on the verdicts and social perceptions of simulated jurors. *Journal of Personality and Social Psychology, 22*, 211–218.

von Winterfeldt, D., & Edwards, W. (1986). *Decision analysis and behavioral research.* Cambridge: Cambridge University Press.

Walster, E., Aronson, E., & Abrahams, D. (1966). On increasing the persuasiveness of a low prestige communicator. *Journal of Experimental Social Psychology, 2*, 325–342.

Walster, E., & Festinger, L. J. (1962). The effectiveness of "overheard" persuasive communications. *Journal of Abnormal and Social Psychology, 65*, 395–402.

Wang, T. H., & Katzev, R. D. (1990). Group commitment and resource conservation: Two field experiments on promoting recycling. *Journal of Applied Social Psychology, 20*, 265–275.

Ware, P. D., & Tucker, R. K. (1974). Heckling as distraction: An experimental study of its effect on source credibility. *Speech Monographs, 41*, 185–188.

Warlop, L., & Alba, J. W. (2004). Sincere flattery: Trade-dress imitation and consumer choice. *Journal of Consumer Psychology, 14*, 21–27.

Watts, W. A. (1967). Relative persistence of opinion change induced by active compared to passive participation. *Journal of Personality and Social Psychology, 5*, 4–15.

Weaver, G. R., & Conlon, D. E. (2003). Explaining façades of choice: Timing, justice effects, and behavioral outcomes. *Journal of Applied Social Psychology, 33*, 2217–2243.

Wegener, D. T., Petty, R. E., & Smith, S. M. (1995). Positive mood can increase or decrease message scrutiny: The hedonic contingency view of mood and message processing. *Journal of Personality and Social Psychology, 69*, 5–15.

Wegner, D. M., Lane, J. D., & Dimitri, S. (1994). The allure of secret relationships. *Journal of Personality and Social Psychology, 66*, 287–300.

Wegner, D. M., Wenzlaff, R., Kerker, R. M., & Beattie, A. E. (1981). Incrimination through innuendo: Can media questions become public answers? *Journal of Personality and Social Psychology, 40*, 822–832.

Wegrocki, H. J. (1934). The effect of prestige suggestibility on emotional attitudes. *Journal of Social Psychology, 5*, 384–394.

Weick, K. E., Gilfillan, D. P., & Keith, T. A. (1973). The effect of composer credibility on orchestra performance. *Sociometry, 36*, 435–465.

Weinstein, E. I., & Deutschberger, P. (1963). Some dimensions of altercasting. *Sociometry, 26*, 454–466.

Werkmeister, W. H. (1948). *An introduction to critical thinking.* Lincoln, NB: Johnsen Publishing.

Werner, C. M., Stoll, R., Birch, P., & White, P. H. (2002). Clinical validation and cognitive elaboration: Signs that encourage sustained recycling. *Basic and Applied Social Psychology, 24*, 185–203.

White, P. H., & Harkins, S. G. (1994). Race of source effects in the elaboration likelihood model. *Journal of Personality and Social Psychology, 67*, 790–807.

Wicklund, R. A. (1970). Prechoice preference reversal as a result of threat to decision freedom. *Journal of Personality and Social Psychology, 14*, 8–17.

Wicklund, R. A., Cooper, J., & Linder, D. E. (1967). Effects of expected effort on attitude change prior to exposure. *Journal of Experimental Social Psychology, 3*, 416–428.

Wilkie, W. L., McNeill, D. L., & Mazis, M. B. (1984). Marketing's "scarlet letter:" The theory and practice of corrective advertising. *Journal of Marketing, 48*, 11–31.

Williams, K. D. (2001). *Ostracism: The power of silence*. New York: Guilford Press.

Williams, K. D., Bourgeois, M. J., & Croyle, R. T. (1993). The effects of stealing thunder in criminal and civil trials. *Law and Human Behavior, 17*, 597–609.

Williams, K. D., & Dolnik, L. (2001). Revealing the worst first: Stealing thunder as a social influence strategy. In J. P. Forgas & K. D. Williams (Eds.), *Social influence: Direct and indirect processes* (pp. 213–231). New York: Psychology Press.

Williams, P., Block, L. G., & Fitzgerald, G. J. (2006). Simply asking questions about health behaviors increases both healthy and unhealthy behaviors. *Social Influence, 1*.

Wood, W., & Quinn, J. M. (2003). Forewarned and forearmed? Two meta-analysis syntheses of forewarning of influence appeals. *Psychological Bulletin, 129*, 119–138.

Worchel, S., Lee, J., & Adewole, A. (1975). Effects of supply and demand on ratings of object value. *Journal of Personality and Social Psychology, 32*, 906–914.

Young, J. W. (1991). *Totalitarian language*. Charlottesville: University of Virginia Press.

Zajonc, R. B. (1965). Social facilitation. *Science, 149*, 269–274.

Zajonc, R. B. (1968). The attitudinal effects of mere exposure. *Journal of Personality and Social Psychology, Monograph Supplement, 9*, 1–27.

Zeff, L. H., & Iverson, M. A. (1966). Opinion conformity in groups under status threat. *Journal of Personality and Social Psychology, 3*, 383–389.

Zimbardo, P. G. (1960). Involvement and communication discrepancy as determinants of opinion conformity. *Journal of Abnormal and Social Psychology, 60*, 86–94.

Zubek, J. P. (Ed.). (1969). *Sensory deprivation: Fifteen years of research*. New York: Appleton-Century-Crofts.

Zukier, H. (1982). The dilution effect: The role of correlation and the dispersion of predictor variables in the use of nondiagnostic information. *Journal of Personality and Social Psychology, 43*, 1163–1174.

3

Omega Approaches to Persuasion: Overcoming Resistance

ERIC S. KNOWLES and DAN D RINER

*M*ost important decisions in life are characterized by ambivalence (Arkowitz, 2002). The reasons for choosing a course of action are accompanied by reasons for not choosing it. Enjoying the benefits of an alternative requires suffering the costs.

This fact that most choices are complex and that each alternative is multivalenced is an axiom of decision theory. If you want to know how someone will choose, list the positives and negatives for each choice alternative, and their likelihood, and see which one has the greater expected utility (Ajzen, 1991; Joyce, 1999). But the ambivalence is also a core proposition for persuasion theory, the science and practice of altering someone's choices (Knowles & Linn, 2004b). The fact that there are desires to approach and desires to avoid an alternative has several implications for persuasion.

TWO WAYS TO PERSUADE

Ambivalence about decision alternatives implies that there are two separate ways to persuade people to accept an alternative. One set of persuasion strategies attempts to increase the attractive features of the alternative; the second set attempts to decrease the negative features of the alternative. We have called the first one the alpha strategies because they seem always to be the first ones attempted (Knowles & Linn, 2004b). We have called the second set the omega strategies because they attempt to reduce the resistance to selecting an alternative, because omega is the universal sign of resistance, and because they seem often to be the last strategies considered. The main focus of this chapter is on defining and describing the different omega strategies, because these have not been defined or described until very recently (Knowles & Linn, 2004b).

The distinction between alpha and omega strategies for persuasion is more than a heuristic categorization of persuasion strategies. The distinction points to a fundamental qualitative distinction that is widely recognized in psychology. It may even be fundamentally represented in different brain structures and processes. Gray (1994), Fowles (1988), Carver and White (1994) and others identify separate neurochemical systems related to sensitivity to benefits and sensitivity to losses. The "behavioral activation system" (BAS) involves the basal ganglia and dopaminergic fibers (Gray, 1994) that seem to become more active in the presence of rewards or the absence of punishments. The functional purpose of the BAS is to be sensitive to and activate action to obtain the benefits and rewards in the environment. The "behavioral inhibition system" (BIS) involves more the amygdala and the serotonin-sensitive receptors that seem to be activated by the presence of punishments or the absence of rewards. The function of the BIS is to be attentive to dangers and costs in the environment and to inhibit action that would encounter them.

In a more motivational realm, Higgins (1999, 2001) has proposed two fundamental orientations that people have toward regulating their actions in the environment. Higgins identifies a "promotive" orientation that is more attentive to the rewards and benefits and attempts to maximize these. A "preventive" orientation, in contrast, is sensitive to the potential dangers and punishments in the environment and attempts to minimize these. These two systems have different emotional consequences. Failure to obtain benefits produces dejection and sadness, whereas failure to avoid costs is associated with agitation and anger.

It appears that nature has provided humans with separate cost assessment and benefit assessment systems, operating through different brain structures, with different neurotransmitters, and with different affective repercussions. The fundamental separation of these systems suggests that the distinction between alpha and omega strategies for persuasion may be similarly fundamental. The alpha strategies that increase the attractiveness of an alternative may be operating on different brain structures and with different neurotransmitters than the omega strategies that serve to reduce the reluctance or dislike of an alternative.

RESISTANCE IS THE FOCUS FOR PERSUASION

The approach–avoidance model of persuasion compels the conclusion that resistance is the key element in the persuasion process (Knowles, Butler, & Linn, 2001; Knowles & Linn, 2004a). Persuasion is required only when people feel "I don't like it!", "I don't believe it!", or "I won't do it!" Without this resistance, a goal would be selected and movement toward that goal would begin. It is the restraint, the resistance, the avoidance forces in the motivational system that inhibit change and make persuasion necessary. All persuasion, therefore, is implicitly aimed at resistance. Because of this, persuasion should rest on an understanding of the different forms of resistance operating to inhibit change. Persuasion should be crafted explicitly to deal with the form of resistance that is operating.

UNDERSTANDING RESISTANCE

Prior research has identified three basic sources for resistance that impede persuasion, compliance, and change. These are (a) resistance to the influence attempt, also known as "reactance", (b) resistance to the proposal, also known as "skepticism", and (c) resistance to change, also known as "inertia."

Resistance to the Influence: Reactance

Jack Brehm (1966; Brehm & Brehm, 1981) coined the term "reactance" to refer to the negative emotional reaction to the usurpation of freedom. Reactance occurs when a person feels that someone else is taking away his or her choices or limiting the range of alternatives. This is an aversive feeling that produces motivation to resist the influence attempt and to restore the threatened freedom. Contrariness, opposition, obstinacy, passive-aggression, and disobedience are all symptoms of reactance. Reactance will initiate actions to restore the freedom in fact or in symbol. Brehm's (1966) research showed that telling someone that they had to select one alternative rather than another reduced liking for the recommended alternative and increased liking for the prohibited alternative.

Brehm (1966) identified two factors that contributed to this form of resistance. The first factor concerns the nature of the threat. Reactance intensifies to the extent that the influence attempt is blatant, coercive, unwanted, or arbitrary. Reactance is diminished to the extent that the influence attempt is subtle, collaborative, indirect, or justified. The second factor concerns the nature of the freedoms that are threatened by the influence attempt. Reactance will be stronger to the extent that the threatened freedoms are more numerous and more important to the person.

The source of resistance to the influence lies in the actions of the agent promoting the change. Reactance is created by the influence attempt. In a sense, this form of resistance has no content. It has little to do with which specific change is proposed. Although reactance will cause people to be against the proposed change and to be nostalgic for the status quo, these are both consequences, not origins, of this form of resistance to persuasion. Changing the nature of the proposal, such as recommending B rather than A, will do little to alter reactance. However, if one softens the influence attempt so that the degree of threat is reduced, then the contrariness to the change and the nostalgia for the past both diminish.

An understanding of reactance produces a variety of effective influence principles. Saying "No you can't!" always produces at least a tinge of reactance. Sometimes this understanding can be used to influence, as in "reverse psychology," where a person prohibits an action that is secretly desired, hoping that the reactance will be strong enough to initiate the prohibited action. As discussed later in this chapter, reverse psychology is not easily recommended. It is uncollaborative and deceitful, and, if that's not enough, it also tends to be ineffective and prone to backfire.

Resistance to the Proposal: Skepticism

A second form of resistance is completely content-focused. It appears as skepticism about the change that is proposed. Its other faces include ambivalence, intensive scrutiny, countering, and doubt.

We know a great deal about this form of resistance from the work of William McGuire (1964), who studied ways to increase resistance to persuasion. McGuire's focus was on how to equip people to resist propaganda, that is, unwanted and coercive influence. McGuire saw that Cold-War propaganda often attacked core societal assumptions, such as "free enterprise promotes prosperity," "democracy is participatory," or "tooth brushing promotes dental health." Because these core beliefs were assumptive and not part of public debate, believers had no experience and little ammunition to call on to resist attacks on these beliefs, making these beliefs particularly vulnerable to propaganda. McGuire (1964) studied ways to create resistance to propaganda.

The model McGuire developed is now standard in the study of persuasion. He believed that to be able to resist propaganda, a person needed two things: (a) the motivation to resist, and (b) the ability to resist. He started by studying the ability to resist, but found that equipping people with arguments and reasons to support their beliefs was often insufficient. People first had to be motivated, by feelings of vulnerability, to attend to the reasons and arguments. McGuire captured the motivational component through forewarning of an attack or administering a "weakened" dose of the attack in an analogy to medical "inoculation."

McGuire had a number of insights about resistance to persuasion. First, he treated resistance as a separate entity from persuasion. The strength of the persuasion attempt and the strength of the resistance could vary independently. Previous researchers had often treated resistance as the reverse of persuasion, believing that less persuasion implied greater resistance. Second, he treated resistance as a potential response (rather than a kinetic response), available to be used whenever called upon. Resistance was more the ability to call on information and logic in repelling an attack than it was the actual action of countering an attack.

You will see from this discussion that McGuire's treatment of resistance dealt more with the cognitive aspects of resistance ("I don't believe it!") than with the affective ("I don't like it!") or behavioral ("I won't do it!") components. As such, this view of resistance blends easily into the cognitive response model of attitudes described by Greenwald, Brock, and Ostrom (1968), Petty, Ostrom, and Brock (1981), and Petty and Cacioppo (1986). In the elaboration likelihood model of attitude change proposed by Petty and Cacioppo (1986), there are two routes to persuasion. The more cognitively central or reasoned route allows one to carefully and deeply scrutinize a proposal or message, checking it for internal consistency, comparing its propositions with one's own beliefs, experiences, and remembered information. This reasoned route produces thoughts about the message – either supportive thoughts, such as "That makes sense!" or "That corresponds to my experience!" or contrary thoughts, such as "I don't believe that!" or "That's not what happens to me!" – and it is these thoughts that determine the final attitude toward the proposal. If a proposal produces mostly positive, supportive thoughts, then it will be accepted; if it produces mostly contrary or counterarguing thoughts, then it will be rejected. For Petty and Cacioppo, the autograph of central route processing is that reasonable arguments are more persuasive than unreasonable arguments. McGuire's resistance-building procedures attempted to provide people with the motivation and information to effectively use the central processing route to critically evaluate and counter unreasonable propaganda.

Petty and Cacioppo (1986) observed that not all persuasion worked through this reasoned route. They realized that people could form a strong attitude even if they didn't think deeply about the issue or the information. They proposed a second, more heuristic route that relied on salient but less informative features of the proposal or message to form a judgment. People could accept a proposal because the spokesperson was attractive or seemed to make many points, or reject a proposal because the words were difficult or the layout was amateurish.

Which route to persuasion was employed rested on how much motivation and ability one had available to critically evaluate a proposal. Petty and Cacioppo found that they could often provide someone with the motivation for reasoned scrutiny of a proposal by making the topic personally relevant (e.g., "This change will affect you soon!"). The ability to scrutinize a proposal included both knowing enough to be able to evaluate the proposal, similar to McGuire's (1964) notion of ability to resist, and being free from distractions so that the proposal could be engaged.

The cognitive response approach implies that there are multiple routes to resistance (Wegener, Petty, Smoak, & Fabrigar, 2004). The reasoned, central route to resistance goes through careful analysis, development of counterarguments, and recall of disconfirming information or experience. The peripheral route to resistance goes through negative contextual associations or other negative aspects of the proposal. In addition, evaluations that are formed through a reasoned route are more inherently stable, and unaffected by counterinfluence, simply because the deeper thought has anchored the evaluation with more of the person's other beliefs. Evaluations formed through a peripheral route are more ephemeral. Change the context or the peripheral features of the proposal and the evaluation also will change.

Wegener and Petty (1995, 1997) have added a metacognitive element to the cognitive response approach to resistance and persuasion. Their flexible correction model suggests that people think about the process of evaluation and make corrections to compensate for hindrances or biases in the evaluation process. If a person thinks that he might be unduly open to influence, he might listen to a proposal, form an opinion of it online, but then adjust his opinion more conservatively in light of his belief that his gullibility may be part of the reason for a belief. Tormala and Petty (2004) have found that people who were successful at resisting a persuasive message became more certain of their initial opinion, and therefore more resistant to further attacks, if they thought that the persuasive message was difficult to resist. If they were led to believe that the same message was easy to resist, then their unchanged opinion was not as firm against a future onslaught.

All of these approaches to resistance focus on the proposal, not on the proposer, and not on nostalgia for the status quo. The common element in these cognitive approaches is that people form an opinion of a proposal, directly through careful evaluation, indirectly through heuristic use of potential signs of quality, or metacognitively through reflection on the process of evaluation. Under these conditions, resistance is not the foregone outcome that it is with reactance or inertia. Resistance to the proposal brings the focus to the proposal. If the features evaluated are negative, then resistance is the outcome. But if the features lead to a positive evaluation – if resistance is not sustainable – then acceptance or attitude change may be the result.

Note that there can be a paradoxical feature to a reasoned focus on the proposal. Greater resistance to the proposal may in fact produce more acceptance of the proposal. When there is little resistance, and therefore little motivation to deal with a proposal, the message may be dismissed out of hand, without much thought or attention. But greater resistance may bring greater scrutiny of the propositions and arguments in a proposal. If these are logical propositions supported by incontrovertible arguments, then the greater scrutiny will produce greater acceptance.

Resistance to Change: Inertia

The final form of resistance is simple inertia, the desire to not change. Inertia is difficult to address precisely because it has little to do with the proposed change. It endorses the status quo. Inertial resistance is focused on the past, not the future. Its goal is to avoid disruption, to avoid spending energy contemplating new ideas or initiating new action. It is unresponsive to the influence agent, and inattentive to the specifics of the proposed change. Consequently, softening the influence attempt or changing the proposal will have little effect on this form of resistance.

The change agent often experiences inertial resistance as passivity, avoidance, or disengagement. This characterization is largely accurate. The influence target has little interest in moving away from the status quo, so doesn't share the persuader's focus on the future possibilities. Clinical resistance has this quality. From a psychodynamic perspective, resistance is usually defined as a motivated reluctance to accept or achieve insight (Messer, 2002). From a more behavioral perspective, it is defined as a noncompliance with a reasonable and doable prescription (Leahy, 2001). The common characteristic is that the persuader and the target of influence have different immediate goals and concerns. Piderit (2000) points out that in organizational settings this difference, while initially frustrating to the persuader, is at the very least informative. Resistance to change in organizations often leads to more carefully considered and formulated changes, where the desires for change and the resistance to making the change each influence the evolving change in a dynamic way.

Another characteristic of inertial resistance is that it doesn't motivate active or effortful consideration of the persuasion attempt. Usually a proposal is rejected out of hand merely because it proposes any change. The reasons, logic, justification, or other particulars of the proposal are of no consequence and are not considered. Inertia can lead to the seemingly paradoxical outcome where the influence target generally agrees with the premises and propositions of an influence attempt (e.g., that the change would be positive, easy to accomplish, with many benefits) but still has no interest in making the change. It is easy to see why persuaders get frustrated with this situation; all the propositions in the message have seemingly been accepted, but the conclusion has not. It doesn't feel logical.

Inertial resistance can be overcome with powerful and personal demonstrations of the need to change, as described by Sagarin and Wood (Chapter 13, this volume). For instance, Sagarin and Cialdini (2004; Sagarin, Cialdini, Rice, & Serna, 2002) found in two studies that training people to be critical of false advertising had little effect on people's susceptibility to false advertising. They reasoned that this lack of effect was due to a kind of inertia: that participants completed the training tasks mindlessly because they thought that they already were immune to any false advertising. Sagarin and Cialdini found that they could break through this inertia by first demonstrating to participants that they were, in fact, vulnerable to false advertising. Confronted by their own susceptibility, people became ready to listen to the training. Aronson (Chapter 4, this volume) describes an awakening from inertia created by becoming aware of one's hypocrisy. People who were made to advocate what they believe in (e.g., safe sex) were not particularly likely to act in accordance with their advocacy, unless they had been made aware of their own contradictory behavior. People confronted with the hypocrisy of their advocacy conformed more closely to the position they had advocated (Aronson, Fried, and Stone, 1991; Stone, Aronson, & Crain, 1994).

OMEGA STRATEGIES FOR PERSUASION: REDUCE RESISTANCE

Omega strategies for persuasion aim to reduce, deactivate, or divert resistance to persuasion. This section of the chapter describes various strategies that have been developed and described, but not really collected together and organized before. You will see that the techniques we describe come from a variety of fields. We organize them here by the type of resistance that they seem to address more directly.

Techniques to Deal with Reactance to the Influence Attempt

The most effective strategy to reduce reactance is not to raise it in the first place. Brehm (1966) defined reactance as a negative reaction to the actual or threatened loss of decisional freedom. The degree of reactance felt is affected by (a) the number and importance of the freedoms that were threatened, and (b) the blatancy or coerciveness of the threat. There are a number of ways to deal with this kind of resistance. Certainly, one can minimize the request that is made and make the request as gently as possible. But when this is not possible, reactance can still be dealt with by acknowledging its existence and/or reframing it from a negative to a positive contributor to the decision. Finally, if the reactance is intractable, it still can be dealt with by creating a counter-reactance. Each of these is described in more detail below.

Minimize the Request   If resistance is created when important alternatives are constrained, one strategy to minimize the resistance is to minimize the request. So, instead of asking someone to buy the whole hog, you ask them to acquire only a small part. This can be done directly, as in the foot-in-the-door technique (Freedman & Fraser, 1966), or indirectly, as in the "even a penny will help" technique (Cialdini & Schroeder, 1976).

Freedman and Fraser (1966) showed clearly that asking people to perform a small task (e.g., putting a sticker in the front window of one's residence, or completing a short opinion poll) led them to be much more likely to agree to a large request (e.g., putting a billboard on their front lawn). Minimal requests are effective change strategies because the minor imposition raises little reactance, but its acceptance starts one on the path of change. A principle at work here is that it is often much easier to create incremental change ("do just a little more") than to initiate abrupt changes ("do something different"). Bob Greene (2002) seems to use this principle in his "Get with the program" diet/exercise book. Rather than ask people to choose to diet and exercise, he begins his book with this coopting statement: "Congratulations! Whether you realize it or not, simply by picking up this book you have taken the first of what I hope will be many steps . . . toward . . . reclaiming your physical health, well-being, and happiness" (p. 9). The subsequent chapters merely continue in small steps the path that, Greene announces, was implied by picking up the book.

Another version of the minimization strategy is to make the same request as others, but to call it less. Cialdini and Schroeder (1976) did this when they went door-to-door in Phoenix, AZ, to collect money for the American Cancer Society. When they made the standard request for a contribution, they received donations from 29% of the households. When they made the same request, but added the minimizing phrase, "even a penny will help", they received donations from 50% of the households. Interestingly, the donation amounts were not much different. "Even a penny will help" lowered people's resistance by making the request seem like less of an imposition (see also Brockner, Guzzi, Kane, Levine, & Shaplen, 1984).

Depersonalize the Request   Reactance to the influence attempt is an interpersonal resistance: "I don't want to be coerced, especially by you!" One way to minimize this form of resistance is to make the request less personal. It is an old finding in the social psychology literature that people overhearing messages are more persuaded than the people to whom the message is directed, presumably because they have less reactance (Brock & Becker, 1965; Walster & Festinger, 1962).

There are many ways to depersonalize a request. The persuader may disavow any personal authorship of a request (e.g., "It's the manager's policy", "The book tells me what to do") or to deny any *ad hominem* element in the request (e.g., "This is the same deal we give everybody"). An interesting example of depersonalizing the request comes out of the law and psychology literature. Wolf and Montgomery (1977) studied the effect of a judge's ruling that negative evidence presented at a trial was inadmissible. When the judge ruled the evidence inadmissible and instructed the jury to ignore it, the jurors instead used the information against the defendant. However, jurors did not use the evidence against the defendant when the judge merely ruled the evidence inadmissible without adding the specific instruction to ignore it. The specific instruction for jurors to ignore the information appeared to create reactance that could be sidestepped by depersonalizing the ruling.

Another way to depersonalize the request is to put it in the form of a parable or a story (Green, Strange, & Brock, 2002) rather than a discursive message. A narrative differs from a discursive message in several ways. A story has protagonists who do things and have things done to them. It has a plot, a temporal sequencing of events, and, in a good story, some tension that is waiting to be resolved. A good narrative transports the listener into the story, leading the listener to visualize the events, take the character's perspective, react emotionally and cognitively to the events, and predict the future (Dal Cin, Zanna, & Fong, 2004). All these features create two effects. First, they increase involvement in the message. Second, they are incompatible with counterarguing or resisting the implicit and even explicit messages in the narrative (Green & Brock, 2000). The consequence is that the messages in stories are more likely to be accepted than the same messages delivered directly.

Redefine the Relationship   A related omega strategy aimed at reducing reactance is to minimize the influence aspects of the relationship. The seller becomes a consultant, an advisor, a collaborator (Straight, 1996). In the 1990s, many of the major brokerage houses created "free" financial planning analyses for their clients. The major recommendation coming out of these analyses was "diversification" into a wide variety of mutual funds, funds that often paid a large commission to the brokerage house. This was quite a different presentation than a phone call saying "I have a number of new products that I'd like to try to sell you." Alessandra (1993), Jolson (1997), and others advise sellers to reconceptualize their task as a collaboration, focusing on establishing a mutual, long-term relationship. The explicit understanding is that it is easier for a consultant to get in the door than it is for a seller.

Redefining a selling relationship as an advisory relationship does several things. First, it minimizes the adversarial quality of the usual exchange relationship, emphasizing instead the mutual and common goals more characteristic of a communal relationship (Clark, Mills, & Corcoran, 1989). Second, it extends the implicit time perspective of the relationship from a one-time exchange to a continuing relationship. Future interactions allow for repair and reciprocity, so that one party's advantage now can be returned by the other party at a later time.

The Power of "Yes"   Reactance occurs when the influence agent says "No" (Brehm, 1966). Therefore, another effective way to avoid reactance is to always say "yes," that is, to not directly limit a person's freedoms or choices. Milton Erickson, who pioneered conversational forms of clinical hypnosis, noted that the hypnotherapist listens for the client's perspective, concerns, and expectations, then adopts and follows these as the beginning assumptions in the interaction, before introducing any change or influence attempt (Erickson, Rossi, & Rossi, 1976). Influence is introduced through "Yes, and . . ." sorts of statements, rather than "No, instead . . ." or even "Yes, but . . ." statements. For instance, when a client asks a real estate agent if he should buy this inexpensive lot, the agent smartly says, "Yes, if you are able to tolerate mosquitoes and can wait several years before you realize significant appreciation in value."

It raises much less reactance to tell people what to do than to tell them what not to do. Therefore, advocating action should lead to higher compliance than prohibiting action (Winter, Sagarin, Rhoads, Barrett, & Cialdini, 2000). For example, researchers have a choice of how to debrief research participants in an experiment involving some deception or omission of information. Often researchers attempt to commit the participant to silence, saying "Please don't tell other potential participants that feedback from the other person was false." This is a prescription that is rife with danger, failing to provide an implementation rule (Gollwitzer, 1999; Gollwitzer, Fujita, & Oettingen, 2004) and raising reactance (Brehm & Brehm, 1981). Much better is to say, "To help make sure that other people provide answers as useful as yours have been, when people ask you about this study, please tell them that you and another person answered some questions about each other." One of the authors saw a delightful and unusual example of this principle at work in an art gallery. A fragile acrylic sculpture had a sign at the base saying, "Please touch with your eyes." The command was clear, yet created much less reactance in this author than "Don't touch!" would have.

Acknowledging Resistance   The previous omega strategies have been aimed at avoiding reactance and sidestepping a person's resistance. If resistance is already raised – particularly the reactance form of resistance – then there are still things that can be done to reduce the resistance. One of the most effective turns out to be one of the simplest: Merely acknowledge the fact that the person might be feeling some resistance. In one of our studies, a student experimenter asked pedestrians heading toward the university post office if they would mail a letter. The requester had a story about being late for class and needing the letter to go out today. When she asked people, "Would you mail this letter for me?", 71% of the people agreed. When she said, "I know you might not want to, but would you mail this letter for me?", 100% of the 23 people agreed. This was a statistically and practically significant difference. We've found similarly dramatic differences, at least among female pedestrians, to requests for parking meter money, 58% giving money in response to a request, but 91% giving money when the request was preceded by an acknowledgment that the person might not want to. Carol Werner and her colleagues have similarly shown that acknowledging – and therefore clini-cally validating – someone's resistance has a dramatic effect on their compliance with aversive recycling tasks (Werner, Stoll, & Birch, 2002).

Acknowledging resistance is a unique influence strategy because it does not alter the request. It does not add more incentives or reasons to the request. Yet an acknowledgment of resistance often has a dramatic effect on compliance rates. We think of it as a way of diffusing someone's resistance by recognizing and honoring it. In a sense, the "buyer beware" form of resistance can be lessened because resistance is now an open topic in the interaction. Of course, there are other consequences of an acknowledgment. The requester communicates empathy and a joining with the person's emotional experience, which help make this technique an effective way to dissipate resistance.

Jujitsu Resistance   When resistance to influence is very strong, it can sometimes be dealt with by refocusing the resistance in a different direction. "Reverse psychology" is one example. Milton Erickson (Erickson & Rossi, 1975; Rosen, 1991) told this story about discovering the power of resistance. As a boy, he saw his father struggling to lead a calf into the barn. The calf was having none of it. Erickson's chuckle drew a challenge from his father to do better. Erickson accepted the challenge, pulled vigorously on the calf's tail, and the calf responded by pulling Erickson through the open barn door.

Reverse psychology only has a chance of working when the resistance is more important to the person than the goal to which it is directed. When a person will resist any request, then one strategy is what Nail and his colleagues (Nail, 2002; Nail, MacDonald, & Levy, 2000; Nail & MacDonald, Chapter 8, this volume) call "strategic self anti-conformity," that is, to advocate publicly against what one privately wants. Of course, one has the practical problem that the position advocated might be accepted rather than resisted and the ethical problem that interaction is based on subterfuge and deception. For both these reasons, reverse psychology is a strategy that we wouldn't recommend.

The more general principle of providing a specific focus for resistance, though, is a useful strategy. Strategic therapies (Haley, 1973) often structure resistance as a way of containing it. A patient who feels a moderate level of dread all day is asked to set aside 30 minutes a day to enumerate, describe, and experience the dread fully. Daniel Wegner (1989) has shown us that attempting to resist thoughts is counterproductive, producing exactly the opposite effect. Paradoxically, the best strategy for not thinking about something is to think about it intensively for a short period of time. These paradoxical effects of unwanted thoughts occur because of the metacognitive processes created by the intent to resist. Wegner's (1989) participants attempting to suppress a thought must check to see whether they are accomplishing their goal. This metacognitive strategy of checking whether they are successful means that the unwanted thought is kept active by the very process of trying to suppress it.

Providing Choices   Providing a choice between two alternatives is another effective way to provide a focus for resistance (Cline & Fay, 1990). Offering only one alternative, on a "take it or leave it" basis, piles all the feelings and motivations on that one alternative. Ambivalence applied to one alternative means that some feelings are always going to be denied. If the alternative is accepted, the desire is satisfied for it, but the resistance is left thwarted. If the alternative is rejected, then the resistance is satisfied, but the desire for it is frustrated. However, when two alternatives are provided, the motive to accept and the motive to resist can each be gratified, the motive to accept satisfied by the chosen alternative and the motive to resist satisfied by the rejected alternative.

One example of the choice strategy is the good cop/bad cop strategy (Davis & O'Donohue, 2004). A witness, even a guilty one, is often ambivalent during police interrogation. He wants to cooperate and ingratiate at the same time that he wants to withhold and protect. A time-tested strategy is for two police interrogators to split the ambivalence so that the kind cop gets the desire to cooperate and the harsh cop gets the desire to withhold.

Choice creates the "alternative choice double-bind" described by Erickson and Rossi (1975). It is a double-bind in the sense that the choice is framed so that either alternative binds the person to the same course of action. So, when the parent says to a dawdling child, "Do you want to put your pants on first, or your shirt on first?", both alternatives move the child toward getting dressed. Of course, the choice alternatives don't have to be so transparently mirrors of each other. A choice between different and consequential alternatives similarly moves the interaction toward completion. A management negotiator sincerely asking the labor union representatives, "Which is the more important issue to you, wages or job security?", is asking for a real and consequential choice, but one where any answer moves the negotiation along. The choice double-bind works best when the choices are distinct and meaningful, because the control implied by the choice restores decisional freedom, which reduces reactance and provides the chooser with a sense of efficacy.

The power of choice as an influence strategy has long been recognized (Cialdini, 2000; Dillard, 1991). The power of choice has been linked to commitment: Choosing one alternative commits the person to a course of action that is then propelled by the desire for consistency. The foot-in-the-door technique (Freedman & Fraser, 1966) is a frequent example of the power of commitment to promote later compliance. Choices certainly have this quality, of committing self to one alternative. But unrecognized, we think, has been the power of choices to effectively handle and satisfy the decision-maker's resistance. Choosing one alternative and spurning another is self-satisfying because the person is both promoting and protecting (Higgins, 1999), both accepting and rejecting.

Resistance is Futile   A final way to deal with someone's resistance to influence is to accept it, but frame it as powerless. This is the "borg maneuver" of *Star Trek* fame: Resistance is futile; you will comply! Davis and O'Donohue (2004) identified this strategy as used in police interrogations. The interrogator says to the witness, with low-key but absolute confidence, "It doesn't really matter what you say, we've got witnesses and crime scene evidence that will put you away for hard time. You might as well tell us your version of what happened." Beware, though – case law allows investigators to lie about such things as evidence and witnesses during interrogation, based on the legal assumption that an innocent witness would know if he or she were innocent and not be swayed by these lies.

Another version of this strategy is to frame a person's resistance as a normal and expected part of the process, nothing special. We will just wait out these feelings, knowing that they are temporary and, in the end, inconsequential. Davis and O'Donohue (2004) point out that the "resistance is futile" maneuver is more implicit and assumptive than direct. The futility of resistance is not a verbal argument presented to the suspect; it is demonstrated in the persuader's calm, confident demeanor, showing no reaction or upset at the resistance, and continuing as if there were no resistance. Obviously, this is a strategy that relies on a power differential and the inability of the target to withdraw from the interaction.

Techniques to Deal with Skepticism about the Proposal

Social psychology and communications have identified a number of strategies that deal with resistance that is focused primarily on the content of the proposal. Unfortunately, many of the most studied are either ineffective or ethically problematic. We will begin by describing three of these less recommended strategies. Counterarguing resistance with rhetoric often turns out to be counterproductive because it is confrontational and creates reactance. Distracting resistance has been well studied, but is difficult to develop into a persuasion technique that is collaborative and ethically satisfying. Similarly, we will present evidence that resistance can be consumed and used up, but only for a short time and only for some people. Fortunately, we will also present four omega strategies that are effective, practical, and more ethically defensible. The most fundamental way of reducing resistance to a proposal is to provide a guarantee that any negative consequence will be rectified. Reframing the proposal attempts to give a person a fuller view of the change, by framing it in a new way. Changing the comparison alters the meaning of a proposal by changing the alternative or counterfact to which the proposal is compared. Finally, changing the time frame for the proposal can change the features of the proposal that become salient and thereby fundamentally alter the meaning of the proposal.

Counterargue Resistance   People have a tendency to try to combat resistance with rhetoric. Strong arguments may change a person's view of the proposal, but this tactic is fundamentally confrontational, which is likely to raise reactance and, in the end, boomerang. The best that can be said for this strategy is that it might work if one has really strong counterarguments and communicates them gently.

To counterargue resistance, one listens for the points of reluctance and then responds to them with disconfirming information and reasoning. The rhetorical skills at countering resistance are the bases of debate and the Socratic method of instruction. The process is fundamentally interactive, involving listening and responding, giving and taking. But in the end, the success rests on having reason, right, and rhetorical skill on your side.

Communications research has addressed a slightly different, non-interactive question: whether a persuasive message is more effective if it sticks solely to explaining the positive benefits of choosing an alternative, or whether a message should also refer to and attempt to refute the negatives of an alternative (Allen, 1991; Faison, 1961). These are typically referred to as one-sided and two-sided messages. The research on this issue got its start with Hovland, Lumsdaine, and Sheffield (1949), who found that two-sided messages were more effective with more educated recipients. Lumsdaine and Janis (1953) concluded that two-sided messages were more effective in creating resistance to propaganda because they (a) forewarned people of the possibility of propaganda and (b) equipped them to counter it (i.e., a two-sided message), a point that was later made in more detail by McGuire (1964). Allen's (1991) meta-analysis of 70 studies that addressed which type of message was most efficacious concluded two things. First, two-sided messages worked only when they were able to refute or counter the negative information they mentioned, and second, the advantage even then was quite small ($r = .07$). In a marketing context, Kamins and Marks (1988) found that two-sided ads were more believable than one-sided ads, but this had no effect on purchase intentions.

Williams (Williams, Bourgeois, & Croyle, 1993; Williams & Dolnik, 2001) has studied two-sided messages in the courtroom. His question was whether a defense lawyer could "steal the thunder" of the prosecution by mentioning negative information about the defendant. Although the negative evidence is not "refuted" or counterargued, it is presumably minimized and normalized when the defendant's lawyer mentions it first. Several experiments have shown that mentioning negative information about one's client dampened the impact when the opposition introduced the evidence.

A variety of evidence suggests that, when the negative information would otherwise be part of the consideration, two-sided messages may confer an advantage over one-sided messages. If people know or would reasonably think of the negative aspects of the alternative, then mentioning and countering the negative information is likely to be more effective than letting the information emerge spontaneously. However, when these negative features would remain unknown, then raising them will insert these negatives into the consideration.

The relatively low effect sizes identified by Allen (1991) suggest that two-sided messages are difficult to make effective. This relative ineffectiveness is probably due at least in part to the subtleties of trying to anticipate what the recipient already knows or will think spontaneously. Undoubtedly, the ineffectiveness of rhetorical responses to resistance is also the result of how much reactance is created by this fundamentally confrontational response. It is hard to hear "You're wrong," especially if you are already skeptical about a presentation.

Distract Resistance   A great deal of communications research has shown that distraction can both interfere with and facilitate persuasion (Petty & Wegener, 1999). Too much distraction can interfere with encoding the message, leaving the person unchanged or uninfluenced. Moderate distraction, however, can allow a message to be encoded, but can interfere with a person's elaboration of that message. Petty, Wells, and Brock (1976) had people watch a televised persuasive message at the same time that lights flashed on and off around the screen. Participants had to listen to the message, but also indicate when a light in one quadrant flashed. This task was easy enough that participants were able to encode the message, but distracting enough to interfere with thoughts that they had concerning the message. Petty et al. showed that distraction made weak messages more persuasive. Distraction interfered with the counterarguing and disparaging thoughts people had about the message. But distraction also made strong messages less persuasive. In this case, the distraction interfered with the supportive and affirming thoughts people had about the strong message.

This elaboration likelihood model of persuasion (Petty & Cacioppo, 1986; Petty & Wegener, 1999) produces the two clear prescriptions: If you have a strong message, minimize the distraction; if you have a weak message, apply enough distracting influences to interfere with criticism of the message. The second prescription may be considered an omega strategy to overcome resistance to a message. This is a strategy that is used many times in advertising and marketing. Reichert, Heckler, and Jackson (2001) showed that sex in advertising acts as a distraction, reducing central route processing. Sagarin, Britt, Heider, Wood, and Lynch (2003), studying the effects of banners and pop-up advertisements on web browsers, found that both distract and persuade. Sagarin et al. also found that people don't protect themselves from banner advertisements, largely because people think they are invulnerable to their effects. When people are distracted, simple aphorisms, maxims, or clichés can be very influential, because they are easily encoded and tap into a rich source of meaning, which can be applied uncritically (Howard, 1997).

We have included distraction as one of the omega strategies because it has a long tradition in social psychology and because it can be used to reduce or avoid the resistance of skepticism. However, as a practical matter, we don't advocate its use for a number of reasons. First, it is ethically unacceptable to distract people away from carefully considering all aspects of a choice. Distraction conjures up images a double-talking salesman who uses gobbledegook to mask facts. Second, distraction is really only a short-term solution. Once the distraction ends and the decision gets reviewed, the thoughtful analysis uncovers the issues that were hidden by the distraction. Thus, distraction is not likely to lead to permanent, confident, integrated choices (Petty & Wegener, 1999; Wegener et al., 2004).

Consume Resistance   Can the exercise of resistance use it up? The assumption of this omega strategy is that it can. Muraven and Baumeister (2000) argued that self-regulation is a limited and finite ego resource that is quickly depleted and slowly replenished, but, like a muscle, can be strengthened through repeated exercise. Resistance to persuasion is a form of self-regulation, where the target attempts to control the impact of the persuasion. We (Knowles, Riner, Brennan, & Linn, 2004) have found evidence for several of Muraven and Baumeister's (2000) ego-depletion propositions.

In a political advertising study, we asked participants to critically evaluate political advertisements. We videotaped advertisements from the November 2000 election that presented local candidates who were unfamiliar to our participants. What we did was ask friends and relatives in other states to record a local channel for 3 evening hours in the week before the election. Each of the selected advertisements presented a candidate (rather than attacked an opponent), describing his or her qualifications or positions. Candidates represented various parties and aspired to various offices. We considered the advertisements as professionally constructed persuasive messages. One focal advertisement was evaluated on several measures, including a 20-item adjective checklist of liking and disliking (the

Bivariate Evaluation and Ambivalence Measures (BEAMs); Cacioppo, Gardner, & Berntson, 1997), ratings of the attractiveness of the candidate, and the likelihood of voting for this candidate if given the opportunity. These measures were highly correlated with each other, so we combined them into a single measure of evaluation. This study varied the position of the focal advertisement. The control condition asked participants to critically evaluate the focal advertisement right after the instructions, at the beginning of the experiment, where resistance was presumed to be strong, and to produce a critical evaluation of the candidate. A depletion condition had participants critically evaluate six political advertisements before evaluating the focal advertisement. In this condition, the repeated critical evaluations were expected to deplete participants' resistance, leading to a more positive evaluation of the focal candidate.

The results showed the expected pattern of evaluations, but only for people who were relatively unpracticed at resisting political ads. We had asked two questions about participants' skepticism concerning political advertisements. First, participants were asked if their view was better represented by the statement "Advertisements can't be trusted" or the statement "Advertisements tell useful information about a product." Second, participants were asked if their view was better represented by the statement "I try to listen to an advertisement with an open mind" or by the statement "I am skeptical of what an advertisement says." Approximately half the sample answered both questions by endorsing the skeptical alternative.

The less skeptical half of the sample exhibited the predicted pattern, with lower evaluations of the focal candidate in the control condition and higher evaluations in the depletion condition. This half of the sample, who presumably had less resistance to begin with and less desire or experience of being resistant, appeared to have their resistance depleted by use. The more skeptical half of the sample, however, showed an opposite effect. They demonstrated greater resistance after they saw six political ads. Their resistance seemed to be mobilized by use rather than depleted.

A commercial advertisement study presented people with ten commercial advertisements videotaped from commercial television broadcasts. We asked participants to view the commercials in one of two ways: uncritically ("list the two most memorable images or ideas from this ad") or critically ("list two ways the ad is deceptive or misleading"). Following the advertisements, participants saw a persuasive message on a very different topic. The message proposed adding a fee to the psychology department research participation requirement. The proposal was supported by several strong reasons (e.g., would allow designing web-based experiments that could be completed at home) or several weak reasons (e.g., experimenter's pay could be increased). We were interested in studying whether the critical review of ten commercials depleted participants' resistance, and if so, whether this reduced resistance would appear as greater acceptance of a message or as less scrutiny of the message.

Resistance, especially in the form of counterarguing, is the stuff of central route processing in the elaboration likelihood model of persuasion (Wegener et al., 2004). Resistance applied to the message exposes the convincing implications of strong arguments and the adverse implications of weak arguments. If resistance depletion reduces elaboration, strong and weak arguments would be evaluated more similarly.

As in the earlier study, we found a difference between people who were generally skeptical about commercials and those who were more accepting. Skeptical people were unaffected by the depletion attempt. They were more persuaded by the strong arguments than the weak arguments regardless of whether they were uncritical or critical of the previous commercials. The less skeptical people also were more persuaded by the strong arguments than the weak arguments. In addition, they showed a simple main effect of depletion. That is, after critically reviewing ten commercials, the less skeptical people were more persuaded by both the strong and the weak arguments than they were after uncritically reviewing the commercials. This pattern was consistent with the earlier study, in that less skeptical people showed depletion of resistance, whereas more skeptical people did not. Moreover, the fact that the less skeptical people showed the same difference between strong and weak arguments in both the critical and uncritical viewing conditions suggests that the depletion did not push the less skeptical people out of central route processing. Rather the depletion made them less able to resist any message, strong or weak.

These studies of the consumability of resistance provide support for two of Muraven and Baumeister's (2000) principles of ego depletion. First, resistance, like a muscle, can be strengthened through repeated use. Our consistent finding that skeptical people were unaffected by resisting commercials suggests that their predisposition had strengthened them against depletion by our relatively minor attempts. Second, resistance can be a finite and depletable resource. Both studies showed that the less skeptical people's ability to resist was depleted by their prior resistance. In the same way that running a mile may be very strenuous to the nonathlete but a simple warm-up to the marathon runner, nonskeptical people were "tired" of resisting after ten commercials, while skeptical people were just hitting their stride. These findings suggest that the application of resistance to persuasion acts in many ways like a self-regulation.

These findings also suggest cautions for the practitioner of influence. Wearing down resistance appears to be, at best, a risky strategy. Attempting to consume resistance may work for resistance weaklings, people who are little practiced in resistance, but it may boomerang for athletes of resistance, people who are practiced, efficient, and eager to resist. Also, as with the strategy of distraction, the strategy of consuming resistance is only temporary. Another of Muraven and Baumeister's principles is that depleted self-regulation capacity will be replenished within a relatively short time. Because of this, choices made when resistance is consumed are likely to be regretted and reversed later. Better to try some other strategy that works more easily, more of the time, more permanently, on more of the people.

Guarantees The guarantee is the most fundamental, straightforward, and effective omega strategy to deal with concerns about an offer or product: Identify the source of resistance to a proposal and provide a guarantee that it will not create a problem. Sam Walton (1992), the founder of Wal-Mart, said, "The two most important words I ever wrote were on that first Wal-Mart sign: 'Satisfaction Guaranteed.' They're still up there, and they have made all the difference" (pp. 316–317). Walton's guarantee meant that Wal-Mart would take back any item, with no hesitation and without a receipt. Walton intuitively knew that only a small percentage of sales actually come back as returns, but a much higher percentage of customers decide to purchase a product knowing that they can return the product if it doesn't work, doesn't fit, is the wrong color, etc.

The guarantee is an effective way to deal with any sort of ambivalence. Identify the reluctance and find a way to assure that it will not be a problem. For example, I recently asked a lawyer to do some work for me. He outlined what was involved and explained his hourly charges. The high hourly fee and indeterminate number of hours led me to express concern about being entrapped in an enterprise that was more than I could afford. This very smart lawyer heard my concern and changed his offer from an hourly charge to a unit price. He heard my reluctance, correctly identified its source, provided a guarantee, and got the job. If a child won't go to the picnic because it might rain, offer to carry an umbrella. If a colleague doesn't want to meet you downtown because parking is so difficult, offer to drive, or to pay for a cab. If a subordinate expresses lack of confidence in taking on a new task, assure him that the task can be reassigned without prejudice if it becomes a burden.

The possibility of having to suffer negative consequences of one sort or another produces a reluctance to accept the proposal. A guarantee works because it diminishes the reluctance created by anticipation of these negative consequences. A guarantee makes a proposal more desirable not by promoting the positive features of the offer (e.g., the product isn't more stylish, or doesn't work any better), but by removing a source of reluctance. Credible guarantees that target a major source of reluctance gain acceptance and reduce ambivalence for a proposal. The cost–benefit ratio seems more advantageous because the possible costs have been reduced.

Looking Ahead   The time frame of an event affects which features of the event are salient (Trope & Liberman, 2000). Liberman and Trope's (1998) research on temporal construal finds that events in the more distant future are thought of in a more general, abstract, principled way, whereas events in the immediate future are thought of in a more detailed, contextualized, and functional way. Distant events are considered at a high level of construal, according to purposes and broad meanings, whereas immediate events are considered at the low level of construal, according to mechanisms and details of implementation (Vallacher & Wegner, 1985, 1987). Distant events are evaluated according to objective (should it be done?), whereas immediate events are evaluated according to function (can it be done?).

These temporal differences in the mental representation of an event imply that the pattern of ambivalence in a decision can be altered by changing the time frame (Sherman, Crawford, & McConnell, 2004). For instance, Trope and Liberman (2000) found that students were more likely to select a difficult but interesting course assignment as a task for the future. For an immediate assignment, however, students preferred the easy but less interesting task. Sagristano, Trope, and Liberman (2002) found time differences in preferences for gambles. Students evaluated a number of gambles that varied independently in the probability of winning (a lower-level consideration of whether one will win) and the payoff for winning (a higher-level consideration of how much one would win). For gambles played right now, the probability of winning the gamble weighed more heavily (standardized regression coefficient $\beta = .58$) than the payoff ($\beta = .36$) in the student's evaluations. However, when choosing gambles to be played two months from now, the students emphasized the payoffs more heavily ($\beta = .52$) than the probability of winning ($\beta = .06$). Sagristano et al. also asked participants to list three reasons why they would or would not want to play each gamble. Participants playing gambles right now offered more probability reasons than payoff reasons 83% of the time. Yet for gambles to be played in the future, probability reasons dominated only 8% of the time.

Temporal differences in construal offer one avenue for changing the way a person considers a choice or offer. When people are ambivalent about a decision – that is, they like the idea but are concerned about its implementation – extending the time perspective out in the future can change the relative weights of the likes and dislikes in predictable ways. We know from personal experience as a book editor that asking people to write chapters next year pulls in more authors to a project than asking them to write chapters this year. The "no payments until next year" advertisements for cars or furniture operate on the same principle. Couching the choice in the more distant future can reduce resistance to the proposal and make its benefits more salient. Both of these consequences make acceptance of the proposal more likely.

Change the Comparison   Another omega strategy that can have a big effect with little cost is to change the comparison. Every judgment involves an implicit comparison. To answer, "How are you?", requires that you assume "Compared to what?" Your answer depends in large part on which comparison you choose – yourself yesterday, the sick friend you are visiting, the athlete who is training for a triathlon, the way you hope to feel. The principle here is that it is often easier to change a decision by changing the comparison than by changing the offer. For example, Levin and Gaeth (1988) found that a grilled hamburger was evaluated much more positively when it was presented as 75% lean than when it was presented as 25% fat.

Resistance can be reduced by introducing a higher reference point, one that creates even more resistance. This technique involves establishing new "counterfactuals" (Roese & Olson, 1995) or changing the "anchor" (Mussweiler, 2000, 2002) for a judgment. Burger (1986) attributes the "that's-not-all" influence technique in part to this mechanism. Burger found that his confederates were able to sell more brownies when they first introduced the price as $1 and then lowered it to 75 cents than when they sold them as 75-cent brownies. Presumably the higher initial price served as a comparison or anchor for the 75-cent price, making the 75 cents seem less costly. Sale prices are effective because they include the original price (Blair & Landon, 1981). Even reference prices that are so high as to be implausible still serve as an implicit comparison and make the sale price seem more attractive (Urbany, Bearden, & Weilbaker, 1988). Comparisons work also for quantity, not only price. For instance, Wansink, Kent, and Hoch (1998) found that setting a higher anchor for quantity of items (e.g., five for $1.00 instead of 20 cents each) increased sales by increasing the quantity of items purchased.

A real estate agent, sensing that her customers are concerned about paying $200,000 for the house they like best, manages to show them another house selling for $300,000. The point is not to sell them the higher price house, but to get them to use the higher price house as a comparison. Instead of using $0 or the price of their last house as the comparison, both of which make $200,000 seem extraordinarily large, the agent introduces the $300,000 house as a possibility, which makes $200,000 seem more reasonable. The customer's resistance to cost has been transferred from the target house to the comparison.

This omega strategy requires a good ear, however. Selecting a higher comparison is effective in overcoming resistance, but it can boomerang if resistance is not a person's main motivation. Consider a customer who wants to get the best possible quality. In a sense, his resistance is to the possibility of poor quality. In this case, the customer's evaluation of a product would be made more confident by introducing a lower comparison, one of lesser quality. The real estate agent should show these customers a $100,000 home, which would make the home they like seem better.

A number of influence strategies have elements of changing the comparison. For instance, the door-in-the-face technique involves first making a large request that is certain to be refused before making the desired request (Cialdini, Vincent, Lewis, Catalan, Wheeler, & Darby, 1975). The teenager asks Dad for $100, which is refused, and followed by a request for $20. The $20 request by itself implies a comparison to $0. But the large request changes the comparison to $100, which makes $20 seem like more of a bargain.

Reframe the Proposal A closely related technique for persuasion is reframing – casting new meanings to an alternative. Armstrong (2004) uses this wonderful example of reframing:

> One monk says "I asked the abbot if I could smoke when I prayed and he said 'No'". "That's funny," said the second monk, "I asked the abbot if I could pray when I smoked and he said 'Yes.'"

Choice alternatives are often considered through a single, implicit frame of reference (Wegner & Giuliano, 1980). The frame selected often provides the comparisons and the standards for evaluating the alternatives. The abbot in the example above was asked twice about smoking and praying, but the first monk framed it as a request about praying, whereas the second monk framed it as a request about smoking. Evaluations can change dramatically depending on which aspects of a choice are held in focal awareness and which aspects are used as the reference (Catrambone, Beike, & Niedenthal, 1996).

Our psychology department changed the frame of reference for thinking about missed appointments in our research subject pool. Years ago, students in general psychology were told that they were required to participate in 4 hours of research, but if they missed any appointment they signed up for, they were assessed a 1-hour penalty and had to complete 5 hours of research. This framing created ill-will whenever the penalty was assessed. In a particularly creative year, our department changed the way the same requirement was framed. Students were subsequently informed that they were required to complete 5 hours of research, but if they completed 4 hours without missing an appointment, they would be granted the fifth hour as a bonus. Same requirement, very different frame, and very different evaluative reactions to meeting and missing appointments.

Rothman and Salovey (1997; Rothman, Kelly, Hertel, & Salovey, 2003) and others (e.g., Wilson, Purdon, & Wallston, 1988) have studied the effectiveness and reactions to choices framed as gain acquisition or as loss prevention. For instance, Banks et al. (1995) framed mammography as the potential for gain (emphasizing the benefits of obtaining mammography) or a potential for loss (emphasizing the risks of not obtaining mammography) in videos shown to 133 women of screening age who had not been receiving regular mammography. Women who viewed the loss-framed message were more likely to have obtained a mammogram within the next year. However, Rothman and Salovey's (1997) extensive review of framing with a variety of health issues shows that no one framing is universally effective. Whether gain-framed or loss-framed messages are more effective depends on the message recipient's level of involvement, prior knowledge, view of the health behavior, and whether the health behavior serves an illness-detecting or a health-affirming function. As with several of these omega strategies, the persuader needs to listen carefully to the person and construct a frame within that specific context.

Techniques to Deal with Inertia

Inertia, the backward-looking form of resistance, is difficult to overcome because it often produces a disinterest and disengagement from the influence attempt. The strongest arguments will have no effect when the recipient daydreams about the status quo. The omega strategies that address inertia have the effect of increasing motivation to engage the persuasion attempt.

Disrupt Inertia   Various research suggests that inertia may be disrupted by something unusual or confusing in the message. Santos, Leve, and Pratkanis (1994) found that asking people for 17 cents or for 37 cents brought panhandlers money 75% of the time (in Santa Cruz, CA), whereas asking people for "some change" was rewarded only 44% of the time. Santos et al. argue that the odd request "piqued" the pedestrian's interest, disrupted their suppositions about the request, and started them searching for reasons for the odd request. In a sense, the odd request violates conversational rules for a panhandle, which initiates a more active search for the true meaning of the request (Fennis, Das, & Pruyn, 2004; Grice, 1975).

The hypnotherapist Milton Erickson was an astute practitioner of social influence. He introduced a number of "conversational" inductions to clinical hypnosis, including a set of strategies that used confusion as mechanism for overcoming resistance (Erickson, 1964; Gilligan, 1987; Sherman, 1988). Erickson knew that even patients who came to him for hypnosis were scared of and resistant to the process. He could sometimes incapacitate the resistance by introducing a confusing element to the hypnotic induction. His thought was that the confusion would occupy a person's resistance ("Why did he say that?"), focusing the resistance away from the induction. Also, the uncertainty created by the confusion would motivate the patient to be more accepting of the structure provided by the hypnotic suggestion. Erickson (1964; Gilligan, 1987) noted that the effective confusion induction started out with a familiar and predictable script, often based on themes originating from the patient. When the patient felt comfortable and complacent with the direction of the story, Erickson would introduce a confusing or contradictory element and follow it immediately with a direct request to go into a trance.

Vallacher and Wegner (1985, 1987) discussed a similar change process as part of their action identification theory. They argued that before a new action identification or framing of the action could be accepted, the old identification had to be disrupted. The disruption caused people to adopt a more detailed and elemental look at the action. The details could be changed into a new understanding in a way that an old understanding could not.

Davis and Knowles (1999) used Erickson's and Vallacher and Wegner's ideas to propose that introducing an odd element to a request and following it by a new reframing of the request might serve to (a) disrupt the inertia form of resistance, and (b) allow a new understanding of the request to be more influential. They had salespeople go door-to-door selling a set of eight note cards for a charity. The standard sales script told a little about the charity, then said "these cards are three dollars, would you like to buy some?" In three different studies, Davis and Knowles found that 35%, 25%, and 30% of the households purchased the cards. The standard script was altered to include a disrupting element ("these cards are 300 pennies") and add a reframe of the transaction from a charitable contribution to an advantageous purchase ("they are a bargain"). With this disrupt-then-reframe script, sales increased to 65%, 70%, and 65% of the households. Other comparison conditions in various studies showed that the reframe by itself ("three dollars, they're a bargain") had no effect (35% and 30%) and that the disruption by itself had no effect (35%). Importantly, a condition where people were told, "They're a bargain at 300 pennies" also showed no effect (25%). This last condition presents the same information as the disrupt-then-reframe, but changes the order of the information. Clearly, the disruption needed to come first. The disruption readied the field in a way that allowed the reframe to root. Davis and Knowles concluded that inertial resistance was plowed under by the unexpected element. Knowles and Linn (2004b) report similar results for a variety of disruptions and reframes. Therefore, the effect generalizes beyond using numbers or bargains in the request (e.g., labeling cup cakes for a sorority sale as "half-cakes" and reframing them as "delicious" similarly increased sales).

The disruption strategy is different from the distraction strategy discussed earlier. Distraction interferes with thinking about a proposal, whereas disruption interferes with the inattention or mindless listening that stems from inertial resistance. When resistance to the proposal can be disrupted, then new information about the offer can be heard and considered.

Increase Self-Efficacy   Sometimes inertial resistance is based in part on fear of choices, fear of unknown, fear of transitions. In these cases, an antidote is a boost of confidence or self-efficacy through some sort of self-affirmation or a self-esteem boost. Providing people with a success experience or the opportunity to think about something in which they believe or of which they are proud seems to dissolve resistance to persuasive messages. Jacks and O'Brien (2004), in three studies, provided some people with the opportunity to affirm personal values, e.g., to write about three times that they were honest. These people were less resistant than other people to a counterattitudinal persuasive message, as long as the affirmation was unrelated to the message topic. Steele and his colleagues (Cohen, Aronson, & Steele, 2000; Sherman, Nelson, & Steele, 2000) have found that self-affirmation strengthens one's self-image and reduces one's need to defensively reject threatening messages. For instance, women who had just affirmed an important but unrelated personal value were more likely to accept threatening health information about links between breast cancer and caffeine (Sherman et al., 2000).

Self-affirmation probably works through several mechanisms. The self-esteem boost may make people feel more invincible and immune to threats (Schimel, Arndt, Pyszczynski, & Greenberg, 2001). The self-affirmation also may imply competence, that is the ability to undo any problem or difficulty. When one feels immune to threats and competent to reverse almost any adversity, then one can be less concerned about protecting oneself and, therefore, more open to exploring alternatives and looking for the opportunities in a situation.

Sagarin and Cialdini (2004) have reported a paradoxical result that may be another example of this self-efficacy effect. Their results are paradoxical because they tried to train people to be critical and resistant to illegitimate advertisements but found that trained people became more easily persuaded by legitimate advertisements. Sagarin and Cialdini trained people to identify when the source of a statement was legitimate (e.g., an expert reporting based on his or her expertise) or illegitimate (e.g., a celebrity or actor advocating a product or service about which he or she had no expertise). In three studies, Sagarin and Cialdini offered trained and untrained participants the opportunity to respond to legitimate and illegitimate advertisements, sometimes immediately, sometimes after a long hiatus, and sometimes not readily connected to the training. Only one of three studies found trained people more resistant to illegitimate ads, and only when the training followed a blatant behavioral demonstration of their personal vulnerability to illegitimate ads. On the other hand, all three studies showed that trained people were more persuaded by legitimate ads. Apparently the training lowered the baseline resistance, allowing people to be more accepting of legitimate sources. The mechanism is likely to be an increased sense of efficacy or competence that the training provided. People became more confident of their ability to identify and resist illegitimate ads. Training, in this sense, took a diffuse resistance, generally applied, and allowed it to be focused on the illegitimate ads, thereby disengaging the resistance from the legitimate ads.

DISCUSSION

Each of the omega strategies described above works by addressing the decision maker's reluctance. This is a relatively new perspective for persuasion, marketing, and advertising (Perloff, 2003). These arenas for social influence are much more attuned to the alpha strategies that work by identifying and promoting the benefits of choosing an alternative. Reducing someone's reluctance to change has several advantages over increasing their desire for the change.

First, omega strategies are relatively inexpensive. Many ways to elevate desire involve increased persuader costs in time and money. Adding bonuses, incentives, or discounts to a marketing campaign all lower profit margins for the seller. Similarly, creating reciprocity or establishing commitment in interpersonal influence add to the time, effort, and commitments of the persuader. Most of the omega strategies involved very little extra cost to the persuader. Even the most costly, providing a guarantee, turns out to be a net profit maker because the added influence outweighs the added cost of fulfilling the guarantee (Walton, 1992).

Second, the strategy of identifying and reducing a person's reluctance also reduces that person's overall ambivalence. The alpha strategies, adding to the reasons to desire an alternative, are effective only because they overwhelm resistance. The resistance, however, is just as strong as before persuasion; it has just been outweighed by the increased attractiveness resulting from the persuasion. In this way, alpha strategies tend not to reduce the ambivalence, but rather to increase it. The omega strategies, on the other hand, reduce a person's resistance, making the decision less conflicted and more satisfying.

We believe that the distinction between alpha and omega strategies for persuasion is a useful one for the science of social influence and for the practice of persuasion. It takes a primary distinction in motivation, neurology, and biochemistry, between activation and inhibition, approach and avoidance, and applies this distinction to persuasion and decision making. The distinction is fundamental to psychology and the implications for persuasion are rich. For the practitioner, this chapter assembles a catalog of new, reasonable, efficient, subtle, and effective strategies for creating change.

When to Use Omega Strategies

Omega strategies for change are most likely to be effective when the target's motivation is ambivalent, that is when the desire and the reluctance are both high. If there is no attraction at all for an alternative, then omega strategies are likely to be ineffective. Omega strategies work by removing reluctance so that the natural attraction can propel action. Without that natural attraction, there is no change. Also, omega strategies, by definition, will not be effective when resistance is low. Of course, when resistance is low, not much persuasion is needed to create acceptance or a change.

This limitation of applicability, that omega strategies are effective only when a person feels ambivalent, turns out to be not much of a limitation. Only trivial decisions or opinions are without ambivalence. Most important choices have both positive and negative features. The hedonic complexity and resultant ambivalence is what makes them important and difficult choices. In these cases, the more effective strategy is to identify the sources of reluctance and then deal openly, effectively, and permanently with the roots of this resistance.

We should also mention that omega strategies are probably widely applicable, to any situation where there is ambivalence. When people think of persuasion, they probably think first of marketing and advertising, propaganda and political persuasion, or social influence and behavioral compliance. Perhaps, with a little more thought, people realize that formal education, skills training, and psychotherapy all have components of persuasion. But the applicability is wider still. Knowles and Linn (2004c) extended persuasion to self-regulation. People in the middle of a difficult decision, aware of their conflicting thoughts and ambivalent feelings, can be both the source and the target of influence. Many of the omega strategies discussed here allow one to look at one's own decision alternatives, identify the sources of resistance, and see if they can be removed, reframed, or resolved. In this way, changing time perspectives, providing choices, choosing another comparison, and reframing the dilemma are potentially helpful and effective strategies for self-management.

Which Omega Strategy to Choose?

One criterion for selecting one omega strategy over another is to match the strategy with the form of resistance that is likely to be encountered. Our organization of the various omega strategies reflects our belief that some strategies might be more effective with one form of resistance than another. As yet, we have no empirical evidence of this principle or of which omega strategies are more and which are less targeted to a particular kind of resistance. Nonetheless, logic suggests to us that the same strategies will be more effective with one form of resistance than another. Minimizing a request or redefining the relationship should avoid reactance, minimizing this form of resistance, but would not deal with the scrutiny form of resistance. Depersonalizing the request by placing it in a narrative, which will distract reactance, may frustrate and exacerbate the scrutiny form of resistance. Similarly, reframing a choice, selecting another comparison, or pushing the consideration into the future should be more effective ways of dealing with the scrutiny form of resistance than with reactance. The fundamental strategic issue for a persuader is to listen carefully to the nature of the resistance and then to adopt a strategy that deals with it.

A second criterion for selecting an omega strategy concerns the permanence and integration of the attitude or behavior change created by persuasion. Some of the strategies described in this chapter are likely to have only a temporary effect – strategies such as distraction, consuming resistance, and jujitsuing resistance. Because these strategies create temporary perturbations in resistance, they are likely to produce regret or choice reversal once the resistance is restored. A number of the strategies, however, have a more permanent effect on resistance. Guarantees are a simple, direct, and prototypic omega strategy. The persuader listens for the content of a person's reluctance, identifies the outcomes that are feared, then issues a contractual assurance to prevent or repair the feared outcome. A guarantee effectively and permanently removes the feared outcome from being a source of resistance to the proposal. Reframing a proposal, choosing another comparison, and looking ahead also are relatively direct and permanent ways of creating change. They have a quality of expanding the myopia of a single framing of a decision. They provide other ways of viewing and thinking about the offer or change. Even when the reframing or alternative comparison is not adopted as the focal frame of reference, its introduction has the effect of increasing, rather than decreasing, a person's options for understanding and acting.

The issue of increasing options brings up the third criterion for selecting an omega strategy – the ethical criterion. Persuasion techniques are tools that can be used for good or for evil, for the benefit of the target of influence or for the benefit of the persuader (Perloff, 2003; Singer & Lalich, 1996). A persuader should consider ethical questions about both the means of persuasion (Have I selected a strategy that increases a person's options and avoids deception?) and the ends of persuasion (Is my intent to help a person make a better decision, rather than conforming to my wishes?). Wallace (1967) identified four core values that defined ethical persuasion: (1) commitment to the worth and dignity of the individual, (2) dedication to equality of opportunity, (3) commitment to an individual's freedom to select and achieve goals, and (4) treat people as free and autonomous agents in society. Ethical persuasion promotes these goals, whereas unethical persuasion hampers these goals. As we look back at the various omega strategies we have delineated in this chapter, we see clear differences among the strategies in the degree to which they meet Wallace's criteria. Issuing guarantees and providing people with choices seem to embody the essence of Wallace's criteria, whereas distracting people from counterarguing or fatiguing their resistance seem to be contrary to Wallace's criteria. Most of the other omega strategies we have discussed have the potential to be used in an ethical or unethical way. Whether they are used ethically or unethically depends not only on the style with which the strategy is used (open about purpose, increasing options, avoiding coercion), but also on the ends toward which the persuasion is directed. Erickson and Rossi (1975), commenting on the ethics and efficacy of therapeutic persuasion, made the point that the two often go hand in hand. Therapeutic persuasion is more effective and satisfying, for both therapist and client, when it is designed to meet the client's purposes and goals, rather than the therapist's purposes and goals.

REFERENCES

Ajzen, I. (1991). The theory of planned behavior. *Organizational Behavior and Human Decision Processes, 50*, 179–211.

Alessandra, A. J. (1993). *Collaborative selling: How to gain the competitive advantage in sales*. New York: Wiley.

Allen, M. (1991). Meta-analysis comparing the persuasiveness of one-sided and two-sided messages. *Western Journal of Speech Communication, 55*, 390–404.

Arkowitz, H. (2002). Toward an integrative perspective on resistance to change. *Journal of Clinical Psychology, 58*, 219–227.

Armstrong, J. S. (2004). *Advertising and the science of persuasion*. Unpublished manuscript, Wharton School of Business, University of Pennsylvania, Philadelphia.

Aronson, E., Fried, C., & Stone, J. (1991). Overcoming denial and increasing the intention to use condoms through the induction of hypocrisy. *American Journal of Public Health, 81*, 1636–1638.

Banks, S. M., Salovey, P., Greener, S., Rothman, A. J., Moyer, A., Beauvais, J., et al. (1995). The effects of message framing on mammography utilization. *Health Psychology, 14*, 178–184.

Blair, E. A., & Landon, E. L., Jr. (1981). The effects of reference prices in retail advertisements. *Journal of Marketing, 45*, 61–69.

Brehm, J. W. (1966). *A theory of psychological reactance*. New York: Academic Press.

Brehm, S. S., & Brehm, J. W. (1981). *Psychological reactance: A theory of freedom and control*. New York: Academic Press.

Brock, T. C., & Becker, L. (1965). Ineffectiveness of "overheard" counterpropaganda. *Journal of Personality and Social Psychology, 2*, 654–660.

Brockner, J., Guzzi, B., Kane, J., Levine, E., & Shaplen, K. (1984). Organizational fundraising: Further evidence on the effect of legitimizing small donations. *Journal of Consumer Research, 11*, 611–614.

Burger, J. M. (1986). Increasing compliance by improving the deal: The that's-not-all technique. *Journal of Personality and Social Psychology, 51*, 277–283.

Cacioppo, J. T., Gardner, W. L., & Berntson, G. G. (1997). Beyond bipolar conceptualizations and measures: The case of attitudes and evaluative space. *Personality and Social Psychology Review, 1*, 3–25.

Carver, S. S., & White, T. L. (1994). Behavioral inhibition, behavioral activation, and affective responses to impending reward and punishment: The BIS/BAS scales. *Journal of Personality and Social Psychology, 67*, 319–333.

Catrambone, R., Beike, D., & Niedenthal, P. (1996). Is the self-concept a habitual referent in judgments of similarity? *Psychological Science, 7*, 158–163.

Cialdini, R. B. (2000). *Influence: Science and practice* (4th ed.). New York: Allyn & Bacon.

Cialdini, R. B., & Schroeder, D. (1976). Increasing compliance by legitimizing paltry contributions: When even a penny helps. *Journal of Personality and Social Psychology, 34*, 599–604.

Cialdini, R. B., Vincent, J. E., Lewis, S. K., Catalan, J., Wheeler, D., & Darby, B. L. (1975). Reciprocal concessions procedure for inducing compliance: The door-in-the-face technique. *Journal of Personality and Social Psychology, 31*, 206–215.

Clark, M. S., Mills, J., & Corcoran, D. M. (1989). Keeping track of needs and inputs of friends and strangers. *Personality and Social Psychology Bulletin, 15*, 533–542.

Cline, F. W., & Fay, J. (1990). *Parenting with love and logic: Teaching children responsibility*. Colorado Springs, CO: NavPress.

Cohen, G. L., Aronson, J., & Steele, C. M. (2000). When beliefs yield to evidence:

Reducing biased evaluation by affirming the self. *Personality and Social Psychology Bulletin, 26,* 1151–1164.

Dal Cin, S., Zanna, M. P., & Fong, G. T. (2004). Narrative persuasion and overcoming resistance. In E. S. Knowles & J. A. Linn (Eds.), *Resistance and persuasion* (pp. 175–191). Mahwah, NJ: Lawrence Erlbaum Associates, Inc.

Davis, B. P., & Knowles, E. S. (1999). A disrupt-then-reframe technique of social influence. *Journal of Personality and Social Psychology, 76,* 192–199.

Davis, D., & O'Donohue, W. T. (2004). The road to perdition: "Extreme influence" tactics in the interrogation room. in W. T. O'Donohue & E. Levensky (Eds.), *Handbook of forensic psychology* (pp. 897–996). New York: Elsevier Academic Press.

Dillard, J. P. (1991). The current status of research on sequential-request compliance techniques. *Personality and Social Psychology Bulletin, 17,* 283–288.

Erickson, M. H. (1964). The confusion technique in hypnosis. *American Journal of Clinical Hypnosis, 6,* 183–207.

Erickson, M. H., & Rossi, E. L. (1975). Varieties of double bind. *American Journal of Clinical Hypnosis, 17,* 143–157.

Erickson, M. H., Rossi, E. L., & Rossi, S. (1976). *Hypnotic realities: The induction of clinical hypnosis and forms of indirect suggestion.* New York: Irvington.

Faison, E. W. J. (1961). Effectiveness of one-sided and two-sided mass communications in advertising. *Public Opinion Quarterly, 25,* 468–469.

Fennis, B. M., Das, E. H. H. J., & Pruyn, A. Th. H. (2004). If you can't dazzle them with brilliance, baffle them with nonsense: Extending the impact of the Disrupt-then-Reframe technique of social influence. *Journal of Consumer Behavior, 14,* 280–290.

Fowles, D. C. (1988). Psychophysiology and psychopathology: A motivational approach. *Psychophysiology, 25,* 373–391.

Freedman, J. L., & Fraser, S. C. (1966). Compliance without pressure: The foot-in-the-door technique. *Journal of Personality and Social Psychology, 4,* 195–202.

Gilligan, S. G. (1987). *Therapeutic trances: The cooperation principle in Ericksonian hypnotherapy.* New York: Brunner/Mazel.

Gollwitzer, P. M. (1999). Implementation intentions: Strong effects of simple plans. *American Psychologist, 54,* 493–503.

Gollwitzer, P. M., Fujita, K., & Oettingen, G. (2004). Planning and the implementation of goals. In R. F. Baumeister & K. D. Vohs (Eds.), *Handbook of self-regulation: Research, theory, and applications* (pp. 211–228). New York: Guilford Press.

Gray, J. A. (1994). Framework for a taxonomy of psychiatric disorder. In S. H. M van Goozen, N. E. van de Poll, & J. Sergeant (Eds.), *Emotions: Essays on emotion theory* (pp. 29–59). Hillsdale, NJ: Lawrence Erlbaum Associates, Inc.

Green, M. C., & Brock, T. C. (2000). The role of transportation in the persuasiveness of public narratives. *Journal of Personality and Social Psychology, 79,* 701–721.

Green, M. C., Strange, J. J., & Brock, T. C. (Eds.). (2002). *Narrative impact: Social and cognitive foundations.* Mahwah, NJ: Lawrence Erlbaum Associates, Inc.

Greene, B. (2002). *Get with the program: Getting real about your weight, health, and emotional wellbeing.* New York: Simon & Schuster.

Greenwald, A. G., Brock, T. C., and Ostrom, T. M. (1968). *Psychological foundations of attitudes.* New York: Academic Press.

Grice, H. P. (1975). Logic and conversation. In P. Cole & J. L. Morgan (Eds.), *Syntax and semantics: Vol. 3. Speech acts* (pp. 41–58). New York: Seminar Press.

Haley, J. (1973). *Uncommon therapy: The psychiatric techniques of Milton H. Erickson, M.D.* New York: Norton.

Higgins, E. T. (1999). Promotion and prevention as a motivational duality: Implications for evaluative processes. In S. Chaiken & Y. Trope (Eds.), *Dual-process theories in social psychology* (pp. 503–525). New York: Guilford Press.

Higgins, E. T. (2001). Promotion and prevention experiences: Relating emotions to nonemotional motivational states. In J. P. Forgas (Ed.), *Handbook of affect and social cognition* (pp. 186–211). Mahwah, NJ: Lawrence Erlbaum Associates, Inc.

Hovland, C. I., Lumsdaine, A. A., & Sheffield, F. D. (1949). *Experiments in mass communication* (pp. 201–227). Princeton, NJ: Princeton University Press.

Howard, D. J. (1997). Familiar phrases as peripheral persuasion cues. *Journal of Experimental Social Psychology, 33*, 231–243.

Jacks, J. Z., & O'Brien, M. E. (2004). Decreasing resistance by affirming the self. In E. S. Knowles & J. A. Linn (Eds.), *Resistance and persuasion* (pp. 235–257). Mahwah, NJ: Lawrence Erlbaum Associates, Inc.

Jolson, M. A. (1997). Broadening the scope of relationship selling. *Journal of Personal Selling and Sales Management, 17*, 75–88.

Joyce, J. M. (1999). *The foundations of causal decision theory.* New York: Cambridge University Press.

Kamins, M. A., & Marks, L. J. (1988). An examination into the effectiveness of two-sided comparative price appeals. *Journal of the Academy of Marketing Science, 16*, 64–71.

Knowles, E. S., Butler, S., & Linn, J. A. (2001). Increasing compliance by reducing resistance. In J. P. Forgas & K. D. Williams (Eds.), *Social influence: Direct and indirect processes* (pp. 41–60). Philadelphia: Psychology Press.

Knowles, E. S., & Linn, J. A. (2004a). The importance of resistance to persuasion. In E. S. Knowles & J. A. Linn (Eds.), *Resistance and persuasion* (pp. 3–9). Mahwah, NJ: Lawrence Erlbaum Associates, Inc.

Knowles, E. S., & Linn, J. A. (2004b). Approach–avoidance model of persuasion: Alpha and omega strategies for change. In E. S. Knowles & J. A. Linn (Eds.), *Resistance and persuasion* (pp. 117–148). Mahwah, NJ: Lawrence Erlbaum Associates, Inc.

Knowles, E. S., & Linn, J. A. (2004c). The promise and future of resistance to persuasion. In E. S. Knowles & J. A. Linn (Eds.), *Resistance and persuasion* (pp. 301–310). Mahwah, NJ: Lawrence Erlbaum Associates, Inc.

Knowles, E. S., Riner, D. D, Brennan, M., & Linn, J. A. (2004). *Consuming resistance to persuasion.* Unpublished manuscript, University of Arkansas, Fayetteville.

Leahy, R. L. (2001). *Overcoming resistance in cognitive therapy.* New York: Guilford Press.

Levin, I. P., & Gaeth, G. J. (1988). How consumers are affected by the framing of attribute information before and after consuming the product. *Journal of Consumer Research, 15*, 374–378.

Liberman, N., & Trope, Y. (1998). The role of feasibility and desirability considerations in near and distant future decisions: A test of temporal construal theory. *Journal of Personality and Social Psychology, 75*, 5–18.

Lumsdaine, A. A., & Janis, I. L. (1953). Resistance to "counterpropaganda" produced by one-sided and two-sided "propaganda" presentations. *Public Opinion Quarterly, 17*, 311–318.

McGuire, W. J. (1964). Inducing resistance to persuasion: Some contemporary approaches. In L. Berkowitz (Ed.), *Advances in experimental social psychology* (Vol. 1, pp. 191–229). New York: Academic Press.

Messer, S. B. (2002). A psychodynamic perspective on resistance in psychotherapy. *Journal of Clinical Psychology, 58*, 157–163.

Muraven, M. R., & Baumeister, R. F. (2000). Self-regulation and depletion of limited resources: Does self-control resemble a muscle? *Psychological Bulletin, 126,* 247–259.

Mussweiler, T. (2000). Overcoming the inevitable anchoring effect: Considering the opposite compensates for selective accessibility. *Personality and Social Psychology Bulletin, 26,* 1142–1150.

Mussweiler, T. (2002). The malleability of anchoring effects. *Experimental Psychology, 49,* 67–72.

Nail, P. R. (2002). *Proposal of a double diamond model of social response.* Unpublished manuscript, Southwestern Oklahoma State University, Weatherford.

Nail, P. R., MacDonald, G., & Levy, D. (2000). Proposal of a four-dimensional model of social response. *Psychological Bulletin, 126,* 454–470.

Perloff, R. M. (2003). *The dynamics of persuasion.* Mahwah, NJ: Lawrence Erlbaum Associates, Inc.

Petty, R. E., & Cacioppo, J. T. (1986). *Communication and persuasion: Central and peripheral routes to persuasion.* New York: Springer-Verlag.

Petty, R. E., Ostrom, T. M., & Brock, T. C. (Eds.). (1981). *Cognitive responses in persuasion.* Hillsdale, NJ: Lawrence Erlbaum Associates, Inc.

Petty, R. E., & Wegener, D. T. (1999). The elaboration likelihood model: Current status and controversies. In S. Chaiken & Y. Trope (Eds.), *Dual-process theories in social psychology* (pp. 37–72). New York: Guilford Press.

Petty, R. E., Wells, G. L., & Brock, T. C. (1976). Distraction can enhance or reduce yielding to propaganda: Thought disruption versus effort justification. *Journal of Personality and Social Psychology, 34,* 874–884.

Piderit, S. K. (2000). Rethinking resistance and recognizing ambivalence: A multidimensional view of attitudes toward an organizational change. *Academy of Management Review, 25,* 783–794.

Reichert, T., Heckler, S. E., & Jackson, S. (2001). The effects of sexual social marketing appeals on cognitive processing and persuasion. *Journal of Advertising, 30,* 13–27.

Roese, N. J., & Olson, G. L. (1995). *What might have been: The social psychology of counterfactual thinking.* Hillsdale, NJ: Lawrence Erlbaum Associates, Inc.

Rosen, S. (1991). *My voice will go with you: The teaching tales of Milton H. Erickson, M.D.* New York: Norton.

Rothman, A. J., Kelly, K. M., Hertel, A. W., & Salovey, P. (2003). Message frames and illness representations: Implications for interventions to promote and sustain healthy behavior. In L. D. Cameron & H. Leventhal (Eds.), *Self-regulation of health and illness behaviour* (pp. 278–296). New York: Routledge.

Rothman, A. J., & Salovey, P. (1997). Shaping perceptions to motivate healthy behavior: The role of message framing. *Psychological Bulletin, 121,* 3–19.

Sagarin, B. J., Britt, M. A., Heider, J. D., Wood, S. E., & Lynch, J. E. (2003). Bartering our attention: The distraction and persuasion effects of on-line advertisements. *International Journal of Cognitive Technology, 8,* 4–17.

Sagarin, B. J., & Cialdini, R. B. (2004). Creating critical consumers: Motivating receptivity by teaching resistance. In E. S. Knowles & J. A. Linn (Eds.), *Resistance and persuasion* (pp. 259–297). Mahwah, NJ: Lawrence Erlbaum Associates, Inc.

Sagarin, B. J., Cialdini, R. B., Rice, W. E., & Serna, S. B. (2002). Dispelling the illusion of invulnerability: The motivations and mechanisms of resistance to persuasion. *Journal of Personality and Social Psychology, 83,* 526–541.

Sagristano, M. D., Trope, Y., & Liberman, N. (2002). Time-dependent gambling: Odds now, money later. *Journal of Experimental Psychology: General, 131,* 364–376.

Santos, M. D., Leve, C., & Pratkanis, A. R. (1994). Hey buddy, can you spare seventeen cents? Mindful persuasion and the pique technique. *Journal of Applied Social Psychology, 24*, 755–764.

Schimel, J., Arndt, J., Pyszczynski, T., & Greenberg, J. (2001). Being accepted for who we are: Evidence that social validation of the intrinsic self reduces general defensiveness. *Journal of Personality and Social Psychology, 80*, 35–52.

Sherman, D. A. K., Nelson, L. D., & Steele, C. M. (2000). Do messages about health risks threaten the self? Increasing the acceptance of threatening health messages via self-affirmation. *Personality and Social Psychology Bulletin, 26*, 1046–1058.

Sherman, S. J. (1988). Ericksonian psychotherapy and social psychology. In J. K. Zeig & S. R. Lankton (Eds.), *Developing Ericksonian Psychotherapy* (pp. 59–90). New York: Brunner/Mazel.

Sherman, S. J., Crawford, M. T., & McConnell, A. R. (2004). Looking ahead as a technique to reduce resistance to persuasive attempts. In E. S. Knowles & J. A. Linn (Eds.), *Resistance and persuasion* (pp. 149–174). Mahwah, NJ: Lawrence Erlbaum Associates, Inc.

Singer, M. T., & Lalich, J. (1996). *Cults in our midst: The hidden menace in our everyday lives*. San Francisco: Jossey-Bass.

Stone, J., Aronson, E., & Crain, A. L. (1994). Inducing hypocrisy as a means of encouraging young adults to use condoms. *Personality and Social Psychology Bulletin, 20*, 116–128.

Straight, D. K. (1996). How to benefit by straight shooter selling. *American Salesman, 41*, 10–15.

Tormala, Z. L., & Petty, R. E. (2004). Resisting persuasion and attitude certainty. In E. S. Knowles & J. A. Linn (Eds.), *Resistance and persuasion* (pp. 65–82). Mahwah, NJ: Lawrence Erlbaum Associates, Inc.

Trope, Y. & Liberman, N. (2000). Temporal construal and time-dependent changes in preference. *Journal of Personality and Social Psychology, 79*, 876–889.

Urbany, J. E., Bearden, W. O., & Weilbaker, D. C. (1988). The effect of plausible and exaggerated reference prices on consumer perceptions and price search. *Journal of Consumer Research, 15*, 95–110.

Vallacher, R. R., & Wegner, D. M. (1985). *A theory of action identification*. Hillsdale, NJ: Lawrence Erlbaum Associates, Inc.

Vallacher, R. R., & Wegner, D. M. (1987). What do people think they're doing? Action identification and human behavior. *Psychological Review, 94*, 2–15.

Wallace, K. (1967). An ethical basis of communication. In R. Johannesen (Ed.), *Ethics and persuasion* (pp. 41–56). New York: Random House.

Walster, E., & Festinger, L. (1962). The effectiveness of "overheard" persuasive communications. *Journal of Abnormal and Social Psychology, 65*, 395–402.

Walton, S. (1992). *Sam Walton: Made in America*. New York: Bantam Books.

Wansink, B., Kent, R. J., & Hoch, S. J. (1998). An anchoring and adjustment model of purchase quantity decisions. *Journal of Marketing Research, 35*, 71–81.

Wegener, D., & Petty, R. E. (1995). Flexible correction processes in social judgment: The role of naive theories in corrections for perceived bias. *Journal of Personality and Social Psychology, 68*, 35–51.

Wegener, D., & Petty, R. E. (1997). The Flexible Correction Model: The role of naive theories of bias in bias correction. In M. P. Zanna (Ed.), *Advances in experimental social psychology* (Vol. 29, pp. 141–208). Mahwah, NJ: Lawrence Erlbaum Associates, Inc.

Wegener, D. T., Petty, R. E., Smoak, N. D., & Fabrigar, L. R. (2004). Multiple routes to resisting attitude change. In E. S. Knowles & J. A. Linn (Eds.), *Resistance and persuasion* (pp. 13–38). Mahwah, NJ: Lawrence Erlbaum Associates, Inc.

Wegner, D. M. (1989). *White bears and other unwanted thoughts: Suppression, obsession, and the psychology of mental control*. New York: Penguin Books.

Wegner, D., & Giuliano, T. (1980). Forms of social awareness. In W. Ickes & E. S. Knowles (Eds.), *Personality, roles and social behavior* (pp. 165–198). Hillsdale, NJ: Lawrence Erlbaum Associates, Inc.

Werner, C. M., Stoll, R., & Birch, P. (2002). Clinical validation and cognitive elaboration: Signs that encourage sustained recycling. *Basic and Applied Social Psychology, 24*, 185–203.

Williams, K. D., Bourgeois, M. J., & Croyle, R. T. (1993). The effects of stealing thunder in criminal and civil trials. *Law and Human Behavior, 17*, 597–609.

Williams, K. D., & Dolnik, L. (2001) Revealing the worst first: Stealing thunder as a social influence strategy. In J. P. Forgas & K. D. Williams (Eds.), *Social influence: Direct and indirect processes* (pp. 213–231). Philadelphia: Psychology Press.

Wilson, D. K., Purdon, S. E., & Wallston, K. A. (1988). Compliance to health recommendations: A theoretical overview of message framing. *Health Education Research, 3*, 161–171.

Winter, P. L., Sagarin, B. J., Rhoads, K., Barrett, D. W., & Cialdini, R. B. (2000). Choosing to encourage or discourage: Perceived effectiveness of prescriptive versus proscriptive messages. *Environmental Management, 26*, 589–594.

Wolf, S., & Montgomery, D. A. (1977). Effects of inadmissible evidence and level of judicial admonishment to disregard on the judgments of mock juries. *Journal of Applied Social Psychology, 7*, 205–219.

4

The Evolution of Cognitive Dissonance Theory: A Personal Appraisal

ELLIOT ARONSON

I am a chronic and habitual storyteller. So what I want to do (primarily) is tell you a story. Part of the story will be fairly traditional for this kind of volume; that is, it will describe a program of research that has come out of my laboratory. But, in addition, the story will include an *homage* to my dear friend and mentor, Leon Festinger, who revolutionized social psychology. It will also include a history of an idea – cognitive dissonance theory – as well as a central aspect of my philosophy of science (such as it is!). But mostly this story is a celebration of social psychology – a field that I have been madly in love with for the past 50 years.

THE BEGINNING OF MY LOVE AFFAIR WITH DISSONANCE THEORY AND SOCIAL PSYCHOLOGY

I was not always in love with social psychology. As a matter of fact, when I entered graduate school in the mid-1950s, it was not my intention to become a social psychologist. I had read a little social psychology as an undergrad, and it struck me as pretty boring stuff. The hot item at the time was the Yale research on communication and persuasion which, among other things, demonstrated that, if you present people with a message indicating that nuclear submarines are feasible, it is more effective if you attribute it to a respected physicist like J. Robert Oppenheimer than if you attribute it to an unreliable source like *Pravda*. I can see now that this was important and necessary research, but at the time, it seemed so obvious that, to an undergraduate, it hardly seemed necessary to perform an elaborate experiment to demonstrate that it was true.

In those days, almost everything done in the field was inspired by a rather simplistic derivation from reinforcement theory. Thus, in the above example, it is clearly more rewarding (in the sense that it is more likely that one's opinions will be correct) to be in agreement with a trustworthy expert than to be in agreement with a biased newspaper run by a totalitarian government. Even classic experiments that weren't specifically inspired by reinforcement theory (e.g. Asch's 1951 experiments on conformity) could easily be recast and explained in terms of that simple and ubiquitous concept. The problem was that there weren't other theories around that could make predictions that couldn't somehow be subsumed under the dominant and apparently more parsimonious wings of reinforcement theory. For example in the Asch experiment, because it was dealing with something as trivial as the size of a line, a reinforcement theorist might suggest that it is simply more rewarding to go along with the unanimous judgment of six other people than to defy that opinion and brave their scorn and ridicule.

Because the field was so thoroughly dominated by this simplistic brand of reward/reinforcement theory, whenever an individual performed a behavior it had to be because there was a concrete reward lurking somewhere in the background – so the name of the game, in those days, was let's find the reinforcer. It goes without saying that there are a great many situations where reinforcement works well as a way of increasing the frequency of a response, but is that all there is to social behavior? One suspected that the human heart and mind were more interesting than that – but, if they were, it didn't seem to be reflected in the bulk of the research that was being done by social psychologists.

Then along came Leon Festinger, and social psychology has not been the same since – thank God. It was my great good fortune to have arrived at Stanford to do my graduate work the same year that Leon arrived there as a professor. I didn't apply to Stanford because of Leon – I didn't even know he was going to be there; needless to say, he didn't know I was going to be there either! I've been very lucky in my life as a social psychologist; I've managed to work with a lot of brilliant and wonderful people – some were my teachers, many were my students – but, in all that time, I've met only one person that I would call a flat-out, honest-to-goodness genius, and that was Leon Festinger.

Interestingly, Leon wasn't attracting a great number of graduate students in those days – his reputation had preceded him; he was considered a very aggressive, harsh, devastating individual, possessed of rapier-like wit, who apparently was capable of devouring tender young graduate students like me for breakfast. I subsequently got to know Leon pretty well – indeed, he was to become one of my closest friends – and I want to tell you that, well, he *was* fully capable of devastating anyone in sight (and often did) and, as I subsequently discovered, he was also capable of enormous sensitivity, warmth, and tenderness.

But I didn't know that then, so it was with great trepidation that I walked into Festinger's office spring quarter and told him I was thinking of enrolling in a seminar that he was teaching. It turned out to be a very small seminar – as I recall, there were four of us – because most of the students were so scared of him. I told Leon I didn't know much about social psychology and I asked him if there was anything I could read in preparation for the seminar. He grunted, rolled his eyes toward the ceiling (as if to say, "just look what they're sending me these days"), and handed me a typed manuscript of a book he had just sent off to the publisher. He told me it was his only copy and he made me promise, under pain of death or dismemberment (whichever I preferred), not to let my young kids get blueberry jam all over it. Needless to say, I kept it well out of their reach.

The manuscript was called A *theory of cognitive dissonance*. I read the damn thing in one sitting. It knocked me out! It was the most exciting thing I had ever read in psychology. That was almost 50 years ago; it's *still* the most exciting thing I've ever read in psychology! Leon started with a very simple proposition: THAT IF A PERSON HELD TWO COGNITIONS THAT WERE PSYCHOLOGIC- ALLY INCONSISTENT, HE WOULD EXPERIENCE DISSONANCE AND WOULD ATTEMPT TO REDUCE DISSONANCE MUCH LIKE ONE WOULD ATTEMPT TO REDUCE HUNGER, THIRST, OR ANY DRIVE. What Leon realized, in 1956, was the importance of forging a marriage between the cognitive and the motivational. Those of us who have survived the more recent era dominated by pure cognition in social psychology are well aware of the fact that, for a great many years, it has become fashionable to pretend that motivation does not exist – but, of course, that was merely a convenient fiction, as we shall see.

DISSONANCE THEORY'S GIFTS TO SOCIAL INFLUENCE RESEARCH

But I'm getting ahead of my story – back to dissonance theory. It is essentially a theory about sense-making – how people try to make sense out of their environ- ment and their behavior, and thus try to lead lives that are (at least in their own minds) sensible and meaningful. Inventing a theory that combined motivation with cognition led Festinger to the most amazing set of predictions, which pro- duced a revitalization of social psychology. In its heyday, the theory generated over a thousand separate experiments – many of which were startling at the time – teaching us hundreds of new things about human behavior. It got us to look in places that we would never have dreamed of looking if it hadn't been for the existence of that theory. Consider the list of influence tactics that my friend Anthony Pratkanis has compiled for his chapter in this volume. Many of them, such as fait accompli, guilt, effort justification, hypocrisy, message discrepancy, insufficient justification, and commitment, came directly from dissonance research. He tells me that for over 50% of the tactics, either they can be explained by dissonance or dissonance theory specifies some of the limiting conditions of the tactics. No single theory in social psychology has contributed this much to social influence research. When surveying the scope of the research generated by dissonance theory, no less a social psychology mavin than Ned Jones (1976) char- acterized what he called the dissonance movement as "The most important single development in the history of social psychology."

I won't argue with that characterization. Indeed, I'll carry it a step further: The impact of dissonance theory went even beyond the generation of new and exciting knowledge. Because of the nature of the hypotheses we were testing, we were forced to develop a new experimental methodology; a powerful, high-impact set of procedures that allowed us to ask truly important questions in a very precise manner. As you know, the laboratory tends to be an artificial environment. But the hypotheses we were generating made it necessary to overcome that artificiality by developing a methodology that would get the subjects enmeshed in a set of events – a drama, if you will – that made it impossible for subjects to avoid taking these events seriously.

In my writing on research methods (Aronson & Carlsmith, 1968; Aronson, Ellsworth, Carlsmith & Gonzales, 1990) I've called this tactic "experimental reality" – where within the admittedly phoney confines of the lab, real things are happening to real people. Because of the nature of our hypotheses, we could not afford the luxury of having subjects passively look at a videotape of events happening to someone else and then make judgments about them. Our hypotheses required the construction of an elaborate scenario that the subject became a part of. Several years ago, at an APA symposium on ethics, I heard a well known social psychologist say that dissonance researchers resembled nothing so much as frustrated playwrights, directors and actors. I'm told he meant this as a criticism. I see it as high praise; the hypotheses to be tested demanded a high degree of realism and we rose to the occasion – with a great deal of passion, I might add.

In addition, dissonance theory provided us with a powerful vehicle for challenging reinforcement theory on its own turf and led us to expose its limiting conditions and, on occasion, to discover that it was flat-out wrong in some of its predictions. For example, reinforcement theory would suggest that, if you reward individuals for saying something, they might become infatuated with that statement (through secondary reinforcement). But, in 1959, the Festinger–Carlsmith experiment exploded that simplistic notion by showing that you believe lies that you tell only if you are under-rewarded for telling them – a process known as *insufficient justification*. Also in 1959, Jud Mills and I performed an experiment demonstrating that people who go through a severe initiation, in order to gain admission to a group, come to like that group better than people who go through a mild initiation. Reinforcement theory would suggest that we like people and groups that are associated with reward; Mills and I showed that we come to like things for which we suffer and that we tend to engage in *effort justification*.

I know this stuff is old hat now, but let me tell you that in the 1950s, simplistic assumptions from reinforcement theory were so dominant that when Jud and I floated our hypothesis and procedure past our fellow graduate students, they laughed. They knew that things become attractive through association with pleasure – certainly not through association with suffering. In 1957, dissonance theory sounded the clarion call for taking cognition seriously in social psychology; dissonance theory produced experimental research that demonstrated convincingly, like no other theory before it, that people think; we are not simple reinforcement machines. And, because we think, we frequently get ourselves into a tangled muddle of self-justification, denial and distortion.

The value of dissonance theory is that it encourages a researcher to look at old problems with a different mind set. If minimum reward for a counterattitudinal behavior brings about insufficient justification and attitude change, would minimum punishment also bring about insufficient justification for a behavior and attitude change? In other words, can the reward theory of the effects of punishment be turned on its head just as Festinger and Carlsmith had done with a reward theory of rewards? Merrill Carlsmith and I wanted to find out, and in doing so conducted an experiment in which we drastically changed children's preferences for various toys (Aronson and Carlsmith, 1963). In our experiment, we allowed pre-schoolers to play with several toys. We then selected one they liked a lot and told them they could play with all the other toys but *not* with that one *forbidden toy*. In one condition, we used a rather severe threat. In the other condition, we used a threat that was relatively mild – just severe enough to get them to refrain from playing with the toy temporarily.

What does dissonance theory predict? Picture the scene: In the severe threat condition, the children refrain from playing with the attractive toy. But they *know* why they are not playing with it – because that grown-up will punish them severely if they do. They do not require any additional justification. But what about the children in the mild threat condition? Like the children in the severe threat condition, they are not playing with the forbidden toy – but when they ask themselves why they are not playing with it, their answer is less clear. That is, the situation does not present them with a high level of justification for not playing with the forbidden toy precisely because the threat is such a mild one. Accordingly, they must supply some additional justification on their own, so to speak – by finding additional reasons to justify their restraint. And that is exactly what we found: Children complying in the face of mild threats subsequently convinced *themselves* that the forbidden toy was less attractive than did those children who were confronted with severe threats.

In a similar vein, dissonance theory challenged psychoanalytic theory – or more specifically, the notion of catharsis. Let me remind you that, in the 1950s, the notion of the catharsis of aggression was widely accepted as axiomatic; that is, most psychologists believed that if you are feeling hostility toward Sam you should get it out of your system – yell at him, call him names or kick the shit out of him – this will release your pent-up anger and you'll feel better about old Sam afterwards. Dissonance theory said no – that, although this kind of behavior might release tension, as psychoanalytic theory suggests, it doesn't reduce your negative feeling about Sam. On the contrary, as several experiments have subsequently shown, if we hurt someone, it causes us to try to justify our actions by derogating our victim. This impels us to feel more hostility toward him, which opens the door for still further aggression (see Davis & Jones, 1960; Glass, 1964; Kahn, 1966).

One of the most powerful influence paradigms under the rubric of dissonance theory has been referred to as *counterattitudinal advocacy* – wherein people are induced to try to convince others of the rightness of a position that differs from their own privately held belief (Cohen, 1962). When offered only a minimal reward for doing so, people must seek additional justification for the position they advocated. They accomplish this by persuading themselves that the position they advocated is not really far from their true position; the end result is a shift in attitude away from their original belief. For example, in one of our experiments (Nel, Helmreich, & Aronson, 1969), we recruited people who were opposed to the use of marijuana, and induced them to compose and deliver a speech, recorded on audiotape, advocating the use of marijuana. Those in the high dissonance condition (i.e., those who made the tape for little reward and who were led to believe that the tape would be played to a persuadable audience) experienced a major softening of their negative attitudes toward the use of marijuana. In short, participants in the high dissonance condition were faced with the undeniable fact that they might be leading their audience into using marijuana. They could justify their action only by persuading themselves that marijuana was not as dangerous as they might have originally believed.

Dissonance theory also gave us a window on the dynamics of social influence in what can be called a *rationalization trap* or the potential for dissonance reduction to produce a succession of self-justifications that ultimately result in a chain of stupid or immoral actions. Once we commit a dissonance-arousing act – say, hurt someone or say something stupid or make a foolish commitment – there is a tendency to engage in an ever-escalating pattern of behavior to somehow justify what we have done. This simple application of dissonance theory can serve to make sense of seemingly senseless behavior such as how seemingly bright people could send thousands of American troops to an unwinnable war in Vietnam or how seemingly normal people could commit mass suicide in a place called Jonestown (see Tavris & Aronson, 2007 for more examples).

Perhaps most importantly, prior to dissonance theory the general wisdom among laypersons and psychologists was that, if you want people to change their behavior, you must first get them to change their attitudes. To take a dramatic example: In 1954, following the Supreme Court decision on the desegregation of schools, a great many psychologists argued that desegregation could not and should not take place – especially in the south – until after some of the prejudiced attitudes had been changed. Dissonance theory burst on the scene and suggested that, while that's one way to go, a more powerful way is to induce people to change their behavior first – and their attitudes will follow. So, our advice would be, the best way to change prejudiced attitudes is to desegregate. Several laboratory and field experiments, as well as the history of desegregation itself, have confirmed this prediction.

I believe that the reason the arousal of dissonance can produce such powerful social influence effects is that it persuades, not by a direct approach, but through the subtle induction of self-persuasion (Aronson, 1999; for more examples of the use of dissonance in influence see Aronson, 2003). In direct persuasion, the target is bombarded with an appeal, and that is the problem. It feels like an influence attempt and thus there is a tendency to resist. Such appeals often produce small influence effects. With dissonance, the target comes to persuade himself or herself by justifying an action or a statement made under conditions of limited justification. In such cases, the person comes to self-persuade that he or she really does believe the self-justification.

A THEORY OF DISSONANCE BASED ON THE SELF

Although Leon once told me that he thought the theory was perfect as originally stated, almost from the very beginning some of us felt it was a little too vague. Several situations arose, in the minds of those of us working closely with the theory, where it wasn't entirely clear what dissonance theory would predict, or indeed whether or not dissonance theory even made a prediction. Indeed, among Leon's graduate students it was frequently said, with tongue only partly in cheek, "If you really want to know whether X is dissonant with Y, ask Leon!" In short, it was becoming increasingly clear that the theory needed its boundaries tightened a bit. Accordingly, just 3 years after the publication of *A theory of cognitive dissonance*, I suggested that dissonance theory makes its strongest and clearest predictions when the self-concept of the individual is engaged (Aronson, 1960). That is, in my judgment, dissonance is greatest and clearest when what is involved is not just any two cognitions but, rather, a cognition about the self and a piece of our behavior that violates that self-concept.

This modification retained the core notion of inconsistency but shifted the emphasis to the self-concept. I believe that this attempt to tighten dissonance theory was of value inasmuch as it increased the predictive power of the theory without seriously limiting its scope. In a subsequent article, Merrill Carlsmith and I argued that Festinger's original statement (and all of the early experiments) rested on the implicit assumption that individuals have a reasonably high self-concept, but that if an individual considered himself to be a "schnook," he might expect himself to do schnooky things – like go through a severe initiation in order to get into a group, or say things that he didn't quite believe (Aronson & Carlsmith, 1962). A few years later, I carried my reasoning a step further (Aronson, 1968; Aronson et al., 1974), elaborating on the centrality of the self-concept in the experience and reduction of dissonance and suggesting that, in this regard, most individuals strive for three things: (a) to preserve a consistent, stable, predictable sense of self, (b) to preserve a competent sense of self, and (c) to preserve a morally good sense of self. Or, in shorthand terms, what leads me to perform dissonance-reducing behavior is my having done something that (a) astonishes me, or (b) makes me feel stupid, or (c) makes me feel guilty.

Needless to say, the three strivings can be in conflict with one another. For example, if, over the years, as a weekend basketball player, I have been a consistently poor free-throw shooter, sinking about 40%, and suddenly in one game I sink twelve in a row, do I feel strange (how could I have done so well when I am really awful at this?) or do I feel wonderful (at last, my true competence is emerging, hurrah!)? My guess is that on the one hand, I would feel wonderful about having performed so well; but, at the same time, there would be some discomfort based on my inability to have gauged and predicted that performance. If our measuring instruments were sensitive enough we would be able to pick up the discomfort lurking underneath the elation.

Moreover, in the real world, whether one or the other of these strivings dominates would depend on the details of the situation. As I have said often in the past (e.g., Aronson, 1991), in both the laboratory and the real world the details of the situation are terribly important. To illustrate, extending the above example, if my self concept as a 40% shooter were not based on much prior experience and my twelve consecutive successful free throws were accomplished in an important game on national television, the rewards associated with my unexpected competence would all but overwhelm any negative cognitive consequences due to its unexpectedness. But if my self concept as a 40% shooter were based on years of experience, and the twelve consecutive successful free throws were accomplished while alone in the gym at the end of a practice session, the discomfort might well predominate.

Because, in our culture, success is such an important and gratifying thing, it is not easy to demonstrate the phenomenon of "discomfort in the face of unexpected success." This does not mean it is not important – only that people have a hard time admitting that they are uncomfortable while they are busily basking in glory or taking bows. In order to demonstrate this phenomenon in the laboratory it would be necessary to exercise a high degree of experimental artistry. Fortunately, the late Merrill Carlsmith was just such an artist. In an experiment that worked largely because of his ingenuity in the laboratory, Carlsmith and I (1962) demonstrated that individuals with low performance expectancy on a given test were made uncomfortable by performing superlatively on that test. As a result of this discomfort, when given the opportunity to re-do the test, they changed significantly more of their answers (most of which were correct) than those who actually performed poorly on the test. Let me state again that the details of that experiment were very important. For example, Carlsmith and I selected a task that was of no great importance to the subject so that the discomfort with unexpected success could be measured.

One of the great advantages of this model is that it opens up the possibility of finding the conditions under which different ways of reducing dissonance are more or less likely to occur. Applying the self-concept model to the Festinger/Carlsmith experiment, what is dissonant is not the cognition that I believe "X" and I said "not X"; what is dissonant is that I see myself as a decent and clever human being and find that I have lied to another person in the absence of adequate justification. This makes me feel both guilty and stupid – so I rush to convince myself that the lie is really true. Note that if I knew myself to be both incompetent and immoral, I would have experienced little or no dissonance in that situation. Similarly, in the Aronson/Mills experiment, what is dissonant is that my cognition about my behavior is dissonant with my self-concept as a sensible, competent person. To have gone through hell and high water to get into a boring discussion group makes me feel stupid. Thus, I try to convince myself that the group was really pretty exciting. If I experienced myself as a generally stupid or incompetent person, I would have experienced little or no dissonance.

For approximately two decades, dissonance theory proved to be an extraordinarily fruitful and powerful explanatory concept both in and out of the laboratory. By the mid-1970s it had transcended the boundaries of academic social psychology and was widely cited in scholarly journals in a variety of disciplines including economics, philosophy, political science and anthropology. The concept also managed to seep into the popular culture, being featured in articles in the *New York Times, Newsweek, Playboy*, and, alas, the *National Enquirer*. It even found its way into daytime soap operas.

THE PREMATURE WANING OF DISSONANCE THEORY

But, ironically, just as a wide range of intellectuals and the general public were beginning to embrace the notion of cognitive dissonance, the pendulum started to swing and interest in dissonance theory among social psychologists began to wane. Indeed, by the end of the 1970s, dissonance experiments all but disappeared from the social psychological literature. Increasingly, during this period, I found myself the reluctant recipient of a great many invitations to appear on symposia entitled "Whatever Became of Dissonance Theory?" How did this come about?

There are several interlocking reasons, which I will mention very briefly. These reasons apply not only to research on dissonance theory, but to much of the research on social influence in general. A revival of dissonance and social influence research – the goal of many of the authors of this edited volume – will require a careful consideration of the implications of each reason.

First, deception, which was an important ingredient in this kind of experimentation, was called into question. This was due, in part, to the blatant lying our government officials were doing about Watergate, the Vietnam War, etc. This made social psychologists very queasy about doing things in the laboratory that seemed similar to what Richard Nixon was doing on national television.

Second, dissonance experiments (and many social influence experiments in general) almost always required high-impact procedures; high-impact procedures frequently cause subjects some discomfort. While dissonance experiments were not as extreme as some (e.g., the Milgram experiment, 1965), they came under attack by those who felt that some subjects could, conceivably, be harmed by these procedures.

Third, at a time when jobs in academic psychology were scarce, young professionals found themselves under a great deal of pressure to increase the quantity of their empirical publications. In this context, high-impact methodology seemed particularly foreboding since it is difficult to pull off, time-consuming and labor-intensive.

Finally, at the same time, just down the corridor of the psychology building, cognitive psychologists had been making enormous strides – it was natural for social psychologists to want to incorporate some of their theories and methods into the area of social cognition. When they did, they discovered that the methodology was easier, less-time consuming and didn't present ethical problems. The motto of the experimentalist shifted from "How do we invent a scenario to convince subjects that such and such is going on?" to "If it moves, prime it!" The video camera became the major presenter of the independent variable; subjects became the audience and judge rather than the participant in a given set of events in the laboratory.

I have strong feelings about this topic, and could go on and on (and, I'm afraid, on and on and on), but I'll spare you that harangue. Suffice it to say that, in my judgment, most social psychologists abandoned high-impact experimentation prematurely and much too docilely and that the discipline lost something very precious in the bargain. In abandoning high-impact experimentation we, unwittingly, all but ruled out the testing of a number of very interesting hypotheses

– hypotheses that simply could not be tested without the use of this kind of methodology. Moreover, almost an entire generation of graduate students did not receive training in this vital skill, or, worse still, developed a negative attitude about it, as something that is "schmutzig," problematic and difficult. Fortunately, the researchers in this volume are attempting to change this state of affairs.

With the rising tide of social cognition, the concept of motivation – and hence the theory of cognitive dissonance – simply became unfashionable like last year's hemline. People were simply not thinking in those terms anymore, not because dissonance theory was replaced by anything better, but only by things that were newer – and a methodology that was quicker and easier.

In his brilliant and influential paper on the shortcomings of the intuitive psychologist, my good friend and favorite interlocutor, Lee Ross (1977), suggested that it might be a good idea to temporarily abandon motivational constructs in order to concentrate on the purely cognitive influences on attributional judgments. This is the "convenient fiction" I mentioned a moment ago. I think this was a useful temporary strategy. But there are unfortunate consequences to this strategy. One of them is that we tend to forget that it was simply a convenient fiction and nothing more. Alas, social psychology has a long history and a very short memory.

During the cognitive revolution in social psychology, researchers not only lost interest in the concept of motivation, they seemed to forget it existed. Interestingly, a great many social psychologists began to reinvent experiments to test cognitive notions that could have easily been done under the rubric of dissonance theory, but now there were different, nonmotivational terms for the phenomena under investigation. Most importantly, the connection between this new body of research and the older research was not noted, and therefore was severed.

There are dozens of examples of this phenomenon in the literature; I'll discuss only one. It is a particularly cogent example because it was a fine piece of research done by people I respect a great deal. Moreover, because the researchers are also friends of mine, I know they will not take offence at my singling them out – at least I *hope* they won't! This is an experiment done by Charlie Lord, Lee Ross and Mark Lepper (1979); they call the phenomenon "biased assimilation." Let me quote from the abstract of that article:

> People who hold strong opinions on complex social issues are likely to examine relevant empirical evidence in a biased manner. They are apt to accept "confirming" evidence at face value while subjecting "disconfirming" evidence to critical evaluation, and as a result to draw undue support for their initial positions from mixed or random empirical findings. (p. 2098)

Clearly that experiment could have been done in 1957; it is easily derivable from dissonance theory. Indeed, in his 1957 book, Festinger made an identical prediction – here's what Festinger said about what would happen to a person if he or she were forced to read a persuasive communication that went against a strong belief:

> One might expect to observe such things as . . . erroneous interpretation or perception of the material . . . [for example], it is only among smokers [not

non-smokers] that one would expect to find skepticism concerning the reported research findings [linking smoking to cancer]. (p. 153)

The article by Lord, Ross and Lepper contains 32 references, not one of which is to dissonance theory or any of the dissonance experiments. That is, Lord, Lepper and Ross were content with a purely cognitive–heuristic explanation for their results. But just because it is possible to explain those results without recourse to motivational constructs does not mean that a motivational explanation is incorrect.

Don't get me wrong – I'm not making a dispositional attribution but a situational one; that is, I'm not accusing my friends Charlie Lord, Lee Ross and Mark Lepper of shoddy scholarship – far from it. I single them out precisely because they are such irreproachably *good* scholars. I use this experiment solely as an illustration of what happens when artificial barriers are erected and related theories get insulated from each other: We decrease our ability to forge vital syntheses and, consequently, our discipline becomes unnecessarily fragmented and disjointed.

A REDISCOVERY OF DISSONANCE PROCESSES

During the past few years, many of the researchers who had been enthralled by social cognition in the 1970s and early 1980s have gradually come to the realization that pure cognition can only carry us so far. Accordingly, several social psychologists seem to have rediscovered the idea of motivation and have come to the conclusion that it might be interesting to try to combine cognition with motivation – in other words, exactly the strategy Leon Festinger employed so brilliantly 50 years ago. In short, the dreaded pendulum has started to swing again. Thus, in the past few years, a plethora of interesting mini-theories has sprung up bearing intriguing names such as self-affirmation theory (Steele, 1988), symbolic self-completion theory (Wicklund & Gollwitzer, 1982), self-evaluation maintenance theory (Tesser, 1988), self-discrepancy theory (Higgins, 1989), action identification theory (Vallacher & Wegner, 1985), self-verification theory (Swann, 1984), self-regulation theory (Scheier & Carver, 1988), and the concept of motivated inference (Kunda, 1990).

Each of these theories is a worthy and interesting effort to combine cognition and motivation but each has a limited scope and, in my judgment, with a little work, every one of them can be contained under the general rubric of dissonance theory, as modified in 1962. This is not meant to imply that they don't add something important. They do. The question I would raise here is: Does it advance the science when we have seven or eight little theories doing the work of one? It doesn't seem very parsimonious – and it's a bitch to remember.

Dissonance without Aversive Consequences

Among the most generative of the neo-dissonance approaches is one developed by Joel Cooper and Russ Fazio (1984), which they sometimes refer to as the new-look dissonance theory. In examining the early forced compliance experiments, like the Festinger–Carlsmith experiment and several others, Cooper and Fazio made an interesting discovery: In these experiments, not only was inconsistency present, but aversive consequences were also present; that is, lying to another person is usually aversive. In a bold theoretical statement, Cooper and Fazio asserted that, in this paradigm, dissonance is not due to inconsistent cognitions at all, but rather is aroused only when an individual feels personally responsible for bringing about an aversive or unwanted event. The astute reader will note that this resembles the third part of my self-concept analysis presented earlier in this chapter – specifically, the commission of an immoral act that makes a person feel guilty.

While I always appreciated the boldness in Cooper and Fazio's theorizing, I could never bring myself to buy into the notion that aversive consequences are essential in this paradigm; that is, I couldn't believe that the other two parts of my "three-part" theory (predictability and the need to feel competent), under the proper conditions, wouldn't be sufficient to arouse dissonance in the forced compliance paradigm. So I went back over the early experiments and found, much to my astonishment, that Cooper and Fazio were right – that in the early experiments on forced compliance, aversive consequences were always present. At the same time, this doesn't prove that aversive consequences are a necessary component. Is it possible to have dissonance without aversive consequences? This is the crucial question. Is there any way to test it? Or are the two factors hopelessly intertwined?

I struggled with this one for a long time – to no avail. And then something interesting happened. I had placed the Cooper–Fazio model on the back burner of my mind while I was working on a challenging problem in the application of social influence processes to problems in the real world. Specifically, I was trying to find a way to convince sexually active college students to use condoms as a way of stemming the epidemic of AIDS and other sexually transmitted diseases. I had tried several of the traditional persuasive techniques – with very little success – and then I thought about using the dissonance–forced compliance paradigm.

In thinking about it, I constructed the following scenario: Suppose you are a college student and you are induced to make a persuasive videotape (to be shown to an audience of sexually active high-school students, as part of a sex education course) in which you proclaim your belief that sexually active people should always use condoms to prevent AIDS. Will you experience any aversive consequences? My guess is that Cooper and Fazio would have to say no. Quite the contrary; far from causing harm, your speech might even save the lives of some of those who hear it. But – wait a minute, there is no dissonance in this situation either, is there?

It seems not. But suppose, in one condition, just after you make the speech, you are made mindful of the fact that there are some situations in which you yourself do not use condoms while having sex. Here we have an interesting situation. According to my version of the theory, this would produce dissonance because you are not practicing what you are preaching. That is, for most people, their self-concept does not include behaving like a hypocrite. Thus, in this situation, we can disentangle what I would call dissonance from any aversive consequences: Your cognition that you are advising others to do things that you yourself do not do would be dissonant with your self-concept as a principled person who practices what he or she preaches. This would cause dissonance even though the algebraic sum of the consequences of your action is overwhelmingly beneficial. How would you reduce dissonance? By resolving to change your behavior in order to bring it into line with your statements so that you will now be practicing what you just got through preaching. In this case, you would increase your resolution to use condoms.

In an experiment I conducted with Carrie Fried and Jeff Stone, we followed the example outlined above (Aronson, Fried, & Stone, 1991). In a 2 × 2 factorial design, in one condition, college students were induced to make a videotape in which they urged their audience to use condoms; they were told that the video would be shown to high-school students. In the other major condition, the college students simply rehearsed the arguments without making the video. Cutting across these conditions was the "mindfulness" manipulation: In one set of conditions, our subjects were made mindful of the fact that they themselves are not practicing what they are preaching, by being asked to think about all those situations where they found it particularly difficult or impossible to use condoms in the recent past. Other students were not made mindful of their past failures to use condoms.

The one cell we expected to produce dissonance is the one high in hypocrisy – i.e., where subjects made the video and were given the opportunity to dredge up memories of situations where they failed to use condoms. Again, how did we expect them to reduce dissonance? By increasing the strength of their intention to use condoms in the future. And that is precisely what we got. Those subjects who were in the high-dissonance condition showed the greatest intention to increase their use of condoms. Moreover, two months later, there was a tendency for the subjects in the high-dissonance cell to report using condoms a higher percentage of the time than in any of the other three cells.

Now, the astute reader may recognize a contradiction in what I said earlier about high-impact experiments – the dependent variable in our condom experiment involves the self-report of intentions and behavior rather than a behavioral measure of actual condom use. As an old "high-impact" experimenter, I'm more than a little uncomfortable with such a dependent variable. After all, I just lectured the field in the first part of this chapter about the value of high-impact research (something that I hope will have positive consequences for your research) and now I am confronted with the fact that I didn't employ such measures in my own experiment. Unfortunately, the problem is, when you are dealing with sexual behavior, you don't have much choice; after all, I (or should I say *even* I), would not be so bold as to try to follow our subjects into their bedrooms to see if they really do use condoms. But I believe that researchers should not allow themselves such easy self-justifications to their apparent hypocrisies, and thus my colleagues and I conducted a second set of experiments employing a behavior measure of condom use in which we found that our subjects placed in a hypocrisy situation would purchase more condoms at the end of the experiment and continue to purchase them over the next few months (see Stone, Aronson, Crain, Winslow, & Fried, 1994)

One way to increase our confidence in the efficacy of the "induction of hypocrisy" paradigm (and to reduce my own dissonance created by telling you to do more high-impact research) is to try to test the paradigm in a different situation – a situation where we stand a chance to demonstrate the phenomenon using a more convincing dependent variable. We found one in the shower room of our campus field house. As you may know, central California has a chronic water shortage. On our campus, the administration is constantly trying to find ways to induce students to conserve water. So we decided to test our hypothesis by using dissonance theory and the induction of hypocrisy to convince students to take shorter showers. What we discovered is that while it is impossible, within the bounds of propriety, to follow people into their bedrooms to observe their condom-using behavior, in our society one can easily follow them into the shower room and watch them take showers.

In this experiment (Dickerson, Thibodeau, Aronson, & Miller, 1992), we intercepted college women at the university field house, who had just finished swimming in a highly chlorinated pool, and were on their way to take a shower. Just like in the condom experiment, it was a 2 × 2 design in which we varied commitment and mindfulness. In the commitment conditions, each student was asked if she would be willing to sign a flyer encouraging people to conserve water at the field house. The students were told that the flyers would be displayed on posters; each was shown a sample poster – a large, colorful, very public display. The flyer read: "Take shorter showers. Turn off water while soaping up. If I can do it, so can you!" After she signed the flyer, we thanked her for her time, and she proceeded to the shower room, where our undergraduate research assistant (blind to condition) was unobtrusively waiting (with hidden waterproof stopwatch) to time the student's shower.

In the mindful conditions we asked the students to respond to a water conservation "survey," which consisted of items designed to make them aware of their proconservation attitudes and the fact that their showering behavior was sometimes wasteful.

The results are consistent with those in the condom experiment: We found dissonance effects only in the cell where the subjects were preaching what they were not always practicing. That is, in the condition where the students were induced to advocate short showers and were made mindful of their own past behavior, they took very short showers. To be specific, in the high-dissonance cell, the length of the average shower (which, because of the chlorine in the swimming pool, included a shampoo and cream rinse) was just over three and a half minutes (that's short!) and was significantly shorter than in the unmindful/uncommitted condition.

Both of these experiments produced changes in important behavior that were beneficial to society. Moreover, when taken together the results indicate that aversive consequences may not be a necessary component of dissonance in the forced compliance paradigm.

Synthesizing Dissonance Theories to Create Dissonance Theory

Why do I think it's better to have one big theory rather than seven or eight little ones? Is it simply a matter of aesthetics? No, it's much more than that. As Leonard

Berkowitz and Trish Devine (1989) have indicated, social psychologists have been much more prone to analysis than synthesis. By analysis, Berkowitz and Devine refer to the careful delineation and differentiation of the theoretical concepts and propositions that lead to the prediction of different outcomes. By synthesis, they refer to the bringing together of apparently disparate observations under a common theoretical umbrella. It goes without saying that both orientations are vitally important to any discipline. But, in my judgment, a problem has arisen in social psychology because there seems to be much more payoff for analysis than for synthesis – a good analysis simply seems more original and creative than a good synthesis. Among other things, this has led to a huge imbalance in the analysis/synthesis ratio during the past several years, resulting in a plethora of small theories with hardly anyone taking the trouble to try to find the common ground among these theories. As Berkowitz and Devine point out, this has been costly because there are great advantages to synthesis in terms of economy of thought and connectivity among approaches – which can serve to help us discover the full meaning of any given theory. Let me give you a few examples, from dissonance theory, to illustrate why I think synthesis might be particularly important here.

As mentioned previously, Merrill Carlsmith and I (1962), working from the "self-concept" revision of dissonance theory, did an experiment in which we found that under certain conditions, college students would rather be able to predict and confirm their own behavior than succeed on a test. Specifically, students who believed themselves to be inept at a given task ended up changing their answers on a successful performance (testing their abilities on that task) as a way of restoring their self-predictability. Twenty-five years later, working from Bill Swann's notion of self-verification, Swann and Pelham (2002) found that people prefer to remain in close relationships with those friends and room-mates whose evaluations of their abilities are consonant with their own (sometimes negative) self-evaluations. In other words, people prefer to be close to someone whose evaluations of them are consonant with their self-concept as opposed to someone whose evaluations of them are more positive than their self-concept.

I see this as not merely an interesting new finding; on the contrary, these results assume great importance precisely because of their linkage to and extensions of the earlier findings described above. That is, when theorists and researchers build on previous theory and data, it enhances our discipline by highlighting its continuity. What these two pieces of research have in common involves that aspect of dissonance that was identified in some of our earliest thinking on this issue – the need people have to form a stable self-concept and to predict their own behavior. Thus, individuals will try to behave in predictable ways (as Carlsmith and I found in 1962) and they will be most comfortable around people who expect neither too much nor too little from them (as Swann & Pelham found in 2002). Twenty-six years is a long time in social psychology. Given our field's proclivity to avoid synthesis, it is little wonder that Swann and Pelham failed to recognize the full meaning of this connection.

Working out of the same framework, Swann and Steven Read (1981) found that people elicit behavior from others that will lead to the verification of their own self-beliefs. To take a central example used by Swann and Read, if a man believes himself to be highly tractable, he will seek out others who treat him as if they expect him to be tractable. This is very interesting – and it assumes even greater importance when we compare it with what Festinger wrote almost 50 years ago. In 1957, Festinger stated that one way to preserve consonance is by changing an environmental cognitive element:

> For example, a person who is habitually very hostile toward other people may surround himself with persons who provoke hostility. His cognitions about the persons with whom he associates are then consonant with cognitions corresponding to his hostile behavior. (Festinger, 1957, p. 20)

The two examples are essentially identical. This sameness makes one wonder why we need a separate theory called "self-verification" to account for the phenomenon being described. As I have said elsewhere (Aronson, 1989), our zeal for the analytical approach (at the expense of the synthetic) tends to blind us to these similarities and induces us to read some of the older theories carelessly – as if they were ancient history and, therefore, of little value to contemporary researchers and theorists. Indeed, as if he were intentionally trying to provide me with data to bolster my feelings about the high price our discipline has been paying for being overly analytical, Swann (1991) has casually dismissed dissonance theory for having ignored the self-verification tendency in humans and, therefore, being "nothing more than a cleverly disguised version of self-enhancement theory" (1991, p. 413). A careful reading of Festinger (1957) might have led Swann to a more generous conclusion.

Let us look briefly at Claude Steele's (1988) notion of self-affirmation in the context of some of the older work. First, the older work: In 1968, Dave Mettee and I did an experiment, inspired by dissonance theory, in which we demonstrated that if we raised an individual's self-esteem, it would serve to insulate him from performing an immoral act like cheating. We found that the higher self-esteem served to make the anticipation of doing something immoral more dissonant than it would otherwise have been. Thus, when our subjects were put in a tempting situation, they were able to say to themselves, in effect, "Terrific people like me don't cheat!" And they succeeded in resisting the temptation to cheat to a greater extent than those in the control condition.

Recently, working from his concept of self-affirmation, Steele and his students found that if people are put in a dissonant situation – a situation where they misled another person (as in the Festinger–Carlsmith experiment) – there was one condition under which they did not reduce dissonance in the usual way (by changing their attitudes). Specifically, those subjects who were given an opportunity to affirm some important aspect of their self-concept – that they were a kind and generous person or a good scientist or whatever – were able to maintain their original attitudes without caving in to the pressures of dissonance to soften their original attitudes. How exciting! The connection between this experiment and the Aronson–Mettee experiment is obvious. Taken together, they show that bolstering the self-concept is both a way of helping the individual avoid performing behavior that will produce a truckload of dissonance (Aronson–Mettee) and a way of reducing dissonance that already exists (Steele). The new findings are interesting and important, but I do not think that we need a new conceptualization to account for them. Indeed, it is precisely by keeping the two sets of findings under the same roof that we can fully appreciate the inter-relatedness of the two experiments and thereby gain a richer understanding of the dissonance phenomenon.

I realize that I'm beginning to sound like the worst kind of smarty pants – I'm taking interesting research and theorizing that's been done in the past two decades and claiming that we did something very similar 40 or 45 years ago. What's worse, I fear I may be coming on like an old curmudgeon, who seems to be longing for the good old days and who is apparently claiming that there is nothing new under the sun. Some might even accuse me of trying to make dissonance theory the kind of all-purpose explanation for everything that I criticized reinforcement theorists for attempting in the 1940s and 1950s. Let me reiterate that I'm not simply saying that there is nothing new under the sun. I don't believe that. Moreover, I hope it is obvious that I don't believe that dissonance theory does or should account for everything. Far from it. I see the scope of dissonance theory as being limited to a clearly defined set of psychological situations (see Aronson, 1969). But where there *are* related phenomena, I believe that it can be of great value to view them under the same rubric – at least until their similarities and differences can be empirically investigated and explored.

In this sense, then, dissonance theory *is* making a comeback – but under a variety of different names. I think the time has arrived for a grand synthesis; now that social psychology has rediscovered the richness in the hypotheses to be generated by combining the cognitive with the motivational, I believe that it would be a serious mistake to diffuse that energy into a series of unconnected mini-theories. I believe that it is appropriate to reach back into our fertile past to achieve continuity as we continue to discover new and interesting things.

The kind of continuity I am pointing toward will not only make our discipline more understandable – it will also generate richer hypotheses. This thinking is a reflection of my basic philosophy of science – such as it is. Needless to say, not everyone will agree with me. For example, Bill Swann (personal communication) has recently criticized my approach. Swann acknowledges that my old tripartite view of dissonance theory managed to embrace both the major assumption of self-enhancement theory and the major assumption of self-verification theory. But for Swann, this is disadvantageous. He writes, in part:

> Here then is the problem with your suggestion that Steele and I are saying the same thing that you said back in '68. I predict one thing, he [Steele] predicts the opposite, and you predict both. How can you say that three theories that have such different properties are saying the same thing? (Swann, 1990, personal communication)

In my response, I wrote, in part:

> Regarding the issue of whether people strive for a consistent sense of self or a good/competent sense of self, I would suspect that most sentient social psychologists would agree that, it's not a matter of whether Bill is right and Claude is

wrong or vice versa. Rather, we know that both in the real world and in the laboratory, either phenomenon *can* occur and frequently *does* occur – depending on the precise details of the situation. As I've said (and said, and said – throughout my whole career, it seems) *the details are always important.*

In sum, to my mind, the attractiveness of the synthetic approach, as illustrated here, is that it highlights a philosophical credo that, as a researcher, I hold dear: that the task of the scientist is not to prove one proposition right and true and the other utterly false, but to painstakingly find the conditions under which one or the other is more likely to occur; in this case, the conditions under which the individual will seek out self-enhancement or stability. So, it is not that my formulation leads me to predict both as Bill Swann indicates – I am suggesting that both a stable sense of self and a competent/moral sense of self are desirable and can be sought out, each under a specific set of conditions. The task of the researcher is to find and demonstrate precisely what those conditions are (see Greenwald, Pratkanis, Leippe, & Baumgardner, 1986). The astute reader will notice that this approach opens the door for analysis – *after* the necessary synthesis has taken place.

This philosophy of science has some advantages – most noteworthy, it turns the research endeavor not into a contest to see who is smarter or righter, but rather into a mutually beneficial, cooperative endeavor to get closer to an understanding of human thought and behavior. And, because I firmly adhere to this philosophy of science, it follows that I also believe that it is very important that, whenever possible, we build on one another's work rather than continually striving to strike out in "original" new directions. This is precisely what I mean by creative synthesis.

The Future of Dissonance and Social Influence Research

It is hard to predict the future of any course of research. To paraphrase Shakespeare, "The course of research ne'er did run smooth." But what I can do is offer some pieces of advice that I think are very useful for doing the very best dissonance and social influence research.

1   *Don't be afraid to do high-impact research.* While it is important to realize the ethical and moral responsibilities that doing high-impact research brings (as well as the ethical and moral responsibilities that *not* doing high-impact research brings), such research has been responsible for almost all the major advances in research on social influence.
2   *Appreciate the history of social influence research.* Sir Isaac Newton once remarked, "If I have seen further it is by standing on the shoulders of giants." Social psychologists should be as bold. Don't be afraid to read classic studies, to reference those works, and most importantly to make use of them in your own research.
3   *Look for synthesis of findings across different domains of research.* In this volume, the chapters by Pratkanis; Knowles and Riner; Nail and

MacDonald; and others pull together what we know about social influence across a range of domains. That is a great first step, but the next step will require synthesis of those findings into new and better theories. I suspect that such an effort will continue to find that dissonance reduction is a fundamental human process and will result in even more interesting research ideas than the ones I had the opportunity to explore.

4   *Take dissonance theory seriously in understanding social influence processes.* As just two examples, given that many influence tactics are based on dissonance then (a) the development of strategies for resisting influence will involve developing techniques for dealing with the underlying dissonance, and (b) dissonance theory will be a major determinant of the conditions under which a given tactic is more or less effective.

5   *Perhaps most importantly, I hope that you will have a love affair with social psychological research as passionate as the one I have enjoyed for the past 50 years.*

REFERENCES

Aronson, E. (1960). *The cognitive and behavioral consequences of the confirmation and disconfirmation of expectancies.* Grant proposal submitted to NSF, Harvard University.

Aronson, E. (1968). Dissonance theory: Progress and problems. In R. P. Abelson, E. Aronson, W. J. McGuire, T. M. Newcomb, M. J. Rosenberg, & P. H. Tannenbaum (Eds.), *Theories of cognitive consistency: A sourcebook.* Skokie, IL: Rand-McNally.

Aronson, E. (1969). A theory of cognitive dissonance: A current perspective. In L. Berkowitz (Ed.), *Advances in experimental social psychology* (Vol. 4, pp. 1–34). New York: Academic Press.

Aronson, E. (1989). Analysis, synthesis, and the treasuring of the old. *Personality and Social Psychology Bulletin, 15,* 508–512.

Aronson, E. (1991). How to change behavior. In R. Curtis and G. Stricker (Eds.), *How people change: Inside and outside therapy.* New York: Plenum.

Aronson, E. (1999). The power of self-persuasion. *American Psychologist, 54,* 875–884.

Aronson, E. (2003). *The social animal* (9th ed.). New York: Worth.

Aronson, E., & Carlsmith, J. M. (1962). Performance expectancy as a determinant of actual performance. *Journal of Abnormal and Social Psychology, 65,* 178–182.

Aronson, E., & Carlsmith, J. M. (1963). Effects of severity of threat on the devaluation of forbidden behavior. *Journal of Abnormal and Social Psychology, 66,* 584–588.

Aronson, E., & Carlsmith, J. M. (1968). Experimentation in social psychology. In G. Lindzey & E. Aronson (Eds.) *The handbook of social psychology* (2nd ed). Reading, MA: Addison-Wesley.

Aronson, E., Chase, T., Helmreich, R., & Ruhnke, R. (1974). A two-factor theory of dissonance reduction: The effect of feeling stupid or feeling awful on opinion change. *International Journal for Research and Communication, 3,* 59–74.

Aronson, E., Ellsworth, P., Carlsmith, J. M., & Gonzales, M. H. (1990). *Methods of research in social psychology.* New York: McGraw-Hill.

Aronson, E., Fried, C., & Stone, J. (1991). Overcoming denial and increasing the intention to use condoms through the induction of hypocrisy. *American Journal of Public Health, 81,* 1636–1638.

Aronson, E., & Mettee, D. (1968). Dishonest behavior as a function of differential levels of induced self-esteem. *Journal of Personality and Social Psychology*, 9, 121–127.

Aronson, E., & Mills, J. (1959). The effect of severity of initiation on liking for a group. *Journal of Abnormal and Social Psychology*, 59, 177–181.

Asch, S. E. (1951). Effects of group pressure upon modification and distortion of judgment. In H. Guetzkow (Ed.), *Groups, leadership and men* (pp. 177–190). Pittsburgh, PA: Carnegie Press.

Berkowitz, L., & Devine, P. G. (1989). Research tradition, analysis, and synthesis in social psychological theories: The case of dissonance theory. *Personality and Social Psychology Bulletin*, 15, 493–507.

Cohen, A. R. (1962). An experiment on small rewards for discrepant compliance and attitude change. In J. W. Brehm & A. R. Cohen, *Explorations in cognitive dissonance* (pp. 73–78). New York: Wiley.

Cooper, J., & Fazio, R. H. (1984). A new look at dissonance theory. In L. Berkowitz (Ed.), *Advances in experimental social psychology* (Vol. 17, pp. 229–266). Orlando, FL: Academic Press.

Davis, K. E., & Jones, E. E. (1960). Changes in interpersonal perception as a means of reducing cognitive dissonance. *Journal of Abnormal and Social Psychology*, 61, 402–410.

Dickerson, C. A., Thibodeau, R., Aronson, E., & Miller, D. (1992). Using cognitive dissonance to encourage water conservation. *Journal of Applied Social Psychology*, 22, 841–854.

Festinger, L. (1957). *A theory of cognitive dissonance*. Evanston, IL: Row, Peterson.

Festinger, L., & Carlsmith, J. M. (1959). Cognitive consequences of forced compliance. *Journal of Abnormal and Social Psychology*, 58, 203–211.

Glass, D. (1964). Changing in liking as a means of reducing cognitive discrepancies between self-esteem and aggression. *Journal of Personality*, 32, 531–549.

Greenwald, A. G., Pratkanis, A. R., Leippe, M. R. & Baumgardner, M. H. (1986). Under what conditions does theory obstruct research progress? *Psychological Review*, 93, 216–229.

Higgins, E. T. (1989). Self-discrepancy theory: What patterns of self-beliefs cause people to suffer? In L. Berkowitz (Ed.), *Advances in experimental social psychology* (Vol. 22, pp. 93–136). Orlando, FL: Academic Press.

Jones, E. E. (1976). Foreword. In Wicklund, R., & Brehm, J., *Perspectives on cognitive dissonance* (p. x). Hillsdale, NJ: Lawrence Erlbaum Associates, Inc.

Kahn, M. (1966). The physiology of catharsis. *Journal of Personality and Social Psychology*, 3, 278–298.

Kunda, Z. (1990). The case for motivated reasoning. *Psychological Bulletin*, 108, 480–498.

Lord, C. G., Ross, L., & Lepper, M. R. (1979). Biased assimilation and attitude polarization: The effects of prior theories on subsequently considered evidence. *Journal of Personality and Social Psychology*, 37, 2098–2109.

Milgram, S. (1965). Some conditions of obedience and disobedience to authority. *Human Relations*, 18, 57–76.

Nel, E., Helmreich, R., & Aronson, E. (1969). Opinion change in the advocate as a function of persuasibility of his audience: A clarification of the meaning of dissonance. *Journal of Personality and Social Psychology*, 12, 117–124.

Ross, L. (1977). The intuitive psychologist and his shortcomings: Distortions in the attribution process. In L. Berkowitz (Ed.), *Advances in experimental social psychology* (Vol. 10, pp. 174–221). Orlando, FL: Academic Press.

Scheier, M. F., & Carver, C. S. (1988). A model of behavioral self-regulation: Translating intention into action. In L. Berkowitz (Ed.), *Advances in experimental social psychology* (Vol. 21, pp. 303–346). New York: Academic Press.

Steele, C. M. (1988). The psychology of self-affirmation: Sustaining the integrity of the self. In L. Berkowitz (Ed.), *Advances in experimental social psychology* (Vol. 21, pp. 261–302). New York: Academic Press.

Stone, J., Aronson, E., Crain, A. L., Winslow, M. P., & Fried, C. (1994). Inducing hypocrisy as a means of encouraging young adults to use condoms. *Personality and Social Psychology Bulletin, 20,* 116–128.

Swann, W. B., Jr. (1984). Quest for accuracy in person perception. A matter of pragmatics. *Psychological Review, 91,* 457–477.

Swann, W. B., Jr. (1991). To be adored or to be known? The interplay of self-enhancement and self-verification. In R. M. Sorrentino & E. T. Higgins (Eds.), *Motivation and cognition.* New York: Guilford Press.

Swann, W. B., Jr., & Pelham, B. W. (2002). Who wants out when the going gets good? Psychological investment and preference for self-verifying college roommates. *Self and Identity, 1,* 219–233.

Swann, W. B., Jr., & Read, S. J. (1981). Acquiring self-knowledge: The search for feedback that fits. *Journal of Personality and Social Psychology, 41,* 1119–1128.

Tavris, C., & Aronson, E. (2007). *Mistakes were made (but not by me): Why we justify foolish beliefs, bad decisions, and hurtful acts.* New York: Harcourt.

Tesser, A. (1988). Toward a self-evaluation maintenance model of social behavior. In L. Berkowitz (Ed.), *Advances in experimental social psychology* (Vol. 21, pp. 181–227). Orlando, FL: Academic Press.

Vallacher, R. R., & Wegner, D. M. (1985). *Action identification theory.* Hillsdale, NJ: Lawrence Erlbaum Associates, Inc.

Wicklund, R. A., & Gollwitzer, P. M. (1982). *Symbolic self-completion.* Hillsdale, NJ: Lawrence Erlbaum Associates, Inc.

5

Emotional See-saw

DARIUSZ DOLINSKI

*I*f you happen to be rather ethereal and unearthly as compared to other women, you are very lucky not to have lived in late medieval or Renaissance Europe. If you had, and if it so happened that your neighbor's dairy cow had stopped producing milk, or the son of some magnate living nearby had become seriously ill, you could have been accused of witchcraft and satanic connections. To "verify" your spiritual chastity, the authorities would most probably have started by checking how much you weighed. If less than a large field stone, your situation would have become much worse. You could have been subjected to another trial, like being thrown into a pond or a river. Should you have floated or reached the other bank – mind you, hardly anybody could swim in those times – you would have provided sufficient evidence of your devilish affiliations. And what if you had drowned? Well, that would have proved you were not a witch, after all.

Not all the methods of dealing with those accused of witchcraft were that radical, however. Sometimes ordinary torture by burning various parts of the suspect's body with hot irons, or breaking her bones, was quite enough to make her acknowledge her "guilt." Sometimes a confession was obtained using psycho-logical methods that played on the emotions (see Pratkanis & Aronson, 2001 for modern-day examples). Consider this typical sequence of events. First the woman was tortured and intimidated by the inquisitor, who threatened her or her children with death; then, right out of the blue, another inquisitor started extending his compassion and taking care of her. The falsely accused woman, dazed and dis-oriented, duly signed the guilt acknowledgement that later served as justification for the "ultimate penalty" sentence.

Many a century later, a very similar procedure was applied in the USSR to those sentenced to imprisonment for "acting against communism" (Herling-Grudzinski, 1965). One of the interrogators would extinguish cigarettes on the prisoner's fore-head, kick him below the belt or break his fingers one by one. Then another officer would replace the sadist. He would offer the prisoner a comfortable seat and a cigarette, and express his deep interest in the prisoner's health or frame of mind. Most often a prisoner who had earlier refused to confess anything would now testify against himself and his closest friends. Many similar examples probably come to the reader's mind. Well-known from both written and filmed detective fiction is what can be labeled the "good cop–bad cop" interrogation: First the subject is brutally mistreated by one policeman – threatened with death, yelled at, and humiliated. Then all of a sudden everything changes. A telephone rings and the "bad" policeman disappears. Another policeman comes in – he is calm and pleasant, suggests a coffee or tea, running a relatively normal conversation. Also in these fictional scenes, subjects who have so far refused to cooperate now most often start to reveal everything and testify against everyone.

We could say that the common denominator in all the above examples is the dynamics of emotions experienced by the people subjected to the described situations. First they experience deep fear caused by an obvious source, like an inhuman interrogator; then, quite unexpectedly, the source of fear retreats.

It should be noted that this dynamics of emotions is not connected exclusively with the situations of forcing the suspects to testify or confess their guilt. Let us imagine, for example, the situation of a woman returning home alone late at night. When she notices a tall man following her, she becomes anxious. But when she suddenly recognizes him as a friend, she immediately feels relieved. Similarly, when we cannot find our wallet after the last night's bender, we are bound to experience a sudden tide of fear, which will retreat immediately after we eventually find it in another pocket.

People interrogated by "good" and the "bad" policemen (or by KGB or "Holy Office" inquisitors) would become extremely vulnerable to suggestions, proposals, or demands presented in the moment when sudden relief replaced the former experience of fear. Would other people, exposed to totally different situations, be equally likely to fulfill requests and commands when undergoing a similar relief of emotion? Richard Nawrat and I (Dolinski & Nawrat, 1998) have made a positive assumption on this thesis and verified our position in a series of experiments.

FEAR-THEN-RELIEF AND COMPLIANCE: EMPIRICAL EXPLORATION

Jaywalkers and people walking along the street became the participants in the first of the experiments by Dolinski and Nawrat (1998), designed to test the consequences of the sudden removal of the source of fear. In the first experimental group, when a jaywalker was in the middle of the road, a police whistle was blown. The participants would reflexively turn their heads toward the sound, only to see there were no policemen on the sidewalk behind them. In the second group, the jaywalking participants were allowed to cross the street undisturbed. In the experimental design, there was also a third group of participants who did not cross the street but only walked along the sidewalk, naturally, without being alarmed by a police whistle. All participants were next accosted by a confederate who asked them to fill out a questionnaire that was to take 10 minutes. It should be noted that the experiment was conducted on a cold autumn day, and it was not possible for the participants to fill out the questionnaire later at home; it had to be completed on the spot.

The questionnaire that the participants were asked to fill out was the Self-Description Inventory (Spielberg, Gorsuh, & Lushene, 1970), which enabled us to measure the current level of the participant's fear. Although the level of fear was almost identical in all experimental conditions, it turned out that the participants who experienced first fear and then relief more frequently agreed to fill out the questionnaire than did the participants in the other groups (see Figure 5.1). In other words, much like the witches of middle ages and the accused of the KGB, we found that fear followed by relief increased compliance with a request.

Armed with this data, we wanted to know if the relief of fear would lead to compliance in other situations and settings. The participants in our second experiment were car drivers who had parked their vehicles in a no-parking zone. Under the wipers of their cars, we placed small leaflets that looked just like police tickets. When the drivers returned and read the leaflets, it turned out these were ads for a hair-growth stimulating shampoo, or appeals for a blood donation. In a different experimental condition, we used adhesive tape to stick the leaflets to the car doors, so the drivers had no reason to become frightened. There was also a control group in the experiment: owners of cars on which we did not place any pieces of paper. When the drivers were about to drive off, they were approached by the confederate, who introduced himself as a student gathering material for his master's thesis and asked whether the participant would fill out a questionnaire on how to optimize the city traffic. As seen in Figure 5.2, drivers under the "fear-then-relief" condition were considerably more likely to fill out the questionnaire than the other drivers.

However, one could ask whether the increased compliance of people who first experience fear and then see its source is gone results from the specific dynamics of emotion or from the very fact of acting under fear. In other words, would it be possible to achieve similar or perhaps greater compliance if – instead of making them experience the fear-then-relief sequence – people were just frightened and left in this emotional state? If the answer to this question were positive, it would

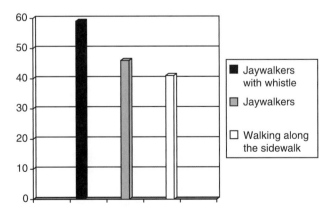

FIGURE 5.1   Percentage of participants who consented to fill out the questionnaire in particular groups. Adapted from Dolinski and Nawrat (1998).

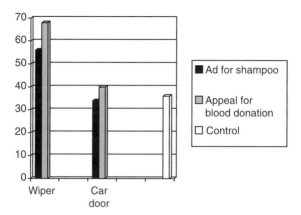

FIGURE 5.2   Percentage of participants who complied with a request in particu-lar groups. Adapted from Dolinski and Nawrat (1998).

imply that the key-factor of increased compliance was the fear itself and not its sudden withdrawal. We devoted another of our experiments to this problem.

The study involved high-school students who were individually invited to our laboratory for "measurements of various skills and abilities". Participants were randomly allocated to one of three experimental conditions: group 1 experienced anxiety, group 2 experienced anxiety that was subsequently reduced, and group 3 (control) was not subjected to any initial procedure. Participants from groups 1 and 2 were informed that they would take part in a study concerning the effect of punishment on learning. They were told: "Your task will be to learn associations of various words. However, should you make an error while learning, you will be given a mild, not very painful electric shock." Participants from group 3 were told that the experiment concerned visual–motor coordination: "Your task will be to throw darts at targets at various distances."

Subsequently, in all the conditions, the students were informed that the experiment would begin in a few minutes and asked to wait in the corridor, near the laboratory. In the case of group 2, after about 2 minutes an experimenter would come up to the participants to tell them that the professor who supervised the laboratory had just decided to postpone the experiment to the following week – so instead of the "electric shock" experiment the students would take part in another study in which they would have to throw darts at various distances. It was explained that this new study required some preparation in the lab, so the students were asked to wait a little longer in the corridor.

During the waiting period before the experiment started, each participant was asked by a female student to join a charity action for an orphanage. She was the experimenter's confederate, but appeared to be totally unattached to the experi-ment. Students who complied with this request were also asked how many work-ing hours they were willing to devote to this action. The results of the study upheld our hypothesis that it was the "fear-then-relief" sequence, and not the emotion of anxiety itself, that led to the higher degree of compliance. In fact, this experiment

TABLE 5.1 Percentage of participants who complied with the request and the average number of days of activity they declared. Adapted from Dolinski and Nawrat (1998)

	Participants who complied (%)	Average days of activity declared
Fear	37.5	.625
Fear-then-relief	75.0	1.150
Control	52.5	1.025

revealed that the participants in group 1 (induced anxiety), who felt the greatest amount of fear, complied less frequently than participants in group 3 (control). Table 5.1 presents the summary data for the study.

As we can see, the increased compliance achieved in our experiments resulted from the experienced sequence of fear followed by relief. However, this raises further methodological doubts: A relief from fear most certainly is a pleasant emotional state. We know from other studies (e.g. Batson, 1991; Isen, 1987; Schaller & Cialdini, 1990) that positive emotions themselves can make people polite and compliant with various requests. Perhaps our participants complied with the requests only because they were in a good mood? Although we asked the drivers participating in our "parking" experiment to fill out the fear questionnaire and we did not find any relevant differences in the fear level across the designed experimental conditions, we could not exclude the possibility that the groups would differ according to the intensity of the positive emotions. To check the impact of the positive emotions on compliance, we returned in our next experiment to the idea of inserting leaflets behind the wipers of cars parked in places where parking was forbidden. This time the experimental design was extended with the condition where real police tickets were inserted behind the wiper. In this way we created the situation when the driver's negative emotions were not removed after reading the "leaflet." (We wanted to make sure that the increased compliance achieved in our experiments resulted from the "fear-then-relief" experience, and not the emotion of fear itself.) In addition to this change in experimental design, we also modified the request. This time a young woman would approach the drivers, introducing herself as a student gathering material for her master's thesis and asking them to fill out a questionnaire that was to take them a quarter of an hour. All drivers who agreed to do this received the PANAS scale (Watson, Clark, & Tellegen, 1988), which in fact is not that time-consuming to fill out. This became our tool to measure the positive and negative emotion levels of participants.

Again it turned out that drivers who found the hair-growth stimulating shampoo leaflet behind the wipers of their cars agreed to fill out the questionnaire more frequently, and those who found the real police tickets and were still under negative emotions hardly ever complied with the confederate's request. In this experiment, however, the focus was the analysis of the PANAS scale results obtained in the different groups of the experiment. As one could have expected, the drivers who got the real ticket experienced higher levels of negative emotions than the participants in the other groups. However, there were no differences in the positive emotion levels. These results show that increased compliance achieved in the "fear-then-relief" conditions cannot be explained by the fact that people relieved from fear experience positive emotions, as these emotions are not any stronger in the "fear-then-relief" condition than in the control group.

Why Compliance after "Fear-then-Relief"? An Attempt at Explanation

The experiments presented above allowed us to make sure that the sudden and unexpected removal of the source of fear makes people who have just experienced the fear more compliant with demands and requests addressed to them. Why? We should probably start searching for the key to understanding this phenomenon by taking a closer look at the very nature of emotion. It is commonly assumed that the central core of any emotion is the change in action readiness (e.g. Frijda, 1986; Oatley & Jenkins, 1996). Every emotion we experience launches a specific action program uniquely designed for this emotion. The feeling of happiness, for example, usually appears as a result of our achievement of a partial goal within a broader action plan; this triggers the program that we follow and – if needed – modify in order to complete the rest of the plan. Anger results from the frustration at being unable to achieve our aim, and as a consequence we either intensify our attempts to reach this aim or we become aggressive. Sorrow usually appears when an important intention has not been realized or when the current target is lost, and the action plan that starts up then is usually based on remaining passive, or making up a new plan, or seeking help.

The emotion of fear, which is the focal emotion in this chapter, launches reactions aimed at stopping all current actions and at the same time increasing cautiousness toward external surroundings – standing still, or running away (e.g., Denny, 1991; Tuma & Maser, 1985). Because in most cases fear appears when the subject feels endangered, these kinds of reaction are usually adequate. However, in a specific fear-then-relief situation, the action program launched by fear ceases to be adequate for the changed circumstances. Before a new and more adequate program is started, there is a very specific (and probably short-lasting) state of a "break between programs." The realization of one program has just been suspended because the stimulus justifying the emotion of fear disappeared, and a new program suitable to the new situation has not yet been coined. We may assume that during this moment of disorientation people function automatically and mindlessly, reacting with ready behavioral models (scripts) assimilated in the past. This interpretation is in accordance with the results of another experiment by Dolinski and Nawrat (1998), inspired by the famous field study by Langer, Blank, and Chanowitz (1978).

The participants in our study were individuals crossing the street where it was not allowed. In half of the cases, the fact was just recorded, but the remaining participants heard a police whistle (produced by the experimenter) as they crossed the street. These participants typically turned round trying to locate the whistle, realized it had been a joke and there was no real threat of being fined, and kept on crossing the street. Next, each participant was approached by a confederate asking for a donation and carrying a moneybox. As in the original experiment by Langer et al. (1978), he formulated the request only ("Excuse me, would you please give us some money?"), or the request with placebic justification ("Excuse me, we are collecting money. Would you please give us some because we have to collect as much money as possible?"), or the request with real justification ("Excuse me, we are from the organization called "Students for the Handicapped." Would you please join our charity action because we have to collect as much money as possible to cover the cost of a holiday camp for mentally handicapped children?").

Results showed that in the emotionally neutral conditions (when participants were not disturbed by the whistle while jaywalking), people usually behaved in a rational and thoughtful manner. They hardly ever decided to drop money into the box when the request was not accompanied by any justification or when the justification was placebic, and frequently made donations when it was explained who collected the money and for what purpose. The participants who found themselves in the fear-then-relief conditions reacted quite differently: It was enough to equip the request with the placebic justification to increase their inclination to reach for their purses, as compared to the situation when no justification for the request was provided. It also turned out that under the fear-then-relief condition, the participants approached with any of the weird messages (e.g. request with placebic justification or without any justification) hardly ever asked any questions about the aim of the action and the organization behind it. However, such questions were common among the neutral emotional-state participants (see Table 5.2).

In terms of the frequency of compliance with the request, as well as the verbal expression of the participants' doubts, this pattern of results is then quite congruent with the assumption that the fear-then-relief technique – along with some

TABLE 5.2 Percentage of participants who offered money spontaneously (without asking any questions) and who asked for additional information concerning charity action. Adapted from Dolinski and Nawrat (1998)

	Jaywalkers with whistle			Jaywalkers		
	Request only	Request plus placebo information	Request plus real information	Request only	Request plus placebo information	Request plus real information
Participants offering money (%)	38.7	76.0	71.9	11.3	15.1	58.5
Participants asking for additional information (%)	20	8	–	49	57	–

other forms of social influence (see Cialdini, 2001) – induces people into a state of mindlessness, which in turn promotes compliance.

Also, the results obtained in two other experiments we conducted support the above thesis. In these experiments, we assumed that if mindlessness underlies increased compliance in a fear-then-relief situation, then the compliance should decrease when the person is forced back to mindful reasoning (Dolinski, Ciszek, Godlewski, & Zawadzki, 2002). To verify this assumption, in the first experiment we created the fear-then-relief condition by suddenly grabbing people coming out of a mall by their shoulders: When they turned around in astonishment, they realized their assailant was a blind man in dark glasses and with a white walking stick. In some cases, the blind man would say only: "Oh, excuse me." In other cases, he added: "How much time is left till [. . .] o'clock?" specifying the time so that the correct answer was "about three-and-a-half hours." The participants in this group usually looked at their watches and calculated the time left till the stated deadline. We assumed that this action demanded certain cognitive activity, which should shift subject's functioning from the mindless to a more mindful level. Having answered the blind man's question, the participant was accosted by another confederate, who asked him or her to spare 5 minutes to fill out a questionnaire. This request was also addressed to participants in the control group who had not met the blind man. The proportion of participants who complied with the request was identical in the control group and the group forced to mindfulness (30%). Participants who experienced the fear-then-relief sequence but were not made to return to mindfulness considerably more often agreed to fill out the questionnaire (53%). A similar pattern of results was obtained in another experiment by Dolinski et al. (2002), where mindfulness of participants was induced in a different way: A blind man suddenly grabbed people coming out of a mall by their shoulders, asking them "Excuse me, is that you?" This made the participants explain that they did not know the man, and also linger on the curio of the whole situation. Hence, mindlessness connected with the experience of the fear-then-relief sequence turns out to be a necessary condition for increased compliance.

Although there is common agreement among psychologists that in many social situations people react mindlessly and automatically, scientists do not agree as to whether this is caused by motivational deficits (e.g. Navon, 1984; Neisser, 1976) or by the limitation of cognitive resources (e.g. Posner & Snyder, 1975; Taylor, 1981).

Personally, I would defend the position that mindlessness can be evoked by either of these factors. In the experiments by Langer et al. (1978), the participants behaved mindlessly only when they agreed to allow a man who provided any sort of justification for his request to make five copies to cut into the line at the copier. It did not matter to the participants whether in this situation he explained: "Because I'm in a rush" or "Because I have to make some copies." However, when they heard that the man wanted to make twenty copies, the justification for the request started to matter. This time the request was granted more often when the man justified himself by saying "Because I'm in a rush" than by saying "Because I have to make some copies." So the participants remained mindless when asked to let the man make five copies, but they became mindful when asked to let him make twenty copies. Langer (1989) assumes that people start to function mindfully whenever remaining in the state of mindlessness would be too costly for them. If someone asks to make five copies without queuing, the amount of time lost is minimal and the people waiting in the line remain in the mindless state. However, when they hear twenty copies they become cautious, as prolonged mindlessness could be too costly.

Does this apply to the situation when the source of fear suddenly disappears? A typical example of a fear-then-relief condition would be the situation that is probably familiar to every car driver. Immediately following a very dangerous traffic commotion, drivers tend to make simple "silly" mistakes. Obviously, very often people have a lot to lose while being under impact of fear-then-relief. According to Langer (1998) they should be highly motivated to avoid mindlessness and, consequently, to shift their functioning to the thoughtful level. Apparently, however, they remain in the mindless state. Why? Not because the drivers no longer care about being cautious (which would be a motivational deficit), but, most probably, because at this very moment they are not able to remain fully cautious (due to cognitive resource deficits).

Although I do agree that mindlessness can occur in routine and recurrent situations (such as those investigated by Langer et al., 1978) and that this mindlessness results mostly from the lack of motivation to behave mindfully, I would suggest that the outcome of a sudden withdrawal of the sources of one's fear can also result in a deficit of cognitive resources. Let us return here to examples brought up at the opening of this chapter. Both the KGB prisoner and the woman accused of witchcraft were most highly motivated to act mindfully, as their lives depended on what they would say to the interrogators. They incriminated themselves not because of lack of motivation to pay attention to what was going on, but because at a certain moment their cognitive capacity was too deficient to let them estimate the situation properly.

Together with Michal Ciszek, Kacper Godlewski and Michal Zawadzki, we carried out a series of experiments and the results were totally in line with the above assumption (Dolinski, Ciszek, Godlewski, & Zawadzki, 2002). In the first of these experiments, we checked whether the fear-then-relief sequence had any impact on the speed and accuracy of the perception of emotion expression. The participants were induced into a state of fear by the procedure described previously: by informing them they would receive an electric shock as a part of the experiment they were to take part in. One of the groups was left with this information to experience continuous fear; the other experimental group was informed that due to some changes in the research schedule they would take part in a different experiment, where they would have to throw darts, and electric shocks were not planned (fear-then-relief condition). In the experimental design, there was also a control group, where the participants were told from the beginning that they would throw darts. Regardless of the type of experimental manipulation applied, all participants were next asked – before the "proper" test was to start – to take part in a short test on the perception of facial expressions of emotion. The idea of the study was based on the original experiment by Hansen and Hansen (1988). Each participant was shown a table of 72 photographs of the same face. There were 71 photos of a smiling face, among which there was one photo of a frightened face (or vice versa in another experimental group). We found out that in the fear-then-relief conditions, participants needed more time to find the "different" face than did the participants in the remaining two groups (i.e. the fear group and the control group). The results indicated, therefore, that the fear-then-relief sequence does affect the simple functions of perception responsible for the speed of detecting the emotion expression. In another experiment, we manipulated emotions in a similar way, but the task set afterwards was cognitively much more complex and had nothing to do with emotions. This time the participants were to do some mental reckoning: to add and subtract lines of three two-digit numbers (e.g.: $34 - 12 + 36 = \ldots$) in their minds only. We found that the fear-then-relief participants managed to solve fewer tasks within 3 minutes than the fear group and the control group participants.

It is noteworthy that the theoretical model outlined here assumes that the compliance evoked by the fear-then-relief sequence is underlain by one's momentary inability to employ an adequate action program. The program connected with the experienced fear is inactive and the new one has not started yet. From this perspective we could expect, however, that increased compliance should be observed not only after the sudden and unexpected withdrawal of the source of fear, but also after the sudden withdrawal of the sources of other emotions. This problem became the subject of another series of experiments in our empirical research project.

HAPPINESS-THEN-DISAPPOINTMENT

If we accept that every emotion starts up a specific action program, then we should also agree that in any specific situation where the sources of the particular emotion suddenly retreat or disappear, the action program launched by this unique affective state ceases to be adequate for the changed circumstances. Consequently, regardless of the type of emotion, the specific state of the "break between programs" should occur: The current program has just been suspended because the stimulus justifying this particular emotion disappeared, and a new program suitable to the new situation has not yet been coined. Being in the "break between programs" state complicates the rational processing of information. But because a human being cannot stay totally passive and inactive, he or she reacts automatically and uses readily available patterns of reactions (scripts) assimilated in the past.

Although on the basis of the discussion presented above one may conclude that compliance effects could be achieved by the sudden withdrawal of any emotion, it should be stressed that our experiments described so far concentrated solely on the consequences of the sequence: fear – then – relief. Therefore, in order to verify whether our previous results could possibly be generalized over other sequences of emotions, we had to conduct experiments where the sources of other emotions were withdrawn. Because fear is considered a negative emotion, it was extremely interesting to see what would happen when some positive emotions suddenly disappear. In our everyday lives this happens quite often; let's take the example of a man who regularly takes part in a lottery. While watching TV in the afternoon, he learns that the numbers he always chooses are the winning ones. Undoubtedly, he experiences great joy. However, when his wife returns home it turns out that this time she forgot to bet the lucky combination at the lottery agency. Needless to say, the husband's joy will cease immediately, and most probably he will become sad or angry.

In our research (Nawrat & Dolinski, in press), we decided to create a similar situation. We intended to induce some of our participants into a positive emotional state, which subsequently would be suddenly changed into disappointment. We expected that people undergoing such a specific emotional sequence should be more willing to comply with a request addressed to them than would the participants of the control group.

People walking along a small street in the city of Wroclaw became the participants of our first experiment on this question. The participants were randomly assigned to one of two groups. In the experimental group, they found a slightly crumpled piece of paper resembling a 50zl banknote (approx. $13). After picking it up they would discover that it was a banknote-like advertisement for a new car wash. The participant's typical reaction was to throw the "false" banknote into a garbage can. The control group participants were not misled with any false banknotes. Then a female confederate waiting round the corner with a travel bag asked each of the participants to watch her luggage for a short time. She explained: "I urgently have to see my friend who lives on the fifth floor of this house and my bag is too heavy, I can't carry it with me upstairs." The results of the experiment showed that people who picked up the banknote-like leaflet agreed almost twice as often to take care of the bag as people who had not found anything resembling a banknote while walking down the sidewalk.

In another experiment, we wanted to check the reactions of German students who learned from their professor that they had received the "excellent" or "1" grade for their tests (the American "A" grade) only to find out after a while that the professor had made a mistake and their actual grade was just the "sufficient" or "3" (the C grade). The reversed situation was also created in this experiment: First the student learned he received the "sufficient" grade (3), and he later learned that actually the grade was "excellent" (1). In the experimental design, there were also groups where the professor did not make mistakes and informed the students about the good or the bad news right away.

The students were then informed that the school would participate in a summer street party in 3 months' time and that an information booth and a buffet with cakes and coffee needed to be prepared. The school administration asked the students for voluntary help and support. To make the planning easier, the students were asked to put their names on a list specifying how many hours (between 1 and 8) they could work at the information booth on the "party" Sunday.

The results of the experiment are shown in Table 5.3. It turned out that in the conditions of the sudden change of the experienced emotion the students were more inclined to offer their contribution to the school event than in the other conditions. Although this effect was especially strong when the information about the bad grade was replaced by the information about the good one, the reversed situation (i.e. when the initial good news was replaced by the

TABLE 5.3 Average number of stated working hours in each experimental condition. Adapted from Nawrat and Dolinski (in press)

Emotional state	Working hours
Negative-then-positive	3.06
Positive-then-negative	2.06
Negative	1.60
Positive	1.13
Control	1.20

information about the lower grade) also made the participant compliant with the final request.

In other words, it can be said that the withdrawal of emotions is an effective instrument of social influence that works no matter whether the participants experience first disappointment and dissatisfaction, and then happiness and the sense of well-being, or whether the sequence of these emotions is reversed. This means that not the valence itself of the experienced emotions but rather the fast change in emotion quality leads to the increased compliance. For this reason we hereby propose the term *emotional see-saw* for all types of this phenomenon. As we all know, a see-saw goes up and down, and this sudden change of opposite directions is in its nature. The term we propose underscores the point that the main feature of such situations is the specific dynamics of emotion resulting from the withdrawal of the stimulus that justified the experience of the emotion in the first place.

In another of our studies, we needed to make sure whether the consequences of the sudden withdrawal of the sources of negative emotions and of positive emotions actually were alike. Additionally, we wanted to check whether the emotional see-saw would "work" in the conditions when the final request was so absurd that its fulfillment would prove mindlessness. This study was conducted by phone. The experimenter phoned randomly chosen people introducing herself as an employee of the Polish Telecom. In some of the experimental conditions, she informed the interlocutor that the computer had calculated an overpayment in his or her account, and he or she would soon receive a return of a considerable sum of money. Other participants were told that the computer had calculated a considerable overdue sum of money to be paid by the participant. Half of the participants were left in this induced emotional state, the other half after a short while were told that the computer had actually identified another telephone owner with the same name but a different address. Regardless of the type of manipulation, the confederate then said: "Polish Telecom is presently testing the permeability of the telephone lines. In connection with the introduction of the TELPOCOL system, I would like you to put the receiver of your telephone to your other ear . . ." After three seconds she asked: "Have you done this?" In the control group, where no emotional state was induced, this message was presented right after the confederate introduced herself as the employee of Polish Telecom. The participants'

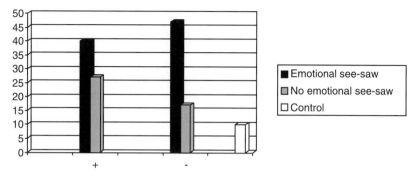

+ Initially induced emotion: POSITIVE
− Initially induced emotion: NEGATIVE

FIGURE 5.3   Percentage of participants who agreed to put the receiver to their other ear under each experimental condition. Adapted from Nawrat and Dolinski (in press).

confirmation that they had put the receiver to their other ear was treated as mindless compliance to an absurd request. While this reaction sporadically occurred in the control group or in the groups where either the positive or the negative emotion was induced, it was considerably more common in the conditions where information justifying negative emotions had been suddenly withdrawn, or where the source of positive emotions had been withdrawn (see Figure 5.3).

The pattern of results obtained in the experiment confirms the thesis that the sudden withdrawal of the source of experienced emotion (no matter whether negative or positive) leads to an increase in compliance. Furthermore, these results can be treated as another confirmation of the thesis that mindlessness underlies the increased compliance observed in the situations explored by our research.

CONCLUSIONS AND PERSPECTIVES FOR FURTHER RESEARCH

In the experimental research of emotion dynamics, it is nearly always assumed that an emotion appears, quickly reaches its peak intensity, and then gradually subsides. This decline of emotion is natural and undisturbed by any external factor. For example, psychologists describe widows' mourning by analyzing the long-lasting process of their adjustment to the new situation (Shontz, 1975), or they describe the dynamics of fear felt by parachutists (Epstein & Fenz, 1965). I have no doubt that this kind of research is highly valuable. It seems, however, that psychology has not paid enough attention so far to the situation in which the stimulus evoking a certain emotion is followed by another stimulus that removes the cognitive justification for having experienced the former emotion. Within the frame of the experiments presented above, my colleagues and I managed to demonstrate that people who experience such situations are particularly susceptible to social pressure. Our latest research provides more specific data on the effectiveness conditions of the emotional see-saw induction social influence technique and the psychological nature of the emotional see-saw state.

In some of these experiments, we verified whether it was relevant that one person induce the emotion and withdraw its source and a different person formulate the request, or whether both activities (i.e. emotion induction–withdrawal and request formulation) could be realized by the same person (Blaszczak, Koterski, & Dolinski, 2003). It turned out that this factor mattered when the subject asked to fulfill a request could assign some malicious intentions to the person who formulated the request and induced–withdrew the emotion ("she wanted to frighten me", "he plays with me", "she doesn't reckon with me"). In such cases the increase of compliance followed only when the person who threatened the subject was different from the one who formulated the request. However, when in another experiment we told the participants we had found a wallet and asked whether they had lost one, the results were quite different. When, after reaching into their bags or pockets, they found their wallets to their great relief, we asked them to mail a letter for us. They would comply with this request with equal frequency regardless of whether the person who induced fear (i.e. suggested they might have lost their wallets) produced the request or whether it was another person who had appeared incidentally there.

In yet another study (Spiewak, 2004), we found some evidence that the efficiency of the emotional see-saw technique could be linked to the deficit of vacant cognitive resources that potentially could enable more rational reactions, such as refusing requests whenever compliance would act against the subject's own interest.

Our research team carried out other experiments where no relation was found between pre-experienced emotional see-saw and compliance with persuasive messages. The experiment by Gusztyla (2005) was carried out during a seminar in psychology. At the beginning of the class, the experimenter entered the room and introduced herself as the representative of the senate of the university. She claimed that the Ministry of Education was performing a random survey of the student knowledge level and hence the students were going to write an unannounced test on the basics of human sciences. In certain cases, it "turned out" that the experimenter forgot the tests and had to go and fetch them (induced fear condition). In other cases, it "turned out" that the tests had been meant only for senior students (fear-relief sequence). There was also a control group in the experimental design: The senate representative did not appear in the class and the necessity of writing the test was not even mentioned. The experiment then developed identically, regardless of the initial experimental condition: The teacher asked the students to read an essay, supposedly written by a professor of geography. The essay presented the numerous threats of the greenhouse effect, caused by increased concentration of certain gases in our atmosphere. The essay suggested that within less than 20 years the effect could lead to global catastrophe. It concluded with a set of indications as to how an average human being could contribute to the reduction of the threat – paper, glass, and metal recycling; moderate usage of motor vehicles; electricity saving; elimination of freon containers; etc. Next, the students were asked to fill out a questionnaire measuring their beliefs in the occurrence of the greenhouse effect and its negative consequences within the nex 20 years. They were also asked if they agreed with the thesis that people should act so as to eliminate the threat. It turned out that while induced fear increased the students' acceptance of the essay theses, the fear-then-relief results did not differ from those obtained in the control group.

Zawadzki (2002) obtained a similar pattern of results in his experiment on the effectiveness of commercials. On a TV screen, participants watched 10 s commercials of various products. Some of the participants watched only the commercials. Others, prior to the commercials, watched a series of photographs; half of those participants were first presented with a series of smiling faces and then a series of terrified faces; the other half viewed the photographs in the reverse (terrified–smiling) sequence. Next, all participants were asked to fill out a questionnaire estimating their willingness to purchase certain goods. One of these was the Barilla pasta advertised in one of the commercials. The key finding of this experiment was that participants' declarations to purchase the advertised product did not depend on their emotional states.

However paradoxical this might seem, the results indicating the absence of any just-experienced emotional see-saw effects on participants' compliance with persuasive messages are totally congruent with our expectations. People in this specific emotional state lack cognitive resources, which makes it difficult for them to pay attention to, process, or remember the new incoming data. Hence, although the emotional see-saw promotes behavioral compliance, it can at the same time impede permanent attitude changes.

Psychology of social influence is by no means the only domain where the experience of the rapid emotional dynamics analyzed here could be of importance. Obviously emotions have an impact on different kinds of human behavior, such as aggression (e.g. Berkowitz, 1981; Williams & Caryl, 2002), decision making (e.g. Bechara, 2004; Gilbert, Morewedge, Risen & Wilson, 2004), risk taking (e.g. Dula & Geller, 2003; Yuen & Lee, 2003), creativity (e.g. Grawitch, Munz, Elliot & Mathis, 2003; Kaufmann, 2003) or, more broadly speaking, information processing (see Oatley & Jenkins, 1996; Forgas, 2001 for review). A worthwhile question to ask could be whether suddenly appearing and disappearing emotions could influence human behavior in the same way as emotions analyzed so far, which last for some time and then gradually fade out. Without further empirical research, such questions cannot be answered.

REFERENCES

Batson, C. D. (1991). *The altruism question: Toward a social-psychological answer.* Hillsdale, NJ: Lawrence Erlbaum Associates, Inc.

Bechara, A. (2004). The role of emotion in judgment and decision-making: Evidence from neurological patients with orbitofrontal damage. *Brain and Cognition, 55*, 30–40.

Berkowitz, L. (1981). On the difference between internal and external reactions to legitimate and illegitimate frustrations: A demonstration. *Aggressive Behavior, 7*, 83–96.

Blaszczak, W., Koterski, M., & Dolinski, D. (2003) Kto wzbudza strach a kto prosi? W poszukiwaniu determinant efektywnosci hustawki emocjonalnej [Who horrifies and who asks for? In search of determinants of the fear-then-relief effectiveness]. *Czasopismo Psychologiczne, 9*, 261–269.

Cialdini, R. B. (2001). *Influence: Science and practice.* Boston: Allyn & Bacon.

Denny, M. R. (Ed.). (1991). *Fear, avoidance, and phobias. A fundamental analysis.* Hillsdale, NJ: Lawrence Erlbaum Associates, Inc.

Dolinski, D., Ciszek, M., Godlewski, K., & Zawadzki, M. (2002). Fear-then-relief, mindlessness, and cognitive deficits. *European Journal of Social Psychology, 32*, 435–447.

Dolinski, D., & Nawrat, R. (1998). "Fear-then-relief" procedure for inducing compliance. Beware when the danger is over. *Journal of Experimental Social Psychology, 34*, 27–50.

Dula, C. S., & Geller, E. S. (2003). Risky, aggressive, or emotional driving: Addressing the need for consistent communication in research. *Journal of Safety Research, 34*, 559–566.

Epstein, S., & Fenz, W. D. (1965). Steepness of approach and avoidance gradients in humans as a function of experience: Theory and experiment. *Journal of Experimental Psychology, 70*, 1–12.

Forgas, J. P. (Ed.). (2001). *Feeling and thinking.* Cambridge: Cambridge University Press.

Frijda, N. H. (1986). *The emotions. Studies in emotion and social interaction.* Paris: Maison de Sciences de L'Homme and Cambridge: Cambridge University Press.

Gilbert, D. T., Morewedge, C. K., Risen, J. L., & Wilson, T. D. (2004). Research report. Looking forward to looking backward: The misprediction of regret. *Psychological Science, 15*, 346–350.

Grawitch, M. J., Munz, D. C., Elliot, E. K., & Mathis, A. (2003). Promoting creativity in temporary problem-solving groups: The effects of positive mood and autonomy in problem definition on idea-generating performance. *Group Dynamics, 7*, 200–213.

Gusztyla, K. (2005). *Wplyw emocji na przetwarzanie i uleglosc wobec komunikatow perswazyjnych* [The influence of emotion on information-processing and compliance with persuasive messages]. Unpublished doctoral dissertation, Maria Curie-Sklodowska University, Lublin, Poland.

Hansen, C. H., & Hansen, R. D. (1988). Finding the face in the crowd: An anger superiority effect. *Journal of Personality and Social Psychology, 54*, 917–924.

Herling-Grudzinski, G. (1965). *Inny swiat* [A different world]. Paris: Institut Literaire S.A.R.L.

Isen, A. (1987). Positive affect, cognitive processes, and social behavior. In: L. Berkowitz (Ed.), *Advances in experimental social psychology* (vol. 20, pp. 203–253). New York: Academic Press.

Kaufmann, G. (2003). Expanding the mood–creativity equation. *Creativity Research Journal, 15*, 131–135.

Langer, E. J. (1989). *Mindfulness.* Reading, MA: Addison-Wesley.

Langer, E. J., Blank, A., & Chanowitz, B. (1978). The mindlessness of ostensibly thoughtful action: The role of "placebic" information in interpersonal interaction. *Journal of Personality and Social Psychology, 36*, 635–642.

Navon, D. (1984). Resources – a theoretical soup stone? *Psychological Review, 91*, 216–234.

Nawrat, R., & Dolinski, D. (in press). "See-saw of emotions" and compliance. Beyond the fear-then-relief rule. *Journal of Social Psychology*.

Neisser, U. (1976). *Cognition and reality*. San Francisco: Freeman.

Oatley, K., & Jenkins, J. M. (1996). *Understanding emotions*. Cambridge, MA: Blackwell.

Posner, M. I., & Snyder, C. R. R. (1975). Attention and cognitive control. In R. L. Solso (Ed.), *Information processing and cognition. The Loyola symposium* (pp. 55–85). Hillsdale, NJ: Lawrence Erlbaum Associates, Inc.

Pratkanis, A., & Aronson, E. (2001). *Age of propaganda. The everyday use and abuse of persuasion*. New York: Freeman.

Schaller, R., & Cialdini, R. B. (1990). Happiness, sadness, and helping: A motivational integration. In: R. M. Sorrentino & E. T. Higgins (Eds.) *Handbook of motivation and cognition: Foundations of social behavior* (Vol. 2, pp. 527–561). New York: Guilford Press.

Shontz, F. C. (1975). *The psychological aspects of physical illness and disability*. New York: Macmillan.

Spielberg, C. D., Gorsuh, R. R., & Lushene, R. E. (1970). *State–trait anxiety inventory: Test manual for form X*. Palo Alto, CA: Consulting Psychologists Press.

Spiewak, S. (2002). Miedzy drzwiami a hustawka: Drenaz poznawczy a skutecznosc wybranych technik wplywu spolecznego [Between the doors and the see-saw. Cognitive depletion and the effectiveness of some compliance techniques]. *Studia Psychologiczne, 40*, 23–47.

Taylor, S. E. (1981). The interface of cognitive and social psychology. In: J. Harvey (Ed.) *Cognition, social behavior, and the environment* (pp. 189–211). Hillsdale, NJ: Lawrence Erlbaum Associates, Inc.

Tuma, A. H., & Maser, J. D. (1985). *Anxiety and the anxiety disorder*. Hillsdale, NJ: Lawrence Erlbaum Associates, Inc.

Watson, D., Clark, L. A., & Tellegen, A. (1988). Development and validation of brief measures of positive and negative affect: The PANAS scales. *Journal of Personality and Social Psychology, 54*, 1063–1070.

Williams, R. B. & Caryl, C. A. (2002). Aggression, competition and computer games: Computer and human opponents. *Computer and Human Behavior, 18*, 495–506.

Yuen, K. S., & Lee, T. M. C. (2003). Could mood state affect risk-taking decisions? *Journal of Affective Disorders, 75*, 11–18.

Zawadzki, M. (2002). *Rola kontekstu w skuteczności reklamy telewizyjnej. Huśtawka emocji i odbiór reklamy* [The role of context in TV ad effectiveness. The emotional see-saw and the reception of TV advertising]. Unpublished master's thesis, Wrocław University, Wroclaw, Poland.

6

Fleeting Attraction and Compliance with Requests

JERRY M. BURGER

*I*f you are like me, you can easily think of a time when you agreed to give someone a ride, made a small donation, bought a raffle ticket, volunteered to stuff envelopes, lent a sweater to a friend or in some way went along with a request only to later ask yourself, "What was I thinking?" In other words, we often find ourselves saying *yes* when we really would have rather said *no*. But why? It's not as if the coworker who needed a ride or the neighborhood kid selling raffle tickets used some slick or high-pressure sales technique on us. And most likely you're not a mindless pushover incapable of making a rational decision. So, what's going on here?

The answer is that we simply don't put as much thought into our responses as we believe. A wealth of research findings confirms that people rarely engage in a rational consideration of arguments before responding to a request. Indeed, it would be odd to spend several minutes pondering the pros and cons of buying a box of Girl Scout cookies. Rather, we rely on rules of thumb – what psychologists call *heuristics* – to deal quickly and (usually) efficiently with requests. For the most part, this is a good thing. Each of us is bombarded throughout the day with demands for our attention and action. We learn to navigate our way through these constant demands by relying on simple rules. Your personal set of heuristics might include, *It must be a good cause if many people support it*, *People who dress and act like me are probably honest and trustworthy*, and *I reciprocate acts of kindness by returning favors*. Thus, if you see several people drop money in a collection jar, it's likely your *It must be a good cause if many people support it* heuristic will lead you to donate as well.

Social psychologists have identified a number of heuristics typically shared by people in our culture (Cialdini & Goldstein, 2004; Cialdini & Trost, 1998). This chapter will focus on one of these, the *liking heuristic*. We'll look at a series of studies several colleagues and I have conducted examining the effects of attraction on compliance. This research not only expands our understanding of social influence processes but also illustrates some of the questions and concerns that investigators confront when conducting this type of research.

RESEARCHING SOCIAL INFLUENCE

Like most good scientific investigations, social influence research usually begins with a prediction. For example, we might hypothesize that people are more likely to comply with a large request if they first agree to a relatively small request (i.e., the classic *foot-in-the-door* effect; Burger, 1999). These predictions come from a number of sources. Interestingly, many predictions in social influence research begin with everyday observations (Cialdini, 1980). It is not uncommon for social psychologists to get ideas about compliance by watching salespeople or recruiters go about their job, or by pondering why they themselves recently purchased some useless office supplies or an unwanted set of knives (Cialdini, 2001; Levine, 2003). However, just because salespeople often use a particular tactic doesn't mean the tactic is effective, even if it appeared to have worked on us. Thus, the first step in a program of research often is to demonstrate empirically the effectiveness of a given influence procedure.

Providing evidence that, for example, a short conversation prior to making a request increases compliance is important. But it's also just a start. Most psychologists want to see whether an effect can be replicated, often using different tasks, in different settings and with different kinds of people. Beyond this, researchers also want to explain the psychological processes underlying the effect. That is, at a conceptual level, *why* does this procedure lead to more or less compliance? Explaining the processes underlying the effect often requires that we eliminate alternative interpretations for the findings.

FLEETING ATTRACTION AND COMPLIANCE

Not surprisingly, researchers find we are more likely to do favors for friends than for strangers (Clark, Ouellette, Powell, & Milberg, 1987; Frenzen & Davis, 1990; Williamson & Clark, 1992). We load furniture onto trucks to help friends who are moving, we give friends rides when their cars are in the shop, and we buy fundraiser candy from neighborhood children. There are good reasons for doing these favors. Helping friends nurtures our relationships, and we like knowing that we can call on our friends when we need a helping hand. Indeed, failure to help a friend in need can damage a relationship (Williamson, Clark, Pegalis, & Behan, 1996). It's not difficult to see why most of us come to rely on a rule of thumb that says *I agree to requests from someone I like*, i.e., the liking heuristic.

But what about requests from someone we don't know who momentarily acts like a friend or the kind of person we like? Let's break this question into two parts. First, is it possible that some simple gesture or action could cause us to develop fleeting feelings of attraction for a stranger? Second, could these passing feelings be sufficient to trigger the liking heuristic and thereby increase the chances that we'll agree to a request we otherwise would have ignored?

The answer to the first question is *yes*. Although true friendships take time and effort to develop, brief feelings of liking between two people can be generated rather easily. Over the years, social psychologists have identified several ways to quickly create feelings of attraction between strangers. For example, learning that you and another person share similar opinions, values or personality characteristics is often sufficient to create measurable increases in liking for this other individual (Byrne, 1997). Other studies find that a short conversation with a stranger leads to feelings of attraction (Insko & Wilson, 1977), especially if the conversation includes an exchange of personal information (Collins & Miller, 1994). In fact, simply seeing the same person day after day can lead to an increased liking for that individual, even if the two of you never say a word to one another (Moreland & Beach, 1992). In other words, there are a number of ways to generate fleeting feelings of attraction between strangers.

But can these flickers of attraction lead to significant increases in compliance? For example, if a recruiter were to engage in a short conversation with you before asking you to volunteer your time, would you find this person sufficiently likeable to activate your *I do favors for people I like* heuristic?

We tested this possibility in a series of studies in which we manipulated fleeting attraction toward a stranger using a variety of procedures (Burger, Soroka, Gonzago, Murphy, & Somervell, 2001). In one study, women undergraduates sat across a table from one another while they worked on a timed puzzle task. For three minutes, they crossed out every *l, k* and *s* they could find on a puzzle sheet. The experimenter was not present during the task, but the participants were instructed to stop working when a timer went off. The experimenter always returned exactly 2 minutes after the sounding of the timer. There were three conditions in the study. In the conversation condition, one woman (actually a confederate working with the experimenter) used this extra time to strike up a short and rather predictable conversation with the real participant ("So, what's your major?"). In the mere exposure condition, the two women were instructed to sit quietly until the experimenter reappeared. Participants in the no-contact control condition worked on the puzzle task alone, but were led to believe that another participant was working on the same task in a nearby room. In this condition, the participant saw the confederate only at the end of the study when they were brought together to receive their participation credit.

The experimenter quickly collected the puzzle sheets, gave the two women participation credit, and left the room. At this point, the participant had every reason to believe that the experiment was over. But as the participant and confederate left the laboratory area, the confederate pulled an essay from her backpack and asked the participant a favor. The confederate explained that her English professor wanted class members to ask someone they did not know to read and critique an eight-page paper they had written. The confederate said that she needed one page of written comments about whether the arguments in the essay were persuasive and why, and that she needed the critique by this time the next day. She waited until the participant either agreed to or declined the favor.

Asking someone to read and critique an eight-page paper is not a trivial request. Students who agreed to the request were committing themselves to a time-consuming chore for someone they had just met (although no one actually had to perform the request). No surprise then that only about a quarter of the participants (26.3%) were willing to help the confederate in the no-contact control condition. However, that number nearly doubled when participants had first engaged in a 2-minute conversation with the requester (48.7%). Moreover, this same increase in compliance was found among participants who simply sat quietly across the table from the requester during the study (48.6%).

Thus, the investigation fulfills the first goal we had for the research, i.e., we demonstrated the predicted effect. Two procedures known to increase fleeting attraction – a short conversation and mere exposure – led to an increase in compliance. Apparently these short-lived feelings of attraction were sufficient to trigger the liking heuristic, which then led the participant to respond to the stranger's request as if responding to a friend. However, as is often the case, other interpretations are possible. For example, one might argue that engaging in a short conversation or sitting in a room with another person is more pleasant than sitting in a room by oneself. Indeed, several studies reveal that people generally find social situations more pleasant than time alone (Larson, 1990). In other words, our attraction manipulations might also have put people in a good mood, and past research finds that people are more likely to help others when in a good mood (Isen, Shalker, Clark, & Karp, 1978). Therefore, it's possible that the participants' mood, rather than feelings of attraction, led to the increased compliance in this study.

We ruled out this alternative explanation and bolstered our own account of the effect in a pair of follow-up studies (Burger et al., 2001). In one of these, we again had participants engage in the puzzle task followed by a few minutes of silent exposure to the confederate. In one condition, the confederate asked the participant to read and critique an English essay, as in the initial study. However, in another condition, a third "participant" who supposedly had been working in a separate room was brought into the scene at the end of the study. It was this previously unseen confederate who then made the request. If the increased compliance seen in the initial study was due to the participants' good mood, then it should not matter who made the request. The participant would be in an equally good mood whether the request came from the familiar person or the new confederate. However, if feelings of attraction are responsible for the effect, then increased compliance should be found only when the confederate with whom the participant is familiar makes the request.

The findings supported the attraction explanation. When participants sat quietly in a room with the requester, 55% agreed with the subsequent request. This was significantly more than in the control group (20%), thus replicating the effect in the first study. More importantly, when the participant sat in the room with one person, yet the request came from someone else, only 22.5% agreed to critique the English paper. In other words, the effect uncovered in the first study cannot be explained simply in terms of mood.

Additional evidence for the liking explanation was found in a study in which we manipulated fleeting attraction with bogus personality test scores (Burger et al., 2001). Under the guise of studying first impressions, women undergraduates were told they and a female participant in another room would learn something about one another without actually meeting each other. Participants were given a list of 50 adjectives (for example, *independent, quiet*) and asked to indicate the

20 adjectives that best described them. Upon completing the task, the experimenter explained that the two participants would now get to see each other's lists. The experimenter took the participant's list and returned a few minutes later with an adjective list supposedly completed by the other participant. In fact, the experimenter had quickly filled out the list to indicate either that the participant had a lot in common with this other individual (17 of 20 matches on the test), very little in common (3 of 20 matches) or only some personality characteristics in common (10 of 20 matches). Based on past research, we expected more attraction when participants believed they had many personality characteristics in common with the other person. After studying the bogus list, participants completed a question-naire asking about their first impressions of this unseen individual. We included several questions designed to measure how much participants liked this person.

Finally, the real participant and the other participant (really a confederate) were brought together and given credit for their participation. As in the earlier study, the experimenter quickly left the scene, and the confederate asked the participant to read and critique her eight-page English paper.

Consistent with past research findings, the more participants thought they had in common with the confederate, the more they liked her. More importantly, when participants thought they and the confederate had very similar personalities, they were significantly more likely to agree to the request (76.7%) than when they perceived only some similarities between them (60.0%) or very few similarities (43.3%). Subsequent statistical analyses demonstrated that the feelings of attrac-tion were at least partly responsible for the increase in compliance. That is, parti-cipants liked the confederate when the two women had similar personalities, and the statistical analyses suggest it was this increase in liking that led to the increase in compliance with the request.

Think about the Implications

The findings from the studies reviewed to this point are rather ominous. They suggest that we are all vulnerable to salespeople, recruiters and the like who know a little something about social psychology. Fleeting feelings of attraction can be generated with relative ease, and a short conversation prior to a sales pitch might be sufficient to move us from "I'm not sure" to "I guess so." Consider a study by Dolinski, Nawrat and Rudak (2001). The experimenters asked passersby a few simple questions (e.g., "How are you feeling today?" "How many [final] exams are you taking?"). The experimenters then asked a small request, such as donating money to a charitable cause. As you might anticipate by now, preceding the request with a few friendly questions significantly increased compliance over a condition in which participants were simply presented with the request or when the experimenter spoke without allowing the participant to comment.

But how far can we take this notion? How little does it take to create enough attraction to get us to buy raffle tickets or agree to work at this year's carnival? Results from several studies suggest that generating fleeting attraction can be surprisingly easy, and that the effects of this attraction can be substantial. For example, passersby in one study were more likely to give a stranger money to make a phone call when that person was dressed in a manner similar to themselves (Emswiller, Deaux, & Willits, 1971). In another investigation, waitresses made better tips when they used their first names with customers (Garrity & Degelman, 1990). Would-be donors in another study gave more money to a charitable cause when the person making the request was physically attractive (Reingen & Kernan, 1993). In each of these examples, we can speculate that participants were more likely to part with their money when the requesters made themselves more likeable. We conducted another set of studies to see how far we could push this idea.

INCIDENTAL SIMILARITIES AND COMPLIANCE

We've all had the experience of discovering that a famous actor or singer was born in our home town or that we and an important historical figure have the same birthday. You may have even found yourself bragging about these associations, as if the celebrity's accomplishments were somehow your own. We say things like "I went to the same high school as . . ." or perhaps "My aunt used to live next door to . . ."

As silly as it may seem, numerous investigations demonstrate that we often form emotional bonds with people with whom we share but an incidental similarity. For example, Canadians felt this type of association with their Olympic hero Ben Johnson. When the track star was accused of using illegal steroids, most Canadians explained away the accusations as if they had been accused themselves (Ungar & Sev'er, 1989). Participants in one study rated Rasputin, the "Mad Monk of Russia," more kindly when they thought they shared a birthday with him (Finch & Cialdini, 1989). People often highlight these incidental bonds as a way of feeling good about themselves, such as when college students associate with successful school sports teams by wearing clothing with team logos or referring to victorious teams as "we" (Burger, 1985; Cialdini, Borden, Thorne, Walker, Freeman, & Sloan, 1976).

Several psychological theories address this tendency to align ourselves with people with whom we have something in common (Greenwald, Pickrell, & Farnham, 2002; Tajfel, 1970; Tajfel & Turner, 1979). Perhaps most relevant for our concerns is the notion of *unit relationships* proposed several decades ago by Heider (1958). According to this theory, we form short-lived bonds with people when we perceive a similarity with them that is shared by few others around us. Thus, a unit relationship is formed when someone from Minnesota meets another Minnesotan in San Francisco, but not when the two meet in Minneapolis. Moreover, this bond often includes an affective component, such that we experience feelings of attraction, however fleeting, for people with whom we share a unit relationship.

But can these incidental similarities create feelings strong enough to trigger the liking heuristic? In other words, are we more likely to agree to a request from someone just because that person comes from our home town or has the same birthday we do? Knowing we share this similarity provides no reasonable information about whether to go along with the request. Yet, in theory, even a trivial similarity with a requester might be sufficient to push us from *no* to *yes*, even if we later regret our response.

We conducted a series of studies to test this possibility (Burger, Messian, Patel, del Prado, & Anderson, 2004). Once again, the first study was designed to simply demonstrate the effect. Undergraduate women were recruited for what they believed to be a study on personality and astrology. The study began with the participant and a confederate filling out a questionnaire that asked, among other things, their date of birth. This information was located in a prominent place on the page, which allowed the confederate to see the participant's birth date with a quick glance. After collecting the questionnaires, the experimenter explained that she would distribute some personality tests, but which test the participant received depended on her zodiac sign. The experimenter then turned to the confederate and asked what her birthday was. Sometimes the confederate gave the birth date she had read on the participant's questionnaire, and other times she gave a different birthday. The experimenter then asked the real participant for her birthday. Not surprisingly, virtually all the participants who thought they shared a birthday with the confederate commented on this similarity. However, beyond this initial observation, neither the confederate nor the participant mentioned the coincidence again, and there was virtually no communication between the two the entire time in the lab room. After the experimenter announced that the study was over and left the room, the confederate made the same essay request used in the earlier investigations.

Before learning the results, remember that sharing a birthday with another person provides no useful information about that individual. One might argue that participants in our earlier studies were simply guilty of arriving at conclusions from too little information. For example, it's possible that the short conversation, however bland and uninformative, provided participants with an opportunity to take measure of the requester. Perhaps the participants relied on body language or the way the requester spoke to form an impression of this other person as trustworthy and likeable. But knowing you and another individual share a birthday provides no logical reason as to why you should agree to read that person's essay.

Nonetheless, the simple manipulation created some dramatic effects. Participants agreed to read and critique the essay only 34.2% of the time when asked by a confederate whose birthday was different from their own. But when they believed the confederate had the same birthday they did, 62.2% of the participants agreed to the request. Thus, it appears that even incidental similarities generate enough fleeting attraction to trigger the liking heuristic and lead to increases in compliance.

However, once again, an alternative explanation can be suggested. As in the earlier research, someone could argue that hearing about the similarity, or perhaps just thinking about one's birthday, might have put the participants in a good mood. In fact, it was common for participants to smile and sometimes laugh when they announced that they and the confederate shared a birthday. Thus, it is possible that mood, rather than liking for the confederate, was responsible for the increase in compliance in the similar-birthday condition.

We conducted a second study to rule out this alternative explanation and to replicate the effect using a different procedure and a different request. We led some participants to believe that they shared the same first name as a woman collecting money for a charitable cause. Participants were asked to bring a series of items with them to the experiment, such as a paper clip and a ballpoint pen. Included in these items were five $1 bills. The purpose of this step was to guarantee that all participants had at least this much money with them when they were approached by the requester. One at a time, participants were asked to engage in a "creativity test" in which they spread the items on a tabletop and then wrote down as many creative uses for the items as they could generate in five minutes. Upon completing the task, participants were given credit and dismissed.

What the participants did not know when they left the lab room was that they were being followed. A student working with the experimenter followed the participant down the stairs and out of the building, then used hand signals to identify the participant for the requester. The requester, who wore a name tag with her first name printed on it and who carried a clipboard with material from the Cystic Fibrosis Foundation, casually approached the participant. In one condition, the name tag indicated that the requester had the same first name as the participant. Without introducing herself or drawing attention to her name tag, the requester showed the participant a photograph of a girl suffering from cystic fibrosis, briefly described the disease, and asked for a donation to the Cystic Fibrosis Foundation. In another condition, the requester wrote her real name on the name tag, but identified the girl in the photograph using the participant's first name. Thus, in this condition, the participant learned that someone shared her first name, but it was not the person making the request. Finally, participants in the control condition encountered a requester with a different first name than theirs and were told the girl in the photograph also had a different first name.

Did the pattern from the earlier study replicate? Participants in the control condition donated an average of $1.00 to the Cystic Fibrosis Foundation. But when participants believed they and the requester shared the same first name, they gave an average of $2.07. This increase was not found in the condition in which participants shared their name with the girl in the photograph. In fact, these participants gave an average of only 81 cents. The findings thus replicate the effect – people are more likely to comply with a request when they share an incidental similarity with the requester. More importantly, the results help to rule out the alternative explanation. Simply hearing that someone shared their name did not lead participants to donate more money.

But what evidence do we have that people in this situation actually formed a unit relationship with the requester, an association that then caused them to go along with the request? To bolster our interpretation of the findings, we conducted a study in which people were led to believe they shared "Type E fingerprints" with another individual. This manipulation was particularly effective because the fingerprint type feedback was totally bogus. We not only failed to actually test for fingerprint type, we also made the concept up. Thus, it was not possible for participants to glean any useful information about this other individual simply by knowing his or her fingerprint type.

As in earlier studies, each session consisted of one real participant and one confederate posing as a participant. Participants were told the study was concerned with the relation between biology and personality, and that the researchers were trying to replicate a study in which fingerprint types were used to predict scores on personality tests. The experimenter took each participant's thumbprint and then distributed some personality tests for the participants to complete. In some conditions, as the experimenter gathered up the completed tests, she commented that both the participant and the confederate had Type E fingerprints. Sometimes this announcement was followed up with, "That's very rare. Only about 2% of the population has Type E fingerprints." Other times she said, "Of course, that's not too surprising. About 80% of the population has Type E fingerprints." Thus, some participants believed they shared an uncommon similarity with the confederate, whereas other participants believed the similarity they shared with the confederate was rather common. Returning to the notion of unit relationships, we would expect that people sharing an uncommon similarity would have more fleeting attraction for one another than those sharing a common similarity.

After the study was supposedly over, the confederate made the English paper request used in earlier studies. Participants in the control condition, in which no information about fingerprint type was provided, agreed to the request 48.3% of the time. However, when participants thought they shared an uncommon, albeit trivial, similarity with the confederate, 82.1% agreed to read and critique the English paper. More importantly, when the similarity was common – and thus not likely to generate strong feelings of attraction – only 54.8% agreed with the request. Subsequent studies verified that hearing that they shared an uncommon fingerprint type indeed caused participants to like the confederate. In short, when combined with the earlier investigations, we have substantial evidence not only that incidental similarities can increase attraction, but also that this attraction can trigger the liking heuristic and lead to increased compliance with a request.

SOME REMAINING QUESTIONS

Another feature of research is worth mentioning. A good program of research not only provides answers to the questions we started with; typically, research also generates new questions and suggests new directions for future investigation. Very often these new questions have to do with limitations of the findings, such as whether the effect can be found in other situations, with other types of people, and in other cultures. We'll look briefly at a couple of questions about fleeting attraction and compliance that arise from the research conducted to date.

Is Attraction Necessary?

We have argued that small manipulations, such as engaging in a short conversation or learning about a shared birthday, often lead to fleeting attraction that then leads to reliance on the liking heuristic when one is responding to a request. However, it is reasonable to ask whether all the steps in this process are necessary. Specifically, are feelings of attraction required to trigger the liking heuristic? Perhaps a requester simply needs to act the way friends typically act. Just seeing people behaving as if they were friends might be sufficient to engage an *I agree to requests from friends* heuristic, even though this other individual is not really a friend. If that is the case, then one could suggest that engaging in a small conversation with a stranger does not necessarily increase liking for that person. The increase in compliance we find after the conversation might be the result of the requester acting like a friend, rather than any feelings of attraction for him or her. Interacting with another person also creates the possibility of triggering a number of emotional and social reactions that could affect whether we agree to a subsequent request. For example, we may be better able to empathize with the person's plight or feel a need to maintain or develop a relationship with this individual. Examining the impact of each of these possible reactions provides the starting point for a series of studies.

Only twice in our studies did we measure attraction directly; that is, by asking the participants how much they liked the other person. In both cases, the amount of liking people felt for the requester fell perfectly in line with how often they agreed with the request. A case can be made from statistical analyses that this attraction contributed to the higher compliance rates. However, whether attraction is *always* necessary to trigger the liking heuristic remains an open question.

Is Awareness Necessary?

In each of the studies reviewed in this chapter, participants were aware of the information that triggered the liking heuristic, even if they were unaware of why they agreed to the request. If asked, some participants might have acknowledged in hindsight that they were swayed by the friendly conversation or the fact that they shared a birthday with the requester. But what if the fleeting attraction is generated in a way that is unrecognizable? Would we still see an increase in compliance?

Although psychologists still debate the extent to which people are aware of the events that affect them, several studies suggest that it may be possible to manipulate attraction in ways that bypass the participants' awareness. For example, researchers find that we often like people who mimic our physical appearance (Chartrand & Bargh, 1999). Participants in these studies sit across from confederates who nonchalantly take on the same posture and gestures as the participants. Researchers find an increase in attraction for these confederates, although the participants typically report that they were unaware of what the confederate was doing. As another example, researchers find that making gestures we usually associate with approval or disapproval can create positive and negative feelings about objects and events we are exposed to while making these gestures. Participants in one study were more likely to select a pen as a gift when they earlier had been nodding their head while using the pen, even though they appeared to be unaware of the association (Tom, Pettersen, Lau, & Burton, 1991).

If our attraction for another person can be manipulated without our awareness, then the research reviewed in this chapter suggests it may be possible to increase compliance through some kind of clandestine manipulation. In other words, perhaps a clever salesperson could act in a way that leads us to say "yes" even when we have no idea that anything is going on. At this point, whether this scenario is a real possibility or merely unsettling speculation awaits the results of some yet-to-be-conducted but probably-should-be-conducted research.

REFERENCES

Burger, J. M. (1985). Temporal effects on attributions for academic performances and reflected-glory basking. *Social Psychology Quarterly, 48*, 330–336.

Burger, J. M. (1999). The foot-in-the-door compliance procedure: A multiple-process analysis and review. *Personality and Social Psychology Review, 3*, 303–325.

Burger, J. M., Messian, N., Patel, S., del Prado, A., & Anderson, C. (2004). What a coincidence! The effects of incidental similarity on compliance. *Personality and Social Psychology Bulletin, 30*, 35–43.

Burger, J. M., Soroka, S., Gonzago, K., Murphy, E., & Somervell, E. (2001). The effect of fleeting attraction on compliance to requests. *Personality and Social Psychology Bulletin, 27*, 1578–1586.

Byrne, D. (1997). An overview (and underview) of research and theory within the attraction paradigm. *Journal of Social and Personal Relationships, 14*, 417–431.

Chartrand, T. L., & Bargh, J. A. (1999). The chameleon effect: The perception–behavior link and social interaction. *Journal of Personality and Social Psychology, 76*, 893–910.

Cialdini, R. B. (1980). Full-cycle social psychology. In L. Bickman (Ed.), *Applied social psychology annual* (Vol. 1, pp. 21–45). Beverly Hills, CA: Sage.

Cialdini, R. B. (2001). *Influence: Science and practice* (4th ed.). Boston: Allyn & Bacon.

Cialdini, R. B., Borden, R. J., Thorne, A., Walker, M. R., Freeman, S., & Sloan, L. R. (1976). Basking in reflected glory: Three (football) field studies. *Journal of Personality and Social Psychology, 34*, 366–375.

Cialdini, R. B., & Goldstein, N. J. (2004). Social influence: Compliance and conformity. *Annual Review of Psychology, 55*, 591–621.

Cialdini, R. B., & Trost, M. R. (1998). Social influence: Social norms, conformity, and compliance. In D. T. Gilbert, S. T. Fiske, & G. Lindzey (Eds.), *Handbook of social psychology* (4th ed., Vol. 2, pp. 151–192). New York: McGraw-Hill.

Clark, M. S., Ouellette, R., Powell, M. C., & Milberg, S. (1987). Recipient's mood, relationship type, and helping. *Journal of Personality and Social Psychology, 53*, 94–103.

Collins, N. L., & Miller, L. C. (1994). Self-disclosure and liking: A meta-analytic review. *Psychological Bulletin, 116*, 457–475.

Dolinski, D., Nawrat, N., & Rudak, I. (2001). Dialogue involvement as a social influence technique. *Personality and Social Psychology Bulletin, 27*, 1395–1406.

Emswiller, T., Deaux, K., & Willits, J. E. (1971). Similarity, sex, and requests for small favors. *Journal of Applied Social Psychology, 1*, 284–291.

Finch, J. F., & Cialdini, R. B. (1989). Another indirect tactic of (self-)image management: Boosting. *Personality and Social Psychology Bulletin, 15*, 222–232.

Frenzen, J. K., & Davis, H. L. (1990). Purchasing behavior in embedded markets. *Journal of Consumer Research, 17*, 1–12.

Garrity, K., & Degelman, D. (1990). Effect of server introduction on restaurant tipping. *Journal of Applied Social Psychology, 20*, 168–172.

Greenwald, A. G., Pickrell, J. E., & Farnham, S. D. (2002). Implicit partisanship: Taking sides for no reason. *Journal of Personality and Social Psychology, 83*, 367–379.

Heider, F. (1958). *The psychology of interpersonal relations.* New York: Wiley.

Insko, C. A., & Wilson, M. (1977). Interpersonal attraction as a function of social interaction. *Journal of Personality and Social Psychology, 35*, 903–911.

Isen, A. M., Shalker, T. E., Clark, M., & Karp, L. (1978). Affect, accessibility of material in memory, and behavior: A cognitive loop? *Journal of Personality and Social Psychology, 36*, 1–12.

Larson, R. W. (1990). The solitary side of life: An examination of the time people spend alone from childhood to old age. *Developmental Review, 10*, 155–183.

Levine, R. (2003). *The power of persuasion: How we're bought and sold.* Hoboken, NJ: Wiley.

Moreland, R. L., & Beach, S. R. (1992). Exposure effects in the classroom: The development of affinity among students. *Journal of Experimental Social Psychology, 28*, 255–276.

Reingen, P. H., & Kernan, J. B. (1993). Social perception and interpersonal influence: Some consequences of the physical attractiveness stereotype in a personal selling setting. *Journal of Consumer Psychology, 2*, 25–38.

Tajfel, H. (1970). Experiments in intergroup discrimination. *Scientific American, 223*, 96–102.

Tajfel, H., & Turner, J. C. (1979). An integrative theory of intergroup conflict. In W. G. Austin & S. Worchel (Eds.), *The social psychology of intergroup relations* (pp. 33–47). Monterey, CA: Brooks/Cole.

Tom, G., Pettersen, P., Lau, T., & Burton, T. (1991). The role of overt head movement in the formation of affect. *Basic and Applied Social Psychology, 12*, 281–289.

Ungar, S., & Sev'er, A. (1989). "Say it ain't so, Ben": Attributions for a fallen hero. *Social Psychology Quarterly, 52*, 207–212.

Williamson, G. M., & Clark, M. S. (1992). Impact of desired relationship type on affective reactions to choosing and being required to help. *Personality and Social Psychology Bulletin, 18*, 10–18.

Williamson, G. M., Clark, M. S., Pegalis, L. J., & Behan, A. (1996). Affective consequences of refusing to help in communal and exchange relationships. *Personality and Social Psychology Bulletin, 22*, 34–47.

7

Using Social Norms as a Lever of Social Influence

NOAH J. GOLDSTEIN and ROBERT B. CIALDINI

After years of seemingly inconsistent findings, and after much debate regarding their explanatory and predictive value (e.g., Berkowitz, 1972; Darley & Latané, 1970; Fishbein & Ajzen, 1975; Sherif, 1936), it is now evident that social norms not only prompt, but also guide people's actions (Aarts & Dijksterhuis, 2003; Kerr, 1995; Schultz, 1999; Terry & Hogg, 2000; Turner, 1991). Having reached something of a consensus on *what* norms are capable of doing, a second generation of research has begun to investigate issues such as *when* their causal impact might be greatest and *how* different kinds of social norms might influence human behavior through different mediating processes. Several perspectives have emerged to address these questions, including deviance regulation theory (Blanton & Christie, 2003), social identity and self-categorization theories (e.g., Abrams & Hogg, 1990), and the focus theory of normative conduct (Cialdini, Kallgren, & Reno, 1991). Although our coverage of the normative literature in this chapter concentrates on focus theory, we first provide a brief overview of each of the other two perspectives. In reviewing the three perspectives, we discuss their theoretical underpinnings, describe research findings relevant to each conceptual framework, and identity future directions for study.

DEVIANCE REGULATION THEORY

Imagine that you're Doc, a well-respected medical practitioner and the unofficial leader of a group of seven close friends. Suppose that someone in your circle of friends never covers his nose or mouth when he sneezes. Also suppose that another friend within your circle has an aversion to germs that makes Howard Hughes seem like Pig-Pen from the comic strip *Peanuts*, but is too Bashful to confront the sneezer directly with his concerns. Given your medical background and your desire to alleviate discomfort, you are motivated to do whatever it takes to curb this potentially injurious microbe-disseminating behavior. How would you run your individual-level behavior-modification campaign? Would you stress to the sneezer the positive aspects of those who cover their faces when they sneeze, or would you emphasize the negative aspects of those who don't? According to deviance regulation theory (DRT; Blanton & Christie, 2003), the correct answer to this question depends on whether Sneezy believes that covering one's face while sneezing is a normative or a non-normative behavior.

Why? One of the central foundations of DRT is that attributes, attitudes, and behaviors that are rare are perceived to be more diagnostic of and central to one's identity than are those that are common (e.g., Ditto & Griffin, 1993; McGuire, McGuire, Child, & Fujioka, 1978; Nelson & Miller, 1995). As a result, individuals should be more attentive to the costs and benefits of associating the self with behaviors that deviate from the perceived norm rather than conform to the perceived norm (Blanton & Christie, 2003). According to Blanton and Christie (2003), this motivates individuals to try to preserve or enhance their favorable self-images, both public and private, by seeking deviation from social norms in positive ways and by avoiding deviation from social norms in negative ways. Thus, DRT predicts that attempts to influence human conduct should be more success-ful when the message characterizes people whose behaviors diverge from, rather than those that conform to, the perceived norm. So, how should a communicator frame his or her message? According to DRT, if a constructive behavior (e.g., covering one's face while sneezing) is believed to be normative, the message should be framed to accentuate the negative characteristics (e.g., irresponsible) of those who deviate from the perceived norm (e.g., "Those who don't cover their face are *very irresponsible*"). In contrast, if a deleterious behavior (e.g., not covering one's face while sneezing) is believed to be normative, the message should be framed to accentuate the positive characteristics of those who deviate from the perceived norm (e.g., "Those who cover their face are *very responsible*"). Messages that focus on the characteristics associated with those who conform to the perceived norm will be less effective.

In an experiment designed to test this hypothesis, Blanton, Stuart, and VandenEijnden (2001, Study 1) had their participants read one of two news-paper articles in which the normativeness of students opting for flu shots was varied. The article conveyed that on the basis of previous research, campus health officials expected that either very many or very few students would choose to receive a flu shot. The participants then read one of two articles reporting on a study investigating the personality correlates of immunization. The findings reported in the second article were framed in a way that either linked the decision to get immunized with positive characteristics (e.g., considerate of others) or linked the decision to not get immunized with negative characteristics (e.g., inconsiderate of others). Participants then rated their intention to get a flu shot.

The findings of the study are wholly consistent with DRT (see Figure 7.1). Participants' intentions to get a flu shot were greater in the conditions that characterized the non-normative rather than the normative actions. That is, when the first newspaper article depicted the decision to get immunized as normative, associating negative attributes with those who choose not to get immunized

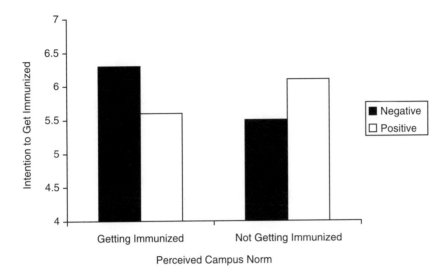

FIGURE 7.1 Intentions to get immunized as a function of perceived student norm and message frame. Higher numbers indicate greater likelihood of getting immunized. Adapted from Blanton et al. (2001) with permission of the authors.

was more effective at strengthening intentions than was associating positive attributes with those who choose to get immunized. However, when the decision *not* to get immunized was depicted as normative, the reverse was true: Associating positive qualities with those who get immunized was more successful at boosting intentions than was associating negative qualities with those who did not get immunized.

Blanton, VandenEijnden, Buunk, Gibbons, Gerrard, & Bakker (2001) provided further support for DRT in an additional study that capitalized on participants' preexisting differences in perceived normativeness of student condom use. Two weeks after reporting their perceptions of the prevalence of condom use on campus, participants read a set of phony testimonials from other students that either ascribed positive traits (e.g., mature, smart) to those who use condoms or negative traits (e.g., immature, stupid) to those who don't use condoms. The researchers found that the more normative participants perceived condom use to be, the more they were influenced by the message that negatively depicted those who don't use condoms. In contrast, the less normative participants perceived condom use to be, the more they were influenced by the message that positively portrayed those who do use condoms.

Thus, according to DRT, if Sneezy believes that most people *do not* cover their faces when sneezing, you might get Happy to say something *positive* about those who *do* cover their faces. On the other hand, if Sneezy believes that most people *do* cover their faces when sneezing, you might get Grumpy to say something *negative* about those who *do not* cover their faces.

SOCIAL IDENTITY AND SELF-CATEGORIZATION THEORIES

Deviating from normative attitudes and behaviors often provides individuals with a sense of uniqueness and personal identity (Blanton & Christie, 2003; Kim & Markus, 1999; Nail, MacDonald, & Levy, 2000), yet people also maintain positive self-evaluations by identifying with and conforming to valued groups (Brewer & Roccas, 2001; Cialdini & Goldstein, 2004; Pool, Wood, & Leck, 1998). Much of the research conducted on this topic over the past two decades has come from the perspective of social identity (Tajfel, 1978; Tajfel & Turner, 1979; see also Hogg & Abrams, 1988) and self-categorization theories (Turner, 1987, 1999).

Although the concept of social identity has taken on a variety of different meanings in various disciplines within social psychology (Brewer, 2001), social identity is often defined broadly as an expansion of the self-concept involving a shift in the level of self-conception from the individual self to the collective self, often based on perceived membership in a social category (Brewer, 2003; Hogg, 2003).

Categorization can occur at various levels of abstraction, from concrete groups of people (e.g., "the Soprano family," "my potato sack racing team," "us guys in Cell Block 4D") to broader concepts (e.g., "citizen," "American," "football referee") (Turner, 1991). Self-categorization theory is an extension of social identity theory that focuses more on the mechanisms and influences of the categorization process (Terry, Hogg, & White, 2000; Turner, Hogg, Oakes, Reicher, & Wetherell, 1987), but the two are often discussed together because of their shared theoretical underpinnings and the similar predictions that are derived from their common perspective.

The social identity and self-categorization perspective contends that behavioral outcomes are influenced by reference group norms, but only for those individuals who consider group membership to be a salient basis for self-representation (e.g., Ellemers, Spears, & Doosje, 2002; Hogg, 2003; White, Hogg, & Terry, 2002). Importantly, one of the primary factors that appears to influence whether group membership is seen as a salient basis for self-conceptualization is the meaningfulness and level of identification that one has for the group (e.g., Terry, Hogg, & White, 1999). For example, researchers found that the perceived norms of participants' reference group of peers and friends was a significant predictor of the participants' intentions to engage in health behaviors (Terry & Hogg, 1996) and household recycling (Terry et al., 1999), but in both cases this was only true for those who strongly identified with the group.

Thus, whereas DRT suggests emphasizing the positive or negative attributes of those who deviate from (rather than conform to) the perceived norm, the social identity/self-categorization perspective suggests highlighting the normative behavior of a psychologically meaningful group – and the more meaningful the group, the greater the likelihood that a target will conform to the norm. Thus, according to this perspective, you might get Sneezy to change his germ-spreading behavior by emphasizing that most members of an ingroup with which he strongly identifies (e.g., the Seven Dwarves) cover their faces when they sneeze.[1] We'll return to the social identity/self-categorization perspective later in the chapter.

FOCUS THEORY OF NORMATIVE CONDUCT

To this point, we have discussed the functions of normative information within two theoretical frameworks, yet one important question still lingers: Just what exactly *are* social norms, anyway? The meaning of social norms has been somewhat amorphous over the decades (for a brief history, see Cialdini & Trost, 1998). Looking both to clarify the definitional nebulousness that had clouded researchers' ability to understand the roles of social norms (see Shaffer, 1983) and to better predict when social norms will influence behavior, Cialdini and colleagues (Cialdini, Reno, & Kallgren, 1990; Cialdini et al., 1991) developed the focus theory of normative conduct. Focus theory has two central postulates. The first is that it is necessary to distinguish between two different types of norms – injunctive and descriptive – that can have drastically different effects on behavior. The second is that a given norm is likely to affect behavior directly to the extent that it is focal in attention. We will consider the evidence for each of these postulates in turn.

Separating Oughts From Is's: Differentiating Injunctive and Descriptive Norms

Much like the distinction that Deutsch and Gerard (1955) made between informational and normative influences, Cialdini et al. (1990) suggested that descriptive and injunctive norms influence conduct through separate sources of human motivation. Akin to what Cialdini (2001) has called "social proof," descriptive norms refer to what is commonly done in a given situation, and they motivate behavior by informing individuals of what is likely to be effective or adaptive behavior in that situation. Injunctive norms refer to what is commonly approved or disapproved within the culture, and they motivate behavior through informal social sanctions. In brief, descriptive norms refer to perceptions of what *is* done, whereas injunctive norms refer to perceptions of what *ought to be* done. The two are sometimes confused as a single construct because what is commonly approved within a culture is also what is commonly done in a culture. However, this is not always the case, as we will see later in the chapter.

The mechanisms through which descriptive and injunctive norms spur and guide people's actions have remained relatively unexplored. However, Cialdini and colleagues (Cialdini, 2003; Cialdini et al., 2007) recently posited that injunctive and descriptive norms influence behavior via different routes. They argued that individuals focusing on descriptive norms need not engage in elaborate cognitive processing of the relevant information because applying the heuristic rule "I should do what most others do" is based primarily on the simple observations of others' situation-specific behaviors. In contrast, acting on information provided by injunctive norms proves a more cognitively demanding course because it is based on an understanding of the culture's moral rules – that is, what others are likely to approve. To test whether injunctive and descriptive norms are mediated through different processes, the researchers had participants watch public service announcements (PSAs) that featured both injunctive and descriptive norms in favor of recycling. Immediately after viewing the ads, participants completed a number of items that assessed their beliefs about recycling norms, their perceptions of the ads, and their recycling intentions. In support of the contention that descriptive and injunctive norms influence behavior through different levels of cognitive analysis, the relationship between recycling intentions and participants' perceptions that the ads conveyed approval for recycling (injunctive norm) was mediated by their cognitive evaluations of the ads' persuasiveness, whereas the effect of descriptive normative information on intentions was direct (i.e., unmediated by considerations of ad persuasiveness). Future work in this area stands to profit from an analysis using behavioral measures rather than intentions.

If the mechanism through which descriptive norms affect conduct is rooted more in perception than in cognition, perhaps its power to motivate behavior might be limited to the setting in which it was originally perceived. Reno, Cialdini, and Kallgren (1993) contended that descriptive norms are more situation-specific in the information they convey, as these norms communicate what others have seen as an effective course of action in that particular setting. Because what constitutes adaptive behavior in a particular setting is not necessarily the same as what constitutes adaptive behavior in a different setting, the researchers suggested that the effect of the descriptive norm is less likely to transfer across situations than is the effect of injunctive norms. This is because injunctive norms more generally convey the kind of behavior that is approved or disapproved within a culture, which is subject to less variation across situations. Therefore, the influence of injunctive norms should transfer across a wide variety of environments. Reno et al. (1993) found that descriptive and injunctive norms against littering were equally successful at reducing littering when the opportunity for their participants to litter occurred in the same setting in which the norm was made salient. However, only the injunctive norm reduced littering rates when the opportunity to litter occurred in an environment that was different from the one in which the norm was made salient.

This is not to say that descriptive norms never transfer across situations or environments, but rather that they are simply less likely to do so than are injunctive norms. Both descriptive norms and injunctive norms are particularly likely to generalize to other situations when they are associated with mnemonic cues that are also present in these other situations, a notion we will return to later in the chapter.

Aligning and Misaligning Norms   One important issue facing communicators who seek to create maximally effective normative messages is whether to attempt to activate injunctive norms, descriptive norms, or both. Recall that two central postulates of focus theory are that norms direct behavior only when they are salient (Kallgren, Reno, & Cialdini, 2000) and that the activation of the injunctive norm or the descriptive norm may elicit considerably different behavioral responses (Reno et al., 1993). Unfortunately, too many communicators fail to be mindful that they must focus the target audience on the type of norm that is aligned with the end objective. For example, officials attempting to raise public awareness of and combat detrimental behavior often make the mistake of characterizing it as regrettably prevalent, and thus unintentionally focus their audience on the unfavorable descriptive norm.

One notable example of a subtle misalignment of injunctive and descriptive norms comes from a commercial produced in the early 1970s by the Keep America Beautiful organization. Designed to infuse America's daily television viewing diet with an extra serving of moral fiber, this public service announcement was considered so moving that *TV Guide* magazine rated it as the sixteenth greatest television commercial of all time ("The fifty greatest," 1999). What set of images did *TV Guide* deem more indelible than the likes of those singing dried grapes from the West Coast, that pitiable early riser who lamented each morning that it was "time to make the donuts," and that pink battery-powered bunny with a penchant for persistent percussion?

The spot begins with a stately and serious looking Native American dressed in traditional garb canoeing across a river. As he paddles through the waterway, we see that the river is effluent-filled and debris-ridden, and that the air is replete with industrial pollutants spewing from smokestacks. After the canoeist pulls his craft along a Styrofoam-laden shore, a driver zooming down an adjacent street tosses a bag of trash out of his car, splattering its contents across the Native American's feet. As a lone teardrop tracks slowly down his previously stoic countenance, a voiceover intones, "People start pollution. People can stop it."

Several years ago, the Keep America Beautiful organization brought back the teary-eyed Native American in another antilittering commercial that in our view retains, indeed amplifies, the potentially problematic feature of the original ad. The camera features several people waiting at a bus stop, engaging in everyday activities such as drinking coffee, reading the newspaper, and smoking cigarettes. After the bus arrives and they all climb aboard, the camera cuts to the empty bus-stop waiting area, now completely covered with cups, newspapers, and cigarette butts. As the camera pans from right to left, it slowly zooms in to a poster of the Native American overlooking the refuse, still with a tear in his eye. As the screen fades to black, the text of the spot's take-home message appears: "Back by popular neglect."

Back by *popular neglect*. What sort of message is conveyed by this phrase and by the litter-filled environments featured in both of these ads? Although the injunctive norm against littering is obvious and powerful, both of the ads present a descriptive norm for littering that indicates that, despite strong disapproval of the behavior, many people do in fact engage in that behavior. Thus, it is possible that the descriptive norm depicting the prevalence of littering behavior may have undermined the potency of the antilittering injunctive norm.

Other examples are abundant. We don't mean to ruffle his feathers, but we question a message conveyed by Woodsy Owl, the lovable but psychologically naïve US Forest Service mascot. In a long-running print ad titled "Gross National Product," Woodsy proclaims, "This year Americans will produce more litter and pollution than ever before." In another example, visitors at Arizona's Petrified

Forest National Park quickly learn from prominent signage that the park's existence is threatened because so many past visitors have been taking pieces of petrified wood from the grounds: "Your heritage is being vandalized every day by theft losses of petrified wood of 14 tons a year, mostly a small piece at a time." Furthermore, to call attention to the need for government intervention against cigarette smoking among children, Federal Drug Administration Commissioner David Kessler publicized the fact that "more than 3 million youths in the US smoke and . . . 3,000 become regular smokers each day" (Scott, 1995). Similarly, a commercial intended to discourage minors from using marijuana depicts a lone middle-school student resisting the pressures of a whole busload of her peers.

Although these pronouncements and depictions may indeed reflect reality and are clearly inspired by good intentions, the influence practitioners behind these campaigns may fail to realize that by using a negative descriptive norm as part of a rallying cry, they might be inadvertently focusing the message recipients on the prevalence, rather than the undesirability, of that behavior. To test this hypothesis, Cialdini and colleagues (Cialdini, 2003; Cialdini, Demaine, Sagarin, Barrett, Rhoads, & Winter, 2006) created two signs designed to deter wood theft at Petrified Forest National Park; one was injunctive in nature and the other was descriptive in nature. The researchers surreptitiously placed marked pieces of petrified wood along visitor pathways, and alternated which of the two signs were posted at the entrance of each pathway. The injunctive normative sign stated, "Please don't remove the petrified wood from the park, in order to preserve the natural state of the Petrified Forest," and was accompanied by a picture of a visitor stealing a piece of wood, with a red circle-and-bar (i.e., the universal "No" symbol) superimposed over his hand. The descriptive normative sign emphasizing the prevalence of theft informed visitors, "Many past visitors have removed the petrified wood from the park, changing the natural state of the Petrified Forest," and was accompanied by a picture of several park visitors taking pieces of wood.

In a finding that should petrify park management, compared to a no-sign control condition in which 2.92% of the pieces were stolen, the descriptive norm message was associated with significantly more theft (7.92%). The injunctive norm message, in contrast, was associated with marginally less theft (1.67%) than the control condition. These results are consistent with the notion that when a descriptive norm for a situation indicates that an undesirable behavior occurs with high frequency, a communicator might indeed cause unintentional damage by publicizing this information. Thus, rather than conveying the descriptive norm, communicators in such circumstances should focus the audience on what kind of behavior is approved or disapproved in that setting.

Of course, norm-based persuasive approaches are most likely to be effective when the descriptive and injunctive norms are presented together and aligned with one another.

To investigate the effect of an information campaign that combined the influences of injunctive and descriptive norms, Cialdini and colleagues (Cialdini, 2003; Cialdini et al., 2007) created a set of three PSAs designed to boost recycling activity in Arizona. Each PSA depicted a scene in which the majority of individuals featured in the ad engaged in recycling, spoke approvingly of it, and spoke disparagingly of a single individual in the scene who failed to recycle. Thus, the act of recycling material was linked to images indicating that recycling activity is both widely performed and widely approved. The PSAs also included humorous dialogue along with information about how to recycle and the benefits of doing so. For example, one of the PSAs featured several cowboys positioned around a campfire:

> Cowboy #1 [holding empty soda can]: "Clem, where'd you put the recycle bin?"
> Clem: "Recycle bin? Just use this here trash barrel."
> Cowboy #2: "Clem, you ig'nant fool. That there sodie can ain't trash. Lots of important things come from stuff we recycle, like Red's cup and Luke's long underwear ... and this here hangin' rope." [Dangles the noose menacingly.]
> Clem [drops the can in the recycle bin]: "Aw, heck, fellers, I was just a-funnin'."
> [A picture of the geographical outline of the state of Arizona then appears on the screen, filled with the faces of scores of different people. The words "Arizona Recycles" accompany the picture.]

In a field test, this PSA and two others like it were played on local TV and radio stations of four Arizona communities. The results revealed a 25.35% net advantage in recycling tonnage over a pair of control communities not exposed to the PSAs.

To return to our earlier example, these findings suggest that it would be effective to inform Sneezy that most people both cover their faces when sneezing and disapprove of those who do not engage in that behavior. It is worth noting that this strategy is not inconsistent with either the DRT or social identity/self-categorization perspectives. In particular, as suggested by DRT, attributing negative characteristics to those who do not engage in the healthy, normative behavior closely mirrors the communication of the injunctive norm in this example. However, focus theory does gain traction over these other perspectives in predicting exactly when descriptive and/or injunctive norms will be adhered to: when they are in focus.

A Focus on Focus: The Importance of Focus

By now, it should be evident that descriptive and injunctive norms are orthogonal constructs that are capable of eliciting considerably different behaviors. However, given that countless social norms have the potential to operate in almost any setting or social situation, what determines which norm or norms will have a direct influence on behavior? Recall that the second postulate of focus theory is that a norm will directly affect conduct to the extent that it is focal (i.e. salient) in consciousness.

Cialdini and colleagues (1990) tested this assertion within the context of littering behavior. Dormitory residents who found a flier in their mailboxes encountered an environment that was prearranged to contain no litter (the control condition), one piece of very conspicuous litter (a hollowed-out, end piece of watermelon rind), or an assortment of different kinds of litter, including the watermelon rind. Why a watermelon rind? The purpose of the large, eye-catching watermelon rind was to ensure that participants would focus on the descriptive norm in that setting regarding the typicality of littering behavior. (Besides, it was safer for the participants than using a banana peel.) Thus, when the environment's only blemish was the watermelon rind, participants would focus on the fact that, with the exception of the rind, littering is uncommon in that setting. On the other hand, when the environment was filled with rubbish in addition to the rind, participants would focus on the fact that littering is common in that setting. Consistent with predictions, the authors found that compared to the littering rate in the clean environment (10.7%), participants in the fully littered environment littered at a significantly higher rate (26.7%), whereas participants who encountered the watermelon rind in the otherwise spotless area littered at a significantly lower rate (3.6%). The finding that the completely litter-free environment actually yielded higher littering rates than the environment containing the lone rind is especially noteworthy because the data cannot be accounted for by other perspectives, such as social learning theory (e.g., Bandura, 1977). That is, if this were simply a modeling effect, participants who observed the discarded rind would have been more likely, not less, to litter than participants in the completely unadulterated environment.

The watermelon study was fruitful in demonstrating how focusing people on a descriptive norm can plant a seed in their consciousness that ultimately sprouts into norm-congruent conduct. However, that study was somewhat limited because the focus was restricted to the descriptive norm. Researchers have also demonstrated the importance of focus when the injunctive and descriptive norms of a setting are not in line with one another. For example, in an experiment conducted by Reno and colleagues (1993, Study 1), library-goers returning to their parked cars passed by a confederate who littered a piece of trash, picked up a piece of trash, or simply walked by. The environment was also manipulated to be either completely devoid or completely full of litter. Much like the rind, the littering of the rubbish was meant to focus participants on the relative presence or absence of other litter in the environment (i.e., the descriptive norm for littering in that setting). The picking up of the litter, on the other hand, was meant to focus participants on the injunctive norm – that is, people generally disapprove of litterbugs and would squash them if they could. The researchers found that compared to those in the control conditions, the library-goers in the descriptive norm focus condition littered less only when the environment was litter-free (see Figure 7.2). However, those in the injunctive norm condition littered less than their control counterparts regardless of the state of the surrounding environment, demonstrating that by focusing the participants' attention on the injunctive norm, the information conveyed by the descriptive norm was rendered uninfluential.[2]

So far, we have discussed some ways in which social norms come to influence behavior. Personal norms, which are an individual's internal standards and principles for particular conduct (Schwartz, 1973, 1977), also have the potential to

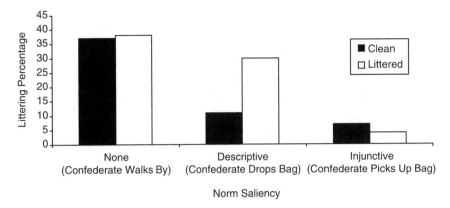

FIGURE 7.2   Littering rates as a function of norm saliency and condition of the environment. Adapted from Reno et al. (1993) with permission of the authors.

direct human conduct. Kallgren et al. (2000) proposed that just as a specific social norm needs to be in focus for it to affect behavior maximally, the same might also be true for personal norms. The researchers administered a questionnaire assessing their participants' personal norms against littering at the beginning of the semester. When participants arrived at the lab later in the semester, half were exposed to a closed-circuit television featuring their own image, whereas the other half watched a closed-circuit television featuring geometric shapes. This focus induction method was rooted in the literature demonstrating that viewing oneself in a television monitor or mirror leads to greater self-awareness, which is associated with increased focus on one's inner traits and states (e.g., Carver & Scheier, 1978; Duval & Wicklund, 1972). Once the participants believed they were done with the study, they were handed a piece of potential litter and were asked to exit through a stairwell. Consistent with focus theory, the investigators found that the strength of participants' personal norms against littering were predictive of their actual littering behavior only when they had focused attention on themselves rather than on the external stimuli. This study helps answer the question, How can people who litter look at themselves in the mirror? At least for those who hold personal norms against littering, the answer appears to be that they don't.

As many of the studies we have discussed to this point suggest, one's behaviors seem to be relatively unaffected by normative information – even one's own – unless the information is highly prominent in consciousness (Cialdini & Goldstein, 2004). Given that relevant norms must be salient to trigger the appropriate norm-congruent behavior, those attempting to persuade others to engage in a particular behavior face the dual challenge of making the norm focal not only immediately following message reception, but also in the future. Cialdini et al. (2007) argue that the long-term effectiveness of persuasive communications such as PSAs is threatened because normative information becomes less accessible over time. They hypothesize that linking an injunctive normative message to a functional

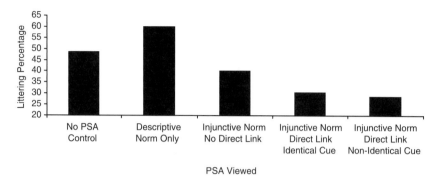

FIGURE 7.3 Littering rates as a function of public service announcement viewed. Adapted from Cialdini et al. (2005) with permission of the authors.

mnemonic cue (see Tulving, 1983) would increase norm accessibility at later times when the norm would not have been focal otherwise. Consistent with their predictions, they found that participants who viewed a PSA in which the wording of an injunctive norm ("You know, people who litter are real jerks") was superimposed directly over a piece of litter (retrieval cue) were significantly less likely to litter a paper towel in a stairwell several hours later than were those who saw the same wording placed elsewhere on the screen (see Figure 7.3). This was the case regardless of whether the retrieval cue featured in the PSA was a paper towel or a newspaper, suggesting that linking social disapproval to the basic category of litter was enough to elicit the desired change (Cialdini et al., 2007). Moreover, in a finding that shows that Woodsy Owl should "give a hoot" about social norms research, participants who saw the phrase "Americans will produce more litter than ever" superimposed on the litter were most likely to litter, demonstrating once again the potential harm caused by characterizing a behavior as regrettably common.

APPLICATIONS OF SOCIAL NORMS RESEARCH TO THE REAL WORLD

Social Norms Marketing Campaigns: "Everybody's Not Doing It"

Should one conclude from the last finding that highlighting descriptive norms is always likely to be a counterproductive tactic in information campaigns? Not at all. In contrast to situations in which destructive behavior is prevalent, highlighting descriptive norms should be effective for those action domains in which less harmful or even beneficial behavior is prevalent. In keeping with this notion, a growing number of college campuses have harnessed a concept that the *New York Times Magazine* named an Idea of the Year: social norms marketing (Frauenfelder, 2001). In utilizing social norms marketing, a college campus might advertise results from a survey revealing that over 70% of students on campus have fewer than three drinks when they party.

Social norms marketing campaigns seek to reduce the occurrence of damaging behavior by correcting people's overestimations of the prevalence of that behavior. These campaigns are particularly popular on college campuses because students tend to overestimate the extent to which their peers abuse drugs and alcohol (Baer, Stacy, & Larimer, 1991; Borsari & Carey, 2003; Perkins & Berkowitz, 1986; Perkins & Wechsler, 1996; Prentice & Miller, 1993). Researchers consider this widespread misperception important because of the causal link between normative beliefs and the student's attitudes and behaviors (e.g., Clapp & McDonnell, 2000; Nagoshi, 1999; Perkins & Wechsler, 1996). Proponents of the plan have argued that if students learn that drug or alcohol abuse is less common than they had thought, they will be less likely to engage in that behavior themselves (Perkins, 2002).

The evidence for the success of such programs is mixed (Campo, Brossard, Frazer, Marchell, Lewis, & Talbot, 2003). A number of studies appear to validate the effectiveness of the social norms approach in changing behavior (e.g., Agostinelli, Brown, & Miller, 1995; Collins, Carey, & Sliwinski, 2002; DeJong & Linkenbach, 1999; Haines & Spear, 1996; Neighbors, Larimer, & Lewis, 2004; Perkins, 2003; see also Schultz, 1999), yet others do not (e.g., Clapp, Lange, Russell, Shillington, & Voas, 2003; Wechsler, Nelson, Lee, Seibring, Lewis, & Keeling, 2003). Unfortunately, very few studies that have investigated the effects of social norms have used control groups (Campo et al., 2003), and often it is impossible to isolate the effects of the social norms campaign from other concurrent programs and campaigns (Neighbors et al., 2004). A number of studies have found that these campaigns do correct the misperceptions but do not influence actual drinking behavior (e.g., Barnett, Far, Mauss, & Miller, 1996; Werch, Pappas, Carlson, DiClemente, Chally, & Sinder, 2000).

Perhaps one reason why some studies examining the effectiveness of social norms campaigns report changes in perceptions but not parallel changes in behavior is that students are focused on the normative information when they are responding to the items on questionnaires, but not when they are in settings that typically elicit that behavior. The results of the retrieval cue study described earlier suggest that if the descriptive norm is not in focus in settings in which these behaviors typically occur, the norms may be less effective or not effective at all at curbing the undesirable conduct. Posters, signs, and other forms of media conveying the campaign's normative message are commonly placed in libraries, classrooms, student unions, health centers, and in areas of residence halls other than the dorm rooms themselves. Although the accurate descriptive norm is quite likely to be in focus for the small minority of individuals who consider getting inebriated during a visit to the university health center or library, the distant voice of the normative appeal may be drowned out by the booming music and crowded drinking areas of bars, clubs, fraternity and sorority parties, and dorm rooms. The foregoing analysis suggests that students' likelihood of focusing on the correct normative information in the appropriate settings could be strengthened by placing the campaign's logo on objects native to those settings (e.g., coasters, entrance bracelets, hand stamps).

A Room with a Viewpoint: Using Normative Messages in a Hotel Setting

The social norms marketing philosophy can also be applied to hotel rooms, where via a strategically placed card placed in their room, guests are urged to reuse their towels to help conserve environmental resources by saving energy and reducing the amount of detergent-related pollutants released into the environment. According to the company that supplies such cards to hoteliers, most guests will recycle at least one towel sometime during their stay, provided that they are asked to do so.

Goldstein, Cialdini, & Griskevicius (2007) set out to investigate whether the efficacy of such signs might be improved through the utilization of norm-focusing appeals. An informal survey of the messages conveyed by dozens of request cards from a wide variety of hotels revealed that the cards most frequently attempt to boost recycling efforts by focusing guests on either basic environmental protection or environmental cooperation (Cialdini & Goldstein, 2002). That is, guests are almost invariably informed that reusing one's towels will conserve energy and help save the environment. In addition, they are frequently told that towel reuse will allow them to become cooperating partners with the hotel in furthering its conservation efforts. To encourage such cooperation, guests may be told that the hotel will donate some of the savings from its towel reuse program to environmental causes. The hotels presumably expect this kind of appeal to increase recycling above the simple environmental protection appeal. Two other common but less pervasive types of messages are those appealing to guests' sense of social responsibility to future generations and those informing the guests of the substantial potential savings to the hotel, which implicitly might be interpreted as passing on the savings to its clientele in the long run.

Notable in its absence from these persuasive appeals was one based on social norms, particularly descriptive norms. Goldstein and colleagues (2007) hypothesized that simply informing guests that the majority of their counterparts do reuse their towels when requested might enhance compliance rates. To examine that question, the researchers placed cards with five conceptually different towel recycling appeals in a large hotel in Arizona, where the room attendants were trained to record the relevant reuse data. All the cards were identical in two respects. First, on the front, they informed guests that they could participate in the program by placing their used towels on the bathroom towel rack or curtain rod. Second, on the back, they provided information regarding the extent to which the environment would benefit and energy would be conserved if most guests participated in the program.

The cards differed, however, in the persuasive appeals designed to stimulate towel recycling. The five messages were chosen to reflect the purest forms of the four most common types of appeals the authors had observed in their informal survey, plus one message explicitly conveying the descriptive norm for towel recycling at that hotel. Each of the five signs communicated its message using a short headline in boldface and capital letters; additional text was located underneath that explicated the appeal.

- One appeal focused guests on *environmental protection*: "HELP SAVE THE ENVIRONMENT. You can show your respect for nature and help save the environment by reusing your towels during your stay."
- A second type of card focused guests on *environmental cooperation*: "PARTNER WITH US TO HELP SAVE THE ENVIRONMENT. In exchange for your participation in this program, we at the hotel will donate a percentage of the energy savings to a nonprofit environmental protection organization. The environment deserves our combined efforts. You can join us by reusing your towels during your stay."
- A third type focused guests on the *benefit to the hotel*: "HELP THE HOTEL SAVE ENERGY. The hotel management is concerned about the rising expense to the hotel of energy, labor, and other resources. You can help the hotel save energy by reusing your towels during your stay."
- A fourth type focused guests on *future generations*: "HELP SAVE RESOURCES FOR FUTURE GENERATIONS. Future generations deserve our concern. Please do your part to protect the environment and conserve dwindling resources for future generations to enjoy. You can help preserve these precious resources for all of us by reusing your towels during your stay."
- Finally, a fifth type of card focused guests on the *descriptive norms* of the situation: "JOIN YOUR FELLOW CITIZENS IN HELPING TO SAVE THE ENVIRONMENT. Almost 75% of guests who are asked to participate in our new resource savings program do help by using their towels more than once. You can join your fellow citizens in this program to help save the environment by reusing your towels during your stay."

The data revealed that the *benefit to the hotel* condition (15.6%), which contained neither an injunctive nor a descriptive component in its message, was least effective in stimulating towel reuse (see Figure 7.4). Compared to this message, the three messages containing an injunctive but no descriptive component (*environmental*

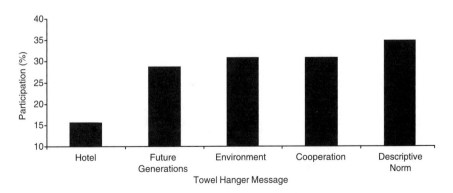

FIGURE 7.4   Towel reuse rates as function of sign in room (Study 1). Adapted from Goldstein et al. (2007) with permission of the authors.

focus, cooperation focus, and *future generations focus* conditions) yielded enhanced compliance (an average of 30.2%). Most notably, the *descriptive norm focus* condition, which contained both an injunctive and a descriptive component, fared best of all (34.8%). The authors noted two interesting aspects of the data. First, the most successful of the communications was one they had never seen employed in the wide range of such messages they had observed, which highlights the utility of employing social science research and theory rather than communicator hunches or best guesses in crafting persuasive appeals.

Second, in the *cooperation focus* condition, the hotel's pledge to donate to an environmental cause when its guests participated in the program did not increase recycling at all. Why not? Although there were several feasible explanations, the researchers posited that this condition failed to augment compliance rates because there is no injunctive norm obligating an influence target to cooperate with individuals who offer the target something only on the condition that the target performs a favor first. However, there is a powerful sense of social obligation in all societies – embodied in the injunctive norm of reciprocation (see Cialdini, 2001; Gouldner, 1960) – to cooperate with individuals who do something for the target first and then ask for a favor in return. This analysis suggests that the *cooperation focus* condition got the concept of the cooperation right but the sequence of the cooperation wrong. Based on the literature, a better way to induce the desired response would be for the hotel to give the donation first and then ask guests to cooperate in this effort by conserving resources (see Berry & Kanouse, 1987; Church, 1993; James & Bolstein, 1992). To test this idea, Goldstein et al. (2007) conducted a second study, this time at a different local hotel. In addition to the *environmental focus* and *cooperation focus* appeals, the researchers included a *reciprocation norm focus* appeal. It stated: "WE'RE DOING OUR PART FOR THE ENVIRONMENT. CAN WE COUNT ON YOU? Because we are committed to preserving the environment, we have made a financial contribution to a nonprofit environmental protection organization on behalf of the hotel and its guests. If you would like to help us in recovering the expense, while conserving natural resources, please reuse your towels during your stay." The data revealed a significant advantage for the *reciprocation focus* condition (45.2%) over the *environmental focus* condition (35.1%) and more importantly, over the *cooperation focus* (30.7%) condition (see Figure 7.5). This finding serves as a reminder that a relatively minor change, informed by social psychological theory, can serve as a corrective to existing practices that may be misguided.

Let's return to the results of the first hotel study with an eye toward how well they fit with the social identity/self-categorization perspective. Goldstein et al. (2007, Study 1) found the highest participation rate with the message informing the guests that the overwhelming majority of others do in fact participate in the program when given the opportunity. But recall that the message asked them to join their "fellow citizens" in this act of environmental protection. Because the wording of the sign in the descriptive norm focus condition may have caused participants to spontaneously categorize themselves as either citizens in general or American citizens in particular (both are categories that seem meaningful and likely to engender strong identification), the extent to which self-categorization

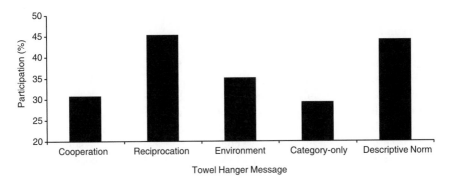

FIGURE 7.5   Towel reuse rates as function of sign in room (Study 2). Adapted from Goldstein et al. (2007) with permission of the authors.

processes contributed to the enhanced compliance rates is not clear. If self-categorization processes did in fact contribute to the more favorable compliance rates, the authors reasoned that this could have occurred via two separate mechanisms. First, it is possible that once the category of *citizen* was made salient to the participants, they were more likely to follow the externally supplied descriptive norm of that category. Second, it is possible that once the category of citizen was made salient to the participants, they were more likely to reuse their towels because they were following the social roles implicit to being a good citizen (American or otherwise). In this second scenario, the enhanced compliance rates could have occurred even if the descriptive normative information provided by the message had no effect whatsoever on the participants.

To address some of these questions, in Study 2, Goldstein and colleagues (2007) added two conditions to the three (*environmental focus, cooperative focus, reciprocation norm focus*) already described for that study.

- The *category-only focus* condition was an appeal that was designed to activate the category of American citizen, but did not provide any descriptive normative information: "HELP SAVE OUR COUNTRY'S NATURAL RESOURCES. We think it is important for American citizens to act to preserve this country's environment. You can help save America's natural resources by reusing your towels during your stay."
- The *descriptive norm focus* condition used exactly the same wording as in Study 1, except that the term "citizens" was removed and replaced with the term "guests": "JOIN YOUR FELLOW GUESTS IN HELPING TO SAVE THE ENVIRONMENT. Almost 75% of guests who are asked to participate in our new resource savings program do help by using their towels more than once. You can join your fellow guests in this program to help save the environment by reusing your towels during your stay."

Two findings are notable (see Figure 7.5). First, similar to the findings of Study 1, the *descriptive norm focus* condition (44.1%) yielded a significantly higher towel reuse rate than the two most common types of appeals, the *environmental focus* (35.1%) and the *cooperation focus* (30.7%) appeals. Second, the towel reuse rates were significantly higher in the *descriptive norm focus* condition than in the *category-only focus* condition (29.2%). Because the message conveying the descriptive norm did not reference a particularly meaningful group or category, yet was still successful, the authors concluded that there was little evidence to suggest that the relative success achieved by the *descriptive norm focus* condition in Study 1 was due to self-categorization processes. Furthermore, the relative failure of the *category-only focus* condition to boost compliance rates beyond the standard signs indicated to the authors that making a meaningful social identity salient without additional descriptive normative information appeared to be ineffective. Thus, compared to the more traditional messages, the *descriptive norm focus* condition that did not use a meaningful social category (from Study 2) appeared to be as effective as the *descriptive norm focus* condition that used a meaningful social category (from Study 1). However, the two could not be directly compared because they were not employed concurrently within the same study.

The researchers were also interested in investigating whether such normative effects might be mediated by the extent to which the hotel visitors perceived that they shared a unit relationship with members of the salient reference group (Heider, 1958). Heider (1958) suggested that meaningful similarities engender strong feelings of association between a person and another entity, but that minor and irrelevant similarities can create an effect of similar magnitude (see Burger, Chapter 6, this volume; Burger, Messian, Patel, del Prado, & Anderson, 2004). Moreover, to keep in a state of balance, individuals might be driven to change their attitudes or behavior in accordance with the person with whom they share a unit relationship. In their study of intergroup relations, Henri Tajfel, who was one of the founders of social identity theory, and his colleagues (e.g., Tajfel, Billig, Bundy, & Flament, 1971) demonstrated in the minimal group paradigm that arbitrary similarities foster ingroup cohesion. Ellemers et al. (2002) noted that individuals' commitments to these minimal groups are low estimates of people's real-world commitments to, and identification with, real groups because these groups are less meaningful than real groups. Similarly, social identity and self-categorization researchers often emphasize that the more meaningful a reference group is, the more an individual's behavior is likely to be in line with the behavioral norms of that group (e.g., Ellemers et al., 2002; Terry et al., 1999). However, if the strength of the perceived unit connection is the true mediator of group-based behavioral conformity, and strong unit connections can be created without the existence of meaningful group identities, an individual should be just as likely to conform to the behavioral norms of a group with which he or she shares a strong unit connection as to the norms of a meaningful group. In contrast, the social identity and self-categorization perspective predicts that individuals should be more likely to follow norms of groups that are meaningful and with which they highly identify.

To explore these issues, Goldstein et al. (2007) conducted a third hotel study that used five different messages. One was the standard *environmental focus* condition. The second and third conditions were the two *descriptive norm focus* conditions used in Study 1 and Study 2; that is, one used the "citizens" terminology and the other used the "guests" terminology. The fourth condition allowed the researchers to pair the descriptive norm with a meaningful category more commonly utilized in social identity and self-categorization research – gender (e.g., Bardach & Park, 1996; Maccoby, 1988; Swan & Wyer, 1997; White et al., 2002). The message for the *gender-based descriptive norm focus* condition stated: "JOIN THE MEN AND WOMEN WHO ARE HELPING TO SAVE THE ENVIRONMENT. In a study conducted in Fall 2003, 76% of the women and 74% of the men participated in our new resource savings program by using their towels more than once. You can join the other men and women in this program to help save the environment by reusing your towels during your stay." The message in the fifth condition was designed to use a completely arbitrary and meaningless similarity between the reference group and the participants to create the feeling of a shared unit relationship: those who had previously stayed in the same room as the participant. The message for the *unit-based descriptive norm focus* condition stated: "JOIN YOUR FELLOW GUESTS IN HELPING TO SAVE THE ENVIRONMENT. In a study conducted in Fall 2003, 75% of the guests who stayed in this room (#xxx) participated in our new resource savings program by using their towels more than once. You can join your fellow guests in this program to help save the environment by reusing your towels during your stay."

The researchers found that the *descriptive norm "guests" focus* condition (44.0%) and the *gender-based descriptive norm focus* condition (40.9%) were each marginally significantly different from the standard *environmental focus* condition (37.2%), whereas the *descriptive norm "citizens" focus* condition (43.5%) and the *unit-based descriptive norm focus* condition (49.3%) were each significantly different from the standard *environmental focus* condition (see Figure 7.6). Although deviance regulation theory and focus theory are mute about these results, these findings do have implications for social identity and self-categorization theories. This perspective suggests that people should be more likely to follow the norms set by certain groups to the extent that the group in question is a psychologically meaningful one. However, the finding that a group with which the guests should

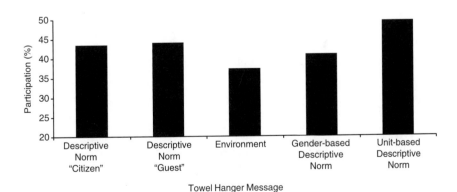

FIGURE 7.6 Towel reuse rates as function of sign in room (Study 3). Adapted from Goldstein et al. (2007) with permission of the authors.

not have felt a strong identification (i.e., others who had previously stayed in their room) yielded the highest compliance rate is inconsistent with predictions flowing from the social identity/self-categorization perspective. Moreover, the data lend credence to the intriguing possibility that the perception of a shared unit relationship is a powerful mediator of conformity effects previously viewed in terms of perceived group importance and the strength of identification with the group.

CONCLUSION

Taken together, the findings reviewed in this chapter support the focus theory of normative conduct. The studies described throughout the chapter are consistent with the notion that a meaningful distinction exists between descriptive and injunctive norms, and that each type of the norm will affect behavior to the extent that it is prominent in consciousness. We also discussed how descriptive and injunctive norms should be aligned not only with one another but also with the goals of the influence campaign. In addition, we touched on some of the burgeoning areas of social norms research, such as the mediating processes of the two kinds of social norms, the long-term effectiveness of normative messages, as well as several other perspectives on norms and social influence, deviance regulation theory and social identity and self-categorization theories.

In conclusion, we hope that we have shown that through the proper implementation of psychologically informed social norms campaigns, we can have a world in which littering is reduced, energy conservation is boosted, drug and alcohol use is curbed, and salad bar sneeze guards are unnecessary. And if that's a little too ambitious, we hope that we have at least conveyed our strong approval for social norms research as well as our belief that everybody's doing it.

ACKNOWLEDGMENTS

Preparation of this chapter was supported by a National Science Foundation Graduate Research Fellowship provided to the first author. We gratefully acknowledge Jenessa Shapiro, Vladas Griskevicius, and Christopher Wilbur for their very valuable comments on an earlier version of this manuscript.

NOTES

1. According to DRT, a communicator who conveyed such a message to Sneezy could additionally increase the likelihood of conformity to the norm by further ascribing negative traits to those who deviate from this group norm.
2. In light of the finding that focusing participants on the injunctive norm reduced littering behavior regardless of the state of the environment (i.e., regardless of the descriptive norm for littering there), one might question whether our analysis of the descriptive norm aspects of the original Keep America Beautiful spot was overly

critical. That is, one might argue that the injunctive norm generated by the tearful Native American was so powerful that it focused the viewers' attention completely on the injunctive norm (i.e., littering is generally disapproved) and not at all on the descriptive norm (i.e., the prevalence of environmentally unfriendly behavior). Although this may in fact be the case, we still find it telling that, nearly 30 years after the spot originally aired, the author of *TV Guide*'s brief summary of this PSA describes the spot in terms of both the injunctive *and* the descriptive norm conveyed by the ad: "a single tear falling down the cheek of Iron Eyes Cody . . . who has just witnessed *various instances* of careless pollution" (emphasis added) ("The Fifty Greatest," 1999, p. 20).

REFERENCES

Aarts, H., & Dijksterhuis, A. (2003). The silence of the library: Environment, situational norm and social behavior. *Journal of Personality and Social Psychology, 84*, 18–28.

Abrams, D., & Hogg, M. A. (1990). Social identification, self-categorization, and social influence. *European Review of Social Psychology, 1*, 195–228.

Agostinelli, G., Brown, J. M., & Miller, W. R. (1995). Effects of normative feedback on consumption among heavy drinking college students. *Journal of Drug Education, 25*, 31–40.

Baer, J. S., Stacy, A., & Larimer, M. (1991). Biases in the perception of drinking norms among college students. *Journal of Studies on Alcohol, 52*, 580–586.

Bandura, A. (1977). *Social learning theory*. New York: General Learning Press.

Bardach, L., & Park, B. (1996). The effect of in-group/out-group status on memory for consistent and inconsistent behavior of an individual. *Personality and Social Psychology Bulletin, 22*, 169–178.

Barnett, L. A., Far, J. M., Mauss, A. L., & Miller, J. A. (1996). Changing perceptions of peer norms as a drinking reduction program for college students. *Journal of Alcohol and Drug Education, 41*, 39–62.

Berkowitz, L. (1972). Social norms, feelings, and other factors affecting helping and altruism. In L. Berkowitz (Ed.), *Advances in experimental social psychology* (Vol. 6, pp. 63–108). San Diego, CA: Academic Press.

Berry, S. H., & Kanouse, D. E. (1987). Physician response to a mailed survey: An experiment in timing of payment. *Public Opinion Quarterly, 51*, 102–114.

Blanton, H., & Christie, C. (2003). Deviance regulation: A theory of action and identity. *Review of General Psychology, 7*, 115–149.

Blanton, H., Stuart, A. E., & VandenEijnden, R. J. J. M. (2001). An introduction to deviance-regulation theory: The effect of behavioral norms on message framing. *Personality and Social Psychology Bulletin, 27*, 848–858.

Blanton, H., VandenEijnden, R. J. J. M., Buunk, B. P., Gibbons, F. X., Gerrard, M., & Bakker, A. (2001). Accentuate the negative: Social images in the prediction and promotion of condom use. *Journal of Applied Social Psychology, 31*, 274–295.

Borsari, B., & Carey, K. B. (2003). Descriptive and injunctive norms in college drinking: A meta-analytic integration. *Journal of Studies on Alcohol, 64*, 331–341.

Brewer, M. B. (2001). The many faces of social identity: Implications for political psychology. *Political Psychology, 22*, 115–125.

Brewer, M. (2003). Optimal distinctiveness, social identity, and the self. In M. R. Leary & J. P. Tangney (Eds.), *Handbook of self and identity* (pp. 480–491). New York: Guilford Press.

Brewer, M. B., & Roccas, S. (2001). Individual values, social identity, and optimal distinctiveness. In C. Sedikides & M. Brewer (Eds.), *Individual self, relational self, collective self* (pp. 219–237). Philadelphia: Psychology Press.

Burger, J. M., Messian, N., Patel, S., del Prado, A., & Anderson, C. (2004). What a coincidence! The effects of incidental similarity on compliance. *Personality and Social Psychology Bulletin, 30,* 35–43.

Campo, S., Brossard, D., Frazer, M. S., Marchell, T., Lewis, D., & Talbot, J. (2003). Are social norms campaigns really magic bullets? Assessing the effects of students' misperceptions on drinking behavior. *Health Communication, 15,* 481–497.

Carver, C. S., & Scheier, M. F. (1978). Self-focusing effects of dispositional self-consciousness, mirror presence, and audience presence. *Journal of Personality and Social Psychology, 36,* 324–332.

Church, A. H. (1993). Estimating the effects of incentives on mail survey response rates: A meta-analysis. *Public Opinion Quarterly, 57,* 62–79.

Cialdini, R. B. (2001). *Influence: Science and practice* (4th ed.). Boston: Allyn & Bacon.

Cialdini, R. B. (2003). Crafting normative messages to protect the environment. *Current Directions in Psychological Science, 12,* 105–109.

Cialdini, R. B., Barrett, D. W., Bator, R., Demaine, L., Sagarin, B. J., Rhoads, K. v. L., et al. (2007). Activating and aligning social norms for persuasive impact. Manuscript in preparation.

Cialdini, R. B., Demaine, L. J., Sagarin, B. J., Barrett, D. W., Rhoads, K. v. L., & Winter, P. L. (2006). Managing social norms for persuasive impact. *Social Influence, 1,* 3–15.

Cialdini, R. B., & Goldstein, N. J. (2002). The science and practice of persuasion. *Cornell Hotel and Restaurant Administration Quarterly, 43,* 40–50.

Cialdini, R. B., & Goldstein, N. J. (2004). Social influence: Compliance and conformity. *Annual Review of Psychology, 55,* 591–622.

Cialdini, R. B., Kallgren, C. A., & Reno, R. R. (1991). A focus theory of normative conduct: A theoretical refinement and reevaluation of the role of norms in human behavior. In L. Berkowitz (Ed.), *Advances in experimental social psychology* (Vol. 24, pp. 201–234). San Diego, CA: Academic Press.

Cialdini, R. B., Reno, R. R., & Kallgren, C. A. (1990). A focus theory of normative conduct: Recycling the concept of norms to reduce littering in public places. *Journal of Personality and Social Psychology, 58,* 1015–1026.

Cialdini, R. B., & Trost, M. R. (1998). Social influence: Social norms, conformity, and compliance. In D. T. Gilbert, S. T. Fiske & G. Lindzey (Eds.), *The handbook of social psychology* (Vol, II, pp. 151–192). New York: McGraw-Hill.

Clapp, J. D., Lange, J. E., Russell, C., Shillington, A., & Voas, R. (2003). A failed norms social marketing campaign. *Journal of Studies on Alcohol, 64,* 409–414.

Clapp, J. D., & McDonnell, A. L. (2000). The relationship of perceptions of alcohol promotion and peer drinking norms to alcohol problems reported by college students. *Journal of College Student Development, 41,* 19–26.

Collins, S. E., Carey, K. B., & Sliwinski, M. J. (2002). Mailed personalized normative feedback as a brief intervention for at-risk college drinkers. *Journal of Studies on Alcohol, 63,* 559–567.

Darley, J. M., & Latané, B. (1970). Norms and normative behavior: Field studies of social interdependence. In J. Macaulay & L. Berkowitz (Eds.), *Altruism and helping behavior* (pp. 83–102). New York: Academic Press.

DeJong, W., & Linkenbach, J. (1999). Telling it like it is: Using social norms marketing campaigns to reduce student drinking. *American Association of Higher Education Bulletin, 32,* 11–16.

Deutsch, M., & Gerard, H. B. (1955). A study of normative and informational social influences upon individual judgment. *Journal of Abnormal and Social Psychology, 51,* 629–636.

Ditto, P. H., & Griffin, J. (1993). The value of uniqueness: Self-evaluation and the perceived prevalence of valenced characteristics. *Journal of Social Behavior and Personality, 8,* 221–240.

Duval, S., & Wicklund, R. A. (1972). *A theory of objective self-awareness.* New York: Academic Press.

Ellemers, N., Spears, R., & Doosje, B. (2002). Self and social identity. *Annual Review of Psychology, 53,* 161–186.

Fishbein, M. L., & Ajzen, I. (1975). *Belief, attitude, intention, and behavior.* Reading, MA: Addison-Wesley.

Frauenfelder, M. (2001, December 9). Social-norms marketing. *New York Times Magazine,* p. 100.

Goldstein, N. J., Cialdini, R. B., & Griskevicius, V. (2007). *A room with a viewpoint: The role of norm specificity in motivating conservation behaviors.* Manuscript submitted for publication.

Gouldner, A. W. (1960). The norm of reciprocity: a preliminary statement. *American Sociological Review, 25,* 161–178.

Haines, M. P., & Spear, S. F. (1996). Changing the perception of the norm: A strategy to decrease binge drinking among college students. *Journal of American College Health, 45,* 134–140.

Heider, F. (1958). *The psychology of interpersonal relations.* New York: Wiley.

Hogg, M. A. (2003). Social identity. In M. R. Leary & J. P. Tangney (Eds.), *Handbook of self and identity* (pp. 462–479). New York: Guilford Press

Hogg, M. A., & Abrams, D. (1988). *Social identifications. A social psychology of intergroup relations and group processes.* London: Routledge.

James, J. M., & Bolstein, R. (1992). Large monetary incentives and their effect on mail survey response rates. *Public Opinion Quarterly, 56,* 442–453.

Kallgren, C. A., Reno, R. R., & Cialdini, R. B. (2000). A focus theory of normative conduct: When norms do and do not affect behavior. *Personality and Social Psychology Bulletin, 26,* 1002–1012.

Kerr, N. L. (1995). Norms in social dilemmas. In D. Schroeder (Ed.), *Social dilemmas: Perspectives on individuals and groups* (pp. 31–48). Westport, CT: Praeger.

Kim, H. S., & Markus, H. R. (1999). Deviance or uniqueness, harmony or conformity? A cultural analysis. *Journal of Personality and Social Psychology, 77,* 785–800.

Maccoby, E. M. (1988). Gender as a social category. *Developmental Psychology, 24,* 755–765.

McGuire, W. J., McGuire, C. V., Child, P., & Fujioka, T. (1978). Salience of ethnicity in the spontaneous self-concept as a function of one's ethnic distinctiveness in the social environment. *Journal of Personality and Social Psychology, 36,* 511–520.

Nagoshi, C. T. (1999). Perceived control of drinking and other predictors of alcohol use and problems in a college student sample. *Addiction Research, 7,* 291–306.

Nail, P. R., MacDonald, G., & Levy, D. A. (2000). Proposal of a four-dimensional model of social response. *Psychological Bulletin, 126,* 454–470.

Neighbors, C., Larimer, M. E., & Lewis, M. A. (2004). Targeting misperceptions of descriptive drinking norms: Efficacy of a computer delivered personalized normative feedback intervention. *Journal of Consulting and Clinical Psychology, 72,* 434–447.

Nelson, L. J., & Miller, D. T. (1995). The distinctiveness effect in social categorization: You are what makes you unusual. *Psychological Science, 6,* 246–249.

Perkins, H. W. (2002). Social norms and the prevention of alcohol misuse in collegiate contexts. *Journal of Studies on Alcohol, Supplement 14*, 164–172.

Perkins, H. W. (Ed.) (2003). *The social norms approach to preventing school and college age substance abuse: A handbook for educators, counselors, and clinicians.* San Francisco: Jossey-Bass.

Perkins, H. W., & Berkowitz, A. D. (1986). Perceiving the community norms of alcohol use among students: Some research implications for campus alcohol education programming. *The International Journal of the Addictions, 21*, 961–976.

Perkins, H. W., & Wechsler, H. (1996). Variation in perceived college drinking norms and its impact on alcohol abuse: A nationwide study. *Journal of Drug Issues, 26*, 961–974.

Pool, G. J., Wood, W., & Leck, K. (1998). The self-esteem motive in social influence: Agreement with valued majorities and disagreement with derogated minorities. *Journal of Personality and Social Psychology, 75*, 967–975.

Prentice, D. A., & Miller, D. T. (1993). Pluralistic ignorance and alcohol use on campus: Some consequences of misperceiving the social norm. *Journal of Personality and Social Psychology, 64*, 243–256.

Reno, R. R., Cialdini, R. B., & Kallgren, C. A. (1993). The transsituational influence of social norms. *Journal of Personality and Social Psychology, 64*, 104–112.

Schultz, P. W. (1999). Changing behavior with normative feedback interventions: A field experiment on curbside recycling. *Basic and Applied Social Psychology, 21*, 25–38.

Schwartz, S. H. (1973). Normative explanations of helping behavior: A critique, proposal, and empirical test. *Journal of Experimental Social Psychology, 9*, 349–364.

Schwartz, S. H. (1977). Normative influences in altruism. In L. Berkowitz (Ed.), *Advances in experimental social psychology* (Vol. 10, pp. 221–279). San Diego, CA: Academic Press.

Scott, W. (1995, December 24). Personality parade. *Parade Magazine*, p. 2.

Shaffer, L. S. (1983). Toward Pepitone's vision of a normative social psychology: What is a social norm? *Journal of Mind and Behavior, 4*, 275–294.

Sherif, M. (1936). *The psychology of social norms.* New York: Harper.

Swan, S., & Wyer, R. S. (1997). Gender stereotypes and social identity: How being in the minority affects judgment of self and others. *Personality and Social Psychology Bulletin, 23*, 1265–1276.

Tajfel, H. (1978). *Differentiation between social groups: Studies in the social psychology of intergroup relations.* New York: Academic.

Tajfel, H., Billig, M. G., Bundy, R. P., & Flament, C. (1971). Social categorization and intergroup behavior. *European Journal of Social Psychology, 1*, 149–178.

Tajfel, H., & Turner, J. (1979) An integrative theory of intergroup conflict. In W. G. Austin & S. Worchel (Eds.), *The social psychology of intergroup relations* (pp. 33–48). Monterey, CA: Brooks-Cole.

Terry, D. J., & Hogg, M. A. (1996). Group norms and the attitude–behaviour relationship: A role for group identification. *Personality and Social Psychology Bulletin, 22*, 776–793.

Terry, D. J., & Hogg, M. A. (2000). *Attitudes, behavior, and social context: The role of norms and group membership.* Mahwah, NJ: Lawrence Erlbaum Associates, Inc.

Terry, D. J., Hogg, M. A., & White, K. M. (1999). The theory of planned behaviour: Self-identity, social identity, and group norms. *British Journal of Social Psychology, 38*, 225–244.

Terry, D. J., Hogg, M. A., & White, K. M. (2000). Attitude–behavior relations: Social identity and group membership. In D. J. Terry & M. A. Hogg (Eds.), *Attitudes, behavior, and social context: The role of norms and group membership* (pp. 67–93). Mahwah, NJ: Lawrence Erlbaum Associates, Inc.

The fifty greatest TV commercials of all time. (1999, July 3–9), *TV Guide*, pp. 2–34.

Tulving, E. (1983). *Elements of episodic memory*. New York: Oxford University Press.

Turner, J. C. (1987). A self-categorization theory. In J. C. Turner, M. A. Hogg, P. H. Oakes, S. D. Reicher, & M. S. Wetherell (Eds.), *Rediscovering the social group: A self-categorization theory* (pp. 42–67). Oxford: Blackwell.

Turner, J. C. (1991). *Social influence*. Milton Keynes, UK: Open University Press.

Turner, J. C. (1999). Some current issues in research on social identity and self-categorization theories. In N. Ellemers, R. Spears, & B. Doosje (Eds.), *Social identity: Context, commitment, content* (pp. 6–34). Oxford: Blackwell.

Turner, J. C., Hogg, M. A., Oakes, P. J., Reicher, S. D., & Wetherell M. S. (Eds.). (1987). *Rediscovering the social group: A self-categorization theory*. Oxford: Blackwell.

Wechsler, H., Nelson, T., Lee, J. E., Seibring, M., Lewis, C., & Keeling, R. (2003). Perception and reality: A national evaluation of social norms marketing interventions to reduce college students' heavy alcohol use. *Quarterly Journal of Studies on Alcohol, 64,* 484–494.

Werch, C. E., Pappas, D. M., Carlson, J. M., DiClemente, C. C., Chally, P. S., & Sinder, J. A. (2000). Results of a social intervention to prevent binge drinking among first-year residential college students. *Journal of American College Health, 49,* 85–92.

White, K. M., Hogg, M. A., & Terry, D. J. (2002). Improving attitude–behavior correspondence through exposure to normative support from a salient ingroup. *Basic and Applied Social Psychology, 24,* 91–103.

8

On the Development of the Social
Response Context Model

PAUL R. NAIL and GEOFF MACDONALD

A s an undergraduate, I (PRN) was fortunate enough to be a member of the varsity tennis team. In my freshman year, I was the #3 player. Following the last tournament that season, Coach Jones informed us that because we had a little extra money left in the budget we were going to eat at a real restaurant on our drive home rather than a fast food restaurant, our usual fare. In fact, Coach Jones said we had so much money left that each of us would be able to order anything on the menu he wanted. He added that he was taking us to a restaurant that had the "best chicken fried steak in the state of Oklahoma." There were seven of us at the restaurant, six players and Coach Jones, all seated together around a large table. The waiter took Coach Jones's order first and then proceeded in turn around the table. I was seated in the sixth chair and thus was slated to give my order second to last. Coach Jones ordered a chicken fried steak and, to my astonishment, so did the first two of my teammates! Chicken fried steak can be very good, but it is usually made from round steak, one of the cheaper and tougher cuts. Being on a college student's budget, this was a rare opportunity, and I had my sights set on something a little more expensive. The fourth in line and #2 player, Don, also ordered chicken fry. Incredulous, I leaned across a corner of the table and whispered to Don, "Didn't you hear what Coach said? You can have whatever you want; you don't have to order chicken fry." Don replied something like, "Well, I just had steak a couple days ago; I want to try the chicken fry." Scrambling for social support, I quickly turned to the fifth in line and #4 player, Danny, who was seated on my right. I asked what he was having. Unfortunately, he too wanted to try the chicken fry. I felt ready to panic as tension built inside me. It was almost my turn to order, and it seemed everyone was having chicken fry. Desperate, I turned to the 7th in line and #1 player, Brad, who was seated on my left, my last hope. Asked what he was having, Brad smiled mischievously and replied, "I don't know about you, but I'm having the 20 oz. sirloin." Immediately I felt completely relieved. With the support of only one teammate, albeit the #1 player, I felt free to order whatever I wanted just as Coach Jones had said we could. Those 20 oz.

sirloins were so large, Brad's and my side orders had to be served on separate plates. It was certainly the largest steak I have ever eaten, one of the best too. To this day, I'm thankful that my friend Brad saved me from the tyranny of the chicken fry.

Students of social psychology will recognize this example as a real-world fac-simile of one of the "partner" variations of the classic Asch (1951, 1956) paradigm. Rather than dealing with an issue of preference, however, like what steak to order, Asch presented research participants with simple perceptual stimuli and asked for judgments regarding objective facts. Specifically, participants were asked which of three line segments on each trial was closest in length to a standard line segment. In so doing, Asch set up a conflict on critical trials between objective reality, as determined by one's own perception, and social reality, as determined by the erroneous judgments of an alleged group of peers (actually Asch's confederates). In his basic paradigm, Asch employed a unanimous majority ($N = 7$) against a single naïve participant. In his initial experiment, Asch (1951) found that 38 of 50 participants (76 per cent) yielded to the erroneous judgments on at least one of 12 critical trials. Further, 32 per cent of the total judgments by participants were in error. This percentage compares to an error rate of only 0.68 per cent for control participants, those who made the same judgments individually and not in the presence of any alleged peers.

It was the consistent partner variation of Asch's (1951) procedure, however, that was so very similar to the situation I faced at the restaurant. Here Asch instructed one of the confederates to consistently deviate from the majority by giving objectively correct answers on all trials. Just as I was able to resist felt group pressure in ordering the steak with the support of one like-minded teammate, Asch found that a single like-minded social supporter dramatically reduced the error rate among his participants, from 32 per cent to only 5.5 per cent, a reduc-tion in errors of 82.8 per cent! Clearly, the support of only one other person can produce rather large effects.

A couple of semesters after my experience at the restaurant, my social psych-ology professor began telling the class about Asch's (1951) research. Because of my restaurant memory and other life experiences, Asch's research resonated deeply with me. I began to be aware for the first time just how much I had been influenced in my life by people around me. I became aware that I had been especially influenced by the groups I had been a member of, like my tennis team. Ever since then, social influence has been one of the main things I have thought, studied, written, and wondered about. It has also been a primary focus of my empirical and theoretical work. In particular, my students, colleagues, and I have been engaged in a series of empirical studies (Levy, 1992; MacDonald & Nail, 2005; Nail, Harton, & Decker, 2003; Nail & Ruch, 1990, 1992; Nail & Thompson, 1990; Nail, Van Leeuwen, & Powell, 1996) and theoretical articles (Levy, Collins, & Nail, 1998; Levy & Nail, 1993; MacDonald, Nail, & Levy, 2004; Nail, 1986; Nail & Helton, 1999; Nail, MacDonald, & Levy, 2000; Nail & Van Leeuwen, 1993) concerned with the following fundamental questions: How can we define con-formity most adequately? Are there different types of conformity? If so, do they follow the same laws of influence? What are the alternatives to conformity? What forms can nonconformity assume? When we began this work in the mid-1980s, we were at first surprised by how little consensus there was among researchers and theorists on these questions, given their fundamental nature and the hundreds of social influence studies that had been published. As we developed a framework to better answer these questions, however, we came to appreciate the many subtleties and complexities involved in adequately describing possible responses to social influence.

To illustrate, consider once more my steak-ordering experience. Some might label Brad's and my behavior with respect to the group as *nonconformity* (e.g., Allport, 1934; Feshbach, 1967), and in a sense this label would be correct. It is true that we did not conform to the strong consensus for chicken fry. Yet, the term nonconformity is not adequately explicit. Working independently, Crutchfield (1962) and Willis (1963) were the first to demonstrate that at least two types of nonconformity are possible (see also Frager, 1970; Nail & Van Leeuwen, 1993). For example, with *independence* a potential influencee nonconforms by giving *zero weight* to the position of others in deciding how to behave or what to believe (Nail et al., 2000; Quinn & Schlenker, 2002; Willis, 1963, 1965a). Operationally, independence is usually defined by the absence of behavioral or attitudinal movement on the part of the influence target after being exposed to social forces. Independence stands in contrast to a different type of nonconformity, *anticonformity* (also known as *counterconformity* or simply *counterformity*; Crutchfield, 1962; Hornsey, Majkut, Terry, & McKimmie, 2003; Krech, Crutchfield, & Ballachey, 1962). Here, the influencee nonconforms by actively rebelling against influence. Operationally, anticonformity is usually defined by behavioral or attitudinal movement *away from* the influence source (Willis, 1965a, see e.g., Argyle, 1957; Frager, 1970; Nail et al., 1996; Wood, Pool, Leck, & Purvis, 1996). Accordingly, in contrast to independence, anticonformity is very much *dependent* on the position of the source of influence as it provides the standard from which the target of influence aims to be different (Nail, 1986; Nail & Van Leeuwen, 1993; Willis, 1965a).

The label "independence" for Brad's and my behavior is more explicit, but in my case at least, it would not be accurate. Without my support, Brad might have been able to resist the consensus of the group, thus showing genuine independence in ordering sirloin. Knowing myself as a freshman and the power of a unanimous majority, however, I have no doubt that I would *not* have been able to resist without Brad's support. Thus, with reference to Brad as an influence source, my ordering sirloin was clearly not independence. Some might classify my response to Brad's influence as *conformity* (cf. Milgram, 1974, p. 118; Osman, 1982). That is, in showing nonconformity to the group, I simultaneously displayed conformity to Brad. Again, in a sense these labels would be correct. I moved from being unsure what to order to ordering sirloin, no doubt because of Brad's influence, and behavioral movement toward an influence source is the most prominent operational definition of conformity in the literature (Kiesler, 1969; Nail et al., 2000; Nail & Van Leeuwen, 1993). There are several important differences, however, between my "conformity" to Brad and "conformity" as it is normally used by social influence researchers, for example, in typical Asch-type conformity studies.[1]

In fact, in one sense these two types of influence are precise opposites of one another (see Nail et al., 2000; Wheeler, 1966). Initially, I wanted to order sirloin, but everyone before me ordering chicken fry raised doubts in my mind and put me in conflict about what I *should* order. Brad freed me from this conflict with his stated intention to order sirloin. Thus, I moved from a state of considerable internal (intrapersonal) conflict and doubt, through Brad's influence, to a state of internal harmony. I wanted to order sirloin and felt empowered by Brad to do just that. The major events in this sequence can be summarized as: conflict → influence → harmony.

For many participants who conformed in Asch's (1951) initial research, however, the sequence regarding conflict, influence, and harmony was exactly reversed: harmony → influence → conflict (cf. Nail et al., 2000; Wheeler, 1966). The participants who most clearly demonstrated this sequence were those Asch referred to as *distortion of action* participants. Harmony existed initially for these participants because the line judgments were easy and the group of confederates unanimously gave *correct* answers on the first two trials. When the group began to give incorrect answers, however, participants were placed in conflict between giving the obviously correct answer and giving the answer that was defined as "correct" by the group. On trials where distortion of action participants conformed, many also ended up in conflict, publicly giving an answer that privately they believed was incorrect. We know that these participants were conflicted in this regard from Asch's (1951, 1956) post-experimental interviews and from similar subsequent research (e.g., Back & Bogdonoff, 1964; Levy, 1992). This type of conformity is widely known specifically as *compliance* (i.e., movement on the part of the influence target to post-influence public agreement with the group but without private acceptance of the group's position; Festinger, 1953; Kelman, 1958; Kiesler & Kiesler, 1969; Nail et al., 2000). In contrast, movement to post-influence public agreement with the group that is accompanied by private acceptance is a type of conformity known as *conversion* (Festinger, 1953; Nail et al, 2000; also known as *internalization*, Kelman, 1958, 1974).

If my response to Brad in ordering sirloin was not a type of conformity, then what was it? In fact, it reflects a textbook case of a recognized type of influence we call *disinhibitory contagion* (Levy, 1992; Nail et al., 2000, 2003; originally labeled *behavioral contagion*, Wheeler, 1966; see also, Redl, 1949). Disinhibitory contagion begins with a potential influencee who is in an approach–avoidance conflict. The individual wants or desires to engage in a certain behavior but is not doing so due to restraints such as social norms, customs, mores, or laws (Wheeler, 1966). When another person, the *model* or *trigger-person*, engages in that very behavior, however, the influencee's avoidance gradient can be significantly reduced. When this occurs, the influencee is freed to engage in the behavior that was previously inhibited – the behavior that was privately desired all along. We prefer the term *disinhibitory* to refer to this type of influence because, in contrast to compliance or conversion, the model reduces or removes the influencee's restraints against a privately desired behavior. Following Redl (1949), we use the term *contagion* because once such a reduction in restraints occurs in a group or crowd, the original trigger-person's influence frequently multiplies and spreads rapidly to others with similar desires. Each influencee becomes a potential trigger for subsequent influencees, with each influencee adding inertia to the social impact of the original trigger in what can be described as a "snowball effect" (Nemeth & Wachtler, 1983). Disinhibitory contagion has been demonstrated in numerous studies (e.g., Baron & Kepner, 1970; Goethals & Perlstein, 1978; Levy, 1992; Russell, Wilson, & Jenkins, 1976; Smith, Murphy, & Wheeler, 1964; Wheeler & Caggiula, 1966; Wheeler & Levine, 1967; Wheeler & Smith, 1967). It is important because it is a common response to influence in the real world. It occurs, for example, (a) when people are freed to dance following those that initiate dancing, (b) when initially inhibited students in a class begin asking questions following the first question, and (c) when rioters engage in looting following the first person who does so. On a much larger scale, disinhibitory contagion applies to the rapid fall of communism among the countries of Eastern Europe in 1989 following the democratic reforms that were initiated in Poland (Nail et al., 2000). Although disinhibitory contagion is frequently confused with conformity, we have demonstrated in previous work, on both axiomatic and empirical grounds, that the two should be regarded as separate and unique types of social influence (see Nail et al., 2000, pp. 460–461).

Before proceeding, it should be acknowledged that Brad's influence on me in ordering sirloin steak illustrates not only disinhibitory contagion but also, more generally speaking, a case of minority influence (see De Dreu, Chapter 10, this volume). Specifically, Brad's position represented a minority view in the group. Thus, my decision to order steak like Brad represents influence despite the minority status of his position. As illustrated in this case, disinhibitory contagion and minority influence often go hand in hand (see Nail et al., 2000, p. 463).

Our primary goal in this chapter is to describe our theoretical work over the past 20 years. This work has focused on developing and proposing integrated descriptive models of response to social influence. In general, the goal of descriptive response models is to include as many recognized types of influence as possible in a model that is as simple as possible. Such models are valuable because they help (a) organize empirical findings, (b) discriminate between closely related phenomena (Nail et al., 2000, p. 454), (c) resolve apparent inconsistencies in the literature (see Nail et al., 2000), and (d) direct the course of research by identifying new or previously undifferentiated types of influence. In describing our work, we will point to some of the inconsistencies, apparent inconsistencies, and paradoxes that initially led us to devote so much attention to the issue of social influence and social response. For example, as noted previously, conformity is usually defined by movement toward the influence source. Yet we have discovered cases where conformity is actually characterized by movement *away from* the source. Conversely, anticonformity is sometimes characterized by movement *toward* the source. We conclude by showing how our most recent model, the Social Response Context Model (MacDonald et al., 2004; see also Nail et al., 2000), might be used as a template to advance future theory and research.

Our work started with reviews of the descriptive social response models literature (Nail, 1986; Nail & Van Leeuwen, 1993). Here, we found that no fewer than fifteen such models had been previously proposed (Allen, 1965; Allport, 1934; Asch, 1951; Brehm, 1966; Festinger, 1953; Hogg & Turner, 1987; Kiesler, 1969;

Krech et al., 1962; Jahoda, 1956, 1959; Montgomery, 1992; Willis, 1963, 1965a, 1965b). Though unique, each model was similar in that it identified one or more responses that could be regarded as conformity, as well as one or more alternative responses. For example, the **conformity–nonconformity** model (Allport, 1934) defines conformity by the single criterion of post-influence behavioral *agreement* between the target and the source of influence. Perfect agreement indicates conformity, and deviations from this position represent different degrees of non-conformity. In contrast, the **independence → conformity** model (Kiesler, 1969; Willis, 1965b) defines conformity by the single criterion of behavioral *movement*. Pre- to post-influence movement by the target toward the source indicates various degrees of conformity, and the total absence of movement represents independence. Upon discovering a high degree of redundancy between such models, we wondered if it would be possible to propose a single more general model that would include and integrate all or most of the distinctions identified in the fifteen models. The first step toward a successful integrated model involved combining two of the more sophisticated of the fifteen models – those proposed by Willis (1963) and Allen (1965).[2]

TWO IMPORTANT DESCRIPTIVE MODELS OF SOCIAL RESPONSE

The Willis (1963) Model

Willis's (1963) model is based on his symbolic scheme for representing possible responses to social influence. The model was first formalized by Nail (1986, see also Nail et al., 2000). It is based on crossing two dichotomous variables: (a) pre-influence (i.e., pre-exposure) agreement or disagreement between a target and source of influence and (b) post-exposure agreement or disagreement between the target and source (see Figure 8.1). Conformity in the model is defined by pre-exposure disagreement (D/) between the target and source that is followed by *inferred* positive movement to a position of post-exposure agreement (/A). Note that the model deftly combines the agreement and movement criteria of the **conformity–nonconformity** and **independence → conformity** models, respectively, by defining conformity as *movement* by the target to a position of post-exposure *agreement* with the source. Note also that even though the model's dimensions in Figure 8.1 are represented as dichotomous, in practice the dimensions for this and other models are frequently continuous. *Independence* in the model is defined by pre disagreement/post disagreement (D/D), *anticonformity* by pre agreement/post disagreement (A/D), and *congruence* by pre agreement/post agreement (A/A). Congruence is sometimes referred to as *uniformity* (Nail, 1986; Willis, 1963, 1965a).

Willis's (1963) model has several strengths. It identifies three widely recognized responses in a single model: conformity, independence, and anticonformity. In so doing, it distinguishes between independence and anticonformity as special types of nonconformity. Further, the model provides for congruence, which

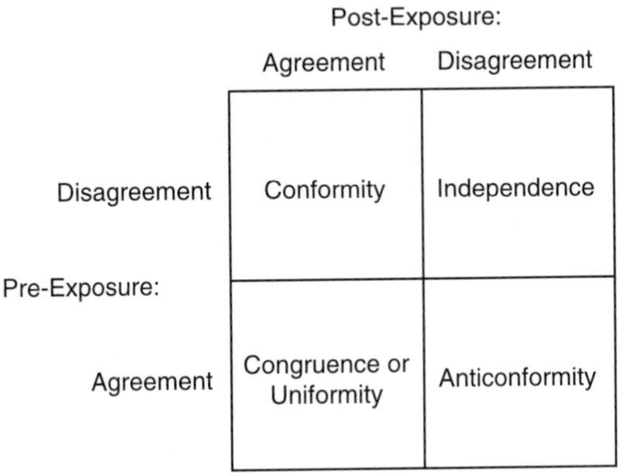

Post-Exposure:

		Agreement	Disagreement
Disagreement		Conformity	Independence
Pre-Exposure:			
Agreement		Congruence or Uniformity	Anticonformity

FIGURE 8.1 A model derived from Willis's (1963) symbolic scheme for symbolizing possible responses to social influence. From Nail et al. (2000). Copyright 2000 by the American Psychological Association. Used by permission.

Willis conceptualized as a type of conformity. Here, because the target and source initially agree, the target can "fit in" without having to dissemble or change his or her views (Nail et al., 2000; Sorrels & Kelley, 1984). The model, however, does not include the important public/private variable. Hence, it has no way of representing the distinction between compliance and conversion as special types of conformity. The model also excludes disinhibitory contagion.

The Allen (1965) Model

Allen's (1965) model (see Figure 8.2) is similar to Willis's (1963). Both models propose that there are four basic responses in social influence settings, and both

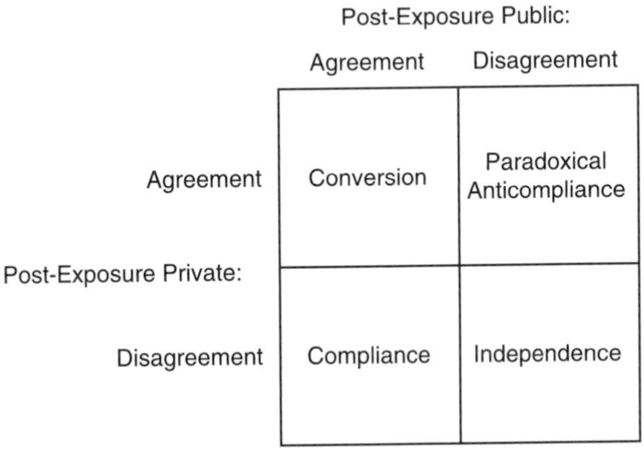

Post-Exposure Public:

	Agreement	Disagreement
Agreement	Conversion	Paradoxical Anticompliance
Post-Exposure Private:		
Disagreement	Compliance	Independence

FIGURE 8.2 The Allen (1965) social response model. From Nail (1986). Copyright 1986 by the American Psychological Association. Adapted by permission.

models are based on a framework that crosses two dichotomous variables. The models are distinct, however, in that Allen's model always assumes initial *disagreement* (D/) between the target and source of influence, whereas Willis's model provides for initial agreement (A/) as well as disagreement (D/). Further, Allen's model distinguishes between post-exposure public and private responses, whereas Willis's does not. As can be seen in Figure 8.2, conversion in the model is defined by inferred positive movement on the part of the target, from initial disagreement with the source to post-exposure public and private agreement (D/AA). In a similar manner, compliance is defined by positive movement to post public agreement, but with continued disagreement in private (D/AD). Independence, in contrast, is defined by the absence of movement, specifically by initial disagreement followed by post-exposure disagreement both publicly and privately (D/DD).

Allen (1965) did not label or discuss the fourth possibility in Figure 8.2, pre-exposure disagreement accompanied by post public disagreement but with post private agreement (D/DA), likely because he found no empirical examples in his literature review. In our more recent reviews, however (MacDonald et al., 2004; Nail, 1986; Nail et al., 2000), we have uncovered several examples (e.g., Abrams, Wetherell, Cochrane, Hogg, & Turner, 1990, Study 2; Eagly, Wood, & Fishbaugh, 1981; Feshbach, 1967; McFarland, Ross, & Conway, 1984; see also Kiesler & Kiesler, 1969, p. 4). For example, Eagly et al. (1981) exposed individual male participants to disagreement from a group of predominantly female participants on a number of opinion items (i.e., implicit pressure to conform). Males who responded in public showed significantly less movement toward the group than males who responded in private. Eagly et al. concluded that the public-responding males may have been reluctant to display conformity because of their desire to live up to the male gender role of dominance and independence from others, perhaps especially females. We refer to this behavior pattern more explicitly, however, as *paradoxical anticompliance*. Based on Eagly et al. (1981) and other empirical examples we located, we coined the term "anticompliance" to connote a special type of anticonformity. In Nail et al. (2000) we added the term "paradoxical" because this response represents a special type of anticonformity despite the fact that it entails inferred *positive* movement toward the influence source (viz., from initial disagreement to post private agreement, D/DA). To clarify, note that even though the Eagly et al. males moved *toward* the female group's opinions at the private level, *between* the private and public levels regarding their post-exposure responses, the males displayed *implicit* movement *away from* the group's position. That is, they seemed to purposely back away from public agreement with the females in order to project autonomy, despite being privately persuaded. By this logic, paradoxical anticompliance qualifies as a special type of anticonformity.

Paradoxical anticompliance (D/DA) is also significant because of its prominence in studies employing the *minority influence* paradigm (De Dreu, Chapter 10, this volume; Moscovici, Lage, & Naffrechoux, 1969), which is also sometimes referred to as the "Asch-backwards" paradigm (see Asch, 1952, pp. 479–480). Here the situation is constructed so that the confederates' position represents a statistical minority in the group, and any movement of majority participants toward the minority is assessed. Interestingly, if the minority is successful, post public disagreement/private agreement with the minority is the modal response (e.g., Doms & Van Avermaet, 1980; Maass & Clark, 1983; Moscovici et al., 1969; Nemeth & Wachtler, 1974, 1983). Apparently, it is easier to persuade members of the majority at the private level than it is to get the first one to publicly defect from the majority position (Maass & Clark, 1984; Wood, Lundgren, Ouellette, Busceme, & Blackstone, 1994). In this context, such behavior is rightly regarded as a form of conversion (Moscovici, 1980; Wood et al., 1994).

Considering studies demonstrating paradoxical anticompliance together, a generalization seems in order. This behavior apparently occurs when targets are persuaded by the *content* of a source's communication but are motivated in the face of public pressure to *not* reveal that they have been influenced. This motivation to resist the appearance of influence has occurred in majority influence settings (a) when males were pressured to conform by females (Eagly et al., 1981), (b) when ingroup members were pressured by outgroup members (Abrams et al., 1990, Study 2), and (c) when marginalized ingroup members were pressured by high-status ingroup members (Feshbach, 1967). Such motivation occurred in a study of anticipated persuasion where participants were apparently reluctant to reveal to the experimenter that they had been influenced by the mere suggestion that they would be exposed to a highly persuasive communication (McFarland et al., 1984). Finally, such motivation has been demonstrated in minority influence settings when privately defecting majority group members were still in the presence of the rest of the majority (e.g., Doms & Van Avermaet, 1980; Moscovici et al., 1969; Nemeth & Wachtler, 1974).

Allen's (1965) model has several strengths. The distinctions between conversion (D/AA), compliance (D/AD), and independence (D/DD) are widely recognized among social psychologists, no doubt because of their continuing theoretical significance and prominence in empirical studies (e.g., Abrams et al., 1990; Asch, 1951; 1956; Baron, Vandello, & Brunsman, 1996; Campbell & Fairey, 1989; Deutsch & Gerard, 1955; Eagly et al., 1981; Insko, Smith, Alicke, Wade, & Taylor, 1985; Lucas, Alexander, Firestone, & Baltes, 2006; Quinn & Schlenker, 2002; Sherif, 1935). It is also desirable that a model can identify a "new" response possibility such as paradoxical anticompliance (D/DA). Although Allen had no empirical evidence for this response at the time, its importance has become obvious with subsequent research. Allen's model is not perfect, however. Because of its structure, it automatically excludes important types of influence such as anticonformity (as in Willis's, 1963, model; Figure 8.1) and disinhibitory contagion.

Willis (1963) versus Allen (1965)

Considering the Willis (1963) and Allen (1965) models together, the reader can perhaps see the apparent contradiction that initially piqued a good deal of our interest. Willis and Allen were both attempting to describe the major ways that people can respond when exposed to a social influence attempt, and both proposed 2 × 2 models wherein four basic responses are theoretically possible. Yet the four responses that each proposed do not appear to match up very well.

Specifically, there is not a one-to-one correspondence between the responses of the two systems. It is fairly clear that Allen's (1965) conversion (D/AA) and compliance (D/AD) can both be correctly regarded as special types of Willis's (1963) conformity (D/A). Further, there appears to be a direct match between Allen's independence (D/DD) and Willis's independence (D/D). Allen simply made explicit what was clearly implied by Willis's conceptual and operational definitions of independence – that the potential influencee is not influenced one way or the other, neither publicly nor privately, by social forces. In majority influence settings, we interpret Allen's fourth cell, paradoxical anticompliance (D/DA), as a special type of anticonformity, yet the match between paradoxical anticompliance and Willis's anticonformity (A/D) is tenuous at best. Paradoxical anticompliance (D/DA) requires initial *disagreement*, movement *toward* the influence source at the private level, and *the distinction* between public and private responding. Willis's anticonformity (A/D), in contrast, entails initial *agreement*, movement *away from* the source, and *no distinction* between public and private responding. Finally, there is no response in Allen's model that matches well with Willis's congruence (A/A). This overall lack of correspondence was what first suggested to us that it should be possible to propose a single more general model, one that would include and integrate all the possible responses suggested in both models. The lack of correspondence also suggested to us that new or previously unidentified responses might be suggested in an integrated model.

The framework of Willis's (1963) model (Figure 8.1) includes both pre-exposure and post-exposure agreement/disagreement between the target and source of influence, but it does not provide for the possibility that the target's public and private post-influence responses might differ. Given the central importance of the public/private variable to social influence theory and research (MacDonald & Nail, 2005), it would seem that no model of social response could hope to be adequate without consideration of this variable. The framework of Allen's (1965) model (Figure 8.2) includes the public/private variable, but it does not provide for the possibility that the target's and source's pre-exposure positions might agree. Given that discovering initial agreement with a group on important issues is so very different phenomenologically than initial disagreement (e.g., Asch, 1951, 1956; Back & Bogdonoff, 1964; Campbell & Fairey, 1989), it would seem that no model could hope to be complete without consideration of the pre-exposure agreement/disagreement variable. Given these considerations, it appeared that an integrated model might be possible by simply extending Willis's (1963) framework to distinguish between post-exposure public and private responses. Alternatively, one could correctly conceptualize such an integrated model as extending Allen's (1965) model to provide for the possibility of pre-exposure agreement between the target and source, as well as pre-exposure disagreement. Such an integrated model is presented in Figure 8.3.

The Nail (1986) Synthetic Model

We refer to the model as "synthetic" because it is quite literally based on a synthesis of the Willis (1963) and Allen (1965) models. Given that both models were

	Postexposure Public:			
	Agreement		Disagreement	
	Postexposure Private:			
	Agreement	Disagreement	Agreement	Disagreement
	#13	#14	#15	#16
Pre-Exposure Disagreement	Conversion	Compliance	Paradoxical Anticompliance	Independence
	#1	#2	#3	#4
Pre-Exposure Agreement	Congruence	Paradoxical Compliance	Anticompliance	Anticonversion

FIGURE 8.3   The Nail (1986) synthetic model of social response. Copyright 1986 by the American Psychological Association. Adapted by permission.

based on crossing two dichotomous factors and that extending either model requires the addition of a third dichotomous factor, the synthetic model provides for 2^3 or 8 response possibilities. The vertical factor in the synthetic model is the same as one of Willis's factors: pre-exposure disagreement/agreement. The horizontal factors are the same as Allen's: (a) post-exposure public agreement/disagreement and (b) post-exposure private agreement/disagreement. For purposes of discussion, the responses have been numbered. Further, for the sake of consistency and to ease the reader's burden, this numbering system follows that of the most complete and final model presented herein, the Social Response Context Model. Responses #13 through #16 are identical to the four responses of Allen's model and require no further elaboration; the synthetic model simply makes it explicit by its framework that each of these responses is possible only assuming initial or pre-exposure *disagreement* between the target and the source of influence. For example, #13 conversion is defined by the confluence of pre-exposure disagreement, post public agreement, and post private agreement (D/AA).

Regarding responses that assume pre-exposure *agreement*, response #1, congruence (A/AA), is very similar to Willis's (1963) congruence (A/A) in Figure 8.1. The synthetic model simply makes it explicit that the target's post response has not changed either publicly or privately. Response #2, *paradoxical compliance* (A/AD), is the mirror image of #15, paradoxical anticompliance (D/DA). As a form of compliance, #2 is characterized by post public agreement/private disagreement between the target and source. Unlike #14 compliance, however, with #2 paradoxical compliance the post private disagreement is arrived at through *negative* movement. Specifically, the target moves from a position of initial agreement with the source to one of post private disagreement, although agreement is still maintained at the public response level. Thus, #2, paradoxical compliance (A/AD), represents a form of compliance despite the fact that it entails negative movement. This is true because #2, paradoxical compliance, also entails implicit positive movement between the target's post-exposure private and public responses. This implicit movement occurs from *post* private disagreement to *post* public agreement (A/AD). That is, the new state of private disagreement is masked with a public face of agreement, and thus this response represents a form of compliance.

A striking example that fits the defining criteria of #2, paradoxical compliance (A/AD), was reported by Janis (1982). The example concerns James Schlesinger's account of the social forces that surrounded President Kennedy's decision to proceed with the Bay of Pigs invasion. Schlesinger reports that he was initially supportive of the operation, being caught up in the mood of "buoyant optimism" that characterized the early days of the Kennedy administration. After learning more of the details of the invasion, however, Schlesinger became increasingly skeptical and suspect of the whole operation. He ultimately became strongly opposed to the invasion but never voiced his opposition in group meetings with Kennedy and other members of the "inner circle." Of these meetings, Schlesinger later wrote, "I can only explain my failure to do more than raise a few timid questions by reporting that one's impulse to blow the whistle on this nonsense was simply undone by the circumstances of the discussion" (cited in Janis, 1982, p. 40). On the whole, then, Schlesinger began with initial public and private agreement with the invasion but ended in public agreement/private disagreement. These are the defining criteria of #2, paradoxical compliance (A/AD). Interestingly, such self-censorship as Schlesinger's is an important component of Janis's concept of *groupthink* (see Turner, Pratkanis, & Struckman, Chapter 9, this volume). Schlesinger's quote above is of particular interest because it points to one of the foundational pillars of contemporary social psychology – the frequent power of situational social forces to overwhelm factors such as reason, logic, facts, attitudes, personality, and values.

Responses #3, anticompliance (A/DA) and #4, anticonversion (A/DD) are mirror images, respectively, of #14, compliance (D/AD) and #13, conversion (D/AA). The symmetry of the model suggests that just as it is important to distinguish between public and private conformity, it is important to distinguish between public and private anticonformity. Response #3, anticompliance (A/DA), begins with pre-exposure agreement. After being exposed to influence, however, the target shows negative movement to a position of post disagreement with the source in public while at the same time maintaining agreement in private. Thus, #3, anticompliance, represents a special type of anticonformity wherein there is negative movement at the public level but no movement at the private level. Response #3, anticompliance (A/DA), has been demonstrated in numerous studies (e.g., Boyanowsky & Allen, 1973; Cooper and Jones, 1969; Frager, 1970; Nail et al., 1996; Plesser-Storr & Tedeschi, 1999; Schlenker & Weigold, 1990; Swim, Ferguson, & Hyers, 1999). A major motive for this behavior appears to be to publicly distance oneself from generally dissimilar, disliked, stigmatized, or unattractive others. For example, Plesser-Storr and Tedeschi (1999) exposed male participants to the attitudes of a physically attractive versus unattractive female. The males were then asked to report their own attitudes either publicly or privately. Some public-condition males were told that their attitudes would be seen by the female, others that their attitudes would be seen only by a group of third-party observers.

Regardless of the public condition, the males reported public disagreement with the attitudes of an unattractive female, but general public agreement with those of an attractive female. In the private condition, there was no difference in the reported attitudes of the males as a function of the female's attractiveness. A different motive for #3, anticompliance (A/DA) appears to be the projection of behavioral freedom and autonomy to others in the face of threats to one's freedoms (Baer, Hinkle, Smith, & Fenton, 1980; Heilman & Toffler, 1976; Nail et al., 1996).

With #4, anticonversion (A/DD), in contrast, there is negative movement both publicly and privately. For example, the motivation to convince oneself of one's autonomy may involve #4, anticonversion (A/DD). A study by Brehm and Mann (1975) found that participants took steps to react against threats to their attitudinal freedom by anticonforming both publicly and privately *vis-à-vis* the source of the threat (i.e., #4, anticonversion). Private anticonformity has also been obtained in studies by Pennebaker and Sanders (1976), Pool, Wood, and Leck (1998); Wood et al. (1996), and Wright (1986). These studies only represent probable occurrences of #4, anticonversion, however, because public behaviors or attitudes were not assessed.

The synthetic model, like the Willis (1963) and Allen (1965) models on which it was based, has some clear strengths. It directly includes all the responses identified by Allen. It also includes all of Willis's responses but offers more refined interpretations of them because of its addition of Allen's critical public/private variable. In particular, the Willis model provides for anticonformity, but it does not distinguish between public anticonformity that is accompanied by private anticonformity (#4, anticonverison (A/DD)) and public anticonformity that is not (#3, anticompliance (A/DA)). The synthetic model provides an improvement given that theory and research concerning anticonformity strongly suggest that the public/private variable is just as important regarding anticonformity as it is with respect to conformity (Baer et al., 1980; Brehm & Mann, 1975; MacDonald et al., 2004; Nail, 1986; Nail et al., 2000). A final strength of the synthetic model is that it led to the identification of one interesting, new response possibility – #2, paradoxical compliance (A/AD). Compelling, real-world examples of this intriguing type of compliance offered in accounts by Schlesinger and others (see MacDonald et al., 2004; Nail et al., 2000) suggest that it is a viable type of social response worthy of study in its own right. Notwithstanding these strengths, a weakness of the synthetic model is that it has no way of accommodating disinhibitory contagion. This limitation led directly to our most recent model, the four-dimensional Social Response Context Model (MacDonald et al., 2004; see also Nail et al., 2000).

The Social Response Context Model

The reader will recall that disinhibitory contagion begins with the potential influencee in an approach–avoidance conflict, desiring to engage in a certain behavior but being inhibited by social forces from doing so. The Willis (1963), Allen (1965), Nail (1986) and all other extant models cannot provide for disinhibitory contagion because, with regard to the potential influencee's *pre-exposure* position, the best that any model does is to consider either uniform agreement or disagreement with the potential influencer. With an approach–avoidance conflict, however, there is not really either. A major advance in our thinking occurred when we eventually realized that an approach–avoidance conflict could be correctly conceptualized with the same public/private, agreement/disagreement variables that we had used in the construction of the synthetic model. The difference, however, is that these labels would now apply not only to a potential influencee's post-exposure position but also to his or her *pre-exposure* position as well. That is, we began to consider the implications of the notion that public and private attitudes may differ even *before* a particular source of social influence is encountered. The degree of pre-influence public and private agreement with the eventual influence source sets the *context* in which various social responses can occur, hence the name "Social Response Context Model." Consider the previous example of disinhibitory contagion where many students in a class ask questions only after the first questioner, the model, does so. Before the model's question, some students are in an approach–avoidance conflict, privately wanting to ask a question but publicly being inhibited from doing so, perhaps because of uncertainty regarding how the teacher might respond. Following the first question, however, when nothing terrible happens to the model, the students' avoidance gradient and inhibitions are reduced and they are thereby freed to ask questions. Thus, the students have moved from (a) pre-exposure public disagreement/private agreement with the behavior of the model, asking a question (DA/), to (b) post-exposure public agreement/private agreement with the model (/AA). In short, the students have moved from intrapsychic conflict, through influence, to harmony (i.e., conflict → influence → harmony (DA/AA)).

Having made these connections, we were nevertheless reluctant to proceed with an expanded model that would include disinhibitory contagion because such a model would apparently necessitate four variables: *pre-exposure* public agreement–disagreement and *pre-exposure* private agreement–disagreement, but also *post-exposure* public agreement–disagreement and *post-exposure* private agreement–disagreement, as in the synthetic model (Figure 8.3). These four dimensions were necessary in order to provide for the possibility of a pre-exposure mismatch in public and private positions, as in disinhibitory contagion. Given four variables, each having two levels, such an expanded model would provide for 2^4 or 16 different response possibilities. Could this increased complexity be justified? Might such a four-dimensional model lead to advances in theory and research? The only thing we knew to do was to put the model together and see what might happen. The resulting four-dimensional model, the Social Response Context Model (SRCM), is presented in Figure 8.4.

The appearance of the SRCM may be a bit daunting at first, but it is actually just a straightforward extension of the synthetic model (Figure 8.3). Again, for purposes of discussion, the responses have been numbered. Responses 1 through 4 of the SRCM, #1 congruence (AA/AA), #2 paradoxical compliance (AA/AD), #3 anticompliance (AA/DA), and #4 anticonversion (AA/DD), are identical to responses 1 through 4 of the synthetic model, respectively. The SRCM simply makes it explicit that these behaviors all begin with pre-exposure public and private *agreement* with the influence source (AA/xx). In a similar way, responses 13 through 16 of the SRCM, #13 conversion (DD/AA), #14 compliance (DD/AD), #15 paradoxical anticompliance (DD/DA), and #16 independence (DD/DD), are identical to responses 13 through 16 of the synthetic model. The SRCM simply makes it explicit that these behaviors all necessitate pre-exposure public and private *disagreement* (DD/xx) with the influence source. Disinhibitory contagion (DA/AA) is represented in Response #9 of the SRCM. It begins with the influencee in an approach–avoidance conflict regarding how to behave, specifically pre public disagreement/private agreement (DA/) with the eventual influence source. It ends with post public and private agreement (/AA) as the model frees the influencee from his or her pre-exposure conflict.

Responses 5 through 8 and 10 through 12 represent the "new" responses of the SRCM. Would any of these behaviors be interpretable and have empirical support? Might any of these behaviors lead to new lines of research or provide integration with existing bodies of knowledge? Somewhat to our surprise, in working on the Nail et al. (2000) and MacDonald et al. (2004) articles, we discovered numerous ties between the new responses of the SRCM and a wide range of basic and applied issues of interest to social psychologists. These include issues such as cognitive dissonance phenomena (e.g., Aronson, Chapter 4, this volume; Festinger & Carlsmith, 1959); self-presentational theory (e.g., Tedeschi, Schlenker & Bonoma, 1971); individual and group psychotherapy (Frankl, 1967; Redl, 1949); prejudice, thought suppression, and the "rebound effect" (Monteith, Spicer, & Tooman, 1998); bystander intervention and nonintervention during emergencies (Darley & Latané, 1968); disobedience to authority (Milgram, 1974); and imitative, "copycat" suicides (Phillips, 1974).

The distinction between #5, *compliance/conversion* (AD/AA), and #6, *continued compliance* (AD/AD) parallels the controversy in the cognitive dissonance/induced compliance literature, respectively, between those who argue that the attitude change obtained in this research is genuine (e.g., Aronson, 1968, 1999; Bem, 1967; Festinger & Carlsmith, 1959) and those who believe that such change is only public in nature, reflecting a self-presentational tactic (e.g., Schlenker, 1980; Tedeschi et al., 1971; see MacDonald et al., 2004; Nail et al., 2000). According to the dissonance camp, if there is insufficient justification to warrant counterattitudinal behavior, pre public agreement/private disagreement defines cognitive dissonance and this dissonance resolves in post public agreement/private agreement (AD/AA). For the self-presentational camp, in contrast, it is only the *appearance* of inconsistency that matters. Thus, pre public agreement/private disagreement yields post public agreement/private disagreement (AD/AD).

Behavior #8, *disinhibitory anticonversion* (AD/DD), corresponds to a technique in psychotherapy known as *paradoxical intention* (Frankl, 1967; Loriedo & Vella, 1992), a technique most frequently employed with clients diagnosed with phobia. Ironically, a therapist commanding such a client that he or she *must* have a panic attack frequently results in the client being unable to have one (see MacDonald et al., 2004). It is "disinhibitory" because the client/influencee's pre-exposure public agreement/private disagreement with the command to have a panic attack (AD/) resolves in post-exposure public and private disagreement

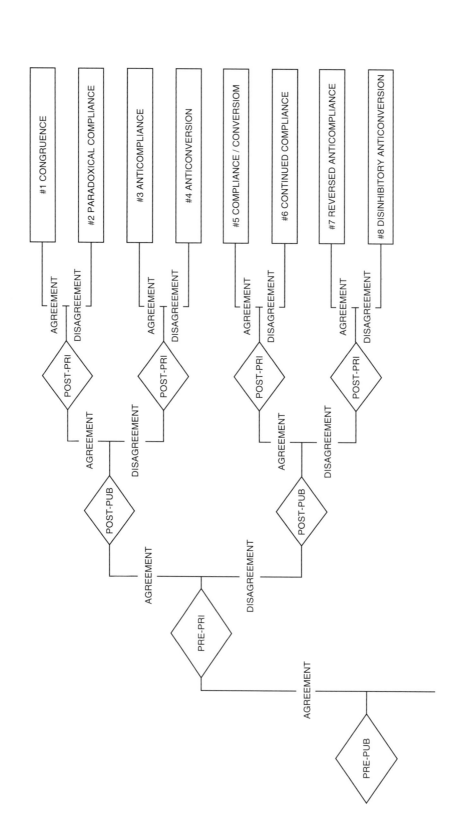

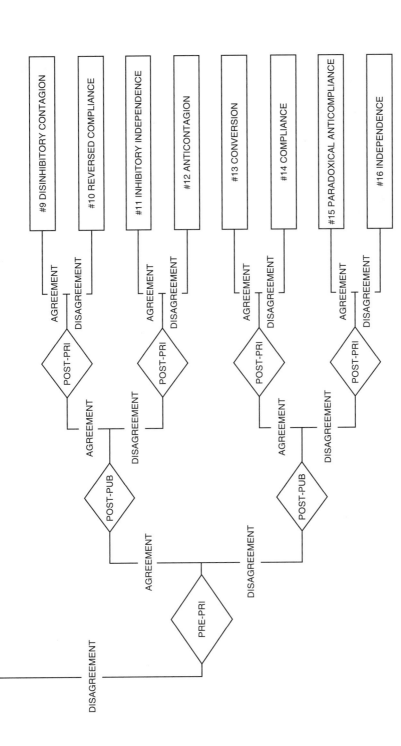

FIGURE 8.4 The Social Response Context Model. PRE-PUB is the potential influencee's pre-exposure, public position relative to the influence source; PRE-PRI is the pre-exposure, private position; POST-PUB is the post-exposure, public position; POST-PRI is the post-exposure, private position. From Nail et al. (2000). Copyright 2000 by the American Psychological Association. Adapted by permission.

(/DD). That is, the influence target's private disagreement (e.g., not wanting a panic attack) is freed for expression at the public level (viz., no panic attack occurs). It is "anticonversion" because the client/influencee moves in a direction opposite to that advocated by the therapist, the influence source. Disinhibitory anticonversion (#8, AD/DD) has also been demonstrated in the prejudice literature. Here, initial public agreement/private disagreement with instructions to suppress prejudicial thoughts among high-prejudice participants has resulted in post-exposure public disagreement/private disagreement with the instructions once they are no longer salient (e.g., Macrae, Bodenhausen, Milne, & Jetten, 1994; Monteith et al., 1998; see MacDonald et al., 2004).

Behavior #9 applies not only to studies explicitly focusing on disinhibitory contagion (DA/AA) but also to studies concerning disobedience to authority and copycat suicides. Briefly, participants' private inclinations to disobey an authority figure are much more likely to be acted upon following the disobedience of peers compared to participants who have no model of disobedience, 90 per cent versus 35 per cent, respectively (Milgram, 1974; see also Gamson, Fireman, & Rytina, 1982). Similarly, suicides are more likely in the days soon after a highly publicized suicide than they are before the suicide (Phillips, 1974, 1989). Not all cases involving pre-exposure public disagreement/private agreement, however, result in #9, disinhibitory contagion (DA/AA). Redl (1949) found that adolescents in group therapy did not always act upon their private hostility for the therapist with overt verbal aggression following such aggression by a peer/model. Such nonaction reflects #11, *inhibitory independence* (DA/DA). It is "independence" because, like #16, independence, the potential influencee remains uninfluenced. It is "inhibitory" because the potential influencee's inhibitions against aggression toward the therapist remain intact. The classic Darley and Latané (1968; Latané & Darley, 1968) work on bystander intervention or non-intervention in emergencies also reflects probable cases of #9, disinhibitory contagion (DA/AA) and #11, inhibitory independence (DA/DA), respectively (see also Bryan & Test, 1967; MacDonald et al., 2004; Rushton & Campbell, 1977). Redl (1949) reports examples that reflect probable #12, *anticontagion* (DA/DD). Some group therapy members would not remain so passive in resisting the influence of a verbally aggressive peer. Occasionally a member would actively resist such influence by removing himself or herself physically from the group. If we assume that such behavioral resistance was accompanied by a private decrease in hostility toward the therapist (e.g., via dissonance processes), such behavior would reflect #12, anticontagion (DA/DD).

Considering all 16 of the SRCM's responses, we have previously failed to find support for only #7, *reversed anticompliance* (AD/DA) and #10, *reversed compliance* (DA/AD). It is not difficult, however, to think of examples that fit these seemingly odd configurations. For instance, #10, reversed compliance might occur in a situation like the riot/brick-throwing example cited previously. Soon after throwing the brick, a rioter might start to feel guilty and privately wish he or she had never thrown the brick. Thus, pre-exposure public disagreement/private agreement with the trigger-person/brick thrower completely reverses to post-exposure public agreement/private disagreement. A probable real-life example #10, reversed compliance (DA/AD) occurred during the 2003 American League

Championship Series between the New York Yankees and Boston Red Sox. Historic and bitter rivals contesting a highly valued series, many members of both clubs may have experienced a relatively constant approach–avoidance conflict during games regarding overt, extra-gameplay aggression toward members of the other team. On October 11, during Game 3 of the series, the aggression was uncorked after a batter was hit by a pitch in a close game. Both dugouts cleared as a brawl quickly ensued. The then 72-year-old assistant manager of the Yankees, Don Zimmer, joined in the mêlée, apparently seeking out and then rushing the Red Sox' ace pitcher at the time, Pedro Martinez, despite the fact that Martinez was not playing that day. Seeing Zimmer's charge, the much younger Martinez extended his arms for defense, stepped to one side, and deftly tossed Zimmer to the ground. If we assume that Zimmer was in an approach–avoidance conflict before the incident, publicly not aggressing against Martinez but privately wanting to (DA/), and if we further assume that his post private position turned to regret following his attack (/AD), his behavior indicates #10, reversed compliance (DA/AD). We know that Zimmer did in all likelihood experience significant anguish over his attack on Martinez because on the following day during a televised news conference Zimmer tearfully expressed what appeared to be sincere regret and embarrassment over the entire incident (Feinsand, 2003). Interestingly, with Zimmer's public renunciation of his attack at the press conference thus bringing his post public and private attitudes in line, his behavior ultimately reflects #12, anticontagion (DA/DD).

DIRECTIONS FOR FUTURE THEORY AND RESEARCH

Progress in many fields of science appears to be directed by four interrelated goals. Considering these goals suggests many potentially fruitful avenues for future theory and research. Once a phenomenon is identified as important for advancing knowledge, a first and fundamental goal is to precisely define the phenomenon in question. What are its critical features; how does it compare and contrast with related phenomena? Precise description, of course, is the primary function of the SRCM and other models in this chapter. Let us call this Goal 1. Another goal (Goal 2) is to identify through empirical research those variables that control a phenomenon (moderators). What variables make the phenomenon increase, decrease, or disappear altogether? What are the rates of change and the forms of the relationships? Goal 3 is to explain why the phenomenon occurs. In psychology, this often means examining the psychological processes that mediate the phenomenon (mediators). Over time, explanatory theories are tempered by empirical evidence collected in the pursuit of Goal 2. At perhaps the highest level of abstraction, Goal 4 is to capture and summarize mathematically the relationships identified by research in connection with the first three goals.

Dating back at least to Sherif (1935), theorists and researchers have been more or less continuously pursuing these goals in the field of social influence – and with considerable success. For example, regarding Goal 1, #14, compliance in the Asch-type situation is defined by DD/AD. Regarding Goal 2, research indicates that the degree of compliance generally increases with variables such as unanimous versus nonunanimous majorities (e.g., Allen & Levine, 1969; Asch, 1952, 1956), high- versus low-status groups (e.g., Walker, Harriman, & Costello, 1980; see Driskell & Mullen, 1990, for a review), and ingroup versus outgroup sources of influence (e.g., Abrams et al., 1990; Guimond, 1999). Further, compliance tends to increase nonmonotonically with the number of confederates making up the majority, up to an asymptotic point (e.g., Gerard, Wilhelmy, & Conolley, 1968; Rosenberg, 1961; Wilder, 1977; see also Insko et al., 1985; Milgram, Bickman, & Berkowitz, 1969). Regarding Goal 3, these effects can all be explained by Deutsch and Gerard's (1955) theory of normative influence wherein compliance is conceptualized as an instrumental response designed to avoid possible social sanctions while gaining group rewards (i.e., social acceptance). Compliance presumably increases under the conditions of responding *vis-à-vis* a large unanimous majority of high-status ingroup members because such conditions foster greater potential sanctions and rewards than if any of these conditions is not met. Regarding Goal 4, all these effects can be described mathematically by Latané's (1981) social impact theory (SIT). Here the degree of social impact (I) is conceptualized as a multiplicative function of the strength, immediacy, and number of influence sources ($I = f[SIN]$). Unanimity, high status, and ingroup membership can all be conceptualized as increasing the strength component in Latané's formula. The number component, specifically, is addressed more precisely by Latané's *psychosocial law*: $I = sN^t$, $t < 1$ (derived from Stevens, 1957), where I, the amount of social impact, is equal to some power, t, of the number of influence sources, N, times a scaling constant, s. The stipulation $t < 1$ indicates that compliance should increase proportionally to some root of the number of influencers present. Latané's (1981) reanalysis of the Gerard et al. (1968) and Milgram et al. (1969) data sets (as well as numerous others) supports the psychosocial law rather well, yielding an r^2 of .80 and .90, respectively.[3]

One elegant feature of Latané's (1981) SIT is that with only a single modification it can be neatly applied to social influence settings where there is negative social impact (i.e., negative influence or movement) rather than positive (Bibb Latané, personal communication, June 3, 2000). Specifically, provision for negative movement can be implemented by simply changing the sign of the strength component in the $I = f[SIN]$ formula from positive to negative. This change makes SIT potentially applicable to any of the behaviors of the SRCM that are defined by negative movement (i.e., #3, anticompliance, AA/DA and #4, anticonversion, AA/DD), although no such published applications of SIT exist to our knowledge. Another elegant feature of SIT is that with only slight modification Latané's psychosocial law can be applied to social influence settings where increasing numbers in the group *decrease*, rather than increase, influence. Such decreases frequently occur in situations where multiple targets are exposed to social influence from a single source, as in Darley and Latané's (1968) research on helping/nonhelping in emergencies. In such settings, Latané (1981) has proposed that the social impact of the source should be divided by some root of the number of targets present, specifically, $I = s/N^t$, which is the same mathematically as $I = sN^{-t}$. In reference to the four goals outlined above, #11, inhibitory independence (DA/DA) describes the frequent nonhelping in emergencies, as in Darley and Latané (1968; Goal 1).

One variable that affects helping in such settings is the perceived number of bystanders available to help (Goal 2). This is known as the *bystander effect* – helping tends to decrease nonmonotonically as the number of bystanders available increases (see Latané & Nida, 1981, for a review in which the bystander effect was obtained in 48 of 56 studies, a percentage of 85.71). This effect can be explained by Darley and Latané's process theory, *diffusion of responsibility* (Goal 3); briefly, the more bystanders present, the less the duty or responsibility for any particular individual to help because the duty is psychologically diffused or divided among the total number of bystanders. This effect can be described mathematically by $I = sN^{-t}$ (Goal 4).

What about the behaviors of the SRCM besides #11, inhibitory independence in bystander intervention/nonintervention studies and #14, compliance (DD/AD) in group pressure studies? A reasonable amount is known about the variables that control the expression of some of the more well-known responses of the SRCM in at least some research paradigms (Goal 2): #1, congruence (AA/AA), #3, anticompliance (AA/DA), #5, compliance/conversion (AD/AA), #6, continued compliance (AD/AD), #9, disinhibitory contagion (DA/AA), #13, conversion (DD/AA), and #16, independence (DD/DD; see Nail, 1986; Nail et al., 2000; MacDonald et al., 2004). For example, #16, independence can be fostered in group pressure settings in a number of ways: by utilizing easy/unambiguous tasks versus difficult/ambiguous tasks (Asch, 1951, vs. Sherif, 1935), by providing incentives for accuracy given easy, Asch-type judgment tasks (Baron et al., 1996), by priming accuracy goals and individual, extragroup accountability for one's judgments (Quinn & Schlenker, 2002), by high levels of self-efficacy, even on difficult (math) tasks (Lucas et al., 2006), by demonstrated expertise and superiority regarding matters of fact (Nail & Ruch, 1992), by providing multiple and better alternatives to conformity on social opinion items (Maslach, Santee, & Wade, 1987; Santee & Maslach, 1982), and by the *pre-experimental* observation of a peer who successfully models independence (Allen & Wilder, 1979; Nemeth & Chiles, 1988).[4] Unfortunately, very little is known about the variables that might control the remaining seven behaviors specified by the SRCM, behaviors #2, #4, #7, #8, #10, #12, and #15 (Goal 2), let alone how these behaviors might be explained (Goal 3), or how the empirical relationships identified in Goal 2 might be described mathematically (Goal 4). If the SRCM is accepted as a general template for describing potential social influence responses and organizing the social influence literature (broadly defined), clearly much work remains to be done.

Given the central importance of #9, disinhibitory contagion (DA/AA) in the development of the SRCM, we close with a probable example of such on a national scale. This example also illustrates a real-world case of minority influence. For most of the history of the United States, homosexuality has been a strong taboo. What more vivid metaphor could there be for a public/private mismatch in behavior and attitudes than to refer to one's sexual orientation as being "in the closet"? Historically, the strongest public taboo of all in this regard, perhaps, has been marriage between members of the same sex. In the winter and spring of 2003–2004, however, all this began to change. Soon after a decision by the Supreme Court of Massachusetts that full, equal rights in that state must include the right of same-sex individuals to legally marry was widely publicized in the media, a small number of gay and lesbian marriages conducted by civil authorities began to happen in places as remote from Massachusetts as San Francisco and New Platz, NY. Soon the number of marriages began to multiply exponentially. For example, in a matter of days, Multnomah County in Oregon issued more than 700 licenses to same-sex couples. Couples from states other than California and New York even traveled to San Francisco and New Platz just to get married, including several from geographically distant states ("Developments on Gay Marriage," 2004). In contagion theory parlance, the Massachusetts Supreme Court and the first same-sex marriages to be publicized were the triggers. When no immediate legal consequences arose for the first couples who married, it apparently signaled to other couples that same-sex marriages would be, for the first time, accepted, at least in cities like San Francisco and New Platz. Accordingly, the number of marriages increased dramatically.

It is interesting to note in the preceding example that if groups and individuals defending the status quo opposing gay marriage were defined as the source of influence rather than the Massachusetts Supreme Court, the multitude of same-sex marriages would reflect #8, disinhibitory anticonversion. To clarify, before the run of marriages began, many same-sex couples presumably lived in conflict, displaying pre public agreement with the public norm opposing gay marriage (i.e., complying by not applying for marriage licenses) while privately disagreeing with it. Seeing the extreme negative response in the media of some of those in society who oppose gay marriage, however, may well have served as a negative referent, or catalyst, for some committed gay couples to defy the norm and marry (i.e., moving to post public disagreement with the norm accompanied by continued private disagreement with it). Pre public agreement/private disagreement that resolves in post public and private disagreement is the defining criterion for #8, disinhibitory anticonversion (AD/DD).

These examples of #8, disinhibitory anticonversion and #9, disinhibitory contagion help demonstrate the potential magnitude and scope of phenomena that come under the rubric *social influence* – phenomena that are identified by the Social Response Context Model.

ACKNOWLEDGMENTS

We thank Helen Harton, Eric Knowles, Mark Leary, Todd Lucas, and Mark Zanna for their support and encouragement in this line of work. Continuing appreciation goes to R. H. Willis. Thanks also go to David Gwinn and Janice Sperle for their technical expertise and assistance.

NOTES

1. Although Asch's work is often cited as an example of the power of social influence, Asch himself considered it a powerful demonstration of nonconformity in that

participants in the original experiment were able to resist the lure of the unanimous majority on 68 per cent of the critical trials (Friend, Rafferty, & Bramel, 1990; Santee & Maslach, 1982).

2. The present chapter is limited to models where social responses can be identified on the basis of a single social influence trial, so-called *one-trial models*. Accordingly, it does not consider *multiple-trial models*, namely, Krech et al.'s (1962) equilateral triangle model, Willis's (1963) isosceles triangle model, Willis's (1965a) diamond model, and Nail and Van Leeuwen's (1993) restructured diamond model. For a discussion of the distinction between one-trial and multiple-trial models, see Nail (1986).

3. Mathematical models that deal with the relative number of influencers and influencees have also been proposed by other theorists. These include Tanford and Penrod's (1984) social influence model (SIM) and Mullen's (1986) other-total ratio. What is more, SIM accounts for Asch's (1951, 1956) data better than Latané's SIT (see Latané, 1981, p. 345). We chose to focus on SIT for illustrative purposes because with its three conceptual variables – strength, immediacy, and number – it appears to provide more links to the empirical literature than either the Tanford and Penrod or Mullen models. A dynamic version of SIT has been proposed by Nowak, Szamrej, and Latané (1990, see also Harton & Bourgeois, 2004).

4. The consistent partner variation of the Asch (1951, 1956) paradigm, however, does not in fact foster genuine independence from the group as is often claimed. Again, technically speaking, the typical increase in nonconformity relative to the group actually represents #9, disinhibitory contagion (DA/AA) relative to the partner.

REFERENCES

Abrams, D., Wetherell, M., Cochrane, S., Hogg, M. A., & Turner, J. C. (1990). Knowing what to think by knowing who you are: Self-categorization and the nature of norm formation, conformity and group polarization. *British Journal of Social Psychology, 29*, 97–119.

Allen, V. L. (1965). Situational factors in conformity. In L. Berkowitz (Ed.), *Advances in experimental social psychology* (Vol. 2, pp. 133–175). New York: Academic Press.

Allen, V. L., & Levine, J. M. (1969). Consensus and conformity. *Journal of Experimental Social Psychology, 4*, 389–399.

Allen, V. L. & Wilder, D. A. (1979). Social support in absentia: The effect of an absentee partner on conformity. *Human Relations, 32*, 103–111.

Allport, F. H. (1934). The J-curve hypothesis of conforming behavior. *Journal of Social Psychology, 5*, 141–183.

Argyle, M. (1957). Social pressure in public and private situations. *Journal of Abnormal and Social Psychology, 54*, 172–175.

Aronson, E. (1968). Dissonance theory: Progress and problems. In R. Abelson, E. Aronson, W. McGuire, T. Newcomb, M. Rosenberg, & P. Tannenbaum (Eds.), *Theories of cognitive consistency: A sourcebook* (pp. 5–27). Chicago: Rand McNally.

Aronson, E. (1999). Dissonance, hypocrisy, and the self-concept. In E. Harmon-Jones & J. Mills (Eds.), *Cognitive dissonance: Progress on a pivotal theory in social psychology* (pp. 103–126). Washington, DC: American Psychological Association.

Asch, S. (1951). Effects of group pressure upon the modification and distortion of judgments. In H. Guetzkow (Ed.), *Groups, leadership, and men* (pp. 177–190). Pittsburgh, PA: Carnegie Press.

Asch, S. (1952). *Social psychology*. New York: Prentice-Hall.

Asch, S. (1956). Studies of independence and conformity: I. A minority of one against a unanimous majority. *Psychological Monographs, 70*(9, Whole No. 416).

Back, K. W., & Bogdonoff, M. D. (1964). Plasma lipid responses to leadership, conformity, and deviation. In P. H. Leiderman & D. Shapiro (Eds.), *Psychobiological approaches to social behavior* (pp. 24–42). Stanford, CA: Stanford University Press.

Baer, R., Hinkle, S., Smith, K., & Fenton, M. (1980). Reactance as a function of actual versus projected autonomy. *Journal of Personality and Social Psychology, 38,* 416–422.

Baron, R. A., & Kepner, C. R. (1970). Model's behavior and attraction to the model as determinants of adult aggressive behavior. *Journal of Personality and Social Psychology, 14,* 335–344.

Baron, R. S., Vandello, J. A., & Brunsman, B. (1996). The forgotten variable in conformity research: Impact of task importance on social influence. *Journal of Personality and Social Psychology, 71,* 915–927.

Bem, D. J. (1967). Self-perception: An alternative interpretation of cognitive dissonance phenomena. *Psychological Review, 74,* 183–200.

Boyanowsky, E. O., & Allen, V. L. (1973). Ingroup norms and self-identity as determinants of discriminatory behavior. *Journal of Personality and Social Psychology, 25,* 408–418.

Brehm, J. W. (1966). *A theory of psychological reactance*. New York: Academic Press.

Brehm, J. W., & Mann, M. (1975). Effect of importance of freedom and attraction to group members on influence produced by group pressure. *Journal of Personality and Social Psychology, 31,* 816–825.

Bryan, J. H., & Test, M. A. (1967). Models and helping: Naturalistic studies in aiding behavior. *Journal of Personality and Social Psychology, 6,* 400–407.

Campbell, J. D., & Fairey, P. J. (1989). Informational and normative routes to conformity: The effect of faction size as a function of norm extremity and attention to the stimulus. *Journal of Personality and Social Psychology, 57,* 457–468.

Cooper, J., & Jones, E. E. (1969). Opinion divergence as a strategy to avoid being miscast. *Journal of Personality and Social Psychology, 13,* 23–30.

Crutchfield, R. S. (1962). Conformity and creative thinking. In H. E. Gruber, G. Terrell, & M. Wertheimer (Eds.), *Contemporary approaches to creative thinking* (pp. 120–140). New York: Atherton.

Darley, J. M., & Latané, B. (1968). Bystander intervention in emergencies: Diffusion of responsibility. *Journal of Personality and Social Psychology, 8,* 377–383.

Deutsch, M., & Gerard, H. B. (1955). A study of normative and informational social influences upon individual judgment. *Journal of Abnormal and Social Psychology, 51,* 629–636.

Developments on gay marriage issue. (2004, March 5). *Yahoo! News*. Retrieved March 9, 2004, from http://story.news.yahoo.com/news?tmpl=story&u=/ap/gay_marriage_developments

Doms, M., & Van Avermaet, E. (1980). Majority influence, minority influence and conversion behavior: A replication. *Journal of Experimental Social Psychology, 16,* 283–292.

Driskell, J. E., & Mullen, B. (1990). Status, expectations, and behavior: A meta-analytic review and test of the theory. *Personality and Social Psychology Bulletin, 16,* 541–553.

Eagly, A. H., Wood, W., & Fishbaugh, L. (1981). Sex differences in conformity: Surveillance by the group as a determinant of male nonconformity. *Journal of Personality and Social Psychology, 40,* 384–394.

Feinsand, M. (2003, October 12). Zimmer issues apology. *Major League Baseball: News.* Retrieved March 17, 2004, from http://www.mlb.com/NASApp/mlb/mlb/news/mlb_news.jsp?ymd=20031012&content_id=576551&vkey=news_mlb&fext=.jsp&c_id=mlb

Feshbach, N. D. (1967). Nonconformity to experimentally induced group norms of high-status versus low-status members. *Journal of Personality and Social Psychology, 6,* 55–63.

Festinger, L. (1953). An analysis of compliant behavior. In M. Sherif & M. O. Wilson (Eds.), *Group relations at the crossroads* (pp. 232–256). New York: Harper.

Festinger, L., & Carlsmith, J. M. (1959). Cognitive consequences of forced compliance. *Journal of Abnormal and Social Psychology, 47,* 203–210.

Frager, R. (1970). Conformity and anticonformity in Japan. *Journal of Personality and Social Psychology, 15,* 203–210.

Frankl, V. E. (1967). Logotherapy. *Israel Annals of Psychiatry and Related Disciplines, 5,* 142–155.

Friend, R., Rafferty, Y., & Bramel, D. (1990). A puzzling misinterpretation of the Asch "conformity" study. *European Journal of Social Psychology, 20,* 29–44.

Gamson, W. A., Fireman, B. & Rytina, S. (1982). *Encounters with unjust authority.* Homewood, IL: Dorsey Press.

Gerard, H. B., Wilhelmy, R. A., & Conolley, E. S. (1968). Conformity and group size. *Journal of Personality and Social Psychology, 8,* 79–82.

Goethals, G. R., & Perlstein, A. L. (1978). Level of instigation and model similarity as determinants of aggressive behavior. *Aggressive Behavior, 4,* 115–124.

Guimond, S. (1999). Attitude change during college: Normative or informational social influence? *Social Psychology of Education, 2,* 237–261.

Harton, H. C., & Bourgeois, M. J. (2004). Cultural elements emerge from dynamic social impact. In M. Schaller & C. S. Crandall (Eds.), *The psychological foundations of culture* (pp. 41–75). Mahwah NJ: Lawrence Erlbaum Associates, Inc.

Heilman, M. E., & Toffler, B. L. (1976). Reacting to reactance: An interpersonal interpretation of the need for freedom. *Journal of Experimental Social Psychology, 12,* 519–521.

Hogg, M. A., & Turner, J. C. (1987). Social identity and conformity: A theory of referent information influence. In W. Doise & S. Moscovici (Eds.), *Current issues in European social psychology* (Vol. 2, pp. 139–182). Cambridge: Cambridge University Press.

Hornsey, M. J., Majkut, L., Terry, D. J., & McKimmie, B. M. (2003). On being loud and proud: Non-conformity, and counter-conformity to group norms. *British Journal of Social Psychology, 42,* 319–335.

Insko, C. A., Smith, R. H., Alicke, M. D., Wade, J., & Taylor, S. (1985). Conformity and group size: The concern with being right and the concern with being liked. *Personality and Social Psychology Bulletin, 11,* 41–50.

Jahoda, M. (1956). Psychological issues in civil liberties. *American Psychologist, 11,* 234–240.

Jahoda, M. (1959). Conformity and independence. *Human Relations, 12,* 99–120.

Janis, I. L. (1982). *Groupthink* (2nd ed.). Boston: Houghton-Mifflin.

Kelman, H. C. (1958). Compliance, identification and internalization: Three processes of attitude change. *Journal of Conflict Resolution, 2,* 51–60.

Kelman, H. C. (1974). Attitudes are alive and well and gainfully employed in the sphere of action. *American Psychologist, 29,* 310–324.

Kiesler, C. A. (1969). Group pressure and conformity. In J. Mills (Ed.), *Experimental social psychology* (pp. 233–306). New York: Macmillan.

Kiesler, C. A., & Kiesler, S. B. (1969). *Conformity*. Reading, MA: Addison-Wesley.

Krech, D., Crutchfield, R. S., & Ballachey, E. L. (1962). *Individual in society*. New York: McGraw-Hill.

Latané, B. (1981). The psychology of social impact. *American Psychologist, 36*, 343–356.

Latané, B., & Darley, J. M. (1968). Group inhibition of bystander intervention in emergencies. *Journal of Personality and Social Psychology, 10*, 215–221.

Latané, B., & Nida, S. (1981). Ten years of research on group size and helping. *Psychological Bulletin, 89*, 307–324.

Levy, D. A. (1992). The liberating effects of interpersonal influence: An empirical investigation of disinhibitory contagion. *Journal of Social Psychology, 132*, 469–473.

Levy, D. A., Collins, B. E., & Nail, P. R. (1998). A new model of interpersonal influence characteristics. *Journal of Social Behavior and Personality, 13*, 715–733.

Levy, D. A., & Nail, P. R. (1993). Contagion: A theoretical and empirical review and reconceptualization. *Genetic, Social, and General Psychology Monographs, 119*, 233–284.

Loriedo, C. & Vella, G. (1992). *Paradox and the family system*. New York: Brunner/Mazel.

Lucas, T., Alexander, S. A., Firestone, I. J., & Baltes, B. B. (2006). Self efficacy and independence from social influence: Discovery of an efficacy–difficulty effect. *Social Influence, 1*, 58–80.

Maass, A., & Clark, R. D. (1983). Internalization versus compliance: Differential processes underlying minority influence and conformity. *European Journal of Social Psychology, 13*, 197–215.

Maass, A., & Clark, R. D. (1984). Hidden impact of minorities: Fifteen years of minority influence research. *Psychological Bulletin, 95*, 428–450.

MacDonald, G., & Nail, P. R. (2005). Attitude change and the public–private attitude distinction. *British Journal of Social Psychology, 44*, 15–28.

MacDonald, G., Nail, P. R., & Levy, D. A. (2004). Expanding the scope of the Social Response Context Model. *Basic and Applied Social Psychology, 26*, 77–92.

McFarland, C., Ross, M., & Conway, M. (1984). Self-persuasion and self-presentation as mediators of anticipatory attitude change. *Journal of Personality and Social Psychology, 46*, 529–540.

Macrae, C. N., Bodenhausen, G. V., Milne, A. B., & Jetten, J. (1994). Out of mind but back in sight: Stereotypes on the rebound. *Journal of Personality and Social Psychology, 67*, 808–817.

Maslach, C., Santee, R. T., & Wade, C. (1987). Individuation, gender role, and dissent: Personality mediators of situational forces. *Journal of Personality and Social Psychology, 53*, 1088–1093.

Milgram, S. (1974). *Obedience to authority: An experimental view*. New York: Harper & Row.

Milgram, S., Bickman, L., & Berkowitz, L. (1969). Note on the drawing power of crowds of different size. *Journal of Personality and Social Psychology, 13*, 79–82.

Monteith, M. J., Spicer, C. V., & Tooman, G. D. (1998). Consequences of stereotype suppression: Stereotypes on and not on the rebound. *Journal of Experimental Social Psychology, 34*, 355–377.

Montgomery, R. L. (1992). Social influence and conformity: A transorientational model. In D. Granberg & G. Sarup (Eds.), *Social judgment and intergroup relations: Essays in honor of Muzafer Sherif* (pp. 175–200). New York: Springer-Verlag.

Moscovici, S. (1980). Toward a theory of conversion behavior. In L. Berkowitz (Ed.),

Advances in experimental social psychology (Vol. 13, pp. 209–239). New York: Academic Press.

Moscovici, S., Lage, E., & Naffrechoux, M. (1969). Influence of a consistent minority on the response of a majority in a color perception task. *Sociometry, 32,* 365–379.

Mullen, B. (1986). Stuttering, audience size, and the other–total ratio: A self-attention perspective. *Journal of Applied Social Psychology, 16,* 139–149.

Nail, P. R. (1986). Toward an integration of some models and theories of social response. *Psychological Bulletin, 100,* 190–206.

Nail, P. R., Harton, H. C., & Decker, B. P. (2003). Political orientation and modern versus aversive racism: Tests of Dovidio and Gaertner's (1998) integrated model. *Journal of Personality and Social Psychology, 84,* 754–770.

Nail, P. R., & Helton, W. B. (1999). On the distinction between behavioral contagion, conversion conformity, and compliance conformity. *North American Journal of Psychology, 1,* 87–94.

Nail, P. R., MacDonald, G., & Levy, D. A. (2000). Proposal of a four-dimensional model of social response. *Psychological Bulletin, 126,* 454–470.

Nail, P. R., & Ruch, G. L. (1990). A demonstration of the reformulated diamond model of social response. *Journal of Social Behavior and Personality, 5,* 711–722.

Nail, P. R., & Ruch, G. L. (1992). Social influence and the diamond model of social response: Toward an extended theory of informational influence. *British Journal of Social Psychology, 31,* 171–187.

Nail, P. R., & Thompson, P. L. (1990). An analysis and empirical demonstration of the concept of self-anticonformity. *Journal of Social Behavior and Personality, 5,* 151–162.

Nail, P. R., & Van Leeuwen, M. D. (1993). An analysis and restructuring of the diamond model of social response. *Personality and Social Psychology Bulletin, 19,* 106–116.

Nail, P. R., Van Leeuwen, M. D., & Powell, A. B. (1996). The effectance versus the self-presentational view of reactance: Are importance ratings influenced by anticipated surveillance? *Journal of Social Behavior and Personality, 11,* 573–584.

Nemeth, C. J., & Chiles, C. (1988). Modeling courage: The role of dissent in fostering independence. *European Journal of Social Psychology, 18,* 275–280.

Nemeth, C. J., & Wachtler, J. (1974). Creating the perceptions of consistency and confidence: A necessary condition for minority influence. *Sociometry, 37,* 529–540.

Nemeth, C. J., & Wachtler, J. (1983). Creative problem solving as a result of majority vs. minority influence. *European Journal of Social Psychology, 13,* 45–55.

Nowak, A., Szamrej, J., & Latané, B. (1990). From private attitude to public opinion: A dynamic theory of social impact. *Psychological Review, 97,* 362–376.

Osman, L. (1982). Conformity or compliance? A study of sex differences in pedestrian behaviour. *British Journal of Social Psychology, 21,* 19–21.

Pennebaker, J. W., & Sanders, D. Y. (1976). American graffiti: Effects of authority and reactance arousal. *Personality and Social Psychology Bulletin, 2,* 264–267.

Phillips, D. P. (1974). The influence of suggestion on suicide: Substantive and theoretical implications of the Werther effect. *American Sociological Review, 39,* 340–354.

Phillips, D. P. (1989). Recent advances in suicidology: The study of imitative suicide. In R. F. W. Diekstra, R. Maris, S. Platt, A. Schmidtke, & G. Sonneck (Eds.), *Suicide and its prevention: The role of attitude and imitation* (pp. 299–312). Leiden, The Netherlands: Brill.

Plesser-Storr, D., & Tedeschi, J. T. (1999). *Self-presentation of men to attractive and unattractive women: Cognitive vs. motivational explanations.* Unpublished manuscript, State University of New York, Albany.

Pool, G. J., Wood, W., & Leck, K. (1998). The self-esteem motive in social influence: Agreement with valued majorities and disagreement with derogated minorities. *Journal of Personality and Social Psychology*, 75, 967–975.

Quinn, A., & Schlenker, B. R. (2002). Can accountability produce independence? Goals as determinants of the impact of accountability on conformity. *Personality and Social Psychology Bulletin*, 28, 472–483.

Redl, F. (1949). The phenomenon of contagion and "shock effect" in group therapy. In K. R. Eissler (Ed.), *Searchlight on delinquency* (pp. 315–328). New York: International Universities Press.

Rosenberg, L. A. (1961). Group size, prior experience and conformity. *Journal of Abnormal and Social Psychology*, 63, 436–437.

Rushton, J. P., & Campbell, A. C. (1977). Modeling, vicarious reinforcement and extraversion on blood donating in adults: Immediate and long-term effects. *European Journal of Social Psychology*, 7, 297–306.

Russell, J. C., Wilson, D. O., & Jenkins, J. F. (1976). Informational properties of jaywalking models as determinants of imitated jaywalking: An extension to model sex, race and number. *Sociometry*, 39, 270–273.

Santee, R. T., & Maslach, C. (1982). To agree or not to agree: Personal dissent amid social pressure to conform. *Journal of Personality and Social Psychology*, 42, 690–700.

Schlenker, B. R. (1980). *Impression management: The self-concept, social identity, and interpersonal relations*. Monterey, CA: Brooks/Cole.

Schlenker, B. R., & Weigold, M. F. (1990). Self-consciousness and self-presentation: Being autonomous versus appearing autonomous. *Journal of Personality and Social Psychology*, 59, 820–828.

Sherif, M. (1935). A study of some social factors in perception. *Archives of Psychology*, 27, 1–60.

Smith, S., Murphy, D. B., & Wheeler, L. (1964). Relation of intelligence and authoritarianism to behavioral contagion and conformity. *Psychological Reports*, 14, 248.

Sorrels, J. P., & Kelley J. (1984). Conformity by omission. *Personality and Social Psychology Bulletin*, 10, 302–305.

Stevens, S. S. (1957). On the psychophysical law. *Psychological Review*, 64, 153–181.

Swim, J. K., Ferguson, M. J., & Hyers, L. L. (1999). Avoiding stigma by association: Subtle prejudice against lesbians in the form of social distancing. *Basic and Applied Social Psychology*, 21, 61–68.

Tanford, S., & Penrod, S. (1984). Social influence model: A formal integration of research on majority and minority influence processes. *Psychological Bulletin*, 95, 189–225.

Tedeschi, J. T., Schlenker, B. R., & Bonoma, T. V. (1971). Cognitive dissonance: Private ratiocination or public spectacle? *American Psychologist*, 26, 685–695.

Walker, M., Harriman, S., & Costello, S. (1980). The influence of appearance on compliance with a request. *Journal of Social Psychology*, 112, 159–160.

Wheeler, L. (1966). Toward a theory of behavioral contagion. *Psychological Review*, 73, 179–192.

Wheeler, L., & Caggiula, A. R. (1966). The contagion of aggression. *Journal of Experimental Social Psychology*, 2, 1–10.

Wheeler, L., & Levine, L. (1967). Observer–model similarity in the contagion of aggression. *Sociometry*, 30, 41–49.

Wheeler, L., & Smith, S. (1967). Censure of the model in the contagion of aggression. *Journal of Personality and Social Psychology*, 6, 93–98.

Wilder, D. A. (1977). Perception of groups, size of opposition, and social influence. *Journal of Experimental Social Psychology*, 13, 253–268.

Willis, R. H. (1963). Two dimensions of conformity–nonconformity. *Sociometry*, *26*, 499–513.

Willis, R. H. (1965a). Conformity, independence, and anticonformity. *Human Relations*, *18*, 373–388.

Willis, R. H. (1965b). *Descriptive models of social response*. Paper presented at the meeting of the American Psychological Association, Chicago.

Wood, W., Lundgren, S., Ouellette, J. A., Busceme, S., & Blackstone, T. (1994). Minority influence: A metaanalytic review of social influence processes. *Psychological Bulletin*, *115*, 323–345.

Wood, W., Pool, G. J., Leck, K., & Purvis, D. (1996). Self-definition, defensive processing, and influence: The normative impact of majority and minority groups. *Journal of Personality and Social Psychology*, *71*, 1181–1193.

Wright, R. A. (1986). Attitude change as a function of threat to attitudinal freedom and extent of agreement with a communicator. *European Journal of Social Psychology*, *16*, 43–50.

9

Groupthink as Social Identity Maintenance

MARLENE E. TURNER, ANTHONY R. PRATKANIS, and
CHRISTINA K. STRUCKMAN

G roupthink refers to the extreme concurrence-seeking displayed by decision-making groups that is hypothesized to result in highly defective judgments and outcomes (Janis, 1982). According to the model, the group decision process is characterized by intragroup pressures toward conformity that are stimulated by specific antecedent conditions such as high stress and directive leadership. Groupthink is purported to be the cause of such spectacular failures as the Bay of Pigs decision, the Watergate cover-up, and the space shuttle disasters.

Groupthink is but one perspective that addresses social influence processes in groups. Other examples include choice shifts, group polarization, and group exacerbation of stereotypic judgment tendencies. In each of these effects, group members tend to exhibit more polarized positions, beliefs, decisions, and so forth after exposure to the group itself. Choice shifts in group decision-making occur when there is a difference between group members' mean initial judgments, opinions, or choices and the group final decision (Isenberg, 1986; Myers & Lamm, 1976). Group polarization refers to the difference between members' initial preferences and their final preferences (which are usually more pronounced) following exposure to the group (Hinsz & Davis, 1984; Kaplan & Miller, 1983; Moscovici & Zavalloni, 1969). Exacerbation of stereotype judgments refers to the tendency for groups to amplify the tendency of individuals to use stereotypes when making evaluations (Friedkin, 1999; Zuber, Crott, & Werner, 1992).

Interestingly, groupthink enjoys an uneasy fame in the social psychological, organizational and management literatures. It is indeed one of the more recognizable concepts ever proposed and is often unquestioningly reported in popular books, periodicals, textbooks, and even scholarly outlets. It is not surprising, then, that groupthink has assumed a central role in popular and organizational culture. What is extraordinary, however, is the limited empirical research on the concept that has produced overwhelmingly equivocal support for the groupthink model (M. E. Turner & Pratkanis, 1998a, 1998b; see also Aldag & Fuller, 1993; Park, 1990).

In this chapter, we present the social identity maintenance (SIM) model of groupthink and review the empirical evidence for the model. This perspective underscores the prominence of the group's social construction of its internal processes and external circumstances. According to this model, groupthink then becomes a process of concurrence-seeking that is directed at maintaining a shared positive view of the functioning of the group in the face of a collective threat.

First, we examine the traditional groupthink model, briefly review the empirical research that the model stimulated, and discuss the responses that the equivocal empirical evidence for the model has produced. We then turn to the SIM model of groupthink, discuss the underlying processes, and present the empirical evidence for the model.

GROUPTHINK DEFINED

Janis's classic formulation (see Janis, 1972, 1982) as well as his more recent articulation (Janis, 1989) hypothesize that decision-making groups are most likely to experience groupthink when they are highly cohesive, are insulated from experts, perform limited search and appraisal of information, operate under directive leadership, and experience conditions of high stress with low self-esteem and little hope of finding a better solution to a pressing problem than that favored by the leader or influential members. Figure 9.1 depicts this model.

When present, these antecedent conditions are hypothesized to foster the extreme consensus-seeking characteristic of groupthink. This in turn is predicted to lead to two categories of undesirable decision-making processes. The first, traditionally labeled symptoms of groupthink, includes illusion of invulnerability, collective rationalization, stereotypes of outgroups, self-censorship, mindguards, and belief in the inherent morality of the group. The second, typically identified as symptoms of defective decision-making, involves the incomplete survey of alternatives and objectives, poor information search, failure to appraise the risks of

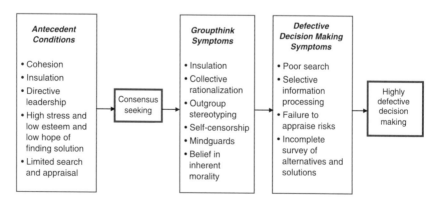

FIGURE 9.1   Janis's model of antecedents and consequences of groupthink.

the preferred solution, and selective information-processing. Not surprisingly, extremely defective decision-making performance by the group is predicted.

As evidence for the groupthink process, Janis (1972, 1982) presented a detailed qualitative analysis of defective decision-making by groups in the cases of the appeasement of Nazi Germany, Pearl Harbor, Bay of Pigs, North Korean invasion, and escalation of the Vietnam War, and compared them to the successful group decisions in the cases of the Marshall Plan and the Cuban Missile Crisis. Tetlock (1979) conducted a more formal test by performing a content analysis of archival records of public statements made by key decision-makers involved in the decisions identified by Janis. Results of this analysis suggested that decision-makers in the groupthink situations possessed more simplistic perceptions of policy issues and made more positive references to the US and its allies but did not engage in more outgroup stereotyping.

A REVIEW OF RESEARCH ON GROUPTHINK

Case Studies of Groupthink

Although Janis's original and some new case analyses provided evidence for the groupthink process, two case analyses raise questions about Janis's original specification of group cohesion. Drawing on a long tradition of group dynamics and social cohesion research (Lott & Lott, 1965), Janis defined cohesion as mutual attraction of group members or as the desire to remain in a prestigious group. However, Raven's (1974) analysis of the Nixon White House handling of the Watergate break-in and Esser and Lindoerfer's (1989) analysis of NASA's decision to launch the *Challenger* space shuttle suggest a different perspective on group cohesion – one that defines cohesion in terms of self-categorization or social identity (Hogg & Abrams, 1988; Tajfel, 1981; J. C. Turner, Hogg, Oakes, Reicher, & Wetherell, 1987).

In his analysis of groupthink in the Nixon White House during the Watergate era, Raven (1974) suggested that cohesion in this instance depended not so much on the presence of an *esprit de corps* as on the desire to maintain group membership at all costs. Raven noted that the Nixon White House demonstrated such groupthink symptoms as illusion of superior morality, illusion of invulnerability, illusion of unanimity, and mindguards. However, the members of the White House team did not form a closely knit group with high *esprit de corps*, nor did they exhibit a high degree of mutual attraction and admiration for each other. Rather, the groupthink stemmed from the low political self-esteem of Nixon's subordinates (none of whom had ever been elected to a political office) and the fact that "despite their personal antagonisms, all of them wanted with all their hearts and souls to be in that group and to be central to that group" (p. 310). In other words, Nixon White House members subscribed to a group or social identity that they collectively sought to maintain at all costs.

In an analysis of the decision to launch the *Challenger* space shuttle, Esser and Lindoerfer (1989) found little evidence for the antecedent conditions of group cohesion (as defined by mutual attraction), lack of impartial leadership, and homogeneity of members' backgrounds but some evidence that the launch team was in a highly stressful situation and for groupthink symptoms of illusion of invulnerability, rationalization, illusion of unanimity, pressure on dissenters, mindguards, and bias in processing information at hand. Evidence for other groupthink symptoms was inconclusive (see Moorhead, Ference, & Neck, 1991 and Dimitroff, Schmidt, & Bond, 2005 for additional analyses of this case). Other analyses suggest that the team was a cohesive group in the sense that they developed a shared identity as members of an elite NASA core and, like the Nixon White House members, wanted to remain part of that group (Feynman, 1988).

Other case studies have included analyses of the World Com accounting fraud incident (Scharff, 2005), the *Columbia* space shuttle tragedy (Dimitroff et al., 2005), and the EU decision about imposing sanctions in the Chechnya conflict (Lintonen, 2004). Following the typical case study methodology, evidence for antecedents, symptoms, and consequences is inferred from archival documents and from interviews with observers and participants. Once again, evidence supporting the complete groupthink model was limited, with varying degrees of support for the existence of antecedent conditions and symptoms of groupthink and defective decision-making.

Experimental Studies of Groupthink

Experimental studies have attempted to manipulate multiple antecedent conditions of groupthink while assessing groupthink symptoms and group decision effectiveness. In general, these studies have found only limited evidence for groupthink symptoms and, with one exception, no evidence for decrements in group decision effectiveness in groupthink treatments.

Three studies examined the effects of cohesion and leadership style on groupthink processes. Flowers (1977) trained appointed leaders of four-person groups to be either participative or directive. Groups composed of either friends (high cohesion) or strangers (low cohesion) proposed solutions to a case involving an elite high school faced with several crises (e.g., financial problems, senile teachers, influx of lower-class students, a possible teacher strike). Groups with directive leaders proposed fewer solutions, shared less case information, and used fewer case facts before and after reaching decisions. However, cohesion (operationalized as prior friendship) did not affect these processes. Other groupthink symptoms such as agreement with the group decision and freedom to express opinions were not affected by leadership style or cohesion. Leana (1985), using a design similar to that of Flowers (1977), found that groups with directive leaders proposed and discussed fewer solutions than did participative groups. In contrast, high-cohesion groups shared more case information than low-cohesion groups. Group evaluation of solution riskiness was unaffected by cohesion or leadership. Finally, Fodor and Smith (1982) asked high-cohesion (given the opportunity to win a reward for the best performance) or low-cohesion (given no such opportunity) groups led by an appointed leader who had either a high or low need for power to solve a business case. Groups with low-power leaders discussed more facts, considered more options, and demonstrated greater moral concern. However, group cohesion did not influence any dependent measures. In general, these three studies found no effects of the manipulated variables on various measures of decision quality.

Three investigations of the effects of cohesion and decision procedures provide similar patterns of results. Procedures designed to limit group discussion (such as instructions to examine few ideas and to achieve cooperation) produce fewer statements of disagreement than do instructions favoring full discussion of ideas (e.g., Courtwright, 1978). Again, this body of research demonstrates no effects of cohesion (typically manipulated as personality compatibility) and discussion procedures on decision quality (Callaway & Esser, 1984; Callaway, Marriott, & Esser, 1985; Courtwright, 1978).

Groupthink Evaluated

Several points about this research should be noted.

1. Inadequacy of Evidence for Causal Relations Among Model Components First, evidence for the full constellation of groupthink antecedents and consequences was limited. For example, Esser and Lindoerfer (1989) found evidence for only six of the thirteen symptoms and for only one of the five antecedents of groupthink. With the exception of the limited evaluation produced by procedures designed to constrict discussion (such as instructions regarding deliberations, directive leadership, and so forth), laboratory research has generally failed to provide convincing evidence for the full range of the groupthink effect.

2. Inadequacy of Conceptualizations of Key Antecedent Variables Second, the nature of the antecedents seems to require further conceptualization. Analyses of both the Nixon White House (Raven, 1974) and the *Challenger* space shuttle decision (Esser & Lindoerfer, 1989) found little evidence for the traditional conception of cohesion as mutual attraction. However, they did find evidence for a conceptualization of cohesion based on the self-categorization and social identity literatures. For example, each group was clearly identified and categorized as a group. A self-categorization and social identity perspective suggests that the perception of others as group members rather than as unique, different persons may be a necessary precondition for group cohesion (Hogg & Abrams, 1988; Tajfel, 1981; J. C. Turner et al., 1987). Hogg and Abrams (1988) also argue that categorization can generate intragroup attraction or social cohesion by allowing the development of conditions traditionally conducive to the development of interpersonal attraction. Further, categorization may also operate by reinforcing the similarities between the individual and other group members. Note that the policy-making groups studied by Janis appear to conform to this precondition. Similarly, it is clear that relatively little experimental evidence for the primary role of cohesion (operationalized using the mutual attraction paradigm) has been produced. This also may be partially due to a lack of consideration of the importance of categorization in producing cohesion. It is quite possible that some manipulations paid insufficient attention to the notion that the perception of others as group members rather than as unique, different persons may be a necessary precondition for group cohesion.

Likewise, the conceptualization of threat in the experimental studies may require further development. In each case analysis, the decision-making group faced a threatening situation for which effective means of resolution were not immediately apparent (see Janis, 1982 for a discussion of the importance of this antecedent). Each group also voluntarily adopted a variety of methods for dealing with the threat. In contrast, the threats used in the experimental studies, while having both face and ecological validity, actually seemed to involve few personal consequences for the group. Rather, threat has been typically controlled by using a task involving some form of crisis for the participants described in the task – but not for the group itself. Thus, the group had little stake in the decision-making process or its outcome. It is possible that more direct and impactful manipulations of threat may produce symptoms associated with the experience of groupthink.

3. Pliability of Groupthink Symptoms

The failure to produce the full constellation of groupthink effects in both case and experimental research suggests that groups may employ a variety of techniques. Clearly, groups can creatively manipulate their perceptions so that these identity protection pressures are resolved. Moreover, these evaluations are not likely to be trustworthy indicators of the group processes. Indeed, many studies demonstrate the futility of attempting to examine self-evaluations as anything other than social constructions of the group. What is even more interesting is the failure of many investigations to document the usefulness of more "objective" measures. Again, we interpret this as a need to develop more fine-grained analyses of the relationships between antecedents and consequences. In support of this idea, one consistency emerges from the experimental findings: Procedures designed to limit group discussion (e.g., directive leadership, instructions emphasizing the importance of avoiding disagreement) tend to produce fewer solutions, less sharing of information, and fewer statements of disagreement. This provides some indirect evidence that particular antecedent conditions may be associated with certain outcomes and that groups may adopt a variety of procedures to resolve groupthink.

4. Failure to Provide Evidence for Defective Decision-making

It is particularly important to note that no experimental evidence for defective decision-making – the hallmark of the groupthink phenomenon – has been obtained in any of these studies. Case studies generally cannot be used to infer the causal relationship between groupthink antecedents and impaired group performance as most cases are selected because they *a priori* fulfill this criterion.

Not surprisingly, the limited empirical evidence for the groupthink model has led some researchers to question the validity and usefulness of the model (see in particular Aldag & Fuller, 1993). However, other responses to this lack of empirical confirmation suggest that more fine-grained conceptualizations of the model might yield fruitful results. These responses have taken two directions: examinations of other factors that might impact groupthink processes, and theoretical reconceptualizations of the groupthink concept and reformulations of the original model.

Examinations of Other Factors Affecting Groupthink Processes

One response to the lack of empirical evidence for groupthink has been to examine the impact of other variables on groupthink processes and outcomes. Once again, results of these investigations generally question the validity of the groupthink model and the utility of additional variables. For example, Ahlfinger and Esser (2001) found that groups whose leaders promoted their own preferred solutions produced more symptoms of groupthink, discussed fewer facts, and reached a decision more quickly than groups with nonpromotional leaders. However, predisposition to conformity did not affect groupthink processes. Other research has demonstrated that certainty orientation affects groupthink symptoms in the opposite direction to that predicted by the groupthink theory and that cohesion affected some group processes but not outcomes (Hodson & Sorrentino, 1997). In a series of qualitative case analyses, Neck and colleagues have examined the role of time pressure and methodical decision-making processes on groupthink processes and outcomes, again finding some support for the role of these variables but equivocal support for the full groupthink model (Moorhead, Ference, & Neck, 1991; Neck, 1996; Neck & Manz, 1994; Neck & Moorhead, 1992). In contrast, Schulz-Hardt, Frey, Lüthgens, and Moscovici (2000) found no evidence for biased information search under consensus decision rule procedures. Kroon and colleagues have found limited support for the effects of accountability on groupthink processes (Kroon, Van Kreveld, & Rabbie, 1992; Kroon, 't Hart, & van Kreveld, 1991). Finally, social cohesion has been related to some but not all groupthink processes whereas task cohesion has reduced the tendency to exhibit some groupthink processes (Bernthal & Insko, 1993).

In addition to examining the role of additional variables in producing groupthink, research has focused on investigating the incidence of groupthink in new contexts. An analysis of archival news articles revealed that the salience of group membership, the positive evaluation of ingroup leaders, the negative evaluation of outgroup leaders and the appearance of self-appointed mindguards were higher during the Northern Ireland conflict than when the conflict was not underway (Hergovich & Olbrich, 2003). Choi and Kim (1999) investigated the perception of groupthink in thirty work teams. Once again, equivocal support for the groupthink model was obtained. Analysis of press reports on the failed globalization decisions of British Airways and Marks & Spencer again finds partial support for the model (Eaton, 2001). Yetiv (2003) interviewed members of the G. H. W. Bush White House group and analyzed primary source documents to investigate the role of groupthink processes in the decision-making regarding the 1991 Gulf War. Some support for the model was obtained, although Yetiv suggests that the defective decision-making predicted by the model was not observed.

In general, the findings of this body of research confirm those of the early studies: Only limited and equivocal support for the model has been obtained. The question of whether additional variables are useful for explicating the groupthink phenomenon clearly requires further research.

Reconceptualizations of the Groupthink Concept and Theory

A second type of response to the lack of empirical verification for the groupthink model has led to the reformulation of the relationships among the antecedents and consequences, and indeed even reconceptualizations of the groupthink concept itself. Both Raven (1998) and Kramer (1998) question the role of groupthink as specified by Janis in the Watergate cover-up. Raven suggests that the need to be part of a highly desirable group was a primary driver of group decisions in the Nixon White House, whereas Kramer highlights the role of political motivations. McCauley (1989) examines the relationship between groupthink and Kelman's three levels of compliance (Kelman, 1958). Whyte (1998) underscores the role of collective efficacy in producing groupthink-like processes. 't Hart (1998) proposes three models of small group functioning in government, each of which highlights different dimensions of collegial policy-making and distinct criteria for evaluating group performance. Moorhead, Neck and West (1998) hypothesize about the potential for groupthink in autonomous work teams. Although promising, these theoretical frameworks and reconceptualizations have yet to be fully empirically tested.

GROUPTHINK AS SOCIAL IDENTITY MAINTENANCE

The social identity maintenance (SIM) model of groupthink (M. E. Turner, Pratkanis, Probasco, & Leve, 1992; M. E. Turner & Pratkanis, 1998a) also was developed in response to the equivocal empirical support for the groupthink model. This perspective underscores the prominence of the group's social construction of its internal processes and external circumstances. According to this model, which is depicted in Figure 9.2, groupthink then becomes a process of concurrence-seeking that is directed at maintaining a shared positive view of the functioning of the group. Empirical evidence provides good support for the model. In the next section, we examine this model in depth and discuss the particular nature of identifiable antecedent conditions and the process by which these conditions lead to the consequences of groupthink. We will then discuss the research that has been conducted on the model.

Cohesion and Collective Threat as Prime Antecedents

The SIM model proposes that groupthink occurs when members attempt to maintain a shared positive image of the group. Two assumptions underlie this notion. First and most simplistically, group members must develop a positive image of the group. Second, that image must be questioned by a collective threat.

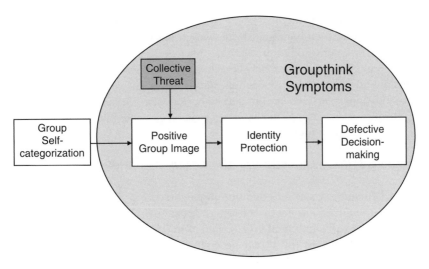

FIGURE 9.2   A social identity maintenance model of groupthink.

These two conditions, then, are essential for the development of groupthink *as social identity maintenance*. Yet how do these conditions arise and what specific components of each antecedent condition are essential?

Developing a Shared Positive Group Image: The Role of Self-categorization and Social Identity

Developing a positive image   How do groups develop a positive image? One route involves the interplay of self-categorization processes and social identity maintenance. According to this perspective (J. C. Turner, 1981; J. C. Turner and Haslam, 2000), group members must categorize themselves as a group (e.g., Kennedy men, Nixon White House, Intel developers) rather than, say, as a set of unique individuals (see Hogg, 1992 for a complete discussion of this). In other words, members must perceive the group as indeed having a social identity. The SIM model suggests that groups who do not meet this precondition will be unlikely to develop groupthink as social identity maintenance. In short, simply drawing together a group of individuals (despite their level of mutual attraction) will be insufficient to produce this form of groupthink. Note that the SIM perspective diverges from some traditional approaches that define cohesion in terms of mutual attraction (e.g., Lott & Lott, 1965) but is consistent with the notion of cohesion as pressure to maintain the group (Cartwright & Zander, 1953). Nevertheless, this categorization, in turn, has crucial implications for the development of groupthink.

The consequences of categorization   Categorization has three consequences for groupthink. First, when categorization occurs, the group tends to develop positive views of itself (J. C. Turner, 1981). Categorization leads groups to seek positive distinctiveness for the ingroup and to exhibit a motivational bias for positive collective self-esteem (J. C. Turner, 1981, J. C. Turner et al., 1987). Thus, we see that members tend to develop a positive image of the group and, importantly, are motivated to protect that image. Categorization may also operate by reinforcing the similarities between the individual and other group members and making the group identity (as opposed to the group members themselves as unique individuals) attractive, thus serving as the basis for cohesion (Tajfel, 1981; J. C. Turner et al., 1987). Finally, categorization provides the basis upon which the collective threat operates.

Collective Threat: Questioning the *Group's* Image

A shared threat   A second condition highlighted by a SIM perspective is that the group should experience a collective threat that attacks its positive image. We define threat as a potential loss to the group (cf. Argote, Turner, & Fichman, 1989). It is critical that the threat be collective in nature and that it question or attack the group's identity. A threat to an individual member of the group is not likely to engender the groupthink-like consequences that a collective threat will. For example, a threat to a single member may result in the dismissal of that member in order to maintain the group's image. With respect to the development of groupthink-like consequences, this shared threat has some critical consequences for group processes.

The consequences of collective threat   When threatened, individuals and groups tend to narrow their focus of attention to threat-related cues (Kahneman, 1973; M. E. Turner, 1992, M. E. Turner & Horvitz, 2000). In instances where the collective identity is threatened, the group tends to focus on those cues that can help maintain the shared positive image of the group that is invoked by social categorization. Thus, the overriding task of the group becomes image protection or even enhancement. Under certain circumstances, this can have detrimental consequences for group functioning. This is especially the case when high cohesion coupled with a social identity exacerbates identity protection motivations.

When the Collective Identity is Threatened: The Independent and Interactive Effects of Cohesion and Threat on Decision Effectiveness and Groupthink Symptoms

Consequences for decision effectiveness   The SIM model holds that threat and cohesion should interactively affect group decision effectiveness. Under nonthreatening circumstances, cohesion, as we have defined it, can in fact have facilitatory effects on group decision performance. When group goals favor effectiveness and productivity, cohesion enhances the accomplishment of those goals. In short, cohesive groups tend to be better at achieving their goals (see M. E. Turner et al., 1992 for a brief review of this literature, see Shaw, 1981 for an extensive treatment).

A collective threat that strongly questions the group identity, however, can fundamentally change those goals because the cohesive group is motivated to protect that identity. Unchecked, this type of threat is likely to induce the group to focus on threat-relevant activities and goals. In this case, the goal of the group is transformed from the pursuit of effective functioning to the maintenance, protection, and even enhancement of the threatened image. Not surprisingly, when the task is complex and uncertain (as in most groupthink decisions), this focusing of attention detracts from the decision-making process to such an extent that performance is impaired. Indeed, experimental evidence provides strong support for this perspective. Highly cohesive groups operating under threatening conditions performed significantly more poorly than did highly cohesive groups operating under nonthreatening conditions (M. E. Turner et al., 1992; M. E. Turner & Pratkanis, 1994a). Moreover, cohesion by itself and threat by itself each had faciliatory effects on group performance.

Consequences for groupthink symptoms The SIM model suggests that groups that have a social identity and that experience a collective threat will have an overriding need to engage in identity protection. Thus, group members' reports of their decision-making processes are likely to reflect that motivation. We would expect then that group members are likely to use defensive strategies designed to protect or even enhance the image of the group. The manifestation of these motivations can vary considerably, with many routes to identity protection possible. Prior research has suggested that cohesion may be associated with more risky decisions (Thompson & Carsrud, 1976), greater social influence, agreement and conformity (e.g., Festinger, Schachter, & Back, 1950), and more discussion of ideas (e.g., Leana, 1985). A collective threat can likewise have a variety of consequences for group processes. Prior research has demonstrated that threat can increase rationalization about the group decision (Janis & Mann, 1977), produce denial (Lazarus & Folkman, 1984), exacerbate premature closure (Janis, 1982; Janis & Mann, 1977), and limit participation in group processes (Hall & Mansfield, 1971; for a review of this literature see M. E. Turner & Horvitz, 2000). Thus, again, the specific components of the group situation are paramount in predicting the effects of the antecedent conditions. Once again, empirical evidence bears this out: Groupthink symptoms tend to be quite pliable and vary depending on particular circumstances (see M. E. Turner et al., 1992, M. E. Turner & Pratkanis, 1998a, 1998b).

The Role of Additional Antecedents and Symptoms

The classic formulation of the groupthink model incorporates three other antecedent conditions: directive leadership, limited search and appraisal of information, and insulation from experts. The SIM model holds that these antecedents will have limited utility under conditions of groupthink as *social identity maintenance* (although they may be important in other forms of groupthink; see Kramer, 1998 and Whyte, 1998). In fact, a review of the existing empirical literature upholds this view. Studies investigating the effects of leadership style and discussion procedures (e.g., restricted vs. participatory discussion) show no adverse effects on performance and few effects on most groupthink symptoms (Callaway & Esser,

1984; Callaway et al., 1985; Courtwright, 1978; Flowers, 1977; Fodor & Smith, 1982; Leana, 1985). Similarly, procedures designed to limit group discussion (e.g., directive leadership, instructions emphasizing avoiding disagreement) tend to produce fewer solutions, less sharing of information, and fewer statements of disagreement but do not affect other outcomes (nor do they adversely affect solution quality measures; e.g., see Flowers, 1977; Leana, 1985). Thus, poor information-processing procedures and insulation tend *not* always to be important for the production of groupthink.

Case Study Evidence for the SIM Model

This model is first illustrated with a case analysis of how the city council of Santa Cruz, California made decisions regarding earthquake safety prior to the 1989 Loma Prieta earthquake disaster that devastated the city (Pratkanis & Turner, 1999). Despite state requirements to develop a mitigation plan and to undertake retrofitting, the city council chose to delay implementation. Unfortunately, the city suffered a 7.1 magnitude earthquake that resulted in five deaths, almost 10,000 homeless, and approximately $1 billion in property damage that would have been mitigated by those retrofitting measures (Quarnstrom, Levy, & Kutzmann, 1989). Pratkanis and Turner (1999) argue that the decision process employed by the city council was an example of groupthink as social identity maintenance.

Evidence for Groupthink Antecedents   Analysis of archival documents indicated that each groupthink antecedent as specified by the social identity maintenance interpretation was indeed a characteristic of the city council. Several characteristics of the council suggest that it was a cohesive group. First, as suggested by self-categorization and social identity approaches, members of the group did label or categorize themselves using a shared identity. It also seems evident that the council operated in isolation, failed to avail itself of other possible sources of information, lacked norms favoring methodical procedures for decision-making, and operated under high stress with little hope of finding a better solution than that favored by the leader or influential members. The nature of the leadership of the council is not entirely clear. However, statements made by the city mayor (the titular head of the council) subsequent to the earthquake show clear support for the chosen course of action.

   These facts paint a picture of a cohesive group confronted with a powerful dilemma. The city council faced a perceived economic threat that seismic retrofitting was expected to induce. This threat was compounded by the fact that the council represented a politically progressive, humanitarian culture. Enacting an ordinance requiring retrofitting and thereby valuing the sanctity of human life over economic gain would be consistent with this ideology. However, such an ordinance was also perceived as exacting great economic harm on both the city and a powerful constituency that controlled a large portion of the city's resources – the city building owners. Consequently, the groupthink process enabled the council to devise a plan that not only maintained its positive image as a progressive group but also allowed it to avoid the perceived adverse economic consequences of retrofitting. An analysis of the symptoms of groupthink and defective decision-making that the group exhibited illustrates this point.

Evidence for Symptoms of Groupthink and Defective Decision-Making An analysis of the decision-making process employed by the council suggests that it displayed many of the symptoms of groupthink, including illusion of invulnerability, collective rationalization, stereotyping of outgroups, pressures toward uniformity, and unanimity. Symptoms of defective decision-making were also apparent. Information search procedures were limited; alternatives and objectives were not evaluated fully; examination of risks was circumscribed; information processing was biased; and contingency plans were not formulated (see Pratkanis & Turner, 1999 for a fuller discussion of the evidence supporting these conclusions).

Thus, the decision-making process employed by the Santa Cruz city council did indeed display most of the symptoms associated with the presence of group-think. The results of this analysis provide support for our hypothesis that the Santa Cruz city council decision to delay the enactment of retrofitting ordinances was a result of groupthink – and of groupthink that served to maintain the threatened image of the group. The council's decision-making process was characterized by all seven defective decision-making symptoms, at least seven of the eight groupthink symptoms, and four (and most likely all) of the five antecedent conditions that are associated with groupthink.

Experimental Tests of Groupthink as Social Identity Maintenance

M. E. Turner et al. (1992) examined the effects of cohesion and threat on decision-making effectiveness and symptoms of groupthink and defective decision-making of three-person groups of college students. The cohesion manipulation drew on both the self-categorization and social cohesion literatures. Consistent with self-categorization and social identity research (Hogg & Abrams, 1988; J. C. Turner et al., 1987), each group received a unique group identity (Eagles, Cougars, etc.). Then, in line with the social cohesion approach, each group in the high-cohesion condition spent five minutes discussing and listing the similarities among the group members. In contrast, subjects in the low-cohesion condition were not given group identities and spent five minutes discussing their dissimilarities. The threat manipulation incorporated personal consequences for the decision-making group and involved a challenge to a positive image of the group. In the high-threat condition, groups were informed that their discussion would be videotaped and, more critically, that the videotapes could be used for training purposes in both classes held on campus and training sessions held in local corporations (this was especially potent for the specific sample, as most students were currently working in local large companies). These tapes were purportedly only to be used if the group engaged in dysfunctional decision-making processes. Thus, failure at the task would in fact involve direct negative consequences for the group that would threaten a positive image of the group – conditions that appear to be characteristic in most groupthink case analyses. In contrast, groups in the low-threat condition were told that the project was in its first stages and that the materials were being pretested.

Subjects worked on a version of the Parasol Subassembly Case (Maier, 1952). The task required participants to propose a solution for the falling productivity of a group of assembly station workers. Production problems centered on an aging worker with limited abilities whose work frequently piled up. The case also included information concerning company procedures and environmental conditions that made some solutions (i.e., hiring additional workers) difficult or impossible to implement. The task is useful for investigating groupthink processes because it involves a wide range of solution quality. Moreover, the range of solutions maps on to the range of decision quality for groups experiencing groupthink (see Steiner, 1982 for a discussion of this task and its relation to groupthink; see also M. E. Turner et al., 1992). Groupthink processes such as incomplete survey of alternatives and objectives tend to result in poorer quality decisions; groups that fully consider and evaluate solution alternatives achieve higher quality solutions (Maier, 1952). After orally discussing the task, subjects responded to a postexperimental survey containing self-reports of symptoms of groupthink and defective decision-making.

Results showed some intriguing patterns. Most critically, the defective decision-making theoretically associated with groupthink was obtained. Group decision effectiveness was *interactively* affected by cohesion and threat. Post hoc comparisons indicated that group solution quality was poorer in the high-threat, high-cohesion (the groupthink treatment) and low-threat, low-cohesion treatments than in the high-threat, low-cohesion treatment. Decision quality was also higher in the low-threat, high-cohesion treatment (although this comparison did not attain conventional levels of significance).

In contrast to decision effectiveness, cohesion and threat *independently* affected symptoms of groupthink and defective decision-making. Cohesion increased confidence in the group solution but decreased reported discomfort with raising points dissenting from the group discussion. Threat increased both rationalization about the solution and agreement with the group decision but reduced self-reported annoyance at other members who raised issues conflicting with the group decisions. Subjects in the high-cohesion treatment evaluated their solutions as less risky than groups in the low-cohesion treatment, and low-threat subjects reported that they stopped searching for a solution once an acceptable alternative was found to a greater extent than high-threat subjects. Other defective decision-making symptoms involving information-processing activities such as the number of solution objectives considered, the number of solution alternatives considered, the number of case facts recalled (a measure of biased information processing), the number of additional items of information requested (a measure of information search), and the development of contingency plans were unaffected by cohesion or threat.

Thus, group decision effectiveness was significantly poorer under the simultaneous presence of cohesion and threat. Yet self-reports of symptoms of groupthink were independently affected by cohesion and by threat. What seems to be happening is that cohesion and threat induce groups to evaluate themselves more favorably on various dimensions than do low cohesion or low threat. (For example, high-threat groups evaluated their solutions more favorably; high-cohesion groups said they felt freer to disagree with other group members.) Although these may be accurate reports when cohesion or threat alone was present (and decision quality was superior), they are clearly inaccurate when both cohesion and threat were present (and decision quality was quite poor). These results reinforce the view that, as Janis (1982) suggests, one outcome of groupthink seems to be a mutual effort among members of the group to maintain emotional equanimity. In other words, groupthink can be viewed as a SIM strategy: a collective effort designed to protect the positive image of the group. This view also suggests that traditional strategies for overcoming groupthink may have some previously neglected pitfalls that may be magnified when groups employ groupthink processes to protect a threatened social identity.

Designing Interventions to Prevent Groupthink as Social Identity Maintenance

According to the SIM model, the prevention of groupthink has two objectives: the reduction of social identity maintenance and the stimulation of constructive, intellectual conflict (see M. E. Turner & Pratkanis, 1994b; 1997). However, the SIM model suggests that the risks of inappropriately implementing interventions can be quite high.

Interventions designed to reduce pressures for identity protection include the provision of an excuse or face-saving mechanism, the risk technique, and multiple role-playing procedures. Providing an excuse for potential poor performance appears to reduce the group's need to engage in identity-protection tactics and increases the group's focus on problem-solving, in turn enhancing performance (M. E. Turner et al., 1992). The risk technique is a structured discussion situation designed to facilitate the expression and reduction of fear and threat (see Maier, 1952 for a complete discussion). Finally, multiple role-playing procedures can be accomplished by having group members assume the perspectives of other constituencies with a stake in the decision (see Fisher, Kopelman & Schneider, 1996 for a good application of this technique) or of another group member.

Procedures for stimulating constructive conflict include structured discussion principles and procedures for protecting minority opinions, as well as linking the role of critical evaluation to the group identity. These recommendations can be given to the group in a variety of ways. One method is to provide training in discussion principles either for the group leader only or, preferably, for all members. This approach may work well when there is sufficient time, resources, and motivation to complete such a program. A second method is simply to expose group members to these recommendations. Research has demonstrated that decision quality may be enhanced with this minimal exposure (M. E. Turner & Pratkanis, 1994a; see M. E. Turner & Pratkanis, 1998a for a more detailed discussion of interventions for overcoming groupthink). Finally, constructive evaluation can be made a part of the normative content of the social identity, as in jury instructions (Neck & Moorhead, 1992).

These approaches do not guarantee success. Much prior research shows that people evaluate conflict extremely negatively (see, for example, O'Connor, Gruenfeld, & McGrath, 1993) and are motivated to avoid it. We can predict that groups operating under groupthink conditions would be especially susceptible to these pressures and might interpret any interventions as threatening the group identity. If so, they will heighten rather than reduce pressures toward groupthink. In such cases, we offer three pieces of advice: (a) make the intervention early in the groupthink-type situation before collective rationalization becomes the norm, (b) introduce strategies that can reduce, obviate, or redirect identity protection motivations, and (c) link the intervention strategy to the identity in a supportive rather than a threatening way.

As with the groupthink model itself, very little research has been conducted to examine the efficacy of these interventions. In the following sections, we examine case and experimental research that specifically examines interventions from a social identity maintenance perspective.

Case Study Evidence on Preventing Groupthink as Social Identity Maintenance

M. E. Turner, Pratkanis, and Samuels (2003) argue that Intel's decision to abandon the memory market was a case of groupthink circumvented. Intel had pioneered the product in 1970, one year after the company's founding; just 15 years later it withdrew from the market, ceding a billion dollar market to its competitors (Burgelman, 1994). This was a dramatic development for a company that, unlike most start-ups, had experienced fourteen consecutive years of profits.

Turner and colleagues go on to suggest that the company clearly faced a situation in which the key components of groupthink as social identity maintenance were characteristic. It had a strong, positive social identity. Intel clearly categorized itself as the memory company. Moreover, this identity was undoubtedly a positive one. Intel viewed itself as an innovative, can-do, technology leader. And it was this identity that was directly and perilously challenged by a collective threat. The situation that Intel faced was perceived as critically threatening, in particular to Intel's identity as the memory company. Grove termed it a "crisis of mammoth proportions" (Grove, 1996, p. 82). Japanese competition and economic recession together had enormous impacts on Intel. Dramatic losses in market share, decreases in unit prices, and dwindling sales had drastic effects on financial performance (see Burgelman, 1994; Cogan & Burgelman, 1989; Graham & Burgelman, 1991 for a complete analysis). What about other antecedent conditions? Consistent with much prior research (see M. E. Turner & Pratkanis, 1998a for a review), little evidence for the role of information processing, directive leadership, and isolation from experts was obtained. Symptoms of groupthink and defective decision-making were apparent. Let us first examine the issue of mindguards and conformity. On one hand, Intel, indeed, did encourage discussion and conflict. Employees described contentious meetings and numerous debates on the issue of just what to do about the memory market. Yet this disagreement was likely more apparent than real. The central belief, that Intel was *the* memory company, was not in contention until very far down the road. Rather, the discussions centered on how to more effectively run the business of memories – a practice that did little to question Intel's identity or the suitability of its course of action. In fact, even after the decision to abandon the market was made, CEO Andrew Grove (1996) reports that a rational, objective discussion of the idea was almost impossible. This practice is consistent with Janis's contention that groups can limit objections to issues that do not threaten to shake the confidence of the group members in the rightness of their collective judgments. Evidence for other symptoms such as collective rationalization, biased information processing, and stereotyping was also apparent.

Yet, in the end, Intel did *not* succumb to groupthink: The company did abandon the market and did go on to achieve spectacular success. So how did the company circumvent groupthink? CEO Andrew Grove (1996) reports it best:

> I remember a time in the middle of 1985, after all this aimless wandering has been going on for almost a year. I was in my office with Intel's chairman and CEO, Gordon Moore, and we were discussing our quandary. Our mood was downbeat. I looked out the window at the Ferris wheel of the Great America amusement park revolving in the distance, then I turned back to Gordon and I asked, "If we got kicked out and the board brought in a new CEO, what do you think he would do?" Gordon answered without hesitation, "He would get us out of memories." I stared at him, numb, then said, "Why shouldn't you and I walk out the door, come back and do it ourselves?" (p. 89)

From the perspective of groupthink as social identity maintenance, this exchange had two key points. First, taking the perspective of a new CEO was clearly an instance of role substitution. Recall that role-playing procedures can provide additional sources of information that can impact the decision itself, provide alternative perspectives on information already at hand, and provide needed perspective on the attack on the group identity. Second, the process of getting out of memories would involve the destruction of Intel's corporate identity and the construction of another. The destruction and reconstruction consisted of several initiatives: the destruction of the old identity, the construction of the new identity, the redeployment of resources to be consistent with the new identity, and reinforcement of the new identity.

Experimental Evidence on Preventing Groupthink as Social Identity Maintenance

To design an intervention that would prevent groupthink as social identity maintenance, M. E. Turner et al. (1992) drew on research that suggests that when faced with a threat to self-esteem, people are likely to self-handicap – that is, they seek to protect against potential failure by actively setting up circumstances or by claiming certain attributes or characteristics (such as reduced effort or alcohol or drug consumption) that may be blamed for poor performance (Frankel & Snyder, 1978; Higgins, 1990; Jones & Berglas, 1978; Miller, 1976; C. R. Snyder, 1990; M. L. Snyder, Smoller, Strenta, & Frankel, 1981). Although this results in poor performance on the task, failure on the task does not reflect poorly on self-esteem because it can be attributed to a volitional self-handicapping.

However, research also demonstrates that providing threatened individuals with another potential explanation for the expected failure (such as poor lighting) may obviate the need to use self-handicapping strategies for maintaining self-esteem and subsequently may ameliorate performance decrements (M. L. Snyder et al., 1981). Similar predictions can be made concerning the performance of highly cohesive, threatened groups that are given an alternative excuse for their performance.

Assuming that threatened groups strive to protect against a negative image of the group suggests that providing them with an excuse for possible poor perform-ance should reduce the need to justify performance: Potential poor performance can be blamed on the distraction. To test these ideas, M. E. Turner et al. (1992) gave three-person groups the high-cohesion manipulation described previously and asked them to work on the same parasol assembly discussion task. One third of the groups were given the identical low-threat manipulation described above. One third received the high-threat manipulation similar to that described above (with modifications to control for potential identifiability concerns). Finally, one third of the groups received this threat manipulation and were provided with a potential excuse for possible poor performance. They were told that background music they heard was potentially distracting.

The results dramatically confirmed the predictions of the SIM model. Groups facing groupthink conditions (i.e., high cohesion and high threat) but given an excuse for potential poor performance performed at the same high-quality level as groups not facing groupthink conditions. And, once again, groups facing groupthink conditions alone (with no excuse) produced the poorest quality deci-sions. Consistent with the particularistic interpretation of the model, symptoms of groupthink were again independently affected by threat (cohesion was not independently manipulated). Thus, the reduction of identity protection pressures seems to allow groups to mitigate groupthink tendencies and to produce higher quality decisions.

CONCLUDING REMARKS

We suggest that groupthink can be interpreted as a collective effort directed at social identity maintenance in the face of a shared threat. This perspective highlights four important aspects of groupthink. First, as a precondition to cohesion, members should categorize themselves as a group. Often, this categor-ization can be supplemented by such factors as a shared ideology or by mutual intragroup attraction (or social cohesion). This shared categorization provides a basis on which the second condition – a collective threat – can operate. Second, the group should experience a collective threat and this threat should, like threats involved in dissonance induction, involve an attack on the positive image of the group. Third, the group may resolve the dissonance induced by the threat in a variety of ways. Just as individuals can employ multiple methods to reduce dissonance, groups may exhibit a variety of groupthink processes and indicators as members attempt to maintain a positive image of the group. Finally, the self-reports of group members engaged in the decision may not be trustworthy indicators of the group process, as members may be engaged in the collective construction of positive social image of the group.

In sum, groupthink as social identity maintenance is not an inevitable consequence of the key antecedent conditions, nor is a progression toward failure predetermined once this form of groupthink has manifested itself. Interventions that reduce pressures toward identity protection, stimulate intellectual conflict, and when necessary, shatter and rebuild identity can be invaluable tools in mitigating groupthink.

REFERENCES

Ahlfinger, N. & Esser, J. (2001). Testing the groupthink model: Effects of promotional leadership and conformity predisposition. *Social Behavior and Personality*, *29*, 31–41.

Aldag, R. & Fuller, S. R. (1993). Beyond fiasco: A reappraisal of the groupthink phenomenon and a new model of group decision processes. *Psychological Bulletin*, *113*, 533–552.

Argote, L., Turner, M. E., & Fichman, M. (1989). To centralize or not to centralize: The effects of uncertainty and threat on group structure and performance. *Organizational Behavior and Human Decision Processes*, *43*, 58–74.

Bernthal, P. R., & Insko, C. A. (1993). Cohesiveness without groupthink: The interactive effects of social and task cohesion. *Group and Organization Management*, *18*(1), 66–87.

Botticelli, P., Collis, D., & Pisano, G. (1997). *Intel Corporation: 1968–1997*. Harvard Business School, Harvard University, Cambridge, MA, Case 9-787-137.

Burgelman, R. A. (1994). Fading memories: A process theory of strategic business exit in dynamic environments. *Administrative Science Quarterly*, *39*, 24–56.

Burgelman, R. A., Carter, D. L., & Bamford, R. S. (1999). *Intel Corporation: The evolution of an adaptive organization*. Stanford Graduate School of Business, Stanford, CA, case SM-65.

Burgelman, R. A., & Grove, A. S. (1996). Strategic dissonance. *California Management Review*, *32*, Winter, 8–28.

Bylinsky, G. (1981). Japan's ominous chip victory. *Fortune*, *104*, December 14, 52–57.

Callaway, M. R., & Esser, J. K. (1984). Groupthink: Effects of cohesiveness and problem-solving procedures on group decision making. *Social Behavior and Personality*, *12*, 157–164.

Callaway, M. R., Marriott, R. G., & Esser, J. K. (1985). Effects of dominance on group decision making: Toward a stress-reduction explanation of groupthink. *Journal of Personality and Social Psychology*, *4*, 949–952.

Cartwright, D. & Zander, A. (1953). *Group dynamics research and theory*. Oxford: Row, Peterson.

Choi, J., & Kim, M. (1999). The organizational application of groupthink and its limitations in organizations. *Journal of Applied Psychology*, *84*(2), 297–306.

Clancy, H. (1997). Dynamic duos: Andrew Grove and Gordon Moore. *Computer Reseller News*, *738*, June 1, 13–18.

Cogan, G. W. & Burgelman, R. A. (1989). *Intel Corporation (A): The DRAM decision*. Graduate School of Business, Stanford University, Stanford, CA, Case BP-256.

Cogan, G. W. & Burgelman, R. A. (1991). *Intel Corporation (C): The DRAM decision*. Graduate School of Business, Stanford University, Stanford, CA, Case BP-256.

Courtwright, J. A. (1978). A laboratory investigation of groupthink. *Communication Monographs, 45*, 229–246.

Day, R. (1984). Intel seeks outside mfrs. to make its older devices. *Electronic News, 30*, January 30, 49.

Dimitroff, R., Schmidt, L., & Bond, T. (2005). Organizational behavior and disaster: A study of conflict at NASA. *Project Management Journal, 36*(2), 28–38.

Donlon, J. P. (1997). Inside Andy Grove. *Chief Executive, 125*, July, 44–52.

Eaton, J. (2001). Management communication: The threat of groupthink. *Corporate Communications, 6*, 183–192.

Esser, J. K., & Lindoerfer, J. S. (1989). Groupthink and the space shuttle *Challenger* accident: Toward a quantitative case analysis. *Journal of Behavioral Decision Making, 2*, 167–177.

Feibus, M. (1987, July 14). Intel, AMD are back in the black. *San Jose Mercury News*, p. 1F.

Festinger, L. (1957). *A theory of cognitive dissonance*. Stanford, CA: Stanford University Press.

Festinger, L. (1987). A personal memory. In N. E. Gruenberg, R. E. Nisbett, J. Rodin, & J. E. Singer (Eds.), *A distinctive approach to psychological research: The influence of Stanley Schachter* (pp. 1–9). Hillsdale, NJ: Lawrence Erlbaum Associates, Inc.

Festinger, L. Schachter, S., & Back, K. W. (1950). *Social pressures in informal groups: A study of human factors in housing*. New York: Harper.

Feynman, R. P. (1988). *What do you care what other people think?* New York: W.W. Norton & Co.

Fisher, F., Kopelman, E., & Schneider, A. K. (1996). *Beyond Machiavelli: Tools for coping with conflict*. New York: Penguin.

Flowers, M. L. (1977). A laboratory test of some implications of Janis's groupthink hypothesis. *Journal of Personality and Social Psychology, 35*, 888–896.

Fodor, E. M., & Smith, T. (1982). The power motive as an influence on group decision making. *Journal of Personality and Social Psychology, 42*, 178–185.

Frankel, A. & Snyder, M. L. (1978). Poor performance following unsolvable problems: Learned helplessness or egotism? *Journal of Personality and Social Psychology, 36*, 1415–1423.

Friedkin, N. E. (1999). Choice shift and group polarization. *American Sociological Review, 64*(6), 856–875.

Graham, B. & Burgelman, R. A. (1991). *Intel Corporation (B): Implementing the DRAM decision*. Graduate School of Business, Stanford University, Stanford, CA, case BP-256B.

Grove, A. S. (1984). How to make confrontation work for you. *Fortune, 110*, July 23, 73–76.

Grove, A. S. (1996). *Only the paranoid survive: How to exploit the crisis points that challenge every company*. New York: Currency Doubleday.

Hall, D. & Mansfield, R. (1971). Organizational and individual response to stress. *Administrative Science Quarterly, 16*, 533–547.

Hayashi, A. M. (1987, November 15). The new Intel: Moore mature, Moore competitive. *Electronic Business*.

Hergovich, A. & Olbrich, A. (2003). The impact of the Northern Ireland conflict on social identity, groupthink and integrative complexity in Great Britain. *Review of Psychology, 10*, 95–106.

Higgins, R. L. (1990). Self-handicapping: Historical roots and contemporary approaches. In R. L. Higgins, C. R. Snyder, & S. Berglas (Eds.), *Self-handicapping: The paradox that isn't*. New York: Plenum.

Hinsz, V. B., & Davis, J. H. (1984). Persuasive arguments theory, group polarization, and choice shifts. *Personality and Social Psychology Bulletin, 10*(2), 260–268.

Hodson, G., & Sorrentino, R. M. (1997). Groupthink and uncertainty orientation: Personality differences in reactivity to the group situation. *Group Dynamics: Theory, Research, and Practice, 1*(2), 144–155.

Hogg, M. A. (1992). *The social psychology of group cohesiveness: From attraction to social identity*. New York: New York University Press.

Hogg, M. A. and Abrams, D. (1988). *Social identifications: A social psychology of intergroup relations and group processes*. New York: Routledge.

Isenberg, D. J. (1986). Group polarization: A critical review and meta-analysis. *Journal of Personality and Social Psychology, 50*(6), 1141–1151.

Jackson, T. (1997). *Inside Intel: Andy Grove and the rise of the world's most powerful chip company*. New York: Plume/Putnam.

Janis, I. L. (1972). *Victims of groupthink*. Boston: Houghton-Mifflin.

Janis, I. L. (1982). *Groupthink: Psychological studies of policy decisions and fiascoes* (2nd ed.). Boston: Houghton-Mifflin.

Janis, I. L. (1989). *Crucial decisions: Leadership in policymaking and crisis management*. New York: Free Press.

Janis, I. L., & Mann, F. (1977). *Decision making*. New York: Free Press.

Jones, E. E. & Berglas, S. (1978). Control of attributions about the self through self-handicapping strategies. *Personality and Social Psychology Bulletin, 4*, 200–206.

Kahneman, D. (1973). *Attention and effort*. Englewood Cliffs, NJ: Prentice Hall.

Kaplan, M. F., & Miller, C. E. (1983). Group discussion and judgment. In P. B. Paulus (Ed.), *Basic group processes* (pp. 189–212). New York: Springer.

Kelman, H. C. (1958). Compliance, identification, and internalization. *Journal of Conflict Resolution, 2*, 51–60.

Kramer, R. M. (1998). Revisiting the Bay of Pigs and Vietnam decisions 25 years later: How well has the groupthink hypothesis stood the test of time? *Organizational Behavior and Human Decision Processes, 73*(2–3), 236–271.

Kroon, M. B. R., 't Hart, P., & van Kreveld, D. (1991). Managing group decision making processes: Individual versus collective accountability and groupthink. *International Journal of Conflict Management, 2*, 91–116.

Kroon, M. B., Van Kreveld, D., & Rabbie, J. M. (1992). Group versus individual decision making: Effects of accountability and gender on groupthink. *Small Group Research, 23*(4), 427–458.

Lazarus, R. S., & Folkman, S. (1984). *Stress, appraisal, and coping*. New York: Springer.

Leana, C. R. (1985). A partial test of Janis' groupthink model: Effects of group cohesiveness and leader behavior on defective decision making. *Journal of Management, 11*, 5–17.

Lintonen, R. (2004). Understanding EU crisis decision-making: The case of Chechnya and the Finnish Presidency. *Journal of Contingencies and Crisis Management, 12*, 29–38.

Longley, J., & Pruitt, D. G. (1980). Groupthink: A critique of Janis's theory. In L. Wheeler (Ed.), *Review of personality and social psychology* (Vol. 1). Beverly Hills, CA: Sage.

Lott, A. J., & Lott, B. E. (1965). Group cohesiveness as interpersonal attraction: A review of relationships with antecedent and consequent variables. *Psychological Bulletin, 64*, 259–309.

McCauley, C. (1989). The nature of social influence in groupthink: Compliance and internalization. *Journal of Personality and Social Psychology, 57*, 250–260.

Maier, N. R. F. (1952). *Principles of human relations.* New York: Wiley.

Miller, R. T. (1976). Ego involvement and attribution for success and failure. *Journal of Personality and Social Psychology, 34*, 901–906.

Moorhead, G., Ference, R., & Neck, C. P. (1991). Group decision fiascoes continue: Space shuttle *Challenger* and a revised groupthink framework. *Human Relations, 44*, 539–550.

Moorhead, G., Neck, C. P., & West, M. S. (1998). The tendency toward defective decision making within self-managing teams: The relevance of groupthink for the 21st century. *Organizational Behavior and Human Decision Processes, 73*, 327–351.

Moscovici, S., & Zavalloni, M. (1969). The group as a polarizer of attitudes. *Journal of Personality and Social Psychology, 12*(2), 125–135.

Myers, D. G., & Lamm, H. (1976). The group polarization phenomenon. *Psychological Bulletin, 83*(4), 602–627.

Neck, C. (1996). Letterman or Leno: A groupthink analysis of successive decisions made by the National Broadcasting Company. *Journal of Managerial Psychology, 11*(8), 3–17.

Neck, C. P., & Manz, C. C. (1994). From groupthink to teamthink: Toward the creation of constructive thoughts patterns in self-managing work teams. *Human Relations, 47*(8), 929–952.

Neck, C. P., & Moorhead, G. (1992). Jury deliberations in the Trial of U. S. v. John DeLorean: A case analysis of groupthink avoidance and an enhanced framework. *Human Relations, 45*, 1077–1091.

O'Connor, K. M., Gruenfeld, D. H., & McGrath, J. E. (1993). The experience and effects of conflict in continuing work groups. *Small Group Research, 24*, 362–382.

Park, W. (1990). A review of research on groupthink. *Journal of Behavioral Decision Making, 3*, 229–245.

Pollack, A. (1985, October 11). Intel posts loss; ends RAM line. *New York Times*, p. D1.

Pratkanis, A. R., & Turner, M. E. (1994). Nine principles of successful affirmative action: II. Branch Rickey, Jackie Robinson, and the integration of baseball. *Nine: The Journal of Baseball History and Social Policy Perspectives, 3*, 36–65.

Pratkanis, A. R., & Turner, M. E. (1999). Groupthink and preparedness for the Loma Prieta earthquake: A social identity maintenance analysis of causes and preventions. In E. A. Mannix & M. A. Neale (Series Eds.) & R. Wageman (Vol. Ed.), *Research on managing groups and teams*, Vol. 2, *Groups in context* (pp. 115–136). Stamford, CT: JAI Press.

Quarnstrom, L., Levy, B., & Kutzmann, D. M. (1989, October 21). Santa Cruz mourns, copes. *San Jose Mercury News*, 21a.

Raven, B. H. (1974). The Nixon group. *Journal of Social Issues, 30*, 297–320.

Raven, B. H. (1998). Groupthink, Bay of Pigs, and Watergate reconsidered. *Organizational Behavior and Human Decision Processes, 73*, 352–361.

Scharff, M. (2005). Understanding WorldCom's accounting fraud: Did groupthink play a role? *Journal of Leadership and Organizational Studies, 11*, 109–118.

Schulz-Hardt, S., Frey, D., Lüthgens, C., & Moscovici, S. (2000). Biased information search in group decision making. *Journal of Personality and Social Psychology, 78*(4), 655–669.

Shaw, M. E. (1981). *Group dynamics* (3rd ed.). New York: McGraw-Hill.

Snyder, C. R. (1990). Self-handicapping processes and sequelae. In R. L. Higgins, C. R. Snyder, & S. Berglas (Eds.), *Self-handicapping: The paradox that isn't.* New York: Plenum.

Snyder, M. L., Smoller, B., Strenta, A., & Frankel, A. (1981). A comparison of egotism, negativity, and learned helplessness as explanations for poor performance after unsolvable problems. *Journal of Personality and Social Psychology, 40,* 24–30.

Steiner, I. D. (1982). Heuristic models of groupthink. In H. Brandstatter, J. H. Davis, & G. Stocker-Kreichgauer (Eds.), *Group decision making* (pp. 503–524). New York: Academic Press.

Tajfel, H. (1981). *Human groups and social categories.* Cambridge: Cambridge University Press.

Tetlock, P. E. (1979) Identifying victims of groupthink from public statements of decision makers. *Journal of Personality and Social Psychology, 37,* 1314–1324.

Tetlock, P. E., Peterson, R. S., McGuire, C., Chang, S., & Feld, P. (1992). Assessing political group dynamics: A test of the groupthink model. *Journal of Personality and Social Psychology, 63,* 403–425.

't Hart, P. (1990). *Groupthink in government.* Amsterdam: Swets & Zeitlinger.

't Hart, P. (1998). Preventing groupthink revisited: Evaluating and reforming groups in government. *Organizational Behavior and Human Decision Processes, 73,* 306–326.

Thompson, J. E., & Carsrud, A. L. (1976). The effects of experimentally induced illusions of invulnerability and vulnerability on decisional risk taking in triads. *Journal of Social Psychology, 100,* 263–267.

Tjosvold, D. (1995). Cooperation theory, constructive controversy, and effectiveness: Learning from crisis. In R. A. Guzzo & E. Salas (Eds.), *Team effectiveness and decision making in organizations.* San Francisco: Jossey-Bass.

Turner, J. C. (1981). The experimental social psychology of intergroup behavior. In J. C. Turner & H. Giles (Eds.), *Intergroup behavior* (pp. 66–101). Chicago: University of Chicago Press.

Turner, J. C. (1982). Towards a cognitive redefinition of the social group. In H. Tajfel (Ed.), *Social identity and intergroup relations* (pp. 15–40). Cambridge: Cambridge University Press.

Turner, J. C., & Haslam, S. A. (2000). Social identity, organizations, and leadership. In M. E. Turner (Ed.), *Groups at work: Theory and research.* Mahwah, NJ: Lawrence Erlbaum Associates, Inc.

Turner, J. C., Hogg, M. A., Oakes, P. J., Reicher, S. D., & Wetherell, M. S. (1987). *Rediscovering the human group: A self-categorization theory.* New York: Basil Blackwell.

Turner, M. E. (1992). Group effectiveness under threat: The impact of structural centrality and performance set. *Journal of Social Behavior and Personality, 7,* 511–528.

Turner, M. E., & Horvitz, T. (2000). The dilemma of threat: Group effectiveness and ineffectiveness in crisis. In M. E. Turner (Ed.), *Groups at work: Theory and research.* Mahwah, NJ: Lawrence Erlbaum Associates, Inc.

Turner, M. E., & Pratkanis, A. R. (1994a). *Effects of structured decision aids on decision effectiveness under groupthink* [Unpublished raw data]. San Jose State University, CA.

Turner, M. E. & Pratkanis, A. R. (1994b). Social identity maintenance prescriptions for preventing groupthink: Reducing identity protection and enhancing intellectual conflict. In E. van de Vliert & C. K. de Dreu (Eds.), Optimizing performance through conflict stimulation [special issue]. *International Journal of Conflict Management, 5,* 254–270.

Turner, M. E., & Pratkanis, A. R. (1997). Mitigating groupthink by stimulating constructive conflict. In C. de Dreu & E. Van de Vliert (Eds.), *Using conflict in organizations* (pp. 53–71). London: Sage.

Turner, M. E. and Pratkanis, A. R. (1998a). A social identity maintenance theory of group-think. *Organizational Behavior and Human Decision Processes, 73*, 210–235.

Turner, M. E. & Pratkanis, A. R. (1998b). Twenty-five years of groupthink research: Lessons in the development of a theory. *Organizational Behavior and Human Decision Processes, 73*, 105–115.

Turner, M. E., Pratkanis, A. R., Probasco, P., & Leve, C. (1992). Threat, cohesion, and group effectiveness: Testing a social identity maintenance perspective on group-think. *Journal of Personality and Social Psychology, 63*, 781–796.

Turner, M. E., Pratkanis, A. R., & Samuels, T. (2003). Identity metamorphosis and groupthink prevention: Examining Intel's departure from the DRAM industry. In S. A. Haslam, D. Van Knippenberg, M. J. Platow, & N. Ellemers (Eds.), *Social identity at work: Developing theory for organizational practice* (pp. 117–138). New York: Psychology Press.

Whyte, G. (1989). Groupthink reconsidered. *Academy of Management Journal, 14*, 40–56.

Whyte, G. (1998). Recasting Janis's groupthink model: The key role of collective efficacy in decision fiascoes. *Organizational Behavior and Human Decision Processes, 73*(2/3), 185–209.

Wilder, C. (1985). Intel to exit dynamic RAM chip mart: Company posts $3.6 million loss in third-quarter 1985. *Computerworld*, October 14.

Wirbel, L. & Ristelhueber, R. (1984). Intel phases out DRAM: Motorola dropping 64K units as price pressure mounts. *Electronic News, 31*, 1, October 14.

Yetiv, S. A. (2003). Groupthink and the Gulf Crisis. *British Journal of Political Science, 33*(3), 419.

Zuber, J. A., Crott, H. W., & Werner, J. (1992). Choice shift and group polarization: An analysis of the status of arguments and social decision schemes. *Journal of Personality and Social Psychology, 62*(1), 50–61.

10

Minority Dissent, Attitude Change, and Group Performance

CARSTEN K. W. DE DREU

Social influence is an inevitable part of human interaction. We rely on others to validate our views of the world, we seek and maintain norms and values about what is appropriate or not, and we try to influence others to serve our personal or group interests. Often, social influence is associated with disagreement and conflict, as the agents and targets of influence disagree about the truth, about proper norms and values, and about whose self-interest should prevail. A common finding in research on conflict and social influence is that people tend to yield to the powerful (De Dreu & Van Kleef, 2004), and adopt the majority point of view (e.g., Asch, 1956; Baron, Kerr, & Miller, 1993; Cialdini & Trost, 1998).

Compliance with the powerful and conforming to the majority perspective are not the only tendencies operating in social influence settings. If conformity and compliance were the dominating social influence processes, groups and societies would, at some point, reach an equilibrium state in which all members look, think, and behave in similar, if not identical, ways. Obviously, this is not what happens. Groups and societies change. At the societal level we see tremendous change in general norms regarding certain types of behavior (what was normal behavior 30 years ago is banned from social life today, e.g., smoking) as well as for underlying beliefs and attitudes (the majority view on voluntary euthanasia, or about genetically manipulated foods, for example, has changed considerably over the past few decades). At the level of small groups, we see similar tendencies. For instance, bringing in newcomers to an *ad hoc* work group changes the strategies the group uses, and thus their ultimate task performance (e.g., Choi & Levine, 2004).

Underlying many of these and other changes we see in the ways group members think and behave is *minority influence*. Minority influence is the possible outcome of *minority dissent*, which occurs when a numerical minority faction in a group or society publicly advocates and pursues beliefs, attitudes, ideas, procedures and policies that go against the "spirit of the times" and challenge the position or perspective assumed by the majority (De Dreu & De Vries, 1997,

2001). Note that minority dissent refers to deviations from the majority point of view, and not to deviations from the majority in terms of social (cultural, religious) or demographic (gender, ethnicity) characteristics. Thus, although cultural or demographic differences may correlate with differences in opinion and point of view, the focus here is on *opinion* minorities and not on *social* minorities.

That minority dissent can be influential follows from the fact that groups do not linearly progress towards a stable and finite equilibrium. What remains is when, how, and why minorities within a group or society influence the majority's way of thinking and doing. It is these and related questions that are covered in this chapter.

As an outline of the things to come, I will first discuss the nature and origins of minority influence: Why is it that some people do not comply with the majority perspective and instead go against the spirit of the times, and under what conditions is it more likely that minority influence emerges and comes into existence? In the second part of the chapter I will review several models, and their evidence, about the influence of minority statements on individual beliefs and attitudes. In the third section I will focus on the ways minority dissent in groups impacts work group processes and performance, and review research showing that minority dissent can actually promote creative thinking and innovative practices in work groups. I conclude with some avenues for future research that I think are worth pursuing.

THE NATURE AND ORIGINS OF MINORITY INFLUENCE

To understand minority influence it is useful to consider various types of minorities, as different types of minorities may have different goals (which may affect the influence strategies they use) and different images (which may influence the way influence strategies are perceived and responded to). Furthermore, it may be useful to understand where minority dissent comes from in the first place – what makes people adopt a dissenting point of view, and voice it? It is these questions that are considered in this section.

Types of Minorities

Levine and Kaarbo (2001) distinguished four types of minorities. *Progressive minorities* advance a new perspective and seek to convince the majority of its value. An example would be the human resource manager who seeks to influence the other members of the management team to stop rewarding performance on an individual basis and instead to adopt a new system for rewarding team-based performance. Another example would be the newly hired medical assistant who consistently advocates implementation of a novel treatment she was taught about at school. *Conservative minorities* attempt to block the majority's tendency to adopt a new, progressive perspective. An example would be a right-wing political party that wants to stop the government from allowing shopkeepers to open their shops on Sundays. Another example would be the small fraction of employees who resist the introduction of a computer-communication system thought to enhance internal communication between management and employees. *Modernist minorities* try to block the majority's tendency to return to previously held attitudes and policies. An example of such a minority is one that tries to persuade the majority that with time the recently implemented organizational change program should become beneficial and therefore ought not to be reversed prematurely. *Reactionary minorities*, finally, try to persuade the majority to return to previously held opinions and perspectives. An example would be the small group of colleagues insisting on dropping affirmative action policies.

Who Engages in Minority Dissent?

Despite a wealth of studies on minority dissent and minority influence, to which I turn in the next sections, we know relatively little about why and when some people are more likely than others to adopt a minority perspective and to advocate a minority position. In a study focusing on "willingness to dissent" in organizational settings, De Dreu, De Vries, Franssen and Altink (1999) found that more extraverted individuals displayed greater willingness to voice dissenting views, and that willingness to dissent was greater when the group had reacted positively to minority dissent in the past. Moreover, willingness to dissent *decreased* when the group had higher clarity of objectives, especially among extraverted individuals. LePine and Van Dyne (1998) similarly found that satisfaction with the group predicted dissent and voice especially in smaller groups, and global self-esteem predicted voice especially in larger groups. These studies thus indicate that the tendency to adopt a minority position within one's group or society depends on personality characteristics (e.g., extraversion, global self-esteem) alone or in combination with context-specific variables such as the way dissent was reacted to in the past, or how satisfied one is with how things go. Clearly, this research area is underdeveloped and we need many more studies to get a good understanding of when and why people decide to adopt a minority position and to stand up against the majority in their group, or in society at large.

MINORITY INFLUENCE ON BELIEFS AND ATTITUDES

The possible effects of minority dissent on beliefs and attitudes have been studied within the context of three leading theoretical accounts – social impact perspectives (e.g., Latané & Wolf, 1981), objective consensus approaches (e.g., Kruglanski & Mackie, 1990; Mackie, 1987), and conversion theory (Moscovici, 1980, 1985; Mugny, 1982). Although these perspectives converge on some aspects of minority influence, they differ in other aspects. Furthermore, in recent years several attempts at integrating these perspectives have been proposed (e.g., Crano & Chen, 1998; Bohner, Moskowitz, & Chaiken 1995; De Vries, De Dreu, Gordijn, & Schuurman, 1996; Martin & Hewstone, 2001).

In this section I will introduce each of these theoretical perspectives and

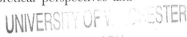

discuss the research evidence and the more recent, integrative models. In essence, social impact and objective consensus models propose a quantitative difference between majority and minority influence, such that majorities are more influential than minorities on whatever influence measure taken. Conversion theory, and later attempts at integration, argue differently. They suggest that there are qualitative differences between majority and minority influence, with majority influence being manifest, immediate, and short-lived (i.e., the result of compliance) and minority influence being latent, delayed, and long-lived (i.e., the result of deep and deliberate processing of information).

Social Impact Models

Consistent with classic studies showing that many people conform to a majority even when this majority is clearly wrong (Asch, 1956), and that people obey an authority even when the authority appears morally and ethically transgressed (Milgram, 1963) are so-called social impact models. These models state, in essence, that the greater a faction size within a group or society, the greater its influence (Latané & Wolf, 1981; Tanford & Penrod, 1984). Social impact models pose normative influence – the influence that communicators have because of the target's desire to belong to, and be identified with these communicators (Deutsch & Gerard, 1955) – as the key mediating mechanism, and they have little to say about informational influence – the influence that communicators have because of its message content. In brief, social impact models state that majority factions will have greater (normative) influence than minority factions.

Objective Consensus Perspectives

Social impact models are about conformity and compliance (yielding to the powerful). In contrast, objective consensus approaches to majority–minority influence (Erb, Bohner, Schmälzle, K., & Rank, 1998; Kruglanski & Mackie, 1990; Mackie, 1987) heavily lean on dual process models of information processing and attitude change (Chaiken & Trope, 1999; Smith & DeCoster, 2000) to predict both normative and informational influence. The idea is that individuals can evaluate persuasive arguments or form impressions of others through a quick, effortless, and heuristic processing of information that rests on well-learned prior associations. Alternatively, individuals may engage in more effortful, deliberate and systematic processing that involves rule-based inferences (Brewer, 1988; Chaiken, 1987; Kruglanski & Webster, 1996; Petty & Cacioppo, 1986; for a critical discussion, see Kruglanski, Thompson, & Spiegel, 1999). Further, it is assumed that individuals are more likely to engage in the systematic processing of information when they have high rather than low accuracy motivation. Accuracy motivation is higher when the topic is personally involving, when personal consequences are important, or when one is held accountable for one's judgments and decisions (Eagly & Chaiken, 1993; Petty & Cacioppo, 1986).

According to objective consensus approaches, majority messages are more persuasive because they are more likely to be processed systematically than minority messages. For example, Mackie (1987) provided students with a set of persuasive arguments in favor of a policy (e.g., reducing military expenditure) that most participants disagreed with. The persuasive arguments were said to be representative of what a majority of 82% of the students believed, or of what a minority of 18% of the students believed. After participants read the arguments, they provided anonymously their private opinion about the attitude topic addressed in the message (focal issue), as well as on some related issues not mentioned in the message but associated with the focal issue. The idea behind measuring both focal and related attitudes was that if majority and/or minority influence was the result of deep and systematic information processing, this would show up not only in message-relevant thoughts collected after the experiment was over, but also on related attitude topics. This is indeed what Mackie (1987) found: Compared to minority arguments, majority arguments led to greater private attitude change on both focal and related topics, and these majority-induced changes were mediated by message-relevant thoughts that participants recorded after the experimental task was over.

Another example of the objective consensus approach is provided by Erb et al. (1998; Erb & Bohner, 2001). In their experiments the authors chose majorities and minorities that were mostly socially irrelevant to research participants and used fictitious attitude objects to minimize any effects of prior attitudes. For example, in one experiment participants were provided with consensus information about a fictitious large-scale building project on which a public discussion meeting had ostensibly taken place. Participants were informed that in this meeting either a majority of 86% or a minority of 14% of attendants had expressed their agreement with the project. In a control condition participants received no consensus information. They then read a persuasive message containing arguments ostensibly provided by those in favor of the project. Later they were asked to list any thoughts they had had while reading the message, and they indicated their own attitudes toward the project. Results showed that respondents perceived the message as more persuasive when consensus was high rather than low. This indicates cognitive bias that led to a more favorable assessment of message content under high than under low consensus. Also, the total number of listed thoughts was lower when consensus information – either high or low – was available, compared to the condition where no consensus information was available. This indicates that participants' use of consensus information had reduced the amount of systematic processing they dedicated to the message. Finally, thoughts were more positive when consensus was high rather than low, and this mediated the effects of consensus on attitudes.

Taken together, social impact models argue that majority influence exceeds minority influence because people comply with larger factions more than with smaller, less powerful factions. Objective consensus approaches add to this that majority messages are also more likely to be seen as credible and relevant, and thus elicit more positive thoughts and more systematic processing. Majority compared to minority messages thus have both more normative and more informational influence.

Conversion Theory

Quite in contrast to the social impact and objective consensus perspectives, Moscovici's (1980) conversion theory proposes that majority and minority influence is the result of two separate processes leading to different levels of public and private influence. Majority influence leads to a *social comparison process*: When confronted with majority influence, individuals compare their own response with that of the majority without considering, in detail, the majority's message. Majority influence thus entails public compliance with little private change. Majorities persuade through threats of censure and ostracism. The social pressure they bring to bear to compel members to acquiesce to the will of the group can be formidable, but it is temporary. When majority surveillance is relaxed, the pressure is off, and the old belief or behavior returns because nothing but appearances are changed by the normative social pressure of the majority (Deutsch & Gerard, 1955).

Minority influence, on the other hand, leads to a *validation process*: Because of their distinctiveness, minorities lead individuals to engage in cognitive processing of the message in order to understand the minority's position. This can lead to conversion behaviour – "a subtle process of perceptual or cognitive modification by which a person gives up his/her usual response in order to adopt another view or response, without necessarily being aware of the change or forced to make it" (Moscovici & Personnaz, 1980; p. 271). Minority influence is thus seen as present, but change in the direction advocated by the minority was expected only after a delay. Moscovici's model assumes that the minority can produce immediate change, but only on beliefs that are associated with, not identical to, the focus of its arguments.

For conversion theory to be accepted as valid, research needs to demonstrate that majority and minority influence have differential impacts on different levels of influence – it is critical to measure both immediate and long-term conformity to the (majority or minority) influence source, and attitudes on the central, targeted issue along with attitudes toward objects that may be associated with, but are not identical to, the attitude object under persuasive attack. Moscovici and Personnaz (1980) refer to two levels of influence, namely the manifest or public and the latent or private levels. The critical difference between the manifest (public) and latent (private) levels of influence is the degree to which the participants are consciously aware of the change in their responses, with the former being at the conscious level and the latter at the unconscious level. The unique contribution of conversion theory is that it goes beyond the manifest or public level, which was the focus of objective consensus perspectives discussed above, and predicts that (a) minority influence is likely to be greater at the latent or private level and (b) this change will be unconscious to the individual. Although conversion theory does not specify how, it implies that exposure to a minority can lead to change without conscious awareness, and therefore the majority view on a particular topic can be altered (Martin & Hewstone, 2001).

Two lines of research emerged to test (parts of) conversion theory. These can be distinguished primarily in terms of the type of dependent variables studied or, to put it differently, the way that levels of influence were measured. Conversion theory is not very specific about this, and allows the theory to be tested by considering (1) changes in after-images during colour perception tasks, (2) change in attitudes and beliefs. The first line of research, concerned with (after-images in) colour perception, was designed by Moscovici and his colleagues (Moscovici & Personnaz, 1980, 1991). It basically argued that minority dissent produces an unconscious change in the after-images of colours. While this is intriguing, and it received some initial support, more recent work clearly showed that social influence on after-images in colour perception is nonexistent, and so is minority influence (Martin, 1995, 1998; Martin & Hewstone, 2001; Sorrentino, King & Leo, 1980).

A second, more promising, line of research considered minority versus majority influence on attitudes and beliefs. Within this tradition, some scholars investigated majority and minority influence on public versus private attitudes, assuming that public attitudes and beliefs are more subject to social pressures whereas private attitudes and beliefs are more subject to conviction (cf. Deutsch & Gerard, 1955). According to conversion theory one would thus expect greater majority influence on public attitudes, and greater minority influence on private attitudes. Indeed, a number of studies found evidence for this idea. For example, Maass and Clark (1984) had people read a transcript of a group discussion about gay rights, at that time a highly controversial issue in the United States. During the transcribed group discussion, a minority of two group members strongly advocated in favour of gay rights, whereas the majority of four group members argued against it. Some participants then had to express their attitudes toward gay rights in public (they were led to believe that their attitudes would be disclosed to others during a group discussion with other participants), whereas others had to express their attitudes toward gay rights in private (they were led to believe that their attitudes would remain private and never be disclosed to anyone). Results showed that in the public attitudes condition participants became less tolerant of gay rights (i.e., majority influence), whereas in the private attitudes condition participants became more tolerant of gay rights (i.e., minority influence).

In addition to the contrast between private and public attitudes, researchers have tested conversion theory by examining the attitude change on focal versus related issues. Focal attitudes are those that are directly mentioned and considered in the persuasive message (e.g., birth control through contraception). Related attitudes are those that are conceptually linked to the focal attitude, but are neither mentioned nor implied in the persuasive message (e.g., abortion). Given this distinction, conversion theory would predict greater majority influence on focal attitudes, and greater minority influence on related attitudes. Thus, when a majority argues in favour of birth control through contraception people with initially negative attitudes towards birth control would become more tolerant with regard to birth control, while their views on abortion remain unaffected. However, when a minority argues in favour of birth control through contraception, people with initially negative attitudes towards birth control remain negative, but at the same time develop more tolerant views about abortion (Mugny, 1982; Pérez & Mugny, 1987).

Twenty years of research has provided considerable support for the idea that minority dissent influences related attitudes. The basic design involves participants reading a counterattitudinal message about an issue that matters to them (e.g., birth control, policies with regard to immigration, arms control) and then responding to a series of attitude questions, some of which concern the focal topic and others concerning some related issues. In one condition the counterattitudinal message is attributed to a minority faction, and in another condition the message is attributed either to no one in particular or to a majority faction. A meta-analysis of this research (Wood, Lundgren, Ouellette, Busceme, & Blackstone, 1994) has shown that majority messages produce more private change than minority messages, a finding that is inconsistent with the notion in conversion theory that majority messages only (or primarily) produce compliance and mindless conformity. However, consistent with conversion theory, and clearly inconsistent with social impact models, is the meta-analytic finding that a persuasive message from a minority produces more private than public change, and more related than focal change. Thus, although a minority clearly has less influence than a majority source on both direct and indirect measures, it does have an impact, and this impact is primarily latent, delayed, and on related issues.

Integrative Models

The above discussion of the early theories of majority–minority influence shows that neither perspective accounts for the bulk of the evidence. The landmark study by Wood and colleagues (1994) has inspired many researchers to try to integrate social impact/objective consensus theories, conversion theory, and research findings. Consecutively, I discuss the models proposed by Crano, and by De Dreu and De Vries.

Leniency Contract   Crano and colleagues (Alvaro & Crano, 1997; Crano & Chen, 1998; for a review see Crano, 2001) developed a leniency model that assumes, much like conversion theory, that majority and minority influence are qualitatively different processes with qualitatively different results. The model holds that a target's reactions to majority messages are conditional on the message's relevance for the target's social identity and sense of belongingness. Consistent with ample evidence, the leniency model thus predicts more majority influence when the majority is seen as ingroup than when it is seen as an outgroup to which the target does not (want to) belong (see Alvaro & Crano, 1997). When the majority is part of the ingroup, and thus relevant to one's social identity, targets are assumed to assess the legitimacy of the majority pressure. When legitimacy is absent or low, or if the issue is deemed irrelevant to the group, outside the boundaries of the majority concern or authority, then the majority's position will be discounted, the target will disengage from the interaction, and the majority may be derogated (Alvaro & Crano, 1997; Crano & Cooper, 1973). However, if the majority concern is legitimate, and the issue is deemed relevant to group concerns, the message will be elaborated systematically, and long-lasting change in attitudes and beliefs is the likely outcome. This prediction is consistent with a number of studies showing majority influence to be long-lasting and deep (Baker & Petty, 1994; Crano & Chen, 1998; De Dreu & De Vries, 1993, 1996; Mackie, 1987).

A different set of processes is proposed in the case of minority influence. According to the leniency contract perspective, the majority target will view the ingroup minority's persuasive position as novel or unexpected. The target will be motivated to understand the position, to understand why the deviants believe as they do. The majority first analyzes any potential threats contained in the minority position; if the conclusion is that the minority position threatens the very existence of the group, it will be ostracized, viewed as outgroup, and derogated or ignored. Otherwise, and in order to maintain (or restore) group cohesion and stability, majority members will treat the deviant (ingroup) minority with dignity and respect. As part of this lenient accommodation accorded the minority, the minority message will be elaborated with little counterargument or source derogation. However, the leniency model also argues that although systematic processing of the minority message will take place, majority members will not (immediately and overtly) change towards the minority position, simply because doing so would allow too much change and instability in the group. Consistent with the basic tenet of conversion theory that minority influence occurs on related issues more than on focal issues, the leniency contract model specifies that the deep and systematic processing of minority messages effectuates at related issues, and in a delayed manner (see, e.g., Alvaro & Crano, 1997).

In a quite sophisticated way, the leniency contract model by Crano and colleagues reveals a limited set of critical moderators of majority–minority influence. Majority messages elicit compliance when they are threatening to the individual, and they elicit deep processing and private attitude change when they have a legitimate message that is relevant to the target's group concerns. Minority messages never elicit compliance, but elicit deep processing and attitude change on related issues as long as the minority position does not threaten the group's existence. The model integrates core elements of social impact/objective consensus perspectives and conversion theory, and is consistent with the bulk of empirical research findings.

Dual Role Model   Although the leniency contract model fares well in experimental tests, it cannot account for research findings showing that in the absence of existential threat minority messages sometimes do and sometimes do not influence attitudes on related topics (see, e.g., Mugny, 1982; Wood et al., 1994). In their dual role model, De Dreu and De Vries (2001; De Vries et al., 1996; De Dreu, & De Vries, 1993, 1996; De Dreu, De Vries, Gordijn, & Schuurman (1999) argued that features of the majority or minority source, the message it sends, and the target of influence, alone or in combination, determine (a) the extent to which targets engage in deep and systematic processing of the message, and (b) the extent to which targets wish to avoid identification with the source by adhering to its position. In terms of the objective consensus perspectives discussed above, the mere fact that a message has majority support makes identification with the source more attractive and makes systematic processing of its message more relevant. The mere fact that a message has minority support makes it unattractive to be identified with the source, and makes systematic processing of the message not all that important.

In their review of majority–minority influence research, De Vries et al. (1996) identified a long list of variables that seemed to promote systematic processing of majority and minority messages, yet also increased the desire to avoid being identified with the source of the message. When a minority message is rigid rather than flexible in its formulation (Mugny, 1982), consistent rather than inconsistent over time (Moscovici, 1980), or surprising rather than expected in content (Baker & Petty, 1994), it likely attracts more attention and is therefore processed systematically. It also increases the desire to avoid being identified with the (rigid, nagging, and weird) minority (Mugny, Kaiser, Papastamou, & Perez, 1984). Likewise, when a majority formulates its message in a threatening, illegitimate, and punitive way it is likely to induce a reactance process – people comply with the majority to avoid being ostracized and expelled yet at the same time continue to hold different beliefs and attitudes in private.

Consistent with objective consensus perspectives, De Dreu and De Vries thus argued that majority sources induce systematic processing and a desire to be identified with the majority. Majority sources by default thus produce attitude change on both focal and related issues in both public and private settings. Because change on focal issues is partly due to the desire to be identified with the (majority) source, features of the situation or the source that reduce the tendency to process majority messages systematically will therefore reduce attitude change on related issues, but not on focal issues. Consistent with conversion theory, and Crano's leniency contract model, the dual role model further assumes that minority messages are ignored unless features of the source or the message stimulate systematic processing of the message. Because people generally do not wish to be identified with the minority source, systematic processing of the message leads to attitude change on related issues more than on focal issues, and its impact will become more pronounced when time elapses (cf. the sleeper effect: Pratkanis, Greenwald, Leippe, & Baumgardner, 1988).

Figure 10.1 shows the relationship between attitude changes away from, or toward, a minority message over time. As can be seen, over time normative pressures to avoid being identified with the minority weaken and, as a result, initially negative impact on public opinions may become positive. Also, because private attitudes – and especially those on related topics – are less susceptible to normative pressures and reluctance of being identified, the minority message impact here is positive, the more so when time elapses (see also De Dreu & De Vries, 1997). In brief, minority influence is immediate and positive on related issues, slightly less so on focal issues assessed in private, and positive only after a delay on focal issues assessed in public.

The dual role model still awaits a full-blown test, although a series of experiments by Gordijn, De Vries and De Dreu (2003) comes quite close. In three experiments these authors examined how change in minority size influenced information processing and attitude change. Experiment 1 showed that a message attributed to an expanding rather than a shrinking minority elicited more issue-relevant thoughts and more related attitude change in the argued direction. Experiment 2 showed more attitude change on related issues when it was unlikely that expanding size was due to the shifting majority members'

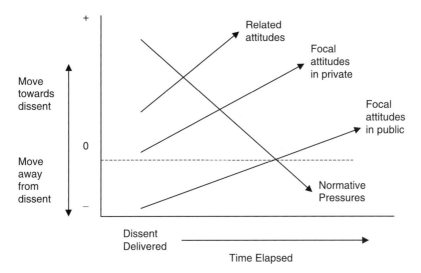

FIGURE 10.1 Impact of minority dissent on related attitudes and on private and public focal attitudes as a function of time elapsed.

self-interest (and thus had to be attributed to the content of the minority message). Experiment 3 replicated these findings and also indicated that change in size interacted differently with majority than with minority status of the source: Related issues remained largely unaffected in the case of majority support, while expanding minorities elicited more related attitude change in the argued direction.

Concluding Thoughts

The effects of majority- versus minority-supported persuasive messages on people's public or private beliefs and attitudes have attracted a great deal of research and theorizing. Few would contest the conclusion that majority supported messages have greater influence than minority supported messages on beliefs and attitudes expressed in public, and few would contest the conclusion that if minority-supported messages have an influence on beliefs and attitudes, this influence is most likely to be seen on related rather than focal issues, in private rather than public measures, and in delayed rather than immediate observations. Clearly, however, more is going on than just these two nowadays well-supported and broadly accepted notions. It is also clear that neither of the original contestants – social impact/objective consensus perspectives, and conversion theory – has the ability to explain most research findings. New models including Crano's leniency contract model and De Dreu and De Vries' dual role model hold promise, but need more and better tests before they can be accepted as providing a valid and comprehensive account of the possible effects of majority versus minority messages on attitudes and beliefs.

MINORITY INFLUENCE AND GROUP PERFORMANCE

Although Moscovici originally designed his conversion theory to account for social influence and change in societies and small groups, his work has primarily spurred an interest in, and tests of, attitude change and persuasion models. Crano's leniency contract model has some relevance to small group settings, but the model has never been examined within the context of small group processes. In fact, quite independently of the works discussed in the previous section, small group researchers have developed an interest in, and theories about, the influences of majority versus minority factions on small group processes and performance. This section reviews some of these models and lines of inquiry, focusing on two related sub-areas within the small groups domain: group decision-making, and group creativity and innovation. As we will see, some of the models discussed in this section complement the ideas advanced in persuasion studies. In some cases, however, the models and studies on small groups have little, if anything, to do with the persuasion studies reviewed above.

Group Decision-making

Preference combination   Rooted in the group performance literature (e.g., Davis, Steiner, 1972) and in formal, mathematical modelling of group processes (e.g., Lorge & Solomon, 1955) is a line of research that bears some similarity to the social impact models discussed above yet applies to minority influence in small groups rather than large collectivities. This so-called "social combination approach" (Laughlin, 1980) tries to predict a product of group interaction (such as a group decision, a group performance, or a group solution to a problem) as a combination of the resources (e.g., group member preferences, levels of performance, or solutions) that members bring to the group.

As Kerr (2001) notes, when there are majority and minority factions in the group, they are simultaneously trying to influence one another, making social influence a highly dynamic process. Second, within small groups there is nearly always an explicit or implicit requirement for some level of ultimate agreement, whether this is based on a majority-decides rule or a unanimity-required rule. The implication is, for instance, that a minority can sometimes block satisfaction of the decision rule and thus compel the majority to consider and try to refute its views. Third, group members are interdependent such that one person's behaviour influences the other person's outcomes.

Within this context, the question emerges as to whether, and when, minorities prevail – is it at all possible that a minority faction within the group persuades the majority to adopt its point of view, and if so, when is this more or less likely to happen? To answer these and related questions, the work of Laughlin and his colleagues (e.g., Laughlin, 1980; Laughlin & Ellis, 1986) is particularly informative. This line of research ordered group tasks on a dimension anchored at one end by purely *intellective* tasks, and at the other end by purely *judgmental* tasks. Intellective tasks have a "correct" answer (i.e., based on a widely shared conceptual system). However, the conceptual systems with which we must evaluate most of the problems or decisions we face are shared incompletely, have missing or ambiguous links, or rely upon nondeterministic reasoning (Kerr, 2001). Our judgments and decisions then become largely a matter of personal preference – the realm of judgmental tasks. Judgmental tasks involve ethical, aesthetic, or attitudinal issues because they have no demonstrably "correct" answer within a shared conceptual system. When demonstrably correct answers are lacking, people are more likely to base their judgments and decisions on socially validated "truths" and this makes the majority perspective prevail. Indeed, many studies in the social combination tradition have shown that minority factions only impact the final group decision if (a) the minority possessed the correct alternative, and (b) the group task was intellectual more than judgmental (Laughlin, 1980; Laughlin & Ellis, 1986).

Information Dissemination The general conclusion derived from the social combination approach is corroborated and further detailed in studies on information sharing in so-called hidden-profile tasks (Stasser & Titus, 1985). In a hidden-profile task, group members have to reach a decision (e.g., on whom to hire for a new job) and each group member has some pieces of information about the available decision alternatives (e.g., job candidates). Whereas some pieces of information are shared among all group members, each group member also has unique pieces of information available. According to the shared information, one decision alternative is superior to all others. However, if group members pool all the shared and unshared information together, the seemingly superior decision alternative turns out to be inferior to a previously considered bad option. By pooling information, groups improve the quality of their decision-making but, unfortunately, group members have a strong tendency to focus on shared information and therefore often perform at suboptimal levels (Stasser & Titus, 1985; Stasser & Stewart, 1992; Wittenbaum & Stasser, 1996).

A number of studies have shown that when prior to group discussion group members differ in their preferred decision alternative, information dissemination and pooling of unshared pieces of information is more likely than when *a priori* preference homogeneity exists (Brodbeck, Kerschreiter, Mojzisch, Frey, & Schulz-Hardt, 2002; Scholten, Van Knippenberg, Nijstad, & De Dreu, in press). To manipulate preference heterogeneity and to study the influence of minority factions, Stasser and Stewart (1992), and McLeod, Baron, Marti, and Yoon (1997) provided one group member with all the information (i.e., the informed minority), and the other group members with parts of the information pointing them toward an inferior decision alternative (uninformed majority). Both studies showed that the arguments put forward by the informed minority influenced individual preferences of the majority members – dissent by an informed minority promoted the quality of the group decision. Brodbeck et al. (2002) replicated this result, but also demonstrated that full heterogeneity of preferences produced even greater improvement in decision quality than minority dissent (see also Hofman & Maier, 1961; Williams & O'Reilly, 1998).

Groupthink A final strand of research on minority dissent has its roots in work on the *groupthink phenomenon* (Janis & Mann, 1977; Turner, Pratkanis, &

Struckman, Chapter 9, this volume), in which group members persuade each other that one decision alternative is superior to all other alternatives, and ignore all contradictory evidence. Groupthink affects groups in a wide variety of settings, including government decision-making and organizational management. It leads groups to make decisions that range between clearly suboptimal and outright disastrous (for examples and discussions, see Aldag & Fuller, 1993; Janis & Mann, 1977; Turner & Pratkanis, 1997). Among the many processes triggered by groupthink, Janis (1972) observed that conformity pressures and (extreme) concurrence-seeking are among the most important. Likewise, Hackman and Morris (1975) argued that an important reason why groups fail to perform well is their premature movement to consensus, with dissenting opinions being suppressed or dismissed.

Researchers interested in (combating) groupthink have spent considerable attention on designing decision-aids that help groups prevent premature consensus formation and groupthink tendencies. Spontaneous as well as induced forms of minority dissent seem to be key. For example, provided there is loyalty and competence within teams, dissent is associated with higher decision quality in strategic decision-making teams (Dooley & Fryxell, 1999), and successful top management teams encouraged dissent in private meetings (Peterson, Owens, Tetlock, Fan, & Martorana, 1998). Other research indicates that exposure to minority dissent increases individual courage to resist group pressures to conformity (Nemeth & Chiles, 1988), and prevents team members from polarizing their attitudes toward extreme viewpoints (Smith, Tindale, & Dugoni, 1996). Finally, research examining the role of a devil's advocate – a team member who criticizes the assumptions and directions of the rest of the team – showed that exposure to a devil's advocate improved the quality of group decision-making (Schweiger, Sandberg & Ragan, 1986; Schweiger, Sandberg, & Rechner, 1989; Schwenk, 1990).

Group Creativity and Innovation

Thus far we have seen that an informed minority may be able to alter the group's decision, and that minority dissent in general prevents premature movement to consensus and thereby promotes the quality of group decision-making. Social psychological research suggests, however, that minority dissent not only prevents defective group decision-making, but also increases individual creativity and innovative capacity in groups. I will first discuss the link between minority dissent and individual creativity, and then move on to discuss recent work revealing how and when minority dissent predicts innovations in work teams.

Recall the idea that minority dissent is surprising and leads majority members to wonder why the minority thinks the way it does (Nemeth, 1986), and that rather than seeking verification and justification of the minority position, majority members seek understanding of the minority position the better to reject it (Moscovici, 1980). In doing so, the majority is able to (a) maintain its position, while (b) preserving harmony and effective intragroup relations (Crano & Chen, 1998). However, the tension produced by minority dissent and the majority's desire to resolve this tension produces divergent thinking: Majority members consider the issues from multiple perspectives, one of which is suggested by the minority (Nemeth, 1986).

Evidence for the idea that minority dissent enhances creativity and divergent thought in majority members comes from a program of research initiated by Nemeth. For example, Nemeth and Wachtler (1983) confronted participants with a series of blue slides that were consistently labeled "green" by either a minority or a majority of confederates. In a subsequent task, participants had to individually generate associations with the word "blue." Results showed that participants confronted with a discrepant minority generated a larger number of original (i.e., unique) associations than participants confronted with a discrepant majority. Likewise, De Dreu and De Vries (1993; Nemeth & Kwan, 1987; Volpato, Maass, Mucchi-Faina, & Vitti, 1990) observed that individuals generated more original word associations when they were confronted with a minority perspective on the subject matter, and Gruenfeld, Thomas-Hunt, and Kim (1998) showed that exposure to minority dissent produced higher levels of cognitive complexity in members of the majority. Thus, this work argues for the importance of minority dissent, even dissent that is wrong. Its import lies not in the truth of its position or even in the likelihood that it will prevail; rather it appears to stimulate divergent thought. Issues and problems are considered from more perspectives and, on balance, people detect new solutions and find more correct answers (Nemeth & Staw, 1989).

That minority dissent increases individual originality suggests that minority dissent may contribute to *innovation*. Innovation is "the intentional introduction and application within a role, group or organization of ideas, processes, products or procedures, new to the relevant unit of adoption, and designed to significantly benefit the individual, the group, the organization or wider society" (West & Farr, 1990, p. 9). Innovation thus is different from creativity because of the application component (Amabile, Conti, Coon, Lazenby, & Herron, 1996; Kanter, 1988; Scott, 1995; Woodman, Sawyer, & Griffin, 1993), and because innovation only has to be new to the relevant unit of adoption, an aspect that has been termed *relative* as opposed to *absolute novelty* in the innovation literature (Anderson, De Dreu, & Nijstad, 2004). An innovation in one team or organization may thus be common practice in other teams or organizations.

The above definition of innovation shows that although creativity and originality are certainly helpful, innovation requires more than just creative thinking and original ideas. In addition to being creative, groups need to critically process creative ideas in order to drop those that appear useless and to implement those that have promise. Group members not only need to communicate their creative insights; they also need work together to transform these creative ideas into workable methods, products, and services. This means that minority dissent may lead individuals to become creative and divergent in their thinking, and that this creativity is turned into innovation especially when group members exchange and process information and ideas in an openminded yet critical way, and work together to implement new ideas and insights.

Two studies with work teams in organizations support this general idea.

De Dreu and West (2001) measured innovation in two different samples of work teams by interviewing team supervisors. Team members received a series of questionnaires that, among other things, assessed the frequency with which minority dissent occurred in their team, and the extent to which group members participated in making decisions in the team. Consistent with the above reasoning, they predicted more innovations in teams with high rather than low levels of minority dissent, but especially when these teams had high rather than low levels of participation in decision-making. Study 1 involved 21 self-managed teams from a parcel service in the Netherlands. Study 2 involved 28 teams from various organizations involved in a diverse set of tasks, including accounting and control, consulting, health care, and manufacturing. Results of both studies provided good support for the hypothesis: Innovation was higher when teams had high rather than low levels of minority dissent, but especially when they also had high levels of participation in decision-making (see also Figure 10.2).

In a follow-up, De Dreu (2002) tested the same basic idea, this time replacing participative decision-making with a measure of team task reflexivity, defined as "the extent to which team members overtly reflect upon the group's objectives, strategies, and processes and adapt them to current or anticipated endogenous or environmental circumstances" (West, 1996, p. 559). The hypothesis was that groups with high rather than low levels of minority dissent would be more innovative, especially when they also had high rather than low levels of task reflexivity. The hypothesis was tested in a study involving 215 individuals in 32 teams. Participants worked in management and (crossfunctional) project teams in different areas, including consulting, financial planning and accounting, and research and development. Results showed a pattern very similar to the one reported earlier – under high levels of task reflexivity, more minority dissent was positively related to team innovations. Under low levels of task reflexivity, no such relationship was found.

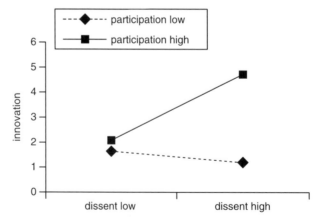

FIGURE 10.2   Team innovations as a function of minority dissent and participative decision-making (based on De Dreu & West, 2001).

Because the data collected by De Dreu and West (2001) and De Dreu (2002) were cross-sectional and correlational in nature, one cannot be sure about the directionality of the findings. To the rescue comes a recent study by Choi and Levine (2004), who, in an experimental setting, showed that a minority of new-comers in a group who propose an innovative strategy can convert the group into adopting this new strategy and, consequently, improve their overall group's performance. With caution we can thus conclude that minority dissent leads to creative thoughts in majority members and that high group-level information exchange and processing turns these creative ideas into beneficial innovations.

Concluding Thoughts

In comparison to the work on minority influence on attitudes and beliefs, far less theoretical controversy and much higher levels of consistency across studies seem to characterize the study of minority dissent in small group performance. Minority factions have a hard time converting majority factions: Only when they are well informed about the truth, and the truth is what the group is looking for, do minor-ities prevail. At the same time, and seemingly regardless of the validity of the minority position, minority dissent prevents groups from moving prematurely to consensus, and forces group members to rethink their assumptions and decision strategies. Minority dissent therefore reduces defective decision-making tenden-cies in groups. Finally, minority dissent triggers divergent thinking and leads majority members to develop creative and original insights. Provided the group works well together and exchanges and processes information in an openminded yet critical way, minority-induced creative thoughts are turned into innovative products and processes serving the group well.

SUMMARY AND CONCLUSIONS

This chapter was divided into two main sections. The first covered minority and majority influence on attitudes and beliefs. Participants in these studies read or listen to a set of persuasive arguments presumably supported by a majority or a minority of a more or less relevant peer group (e.g., fellow students, the general public). Subsequently attitudes are measured, either in public or in private, and either on the focal issue only or also on related issues. For a long time more or less competing models coexisted; only recently have we witnessed attempts at integra-tion of objective consensus approaches, conversion theory, and somewhat isolated research findings (e.g., Crano & Alvaro, 1998; De Vries et al., 1996). Although these integrations hold promise, they cannot account for all empirical research findings (e.g., Martin & Hewstone, 2001), and in a few cases more sophisticated tests would be in order. Nevertheless, with regard to majority and minority influ-ence on attitudes and beliefs we can safely conclude that (1) majority influence exceeds minority influence on both public and private attitudes, and on both focal and related attitudes; (2) majority influence on public and focal attitudes exceeds its influence on private and related attitudes, especially when the majority is, in one way or another, threatening to the recipient's social identity; (3) minority influence on private and related attitudes exceeds its influence on public and focal attitudes, especially when the minority is, in one way or another, raising recipients' motivation to engage in deep and systematic information processing, yet it also makes recipients reluctant to overtly identify with the minority.

The second area of research and theory reviewed here was concerned with small group dynamics and performance when minority and majority factions emerge within the group. Work within the social combinations approach suggests that in these situations minority factions only prevail – convert the majority – when the group works on an intellective task and the minority possesses the correct answer. Work on information sharing and group decision-making further suggests that in other cases minority dissent produces conversion to a lesser extent but still increases the quality of group decisions by enhancing individual- and group-level information exchange and processing. Finally, studies in the social psychological laboratory as well as in organizational teams show that exposure to minority dissent increases creative and divergent thought, and that this turns into innovation when group members openmindedly yet critically process information.

Each of these two sections in its own right thus shows the power of minority factions in small groups and in society. Given the right conditions, minority dissent can have substantial impact on majority beliefs and attitudes, work practices, and group decisions. Minority influence is not always immediately noticeable, and usually requires time. The irony often is that by the time minority influence becomes manifest and noticeable, the message and its implications are no longer attributed to the minority but instead seen as "the spirit of the times", as "in the air", and so on. Clearly, more research and better theories are needed to understand minority and majority influence on attitudes and beliefs, and to integrate these insights with work on small group dynamics, group decision-making, and group innovation. This will allow us to understand when and why majority influence goes beyond mere compliance and minority influence acts as the premier driver of change and innovation in society and small groups.

REFERENCES

Aldag, R., & Fuller, S. R. (1993). Beyond fiasco: A reappraisal of the groupthink phenomenon and a new model of group decision processes. *Psychological Bulletin, 113,* 535–552.

Alvaro, E. M., & Crano, W. D. (1997). Indirect minority influence: Evidence for leniency in source evaluation and counter argumentation. *Journal of Personality and Social Psychology, 72,* 949–964.

Amabile, T. M., Conti, R., Coon, H., Lazenby, J., & Herron, M. (1996). Assessing the work environment for creativity. *Academy of Management Journal, 39,* 1154–1184.

Anderson, N., De Dreu, C. K. W., & Nijstad, B. A. (2004). The routinization of innovation research: A constructively critical review of the state-of-the-science. *Journal of Organizational Behavior, 25,* 147–174.

Asch, S. E. (1956). Studies of independence and conformity: A minority of one against a unanimous majority. *Psychological Monographs: General and Applied, 70,* 1–70.

Baker, S. M., & Petty, R. E. (1994). Majority and minority influence: Source-position imbalance as a determinant of message scrutiny. *Journal of Personality and Social Psychology*, 67, 5–19.

Baron, R. S., Kerr, N., & Miller, N. (1993). *Group process, group decision, group action.* London: Open University Press.

Bohner, G., Frank, E., & Erb, H.-P. (1998). Heuristic processing of distinctiveness information in minority and majority influence. *European Journal of Social Psychology*, 28, 855–860.

Bohner, G., Moskowitz, G., & Chaiken, S. (1995). The interplay of heuristic and systematic processing of social information. In W. Stroebe & M. Hewstone (Eds.), *European Review of Social Psychology* (Vol. 6, pp. 33–68). Chichester, UK: Wiley.

Brewer, M. B. (1988). A dual process model of impression formation. In R. S. Wyer, Jr., & T. K. Srull (Eds.), *Advances in social cognition* (Vol. 1, pp. 1–36). Hillsdale, NJ: Lawrence Erlbaum Associates, Inc.

Brodbeck, F. C., Kerschreiter, R., Mojzisch, A., Frey, D., & Schulz-Hardt, S. (2002). The dissemination of critical unshared information in decision-making groups: The effect of pre-discussion dissent. *European Journal of Social Psychology*, 32, 35–56.

Chaiken, S. (1987). The heuristic model of persuasion. In M. P. Zanna, J. M. Olson, & C. P. Herman (Eds.), *Social influence: The Ontario symposium* (Vol. 5, pp. 3–39). Hillsdale, NJ: Lawrence Erlbaum Associates, Inc.

Chaiken, S. & Trope, Y. (Eds.). (1999). *Dual-process theories in social psychology.* New York: Guilford Press.

Choi, H.-S., & Levine, J. M. (2004). Minority influence in work teams: The impact of newcomers. *Journal of Experimental Social Psychology*, 40, 273–280.

Cialdini, R. B. & Trost, M. R. (1998). Social influence: Social norms, conformity and compliance. In D. T. Gilbert, S. T. Fiske, & G. Lindzey (Eds), *The handbook of social psychology* (4th ed., Vol. 2), pp. 151–192. New York: McGraw-Hill.

Clark, R. D. III, & Maass, A. (1988). Social categorization in minority influence: The case of homosexuality. *European Journal of Social Psychology*, 18, 347–364.

Crano, W. D. (2001). Social influence, social identity, and ingroup leniency. In C. K. W. De Dreu & N. K. De Vries (Eds.), *Group consensus and minority influence: Implications for innovation* (pp. 122–143). Oxford: Blackwell.

Crano, W. D., & Alvaro, E. M. (1998). The context/comparison model of social influence: Mechanisms, structure, and linkages that underlie indirect attitude change. In W. Stroebe & M. Hewstone (Eds.), *European review of social psychology* (Vol. 8, pp. 175–202). Chichester, UK: Wiley.

Crano, W. D., & Chen, X. (1998). The leniency contract and persistence of majority and minority influence. *Journal of Personality and Social Psychology*, 74, 1437–1450.

Crano, W. D., & Cooper, R. E. (1973). Examination of Newcomb's extension of structural balance theory. *Journal of Personality and Social Psychology*, 27, 344–353.

Davis, J. H. (1973). Group decision and social interaction: A theory of social decision schemes. *Psychological Review*, 80, 97–125.

De Dreu, C. K. W. (2002). Team innovation and effectiveness: The importance of minority dissent and reflexivity. *European Journal of Work and Organizational Psychology*, 11, 285–298.

De Dreu, C. K. W., & De Vries, N. K. (1993). Numerical support, information processing and attitude change. *European Journal of Social Psychology*, 23, 647–662.

De Dreu, C. K. W., & De Vries, N. K. (1996). Differential processing and attitude change following majority and minority arguments. *British Journal of Social Psychology*, 35, 77–90.

De Dreu, C. K. W., & De Vries, N. K. (1997). Minority dissent in organizations. In C. K. W. De Dreu and E. Van de Vliert (Eds.), *Using conflict in organizations* (pp. 72–86). London: Sage.

De Dreu, C. K. W., & De Vries, N. K. (Eds.). (2001). *Group consensus and minority influence*. Oxford: Blackwell.

De Dreu, C. K. W., De Vries, N. K., Franssen, H., & Altink, W. (1999). Minority dissent in organizations: Factors influencing willingness to dissent. *Journal of Applied Social Psychology, 30*, 2451–2466.

De Dreu, C. K. W., De Vries, N. K., Gordijn, E., & Schuurman, M. K. (1999). Convergent and divergent processing of majority and minority arguments: Effects on focal and related attitudes. *European Journal of Social Psychology, 29*, 329–348.

De Dreu, C. K. W., & Van Kleef, G. A. (2004). The influence of power on the information search, impression formation, and demands in negotiation. *Journal of Experimental Social Psychology, 40*, 303–319.

De Dreu, C. K. W., & West, M. A. (2001). Minority dissent and team innovation: The importance of participation in decision making. *Journal of Applied Psychology, 86*, 1191–1201.

Deutsch, M., & Gerard, H. B. (1955). A study of normative and informational social influence upon individual judgment. *Journal of Abnormal and Social Psychology, 51*, 629–636.

De Vries, N. K., de Dreu, C. K. W., Gordijn, E., & Schuurman, M. (1996). Majority and minority influence: A dual role interpretation. In W. Stroebe & M. Hewstone (Eds.), *European review of social psychology* (Vol. 7, pp. 145–172). Chichester, UK: Wiley.

Dooley, R. S., & Fryxell, G. E. (1999). Attaining decision quality and commitment from dissent: The moderating effects of loyalty and competence in strategic decision-making teams. *Academy of Management Journal, 42*, 389–402.

Eagly, A. H., & Chaiken, S. (1993). *The psychology of attitudes*. Fort Worth, TX: Harcourt Brace Jovanovich.

Erb, H.-P., & Bohner, G. (2001). Mere consensus effects in minority and majority influence. In C. K. W. De Dreu & N. K. De Vries (Eds.), *Group consensus and minority influence: Implications for innovation* (pp. 40–59). Oxford: Blackwell.

Erb, H.-P., Bohner, G., Schmälzle, K., & Rank, S. (1998). Beyond conflict and discrepancy: Cognitive bias in minority and majority influence. *Personality and Social Psychology Bulletin, 24*, 620–633.

Gordijn, E., De Vries, N. K., & De Dreu, C. K. W. (2002). Minority influence on focal and related attitudes: Change in size, attributions, and information processing. *Personality and Social Psychology Bulletin, 28*, 1315–1326.

Gruenfeld, D. H., Thomas-Hunt, M. C., & Kim, P. H. (1998). Cognitive flexibility, communication strategy, and integrative complexity in groups: Public versus private reactions to majority and minority status. *Journal of Experimental Social Psychology, 34*, 202–226.

Hackman, J. R., & Morris, C. G. (1975). Group task, group interaction process and group performance effectiveness: A review and proposed integration. In L. Berkowitz (Ed.), *Advances in experimental social psychology* (Vol. 8, pp. 45–99). New York: Academic Press.

Hoffman, L., & Maier, N. (1961). Quality and acceptance of problem solutions by members of homogeneous and heterogeneous groups. *Journal of Abnormal and Social Psychology, 62*, 401–407.

Janis, I. L. (1972). *Victims of groupthink: A psychological study of foreign-policy decisions and fiascoes*. Boston: Houghton-Mifflin.

Janis, I. L., & Mann, F. (1977). *Decision making.* New York: Free Press.

Kanter, R. M. (1988). When a thousand flowers bloom: Structural, collective, and social conditions for innovation in organizations. In B. Staw & L. L. Cummings (Eds.), *Research in organizational behavior* (Vol. 10, pp. 169–211). Greenwich, CT: JAI Press.

Kerr, N. L. (2001). Is it what one says or how one says it? Style vs. substance from an SDS perspective. In C. K. W. De Dreu & N. K. De Vries (Eds.), *Group consensus and minority influence: Implications for innovation* (pp. 201–228). Oxford: Blackwell.

Kerr, N. L., MacCoun, R. J., Hansen, C. H., & Hymes, J. A. (1987). Gaining and losing social support: Momentum in decision-making groups. *Journal of Experimental Social Psychology, 23,* 119–145.

Kruglanski, A. W., & Mackie, D. M. (1990). Majority and minority influence: A judgmental process analysis. In W. Stroebe & M. Hewstone (Eds.), *European review of social psychology* (Vol. 1, pp. 229–261). Chichester, UK: Wiley.

Kruglanski, A. W., Thompson, E. P., & Spiegel, S. (1999). Separate or equal? Bimodal notions of persuasion and a single-process "unimodel". In S. Chaiken & Y. Trope (Eds.), *Dual-process theories in social psychology* (pp. 293–313). New York: Guilford Press.

Kruglanski, A. W., & Webster, D. M. (1996). Motivated closing of the mind: "Seizing" and "freezing". *Psychological Review, 103,* 263–283.

Latané, B., & Wolf, S. (1981). The social impact of majorities and minorities. *Psychological Review, 88,* 438–453.

Laughlin, P. R. (1980). Social combination processes of cooperative problem-solving groups on verbal intellective tasks. In M. L. Fishbein (Ed.), *Progress in social psychology* (Vol. 1). Hillsdale, NJ: Lawrence Erlbaum Associates, Inc.

Laughlin, P. R., & Ellis, A. L. (1986). Demonstrability and social combination processes on mathematical intellective tasks. *Journal of Experimental Social Psychology, 22,* 177–189.

LePine, J., & Van Dyne, L. (1998). Predicting voice behavior in work groups. *Journal of Applied Psychology, 83,* 853–868.

Levine, J. M., & Kaarbo, J. (2001). Minority influence in political decision-making groups. In C. K. W. De Dreu & N. K. De Vries (Eds.), *Group consensus and minority influence: Implications for innovation* (pp. 229–257). Oxford: Blackwell.

Lorge, I., & Solomon, H. (1955). Two models of group behavior in the solution of eureka-type problems. *Psychometrika, 20,* 139–148.

Maass, A., & Clark, R. D. III (1984). Hidden impact of minorities: Fifteen years of minority influence research. *Psychological Bulletin, 95,* 428–450.

Mackie, D. M. (1987). Systematic and nonsystematic processing of majority and minority persuasive communications. *Journal of Personality and Social Psychology, 53,* 41–52.

McLeod, P., Baron, R. S., Marti, M. W., & Yoon, K. (1997). The eyes have it: Minority influence in face-to-face and computer-mediated group discussions. *Journal of Applied Psychology, 82,* 706–718.

Martin, R. (1995). Majority and minority influence using the afterimage paradigm: A replication with an unambiguous blue slide. *European Journal of Social Psychology, 25,* 373–381.

Martin, R. (1998). Majority and minority influence using the afterimage paradigm: A series of attempted replications. *Journal of Experimental Social Psychology, 34,* 1–26.

Martin, R., & Hewstone, M. (1999). Minority influence and optimal problem solving. *European Journal of Social Psychology, 29,* 825–832.

Martin, R., & Hewstone, M. (2001). Afterthoughts on afterimages: A review of the after-image paradigm in majority and minority influence research. In C. K. W. De Dreu & N. K. De Vries (Eds.), *Group consensus and minority influence: Implications for innovation* (pp. 15–39). Oxford: Blackwell.

Milgram, S. (1963). Behavioral study of obedience. *Journal of Abnormal and Social Psychology, 67,* 371–378.

Moscovici, S. (1980). Toward a theory of conversion behavior. In L. Berkowitz (Ed.), *Advances in experimental social psychology* (Vol. 13, pp. 209–239). New York: Academic Press.

Moscovici, S. (1985). Social influence and conformity. In G. Lindzey and E. Aronson (Eds.), *The handbook of social psychology* (3rd ed., pp. 347–412). New York: Random House.

Moscovici, S., & Personnaz, B. (1980). Studies in social influence: V. Minority influence and conversion behavior in a perceptual task. *Journal of Experimental Social Psychology, 16,* 270–282.

Moscovici, S., & Personnaz, B. (1991). Studies in social influence: VI. Is Lenin orange or red? Imagery and social influence. *European Journal of Social Psychology, 21,* 101–118.

Mugny, G. (1982). *The power of minorities.* London: Academic Press.

Mugny, G., Kaiser, C., Papastamou, S., & Perez, J. A. (1984). Intergroup relations, identification and social influence. *British Journal of Social Psychology, 23,* 317–322.

Nemeth, C. (1986). Differential contributions of majority and minority influence. *Psychological Review, 93,* 23–32.

Nemeth, C., & Chiles, C. (1988). Modelling courage: the role of dissent in fostering independence. *European Journal of Social Psychology, 18,* 275–280.

Nemeth, C., & Kwan, J. (1987). Minority influence, divergent thinking and detection of correct solutions. *Journal of Applied Social Psychology, 17,* 786–797.

Nemeth, C. J., & Staw, B. M. (1989). The tradeoffs of social control and innovation in groups and organizations. In L. Berkowitz (Ed.), *Advances in experimental social psychology* (Vol. 22, pp. 175–210).

Nemeth, C. J., & Wachtler, J. (1983). Creative problem solving as a result of majority vs minority influence. *European Journal of Social Psychology, 13,* 45–55.

Pérez, J. A., & Mugny, G. (1987). Paradoxical effects of categorization in minority influence: When being an out-group is an advantage. *European Journal of Social Psychology, 17,* 157–169.

Peterson, R. S., Owens, P. D., Tetlock, P. E., Fan, E. T., & Martorana, P. (1998). Group dynamics in top management teams: Groupthink, vigilance, and alternative models of organizational failure and success. *Organizational Behavior and Human Decision Processes, 73,* 272–305.

Petty, R. E., & Cacioppo, J. (1986). The elaboration likelihood model of persuasion. In L. Berkowitz (Ed.), *Advances in experimental social psychology* (Vol. 19, pp. 123–205). New York: Academic Press.

Pratkanis, A. R., Greenwald, A. G., Leippe, M. R., & Baumgardner, M. H. (1988). In search of reliable persuasion effects: III. The sleeper effect is dead: Long live the sleeper effect. *Journal of Personality and Social Psychology, 54,* 203–218.

Scholten, L., Van Knippenberg, D., Nijstad, B. A., & De Dreu, C. K. W. (in press). Motivated information processing and group decision making: Effects of process accountability and information dissemination. *Journal of Experimental Social Psychology,* in press.

Schweiger, D. M., Sandberg, W. R., & Ragan, J. W. (1986). Group approaches for improving strategic decision making: A comparative analysis of dialectical inquiry, devil's advocacy, and consensus. *Academy of Management Journal, 29*, 51–71.

Schweiger, D., Sandberg, W., & Rechner, P. (1989). Experimental effects of dialectical inquiry, devil's advocacy, and other consensus approaches to strategic decision making. *Academy of Management Journal, 32*, 745–772.

Schwenk, C. R. (1990). Effects of devil's advocacy and dialectical inquiry on decision making: A meta-analysis. *Organizational Behavior and Human Decision Processes, 47*, 161–176.

Scott, R. K. (1995). Creative employees: A challenge to managers. *Journal of Creative Behavior, 29*, 64–71.

Smith, E. R., & DeCoster, J. (2000). Dual process models in social and cognitive psychology: Conceptual integration and links to underlying memory systems. *Personality and Social Psychology Review, 4*, 108–131.

Smith, C. M., Tindale, R., & Dugoni, B. L. (1996). Minority and majority influence in freely interacting groups: Qualitative versus quantitative differences. *British Journal of Social Psychology, 35*, 137–150.

Sorrentino, R. M., King, G., & Leo, G. (1980). The influence of the minority on perception: A note on a possible alternative explanation. *Journal of Experimental Social Psychology, 16*, 293–301.

Stasser, G. & Stewart, D. D. (1992). Discovery of hidden profiles by decision-making groups: Solving a problem versus making a judgment. *Journal of Personality and Social Psychology, 63*, 426–434.

Stasser, G., & Titus, W. (1985). Pooling of unshared information in group decision making: Biased information sampling during discussion. *Journal of Personality and Social Psychology, 48*, 1467–1478.

Stasser, G., & Titus, W. (1987). Effects of information load and percentage of shared information on the dissemination of unshared information during group discussion. *Journal of Personality and Social Psychology, 53*, 81–93.

Steiner, I. (1972). *Group process and productivity.* New York: Academic Press.

Tajfel, H., & Turner, J. T. (1986). The social identity theory of intergroup behavior. In S. Worchel & W. Austin (Eds.), *Psychology of intergroup relations* (pp. 7–24). Chicago: Nelson-Hall.

Tanford, S. & Penrod, S. (1984). Social influence model: a formal integration of research on majority and minority influence processes. *Psychological Bulletin, 95*, 189–225.

Turner, M. E., & Pratkanis, A. R. (1997). Mitigating groupthink by stimulating constructive conflict. In C. K. W. De Dreu & E. Van de Vliert (Eds.), *Using conflict in organizations* (pp. 53–71). London: Sage.

Van Dyne, L., & Saaverda, R. (1996). A naturalistic minority influence experiment: Effects on divergent thinking, conflict, and originality in work-groups. *British Journal of Social Psychology, 35*, 151–168.

Volpato, C., Maass, A., Mucchi-Faina, A., & Vitti, E. (1990). Minority influence and social categorization. *European Journal of Social Psychology, 20*, 119–132.

West, M. A. (1996). Reflexivity and work group effectiveness: A conceptual integration. In M. A. West (Ed.), *Handbook of work group psychology* (pp. 555–579). Chichester, UK: Wiley.

West, M. A. & Farr, J. L. (1990). Innovation at work. In M. A. West and J. L. Farr (Eds.), *Innovation and creativity at work: Psychological and organizational strategies* (pp. 3–13). Chichester, UK: Wiley.

Williams, K. Y., & O'Reilly, C. A. III (1998). Demography and diversity in organizations:

A review of 40 years of research. *Research in Organizational Behavior, 20,* 77–140.

Winquist, J. R., & Larson, J. R., Jr. (1998). Information pooling: When it impacts group decision making. *Journal of Personality and Social Psychology, 74,* 371–377.

Wittenbaum, G. M., & Stasser, G. (1996) Management of information in small groups. In J. L. Nye & A. M. Brower (Eds.), *What's social about social cognition? Research on socially shared cognition in small groups* (pp. 3–28). Thousand Oaks, CA: Sage.

Wood, W., Lundgren, S., Ouellette, J. A., Busceme, S., & Blackstone, T. (1994). Minority influence: A meta-analytic review of social influence processes. *Psychological Bulletin, 115,* 323–345.

Woodman, R. W., Sawyer, J. E., & Griffin, R. W. (1993). Toward a theory of organizational creativity. *Academy of Management Review, 18,* 293–321.

11

Rumors Influence: Toward a Dynamic Social Impact Theory of Rumor

NICHOLAS DIFONZO and PRASHANT BORDIA

While teaching my social psychology class recently, I (ND) asked students to use social influence tactics in designing a campaign to persuade people to obtain a free flu shot. "Incidentally," I asked, "How many of you have *not* received your free flu vaccination?" To my surprise, almost everyone raised their hand. "Why not?" I inquired. "I've heard stories of bad side-effects for young people," Peter in the front row responded. "Really," I said (I was surprised because I had not heard these tales; my physician later told me that there are no such bad side-effects for youth). "How many of you have heard stories like this?" Again, almost all raised their hands. I pursued further: "And how many of you don't get your flu shot because of this?" A third time, almost all raised their hands. "Hmm," I mused aloud; "*Rumors influence.*"

Rumors influence indeed. In March of 1991, false rumors circulated that Tropical Fantasy Soda Pop was manufactured by the Ku-Klux-Klan and caused black men to become sterile; sales plummeted 70%, delivery trucks were attacked, and vendors dropped the product (Freedman, 1991). Similarly, false allegations that Pop Rocks candy, when eaten with soda, would explode in the stomach resulted in a substantial reduction in Pop Rocks purchases (Unger, 1979). Belief in such *contamination* rumors is not always necessary for influence to occur; even though false rumors that McDonald's used worm-meat in its hamburgers were disbelieved, merely hearing them appeared to have a negative effect on intention to visit the fast-food chain (Tybout, Calder, & Sternthal, 1981). Rumors often increase distrust (DiFonzo, Bordia, & Rosnow, 1994) and aggravate conflict between groups. The Report of the American National Advisory Commission on Civil Disorders cited rumor as responsible for exacerbating racial tensions in "more than 65% of the disorders studied by the Commission" (Kerner et al., 1968, p. 173). Rumors like these continue to spark riots between opposing ethnic groups (Horowitz, 2001); for example, false rumors circulated among Pakistani Muslims that no Jew attended work at the World Trade Center on September 11, 2001 (Hari, 2002). Rumors also affect expectations. German agents in the Second World War propagated rumors among the French to demoralize them (Knapp, 1944). More recently, rumors in corporations were found to be ubiquitous and frequently caused a loss of morale in the workplace, especially during change (DiFonzo & Bordia, 1998, 2000). Finally – as in our example above – medical rumors may substantially affect important health detection and disease-prevention behaviors (Suls & Goodkin, 1994). In short, rumors influence a wide variety of human actions, expectations and attitudes.

Social psychologists have been interested in rumor for over 70 years. Rumor researchers have included some of the best-known leaders of the field: Floyd Allport, Gordon Allport, Leon Festinger, Kurt Back, Stanley Schachter, Dorwin Cartwright, and John Thibaut. With some notable exceptions, however (e.g., see the work of Ralph L. Rosnow and colleagues summarized in Rosnow, 1991; also see Pratkanis & Aronson, 1991), interest in rumor has tended to wane. Why? We have argued elsewhere (Bordia & DiFonzo, 2002) that social psychology has typically employed an individual level of analysis – this approach has not been well suited for the multilevel and dynamic nature of rumor phenomena. For example, Allport and Postman, in their classic *The Psychology of Rumor* (1947), studied rumor distortion using what is commonly known as "the telephone game." Subjects transmitted a message – without discussion – serially down a chain of individuals; the final message was always severely shortened and distorted. From this *serial transmission* methodology we learned much about the role of *individual* memory limitations and projections, but could not hope to capture distortion effects that occur because of interpersonal or group processes. A second example: Festinger et al. (1948) approached belief in rumor from the level of the individual to explain why rumors occurred following a natural disaster. They speculated that persons in such situations felt anxious; to legitimate their anxiety they transmitted anxiety-provoking rumors. Festinger's work taught us much about the role of *cognitive consistency* in rumor content, but did not address how cultural and social representations inform content (Prasad, 1950). In addition, experimental research on rumor activity has typically been static, analyzing associations between situational variables (e.g., uncertainty), psychological states (e.g., anxiety), and rumor transmission at a single point in time (see review in Bordia & DiFonzo, 2002). While this research has made helpful contributions to our understanding of psychological factors affecting rumor spread, we know little about the *dynamic* processes involved here: how rumors and psychological states interact and evolve *over time*. The point is that real-life rumor phenomena (transmission, belief, distortion) almost certainly involve *multiple level* – micro, meso, and macro – *dynamic* processes (similar arguments have been applied to small group research in Arrow, McGrath, & Berdahl, 2000, and Wheelan, 1994).

This chapter aims to advance a multilevel and dynamic understanding of rumor as social influence. We'll do this by focusing on three key phenomena: *rumor as shared sensemaking, rumor propaganda*, and *rumor spread*. We first define rumor and focus on its function of shared sensemaking. We then touch upon the neglected topic of rumor propaganda – the intentional use of rumor. The greater part of the chapter, however, will explore rumor spread within a multilevel and dynamic model of social influence: *dynamic social impact theory* (DSIT; Latané & Bourgeois, 2001). DSIT is about how individual-level social influence leads to self-organization at the group level over time. Guided by DSIT, we review individual-level factors related to rumor transmission. Then, we consider group-level forms of rumor self-organization and we explore how rumor activity within and across social networks over time might affect this self-organization. Along the way, we propose some new theoretical paths that social psychologists can fruitfully follow to investigate this complex and dynamic social phenomenon. In particular, we theorize about how rumors self-organize across groups, how rumors can rapidly disperse far and wide, and why some rumors recur periodically. We begin by defining rumor.

RUMOR AS SHARED SENSEMAKING

We define rumor as *unverified and instrumentally relevant information statements in circulation that arise in contexts of ambiguity and that function primarily to help people make sense and manage threat.* Let's unpack this definition. Rumors are first of all *information statements*; they tell rather than interrogate or command. "Paul McCartney is dead" (Rosnow, 1991) *informs* us. Second, these information statements are *in circulation* among some group; they are not merely thoughts held privately. Rumors are a type of *meme*: an idea that may adapt, survive, or die among people just as species may adapt, survive, or die among environments (Heath, Bell, & Sternberg, 2001). Some rumors seem especially "fit" and thrive; others become extinct. Third, these communicated information statements are *unverified* in some context: They lack "secure standards of evidence" (Allport & Postman, 1947, p. ix) for at least some group of people. *Unverified* is not the same as being *untrue*; a rumor may in reality be true or false. Rather, it is simply in doubt. The rumor transmitter herself may possess this doubt – "I'm not sure if this is true, but I heard that . . ." – or she may pass it along as a true statement; it is nonetheless still a rumor because in other contexts (e.g., the larger group) the statement is held in doubt.

Fourth, these communicated and unverified information statements are *instrumentally relevant* – they tend to be viewed as important/significant/urgent bits of information. Why? People have a basic desire to make sense and to manage threat – rumors help them do both. Rumors sometimes help people make sense of ambiguous, confusing, and uncertain situations. "Why are department offices being renovated?" may well be answered by "Because the division is being reorganized" (DiFonzo et al., 1994). The rumor is a hypothesis proposed to explain a situational puzzle. Thus, rumor discussions in ambiguous contexts are a *group sensemaking* activity (Shibutani, 1966). At other times, people feel threatened and rumors help them prepare for or manage that threat (Bordia, Hunt, Paulsen, Tourish, & DiFonzo, 2004; Walker & Blaine, 1991). The threat may be to their welfare – "I heard that the Port Jervis dam will burst; leave town immediately!" (Turner, 1964). A more recent example of a rumor functioning to warn people of a physical threat circulated in Sri Lanka after the devastating tsunami of 2004: "Fish should not be eaten, as they have eaten human remains and are therefore likely to be carrying diseases" (Sarkar, 2005). Or the threat may be to one's sense of self – to anything one holds dear. "Eleanor Club" rumors that black servants were found using the "lady of the house's" combs occurred during times of racial turbulence in American history (Allport & Postman, 1947). The context of these rumors was a sense that one's identity as a white person was under attack. *Wedge-driving* rumors – rumors that derogate other groups or classes of people (Knapp, 1944) – express defensive sentiments; one *feels* threatened. To cope with such feelings, the wedge-rumormonger enhances their sense of self by putting others down.

Classic rumor differs from gossip and urban legend, though these differences often blur. *Gossip* is evaluative idle talk about individuals – usually not present – often shared for amusement, to communicate social mores, and to exclude someone from a social group (Gluckman, 1963; Rosnow & Fine, 1976; Smith, Lucas, & Latkin, 1999). An example of gossip: "Did you hear that Sally is having an affair?" When we object "That's gossip!" we are saying that it slanders and it is idle talk; when we object "That's rumor!" we mean that it is unverified (Sabini & Silver, 1982). Rumor is a morsel of food in an information famine; gossip is a tasty juicy treat at a cocktail party.

Urban legends are narratives – they have a story-like structure – of unusual, humorous, or horrible events that contain modern themes and moral implications. Urban legends are told as something that did happen or may have happened and variations of which are found in numerous places and times (Cornwell & Hobbs, 1992; Fine, 1992; Kapferer, 1990). For example, the tale entitled "The Hook" criticizes adolescent promiscuity: A teenage couple in a parked car in the dead of night stops necking after hearing scratching noises – upon their arrival home, the prosthetic hook of an escaped mental patient is found hanging on the car door handle (Brunvand, 1981). The tale has a setting, plot, characters, climax, and moral (don't park!), and variants of this tale have been documented. Urban legends may "touch down" as rumor or gossip when invested with particular details about time and place (Allport & Postman, 1947) – "I heard that Sally and Joe were necking out by Asylum Avenue last weekend and an escaped mental patient scratched up their car door!" Strictly speaking, however, rumors are about group sensemaking in ambiguity; urban legends are good stories. If rumor is a morsel and gossip is a treat, then urban legends are dessert after the evening meal: Dessert still nourishes (helps people make sense of the world through storytelling) but the diner is no longer famished (the sense made is not so urgent and it often points to a broader cultural value).

Though they are sometimes blurred, we think the distinctions between rumor, gossip, and urban legends are important because they may affect transmission processes differently at both individual and network levels; this is currently an open question. For example, when rumors are primarily motivated by fact-finding (see below), belief in the rumor will play a central role in deciding whether or not to transmit it (Bordia & DiFonzo, 2005). In contrast, gossip is most often spread without regard to the transmitter's belief in it. Indeed, gossip is told with the idea of building, changing, or maintaining social structures such as norms, hierarchy, and group identification (Foster, 2004); for example: "Joey is a wimp – don't play with him!" Nor is belief important in spreading urban legends; they are often told primarily for entertainment motives. For example, the tale that a highly stressed college student committed suicide during a final exam by shoving pencils up his nostrils and into his brain plays well among collegians (Mikkelson & Mikkelson, 2004).

Elsewhere (DiFonzo & Bordia, 2007) we carefully conceptualized contextual, content, and functional similarities and differences between these communication genres and presented some empirical results about these differences and how they differentially affect transmission likelihood. For example, we found that rumors of downsizing were more likely to be spread in a "serious conversation with one's boss" than was gossip about coworkers or urban legends about stunned kangaroos (Mikkelson, 2004). Also, these rumors were rated as more important and useful, but less entertaining, than both gossip and urban legends. And though all three genres were rated as having little evidentiary basis, rumor was rated as being less about individuals and less slanderous than gossip. This work is preliminary but suggestive; the effects of genre differences on transmission – at both the individual and network levels – are a topic ripe for further investigation.

Thus, central to our definition of rumor – and its distinguishing characteristics – is its group sensemaking function. Rumors are "shared understandings in progress" that may influence behavior in dramatic ways. Consider ethnic tensions between rival groups. Criminal acts by a few individuals are perceived as aggression by the entire group, thus justifying a retaliatory response (Horowitz, 2001). The susceptible – those who are anxious and uncertain – define a situation according to the rumor. In turn, the rumor makes impending threats salient and helps rally group members to take hostile action. Rumors explain and thereby foster expectations. When they were trading stock in a simulated market game, causal explanations embedded in rumors – "Goodyear profits up" – led student traders to expect share price movement (a price increase) in agreement with the rumor (DiFonzo & Bordia, 1997, 2002a). These expectations dramatically influenced trading behavior. Part of how rumors influence, then, is that they *make sense*. Elsewhere (Bordia & DiFonzo, 2004), we have explored the group dynamics of this sensemaking activity over the life of rumor discussions on the Internet.

Our conception of rumor has focused on the sensemaking and threat management needs that people have. These needs can be exploited by propagandists. In the next section we touch upon how rumors have been intentionally used to affect attitudes and actions.

RUMOR AS PROPAGANDA

Rumors have been used intentionally to influence others via misinformation and propaganda campaigns. Although this is underemphasized, rumor literature has acknowledged that rumors may originate or spread as part of a motivated – even malicious – *whispering campaign* (Allport & Postman, 1947; Kapferer, 1990;

Rosnow, 2001; Sinha, 1952). When much is at stake – such as an election to political office or product sales in a highly competitive consumer market – rumor becomes the means to a tangible gain. In wartime, rumors are used to demoralize enemy forces (Allport & Postman, 1947). In organizational settings, managers use rumors to float an idea and gauge employee reactions before formally proposing the idea (Esposito & Rosnow, 1983). Sales agents use rumors to steer consumers away from rival products and toward their own products; rumors become grist for the word-of-mouth advertising mill (Kapferer, 1990). Similarly, rumors may be used as an excuse, as when a failing student spreads a false allegation that the professor sexually harassed or was biased against her. Such existing rumors may be further promoted by rival factions – in our example, a rival professor.[1] During elections, rumors are used to sully the reputation of rival candidates (Kapferer, 1990; Sinha, 1952). For example, in recent elections in the Indian state of Madhya Pradesh, the Congress Party spread false statements alleging that the Indian Prime Minister, who belongs to the rival Bharatiya Janata Party, eats beef (Verma, 2003). Cows are sacred to Hindus and beef eating is anathema. The allegations created enough trouble that the Prime Minister had to announce dramatically: "I would rather die than eat beef." As our examples indicate, we suspect that rumor propaganda is often employed in the domain of politics.

These anecdotes tell a depressing tale, but are such uses of rumor for propaganda really so effective? That is, from the propagandist's point of view, is rumor truly a useful weapon in the arsenal of deceit? Surprisingly little empirical research has directly investigated this question. Two exceptions are research on the effects of *innuendo* and *projection*. First, innuendo: A negative rumor about a political candidate – presented as a newspaper headline – damages that candidate's reputation (Wegner, Wenzlaff, Kerker, & Beattie, 1981). Second is research on the use of projection as an influence tactic. Projection – accusing another person of the same things that the accuser is guilty of – leads to higher evaluations of the accuser (projectionist) and lower evaluations of the accused (Rucker & Pratkanis, 2001). These counterintuitive results occurred even when observers were suspicious of the projectionist's motive and were presented with evidence that the projectionist was indeed the guilty party! The implications of this research should bring glee to the black heart of the rumor propagandist: They suggest that spreading malicious rumors – even ones that are discredited and even when the propagandist's own culpability is clear – is effective in denigrating the target and elevating the spreader. It seems rather unfair.

However, it may be that rumor propaganda effects can be mitigated by several factors. We suggest a couple here for further investigation: motivational posture of the rumor public, and time. Consider motivational posture. We suspect that propaganda rumors are less effective when the target is one's ingroup than one's outgroup. Adapting Wegner et al.'s (1981) example: If "Bob Talbert" is a member of one's clan, the propaganda rumor ("I heard that Bob Talbert is part of the Mafia") seems unlikely to diminish Bob's reputation and improve the status of the rumormonger. Such a thesis could easily be tested by manipulating ingroup status in an adaptation of Wegner et al. Second, consider the effects of time. Would a propagandist's efforts be so effective over several rounds of propaganda? It seems plausible that the credibility of the propagandist – a factor crucial to her success (Pratkanis & Aronson, 1991) – would diminish. Reductions in her credibility would be aided by rumor refutations that made salient her malicious motivation. This hypothesis could be tested in an extension of Rucker and Pratkanis's (2001) projection studies that incorporated several rounds of propaganda incidents in a series, in which a rumor propagandist repeatedly accused others, and where the rumor-target increasingly made the propagandist's motivation salient.

If indeed rumor propaganda is so effective, findings from at least two lines of social psychological research help to inform us about *why* this might be so. First is research on *belief perseverance*: First impressions tend to persist, even when the initial evidence on which these impressions were based is discredited. For example, subjects who – after being presented with biased case histories – formed a belief about the relationship between score on a measure of risky behavior and success as a firefighter, adhered to that belief (albeit more weakly) *even after being informed that the case studies were fictitious* (Anderson, Lepper, & Ross, 1980). These researchers explain this result partly as a manifestation of *confirmation bias*: the tendency to interpret incoming, contradictory data so that it does not challenge existing impressions (Nisbett & Ross, 1980). Applied here, propaganda rumors lead to an initial belief and subsequent information tends to be selectively attended to so as to support that belief; in a word, propaganda rumors may effectively *bias* the interpretation of subsequent information.

In spite of the variety of contexts in which deliberate rumor spread may occur, and the work on the effects of innuendo and projection notwithstanding, rumor propaganda has generally been ignored as a variable of interest. Perhaps conscious and malicious rumor spread reveals a repugnant characteristic of human nature and forms "the ugly underbelly of interpersonal life" (Leary, 1995, p. 9). Also, intentional rumor spread does not tell us a great deal about the social dynamics of rumor spread, as undoubtedly it cannot by itself sustain a rumor (Horowitz, 2001). For a rumor to take hold, it has to find fertile ground and catch the imagination of many people: It must *spread*.

Rumor spread is an important part of how rumors influence. A rumor's influence is dependent on how extensively it has dispersed. A rumor that I share with only one person and is never transmitted further has negligible influence. Conversely, widespread rumors that "The flu vaccine has side-effects for young people" are likely to influence many to forgo this health prevention behavior. Rumors seem to have *built-in* spreading mechanisms. What are they? For the remainder of this chapter, we explore a multilevel and dynamic understanding of rumor spread. We begin at the level of the individual: Viewed from the perspective of the person, what are the factors involved in rumor spread?

INDIVIDUAL-LEVEL MECHANISMS OF RUMOR SPREAD

Research exploring the *micro level* antecedents of rumor transmission has investigated several important factors: uncertainty, anxiety, outcome-relevant involvement, and belief in the rumor (Rosnow, 1991). Motivational factors in transmission – fact-finding, relationship-enhancement, and self-enhancement – have also been considered (Bordia & DiFonzo, 2005).

Uncertainty

We think of uncertainty as the psychological state of doubt about what current events mean or what future events are likely to occur. Schachter and Burdick (1955) referred to uncertainty as "cognitive unclarity"; in a fascinating field study they induced uncertainty in an all-girls grade school by suddenly withdrawing a student from class without explanation. The school was abuzz with rumor. Uncertainty is thus the psychological experience of the individual in ambiguous and undefined situations (Rosnow, 1991). Uncertainty has consistently been linked to rumor transmission; Rosnow (1991) meta-analysed five studies and found a small to moderate ($r = .19$) average linear effect for uncertainty. Why? Uncertainty is an aversive state and people are motivated to reduce it; stated positively, people have a core social motive to understand (Fiske, 2004). Attempting to reduce uncertainty, people communicate with one another (Berger, 1987). According to Tamotsu Shibutani (1966), rumors are "improvised news" necessitated by uncertain situations: When formal information is not available or not trusted, people compensate with informal speculation. Indeed, he – and other sociologists – advocated thinking of rumor as collective problem-solving to define (i.e., make sense of) undefined situations (Turner & Killian, 1972); "undefined" situations are by definition filled with uncertainty. Turner (1994) equated rumor activity to information gathering; when group standards for evidence are high, the process looks like careful fact-finding. For example, rumor-related discussions on the Internet often involve fact-finding in the form of information seeking, sharing, and evaluating (Bordia & DiFonzo, 2004). When group standards for evidence are low – as with situations filled with intense anxiety – the process resembles contagion.

Anxiety

Whereas the experience of uncertainty is the cognitive side of ambiguous situations, anxiety is the emotional *angst* that one feels about a dreaded consequence. Uncertainty may lead to anxiety through a reduced sense of control (Bordia et al., 2004; DiFonzo & Bordia, 2002b). Uncertainty and anxiety naturally occur in ambiguous situations involving dreaded events. For example, information about corporate restructuring is often poorly communicated, resulting in uncertainty; the restructuring may cause departmental layoffs over which I have no control, resulting in anxiety.

Individual anxiety, whether it is a personality trait (Anthony, 1973) or a situational variable (Esposito, 1986/1987), has been linked to rumor transmission (Anthony, 1992; Bordia & Rosnow, 1998); Rosnow's (1991) seven-study meta-analysis found a large average linear effect ($r = .48$) for the personal anxiety–transmission relationship. In one of the few experimental studies investigating anxiety, students made to feel anxious over an impending unpleasant interview with a professor spread rumors more quickly than controls (Walker & Beckerle, 1987). Why should this be so? Two explanations have been offered. First, the *dissonance* explanation: Anxious feelings may be justified or legitimated by rumor as a way of reducing cognitive dissonance (Festinger, 1957; Turner, 1994). "I feel anxious; this rumor of a dreaded event makes sense of my anxiety." In this view, anxious individuals are especially receptive to rumors portending bad events. Second, the *hydraulic* explanation: anxious people share rumors in hopes of reducing anxiety by gaining a sense of control. How would rumors be used to gain a sense of control? Rumors help people prepare for and/or understand events (Walker & Blaine, 1991). For example, in a recent sample of psychiatric hospital staff undergoing organizational change, most of the anxiety (or psychological strain) variance was mediated by a reduced sense of control (Bordia et al., 2004). We found this same result in a survey of rumor episodes recalled by experienced corporate public relations officers (DiFonzo & Bordia, 2002b).

The relation between anxiety and rumor may not be linear; Rosnow (1980) speculated a curvilinear – an inverted "U" shape – relation. Moderate levels of anxiety may produce the highest likelihood of transmission. As with arousal in general, too little anxiety may not motivate an individual to spread a rumor – he simply doesn't care – but too much may result in an aversion to communicate at all. Rosnow, Esposito, and Gibney (1988) didn't find this curvilinear relation in a subsequent study of rumors surrounding a campus murder. However, two recent unpublished investigations by Mark Pezzo and John Yost (2003) do. In two high-anxiety sets of rumors concerning campus crime and an unexpected student death from spinal meningitis, a curvilinear relationship obtained between anxiety and the number of people to whom participants passed the rumor. The exact shape of the anxiety–transmission relationship thus remains an open question.

The anxiety–transmission relation may also be due to loss aversion tendencies and this may explain why *dread* rumors seem to be more prevalent than *wish* rumors. Dread rumors are those forecasting negative consequences; wish rumors, hoped-for events (Knapp, 1944). Dread rumors appear to be more likely to be transmitted than wish rumors in Internet discussions (Bordia & DiFonzo, 2004) and among collections of campus rumors (Walker & Blaine, 1991). Why might this be so? Prospect theory (Kahneman & Tversky, 1979) provides a possible answer. Prospect theory posits that losses are felt more keenly than equivalent gains. A dread rumor conveying the possibility of a loss would therefore motivate transmission more than a wish rumor conveying the possibility of an equivalent gain. Under this framework, the rumor of an impending $1 per share loss in stock value would be more likely to be transmitted than a $1 gain rumor. Similar reasoning supports the idea that dread rumors are *attended to* more easily than wish rumors – we are more alert to loss information than gain information. These hypotheses have not been investigated.

Similarly, the anxiety–transmission relation may also stem – paradoxically – from a core social motive to trust others; to view them as "basically benign" (Fiske, 2004). Most of the time we do trust others, but sometimes it is maladaptive to do so, as when they are not interested in our welfare. Individuals are, on average, very poor at detecting deception (DePaulo, Stone, & Lassiter, 1985). Rumors may be an important – and understudied – group deception detection mechanism; they serve to alert unsuspecting group members about persons and actions that should not be trusted. A recent longitudinal study (DiFonzo, Bordia, & Winterkorn, 2003) that we conducted in an organization undergoing radical downsizing is consistent with this idea: Individuals who did not trust the company transmitted negative rumors more than those who did, regardless of anxiety.

Outcome Relevant Involvement (ORI)

ORI refers to how important or significant the rumor topic is *to an individual*; more important topics (e.g., job layoffs in my department) are presumably more involving (Rosnow, 1991). Let's first review the findings on importance. Allport and Postman's (1947) *basic law of rumor* (rumor transmission = importance of the rumor multiplied by the ambiguity of the situation) points toward the necessity of both importance and uncertainty in rumor transmission. They stated: "An American citizen is not likely to spread rumors concerning the market price for camels in Afghanistan because the subject has no importance for him, ambiguous [uncertain] though it certainly is" (p. 34). Importance has indeed been linked to rumor transmission (Kimmel & Keefer, 1991; Schachter & Burdick, 1955). Esposito (1986/1987) found a positive association between importance and transmission of rumors among patrons of a transit system on strike. We also found the same direct association in a sample of rumors obtained from our survey of top corporate public relations personnel (DiFonzo & Bordia, 2002b). In a small number of studies, however, importance has not been linked with transmission. For example, subjects hearing a rumor about a student caught smoking marijuana during a final exam tended to spread the rumor if they thought the drug issue to be *less* important (Jaeger, Anthony, & Rosnow, 1980). Rosnow (1991) posited that "importance" in these studies might not have been operationally defined as "personally involving." In support of this idea, we found evidence that the effect of importance on transmission was mediated by anxiety (DiFonzo & Bordia, 2002b).

Belief

Belief refers to how much confidence an individual puts in the truth of a rumor. Belief in a rumor has been linked with its transmission. Rosnow (1991) meta-analyzed six studies and found a moderate average linear effect ($r = .30$) for the belief–transmission relationship. Rumors that were firmly believed during a strike by university faculty were transmitted more than those in which there was less confidence (Rosnow, Yost, & Esposito, 1986). Similar results were reported in the field study of a campus murder mentioned above (Rosnow et al., 1988) and in our sample of rumors from corporate public relations officers (DiFonzo & Bordia, 2000). Why would belief relate to transmission? Researchers have posited a *social reputation* explanation: Passing a false rumor along raises false hopes and alarms, and thus hurts my credibility and social standing (Caplow, 1947). Similarly, Higgins (1981) and Grice (1975) have noted that an important social norm of conversation is to pass on accurate information.

Belief in rumor is, of course, an interesting variable as well. What causes people to place confidence in such fantastic – and false – rumors as "Coca-Cola is contaminated with carcinogenic food additives" (Kapferer, 1991) and "The African AIDS pandemic occurred because the AIDS virus was created in a Western laboratory and tested on Africans" (Lynch, 1989)? How do people judge a rumor's truthfulness? Our review of the literature suggests several "cues" that people use to estimate the likelihood of a rumor's verity: First, *does the rumor agree with a currently held attitude?* Knapp (1944) speculated that prejudice lay behind the large percentage (65.9%) of Second World War rumors that were wedge-driving, such as "the Catholics in America are trying to evade the draft" (p. 25). Prasad (1950) posited that belief in rumors increased if they agreed with local superstitions. Allport and Lepkin (1945) found that belief in rumors of government waste or privilege (e.g., "A certain prominent government official has 3 cars and a large underground storage tank filled with gasoline for his own use," p. 5) were correlated with negative attitudes toward the Roosevelt administration.

A second cue is *how credible is the source of the rumor?* Knapp (1944) compiled 1,089 Second World War rumors and found that flourishing rumors tended to be attributed to a credible source that gave them the appearance of validity (Bird, 1979; Blake, McFaul, & Porter, 1974). Porter (1984) found that rumor communicator credibility was strongly related to belief in negative rumors about birth control in the Dominican Republic. A third cue is *how often have I heard this rumor?* Undergraduates tended to hear a campus rumor about a hit-and-run accident two or three times before spreading it (Weinberg et al., 1980). Allport and Lepkin (1945) found that people believed government waste rumors more if they had previously heard them than if they had not. A fourth (negative) cue is *has the rumor been denied?* Hearing President Roosevelt deny a rumor that Pearl Harbor damage was worse than reported reduced belief in that rumor (Allport & Postman, 1947). Belief in a rumor that secondhand tobacco smoke is harmful decreased after hearing a denial, especially a denial from a neutral source (Iyer & Debevec, 1991). Belief in a campus rumor – that a high grade point average would be required for entrance into upper-level psychology courses – was reduced by reading a refutation (Bordia, DiFonzo, & Travers, 1998). Other cues exist, such as whether or not the rumor fits a larger trend of events (DiFonzo, 1994, Study 2). Identification of such cues within specific domain areas, as well as how these cues may serve as self-fulfilling prophecies, is a promising future avenue of research. For example, dramatic stock price changes may give rise to rumors; investors then pay attention to price changes as cues to the rumor's validity and trade so as to spur further changes in the security's price (DiFonzo & Bordia, 1997, 2002a).

Motivational Factors

Individual-level antecedents to rumor transmission may also be considered from a motivational frame (Bordia & DiFonzo, 2005). We consider three broad motivations in rumor spread here: fact-finding, self-enhancement, and relationship enhancement.

Fact-finding   One broad motivation in social interchange is the desire to *act effectively*, that is, to respond to one's environment in a way that will ultimately maximize the chances for survival (Cialdini & Trost 1998; Wood 1999, 2000). This motivation leads to the search for *accurate* judgments. Applied to rumor, wanting to act effectively engenders what Shibutani (1966) dubbed *deliberative* rumor discussion. People check the credibility of sources, evaluate propositions based on what is known, and test their judgments against what they perceive to be objectively true. In short, people are at times motivated to be *accurate* and to *find facts*. The individual level antecedents of uncertainty, anxiety, and ORI are probably most conducive to this motivational state: Uncertainty about outcome-relevant issues involving dreaded outcomes results in anxiety. When dominated by this motivation, people engage in rumor discussions as a type of collective problem-solving process; they work together to "ferret out the facts." Our recent analysis of Internet rumor discussions showed evidence of this: Nearly 60% of rumor discussions were related to finding the facts of the matter at hand; for example, proposing hypotheses, checking sources, and arguing about plausibility (Bordia & DiFonzo, 2004). Participants sought veridical information.

Self-Enhancement   An individual's desire to enhance his or her sense of self has been linked to rumor transmission. Self-enhancement is a core social motive to view ourselves as "basically worthy and improvable" (Fiske, 2004). Rumors help us do this in at least two ways. First, sharing a rumor may enhance one's status within the ingroup – the group with which one closely identifies; we become, at least for a time, "in the know" (Turner, 1964). Scarce or secret information is valued more highly than commonly known information (Brock, 1968; Lynn, 1991); possessing such information enhances our sense of uniqueness and worth (Fromkin, 1972). Such motivations are quite powerful and may lead us to resist disconfirming data that would discredit "our" rumors. Second, rumors manage threats to our self-esteem by disparaging outgroups – groups with which we do not closely identify. For example, rumors that a rival school had been rated less favorably than one's own were more likely to be spread than the opposite rumor (Kamins, Folkes, & Perner, 1997). We have already mentioned how such defensive maneuvers underlay *wedge-driving* rumors that African-American servants were found using the "lady of the house's" combs; these occurred during times of racial turbulence in American history (Allport & Postman, 1947).

Relationship Enhancement   An individual's desire to enhance or maintain his or her relationship with the rumor recipient has been linked to rumor transmission. In a recent data set we found that when talking to members of one's outgroup, rumors that the outgroup member's school ranking had increased were more likely to be transmitted than rumors that the ranking had decreased; this effect was mediated by the desire to make the rumor recipient *like* and *think better of* the rumor transmitter (DiFonzo & Bordia, 2007). People actively strive to manage good impressions in others (Leary, 1995). Undoubtedly, this desire stems from a core social motive to belong (Fiske, 2004). Sharing rumors may fulfill our need to belong in at least three ways. One way it does this is by endowing individuals with a social role in the group sense-making process: We are *part of the group* as we pitch in to perform the collective tasks involved in making sense and managing threat (bringing information, evaluating information, challenging information, expressing anxiety about information, and exploring implications of information; Bordia & DiFonzo, 2004). Another way it does this is via reciprocity: Rumors are a commodity in the framework of *exchange theory* (Rosnow, 2001). If I share valuable uncertain information with you, you feel obligated to do a favor for me. A third way it does this is via *affect infusion* (Forgas, 1995): Sharing rumors may produce positive feelings or reduce negative feelings; these positive changes in affective state become associated with other people and increase our sense of belonging.

We have been reviewing individual-level factors in rumor transmission. Before exploring social network factors involved in rumor spread, we need to address two questions: (a) What framework will guide our exploration and (b) what group-level outcome variables are we concerned with? Regarding (a), whatever framework we choose should be able to incorporate rumor sensemaking and spread aspects of influence over time. Dynamic social impact theory (DSIT; Latané & Bourgeois, 1996) is just such a model.

DYNAMIC SOCIAL IMPACT THEORY

DSIT is a theory about how bottom-up social impacts self-organize over time (Latané, 1996). Let's unpack this statement. The key question is: How do *spatial* patterns of attitudes arise? Why, for example, did "Blue" states (those that voted Democrat in the 2000 – and even more so in the 2004 – US Presidential election) tend to be geographically next to one another, and the same for Red (Republican) states? Surely campaign managers from each party did not orchestrate these differences from the *top down*. Rather, these patterns organized by themselves over time from the *bottom up* (Harton & Bourgeois, 2004; Latané & L'Herrou, 1996; Schelling, 1978; Strogatz, 2003). "Bottom up" in this context means that individual-level social impacts – individual persons influencing another person to vote Blue or Red – occurred over time and resulted spontaneously in group-level patterns: Red vs. Blue geographical regions.

How does this occur? Let's consider *social impacts* first. *Social impact theory* (SIT; Latané, 1981) posits three general factors that affect influence: *strength* of influence tactic, *immediacy* of influence agent, and *number* of influence agents. Thus, a person will be most likely to be persuaded on an issue if a strong influence tactic is exerted by many persons close to him. To continue with our Presidential example, if "Vote Blue" signs appear on *all* (high number of influence agents) the lawns of my neighbors (immediate influence agents), to all of whom I *owe a favor* (reciprocity is a strong influence tactic), then I'm likely to put a "Vote Blue" sign on my own lawn. Similarly, if *most* of my *coworkers* in our highly *cohesive* work group begin using IBM-compatible computers, then I'm likely also to choose a PC.

Dynamic SIT examines how these social impacts – over time – spontaneously result in four group phenomena: clustering, consolidation, continuing diversity, and correlation (Latané & Bourgeois, 1996, 2001; Latané, & L'Herrou, 1996). *Clustering* means that pockets of shared opinion form. Over time, a sea of "Vote Blue" signs will expand in my neighborhood until meeting a growing patch of "Vote Red" signs; the result is homogenous patches of signs. *Consolidation* means that opinion diversity decreases – the majority tends to grow. At my workplace, for example, PCs will tend to dominate and Macs will wane. However, Macs may not disappear: *Continuing diversity* means that, despite consolidation, opinion minorities persist. Mac users will "circle wagons" and resist extinction. These processes occur simultaneously for unrelated attitude domains (e.g., Presidential and computer preferences) and the attitudes thereby become (randomly) *correlated*. For example, Mac users will tend to put "Vote Red" signs on their lawns; PC owners will erect "Vote Blue" (or vice versa). Correlation explains associations between conceptually unrelated attitudes – such as eating bagels and saying "y'all" (Latané, 1997).

RUMOR SPREAD OUTCOME VARIABLES: THE FIVE "Cs"

Our second question is: What are the group-level outcome variables of interest in a multilevel framework? Obviously, we are concerned with the extent of *rumor circulation*, by which we mean how widely the rumor has been dispersed. A rumor will exert greater social influence if it enjoys wide – as opposed to narrow – circulation. Beyond this, DSIT suggests four additional outcome variables discussed above. We here adapt them to rumor and coin four new terms: *rumor clustering, rumor consolidation, continuing diversity of rumors*, and *rumor correlation*. Adding *rumor circulation*, these five "Cs" constitute group-level outcome variables of interest in a dynamic social impact understanding of rumor spread.

Rumor clustering is when pockets of rumors or rumor variants form. There is some evidence for rumor clustering. Rumors often spread within – but not across – closely connected groups (Caplow, 1947; Davis, 1972). For example, rumors circulating in the African-American community that a young boy had been mutilated in a shopping mall lavatory specified the perpetrators as white; the same rumors circulating in the white community specified them as black (Rosenthal, 1971). In the language of DSIT, pockets of "Perpetrator is black!" and "Perpetrator is white!" rumors appeared. Similarly, Patricia Turner (1993) has documented rumors circulating in the African-American community that are rarely heard outside this community – they cluster along color lines (Turner & Fine, 2001). In addition, urban legends have "touched down" as rumors that contain different details to match the locale and time period (Allport & Postman, 1947). In general, however, though rumor researchers have noted the existence of rumor variants, they have not typically located them in social or geographical space. For example, in our own recent research we have noted variations of downsizing rumors ("There will be 25 to 30 layoffs" and "There will be 40 to 50 layoffs") collected in a company experiencing a radical downsizing (DiFonzo et al., 2003), but we did not investigate if they existed in pockets. Rumor collection studies that note the social and geographical location of each participant could ascertain whether or not rumor clustering occurs.

Rumor consolidation is when one rumor or rumor variant gains ascendancy and the diversity of rumors decreases. Rumor consolidation has often been observed as part of the group sensemaking process: Various rumor hypotheses are considered; often one solution survives and competing rumors die. Rumor consolidation often happens because of uniformity pressures. Once consensus about the veracity of a rumor is formed, conformity is demanded (Festinger et al., 1948; Firth, 1956; Turner & Killian, 1972). For example, in attempting to ascertain which prison inmates "snitch," hypotheses are tested and sources checked; once a hypothesis is accepted, however, data are reorganized and conformity pressures are brought to bear (Åckerström, 1988). The diversity of competing rumors set forth to explain an ambiguous situation is therefore reduced; in other words, consolidation occurs.

Continuing diversity of rumors refers to the persistence of "minority opinion" rumors or rumor variants. Continuing rumor diversity has been observed in at least two forms. First, some rumors persist over time. For example, rumors surrounding the assassination of John F. Kennedy are still with us (though they have changed over time; Polidoro, 2005). Second, rumors that resist consensus also persist. Rumors that *snowball* (become more detailed with time) seem especially applicable here. For example, snowballing rumors surrounding the sensational murder of a babysitter resisted consensus; though a majority of rumor participants believed that the murder had been committed by the husband who hired the babysitter, some continued to speculate that the deed was done by a passing vagrant (Peterson & Gist, 1951).

Finally, *rumor correlation* is when conceptually unrelated rumors or rumor variants become randomly associated: for example, if rumors that Paul McCartney is dead were correlated with rumors that JFK was really assassinated by the Mafia. We know of no research investigating this idea.

With these five outcome variables and DSIT as our backdrop we can now more fruitfully explore one important class of meso-level factors in rumor spread: social networks.

NETWORK FACTORS IN RUMOR SPREAD

"Clumpiness" of Social Space Configuration

Rumors occur in the context of *social space configurations* – patterns of relationships between people (Latané & Bourgeois, 1996). These are also known as types of *social networks* (Rogers & Agarwala-Rogers, 1976). Social space configurations are important because they directly affect immediacy and numbers of influence sources, two key social impact factors. Consider the various types of social space configurations. They include torus, "family," "ribbon," "scale-free," and random spatial configurations (Latané & L'Herrou, 1996; Watts, 2003). Twelve-person torus, family, and ribbon networks are diagrammed in Figure 11.1. Each of the

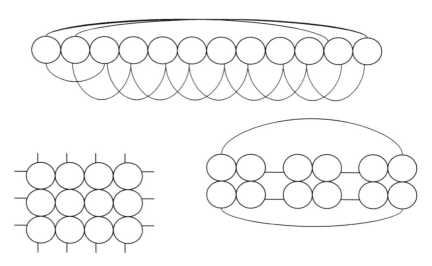

FIGURE 11.1   Ribbon (top), torus (lower left), and family (lower light) configurations. We thank Martin J. Bourgeois for these diagrams.

circles represents an individual. Social connections are indicated when circles touch or are connected with a line. In the torus network depicted, each individual is connected to four "neighbors" – north, south, east, and west – in a two-dimensionally uniform distribution. The ribbon configuration shows how an individual may be connected to four neighbors aligned as on a street – two on the left and two on the right. The family configuration depicted shows how the majority of one's social interactions may be with one's "family" or local cluster of contacts. Each of these configurations differs in "clumpiness" in that the chances of interacting with some neighbors, as opposed to others, differ dramatically. Families, for example, are very clumpy. Random configurations, as the name implies, are arranged so that the probability of connections between individuals is random; random configurations would be the least clumpy and have been used in DSIT empirical research (Latané & L'Herrou, 1996) as controls.

How might clumpiness affect the five rumor Cs? Consider rumor circulation first. As we have already noted, rumors tend to circulate within closely connected groups rather than between them (Buckner, 1965; Festinger, Schachter, & Back, 1950). People closely involved in friendship networks were more likely to have heard a rumor that a community worker was a communist (Festinger et al., 1948). Military rumors tended to diffuse within established groups rather than between them (Caplow, 1947). Therefore rumors tend to circulate less *across* highly "clumped" social networks and more *within* the clumps. Beyond this very general finding, little is known about the effects of network configuration on rumor circulation.

Clumpy social networks tend to exhibit less consolidation and more continuing diversity of *attitudes* than random networks (Latané & L'Herrou, 1996); we think the same patterns should be exhibited with *rumor* consolidation and diversity.

That is, clumpier social space configurations should reduce consolidation of rumors and should increase continuing diversity of rumor over time. For example, a social clan consisting of close-knit families that are weakly connected to one another would be likely to *resist* coming to a consensus across the clan and to *preserve* a higher number of rumor variants. Sense-making activities and spread of rumors should tend to be partially "contained" within families; "minority" rumor solutions should thus be less susceptible to the influence of the larger clan. For similar reasons, clumpy social networks tend to exhibit more attitude clustering than random networks (Latané & Bourgeois, 1996); we think that clumpier networks should also exhibit greater rumor clustering. To continue with our example, more patches of rumor variants should be observed between families across our hypothetical clan than in a very non-clumpy configuration such as a torus.

Distribution of Network Connections

Some people have many social connections and others are hermits. It turns out that the number of network connections in real networks – such as pages on the World Wide Web, scientific article coauthors, and movie actors – is often not distributed normally, but rather according to a *power-law* function ($y = c/x^p$, where c and p are constants); such networks are called *scale-free* (Watts, 2003). Scale-free networks are characterized by a few very well connected persons – called *hubs* (Watts, 2003), *liaisons* (Davis, 1972), or *opinion leaders* (Rogers, 1995) – and many people with a meager number of connections. The result is a *small world* where the average number of *degrees of separation* between any two persons in the network is surprisingly small (Milgram, 1969). A nonsocial example of a small-world network would be the distribution of airline connections between cities; there are a few well-connected hubs (Chicago, Los Angeles) and a very large number of smaller airports (Rochester, Albuquerque). To get from Rochester to Albuquerque would require only three connections (Rochester → Chicago → Los Angeles → Albuquerque). A social example: Milgram asked 160 people in Omaha to deliver a letter to a stockbroker in Boston by passing it along to a friend or acquaintance; of the 42 letters that were successfully delivered, the median number of degrees of separation was 5.5 – a remarkably small number.

Network studies of organizational rumor circulation often show a pattern of transmission that resembles the small world: Transmission episodes consist of a few well-connected persons (liaisons or opinion leaders) dispersing the rumor widely but most people spread it to zero (*dead-enders*) or only one other person (Hellweg, 1987). Davis (1972) called this a *cluster* pattern of transmission (not to be confused with *clustering* in DSIT).

The scale-free structure of small-world social networks would explain a couple of well-known features of rumor circulation. First, rumors can travel quickly and disperse widely. Small-world network theory points toward the key role played by hubs in a rapid diffusion of information (Barabási, 2002; Rogers, 1995; Watts, 2003). Like the spread of a virulent disease, rumors quickly make their way to hubs who then broadcast them widely, rapidly saturating the network. Hubs therefore exert a disproportional influence in rumor circulation. This suggests a means of affecting rumor circulation: Identify hubs and "inoculate" them to the rumor by dispelling uncertainty. This is similar to Barabási's (2002) proposal for counteracting the spread of AIDS: Treat highly promiscuous people first. The point is that hubs are key to spread.

Second, the scale-free structure of social networks also suggests a reason why some rumors persist or recur in an episodic fashion. That is, rumor activity seems to rise quickly, peter out, and then recur in similar episodes at later times. Allport & Postman (1947) called these *diving* rumors – like dolphins they "dive" (seem inactive) and resurface (become active) periodically. Again, hubs play a key role. Watts (2003) has theorized that the persistence of disease or computer viruses is due to occasional infections of hubs. The virus, never completely killed off, eventually makes its way back to a non-immunized hub, who broadcasts it widely. This suggests that persistent rumors – to which some portion of the population are never fully immunized – are occasionally heard and transmitted by a few well-connected, but susceptible, individuals. The rumor then recurs periodically. The recurrence of the "Good Times" email hoax exemplifies this pattern. The hoax consists of an email that warns users of the "Good Times" virus, and directs them to delete any message bearing the subject line "Good Times!" and to spread the warning to friends and family. The hoax periodically surfaces, in part we think because it reaches an unsuspecting – though well-meaning – hub (person with large email address list).

Local Network Homogeneity

Local network homogeneity is our term for the extent to which one's "clump," clique, or "family" – the local part of a network with which one has most interaction – is composed of *ingroup* members. Ingroups are those groups with which we strongly identify; outgroups those with which we do not. A highly homogenous local network would consist solely or mostly of ingroup members; most local structures are probably so composed. Friendship cliques, for example, are often divided along racial lines. Stated negatively, cliques are typically not diverse.

Local network homogeneity may interact with motivational factors associated with group membership to affect rumor circulation. Rumors in a highly homogenous local network will face selection pressures toward ingroup-positive and outgroup-negative rumors because such rumors are self- and relationship-enhancing. Groups often differ in this way with respect to the contents of rumors that circulate within them. For example, false rumors circulated among some Pakistani Muslims that no Jew attended work at the World Trade Center on September 11, 2001 (Hari, 2002) – these rumors undoubtedly did not circulate among Jewish circles. A second example: One-third of African-Americans believe strongly that the AIDS virus originated in a Western laboratory and that the African AIDS pandemic resulted from covert testing of the virus on Africans ("Black beliefs," 1995); these types of rumors appear to be propagated in African-American communities only (Turner & Fine, 2001). The strongly divergent "shared realities" that sometimes exist between groups (e.g., divergent opinions of the O. J. Simpson trial across race) may indeed be due to consensus arising within locally homogenous networks. Wedge-driving rumors find fertile soil in these homogenous networks.

Rumor Activity

We have been exploring how social networks affect rumor circulation, but the effects are interactive: Rumors themselves may markedly affect social networks. Turner's study of earthquake rumors (1994) and Shibutani's work on rumors transmitted during times of natural disasters (1966) showed that rumor is an information-gathering activity undertaken after normal channels are not available or not trusted. People then gather information and rumors from any source – even incredible ones. Another way of saying this is that people forge *new network connections*. Networks then become more highly interconnected – further explaining the ability of rumor to disseminate very quickly and widely. "Percolation theory" (Barabási, 2002) explores what happens when more and more randomly selected nodes (i.e., single units in the network, such as people or atoms) become connected in network. At a certain point – called a *phase transition* – the nodes suddenly coalesce into one large, highly interconnected network (Watts, 2003). After the phase transition, any node in the network can be linked to any other node. This may be the manner in which anxiety affects rumor circulation collectively: Anxiety causes random connections to occur. During times of crisis, highly anxious persons may reach out and connect with others for information-seeking purposes – even randomly – thus causing a phase transition of the percolation type; one huge interconnected network results. In such a network, rumor diffusion would of course be rapid and widespread. Thus, anxiety may not only affect an individual's susceptibility to a rumor but, if experienced collectively, may also lead to sudden interconnections between large networks of people.

SUMMARY

In this chapter we have considered three phenomena key to understanding rumor as social influence, and have considered rumor transmission within a multilevel and dynamic framework. Rumor is a sense-making activity that groups engage in when trying to explain ambiguity or managing threat. Rumors have been used intentionally as propaganda. Individual-level factors involved in rumor spread are uncertainty, anxiety, outcome-relevant involvement, belief in the rumor, and motivations (fact-finding, self-enhancement, and relationship-enhancement). We conceptualized five "Cs" of group-level outcome variables: rumor circulation, consolidation, clustering, continuing diversity, and correlation. At the meso level, we drew from dynamic social impact theory as a useful framework for exploring social network factors in rumor transmission. These were: clumpiness of social space configuration, distribution of network connections, local network homogeneity, and rumor activity.

Along the way we have addressed some older questions; for example, what leads a person to pass a rumor? We have also raised some newer ones such as:

What are the spatial *patterns* of rumor activity, how does social space configuration affect rumor transmission, how do rumors travel so quickly (especially under conditions of collective anxiety), why do some rumors expand and recur over time, and why do groups differ so dramatically with respect to rumor content? These questions are ripe for fruitful investigation. We hope that they will aid in furthering a multilevel and dynamic understanding of how rumors influence.

NOTE

1. We thank Anthony Pratkanis for suggesting these last two uses and examples of rumor as propaganda.

REFERENCES

Åckerström, M. (1988). The social construction of snitches, *Deviant Behavior, 9,* 155–167.

Allport, F. H., & Lepkin, M. (1945). Wartime rumors of waste and special privilege: Why some people believe them. *Journal of Abnormal and Social Psychology, 40,* 3–36.

Allport, G. W., & Postman, L. J. (1947). *The psychology of rumor.* New York: Holt, Rinehart & Winston.

Anderson, C. A., Lepper, M. R., & Ross, L. (1980). Perseverance of social theories: The role of explanation in the persistence of discredited information. *Journal of Personality and Social Psychology, 39*(6), 1037–1049.

Anthony, S. (1973). Anxiety and rumour. *Journal of Social Psychology, 89,* 91–98.

Anthony, S. (1992). The influence of personal characteristics on rumor knowledge and transmission among the deaf. *American Annals of the Deaf, 137,* 44–47.

Arrow, H., McGrath, J. E., & Berdahl, J. L. (2000). *Small groups as complex systems: Formation, coordination, development, and adaptation.* Thousand Oaks, CA: Sage.

Barabási, A. (2002). *Linked: The new science of networks.* Cambridge, MA: Perseus Publishing.

Berger, C. R. (1987). Communicating under uncertainty. In M. E. Roloff & G. R. Miller (Eds.), *Interpersonal processes: New directions in communication research* (pp. 39–62). Newbury Park, CA: Sage.

Bird, D. A. (1979). *Rumor as folklore: An interpretation and inventory.* Unpublished doctoral dissertation, Indiana University, Bloomington.

Black beliefs on AIDS tallied. (1995, November 2). *Rochester Democrat and Chronicle,* p. B1.

Blake, R. H., McFaul, T. R., & Porter, W. H. (1974). *Authority and mass media as variables in rumor transmission.* Paper presented at the Western Speech Communication Association, Newport Beach, CA.

Bordia, P., & DiFonzo, N. (2002). When social psychology became less social: Prasad and the history of rumor research. *Asian Journal of Social Psychology, 5,* 49–61.

Bordia, P., & DiFonzo, N. (2004). Problem solving in social interactions on the Internet: Rumor as social cognition. *Social Psychology Quarterly, 67*(1), 33–49.

Bordia, P., & DiFonzo, N. (2005). Psychological motivations in rumor spread. In G. A. Fine, C. Heath, & V. Campion-Vincent (Eds.), *Rumor mills: The social impact of rumor and legend* (pp. 87–101). New York: Aldine.

Bordia, P., DiFonzo, N., & Travers, V. (1998). Denying rumors of organizational change: A higher source is not always better. *Communications Research Reports, 15*(2), 189–198.

Bordia, P., Hunt, L., Paulsen, N., Tourish, D., & DiFonzo, N. (2004). Communication and uncertainty during organizational change: Is it all about control? *European Journal of Work and Organizational Psychology, 13*(3), 345–365.

Bordia, P., & Rosnow, R. L. (1998). Rumor rest stops on the information highway: Transmission patterns in a computer-mediated rumor chain. *Human Communication Research, 25*(2), 163–179.

Brock, T. C. (1968). Implications of commodity theory for value change. In A. Greenwald, T. C. Brock, & T. M. Ostrom (Eds.), *Psychological foundations of attitudes* (pp. 243–276). New York: Academic Press.

Brunvand, J. H. (1981). *The vanishing hitchhiker*. New York: Norton.

Buckner, H. T. (1965). A theory of rumor transmission. *Public Opinion Quarterly, 29*, 54–70.

Caplow, T. (1947). Rumors in war. *Social Forces, 25*, 298–302.

Cialdini, R. B., & Trost, M. R. (1998). Social influence: Social norms, conformity, and compliance. In D. T. Gilbert, S. T. Fiske, & G. Lindzey (Eds.), *The handbook of social psychology* (4th ed., pp. 151–192). New York: McGraw-Hill.

Cornwell, D., & Hobbs, S. (1992). Rumour and legend: Irregular interactions between social psychology and folklorists. *Canadian Psychology, 33*(3), 609–613.

Davis, K. (1972). *Human behavior at work: Human relations and organizational behavior* (4th ed.). New York: McGraw-Hill.

DePaulo, B. M., Stone, J. I., & Lassiter, G. D. (1985). Deceiving and detecting deceit. In B. R. Schlenker (Ed.), *The self and social life* (pp. 323–370). New York: McGraw-Hill.

DiFonzo, N. (1994). *Piggy-backed syllogisms for investor behavior: Probabilistic mental modeling in rumor-based stock market trading*. Unpublished Doctoral Thesis, Temple University, Philadelphia.

DiFonzo, N., & Bordia, P. (1997). Rumor and prediction: Making sense (but losing dollars) in the stock market. *Organizational Behavior and Human Decision Processes, 71*(3), 329–353.

DiFonzo, N., & Bordia, P. (1998). A tale of two corporations: Managing uncertainty during organizational change. *Human Resource Management, 37*(3&4), 295–303.

DiFonzo, N., & Bordia, P. (2000). How top PR professionals handle hearsay: Corporate rumors, their effects, and strategies to manage them. *Public Relations Review, 26*(2), 173–190.

DiFonzo, N., & Bordia, P. (2002a). Rumor and stable-cause attribution in prediction and behavior. *Organizational Behavior and Human Decision Processes, 88*, 785–800.

DiFonzo, N., & Bordia, P. (2002b). Corporate rumor activity, belief, and accuracy. *Public Relations Review, 150*, 1–19.

DiFonzo, N., & Bordia, P. (2007). *Rumor psychology: Social and organizational approaches*. Washington, DC: American Psychological Association.

DiFonzo, N., Bordia, P., & Rosnow, R. L. (1994). Reining in rumors. *Organizational Dynamics, 23*(1), 47–62.

DiFonzo, N., Bordia, P., & Winterkorn, R. (2003). *Distrust is a key ingredient in negative rumor transmission*. Paper presented at the 4th Annual Meeting of the Society for Personality and Social Psychologists, Los Angeles.

Esposito, J. L. (1986/1987). Subjective factors and rumor transmission: A field investigation of the influence of anxiety, importance, and belief on rumormongering (Doctoral dissertation, Temple University, Philadelphia, 1986). *Dissertation Abstracts International*, *48*, 596B.

Esposito, J. L., & Rosnow, R. L. (1983). Corporate rumors: How they start and how to stop them. *Management Review*, April, pp. 44–49.

Festinger, L. (1957). *A theory of cognitive dissonance*. Evanston, IL: Row, Peterson.

Festinger, L., Cartwright, D., Barber, K., Fleischl, J., Gottsdanker, J., Keysen, A., et al. (1948). A study of rumor: Its origin and spread. *Human Relations*, *1*, 464–485.

Festinger, L., Schachter, S., & Back, K. (1950). *Social pressures in informal groups: A study of human factors in housing*. New York: Harper and Brothers.

Fine, G. A. (1992). *Manufacturing tales: Sex and money in contemporary legends*. Knoxville, TN: University of Tennessee Press.

Firth, R. (1956). Rumor in a primitive society. *Journal of Abnormal and Social Psychology*, *53*, 122–132.

Fiske, S. T. (2004). *Social beings: A core motives approach to social psychology*. Hoboken, NJ: Wiley.

Forgas, J. P. (1995). Mood and judgment: The affect infusion model (AIM). *Psychological Bulletin*, *117*(1), 39–66.

Foster, E. K. (2004). Research on gossip: Taxonomy, methods, and future directions. *Review of General Psychology*, *8*(2), 78–99.

Freedman, A. M. (1991, May 10). Rumor turns fantasy into bad dream. *The Wall Street Journal*, pp. B1, B5.

Fromkin, H. L. (1972). Feelings of interpersonal undistinctiveness: An unpleasant affective state. *Journal of Experimental Research in Personality*, *6*(2–3), 178–185.

Gluckman, M. (1963). Gossip and scandal. *Current Anthropology*, *4*, 307–316.

Grice, H. P. (1975). Logic and conversation. The William James Lectures. In P. Cole & J. L. Morgan (Eds.), *Syntax and semantics* (Vol. 3, pp. 41–58). New York: Academic Press.

Hari, J. (2002, December 31). Well, they would say that, wouldn't they? *Australian Financial Review*, p. 42.

Harton, H. C., & Bourgeois, M. J. (2004). Cultural elements emerge from dynamic social impact. In M. Schaller & C. Crandall (Eds.), *The psychological foundations of culture*. Hillsdale, NJ: Lawrence Erlbaum Associates, Inc.

Heath, C., Bell, C., & Sternberg, E. (2001). Emotional selection in memes: The case of urban legends. *Journal of Personality and Social Psychology*, *81*, 1028–1041.

Hellweg, S. A. (1987). Organizational grapevines. In B. Dervin & M. J. Voigt, *Progress in communication sciences* (Vol. 8, pp. 213–230). Norwood, NJ: Ablex.

Higgins, E. T. (1981). The "communication game": Implications of social cognition. In E. T. Higgins, C. P. Herman, & M. P. Zanna (Eds.), *Social cognition: The Ontario Symposium* (Vol. 1, pp. 343–392). Hillsdale, NJ: Lawrence Erlbaum Associates, Inc.

Horowitz, D. L. (2001). *The deadly ethnic riot*. Berkeley: University of California Press.

Iyer, E. S., & Debevec, K. (1991). Origin of rumor and tone of message in rumor quelling strategies. *Psychology and Marketing*, *8*(3), 161–175.

Jaeger, M. E., Anthony, S., & Rosnow, R. L. (1980). Who hears what from whom and with what effect: A study of rumor. *Personality and Social Psychology Bulletin*, *6*, 473–478.

Kahneman, D., & Tversky, A. (1979). Prospect theory: An analysis of decision under risk. *Econometrica*, *47*, 263–291.

Kamins, M. A., Folkes, V. S., & Perner, L. (1997). Consumer responses to rumors: Good news, bad news. *Journal of Consumer Psychology*, *6*(2), 165–187.

Kapferer, J. N. (1990). *Rumors: Uses, interpretations, and images*. (B. Fink, Trans.).

New Brunswick, NJ: Transaction Publishers. (Original work published 1987 as *Rumeurs: Le Plus Vieux Média du Monde* [Rumors: The world's oldest media]. Paris: Editions du Seuil)

Kapferer, J. N. (1991). A mass poisoning rumor in Europe. *Public Opinion Quarterly, 53*, 467–481.

Kerner, O., Lindsay, J. V., Harris, F. R., Abel, I. W., Brooke, E. W., Thornton, C. B., et al. (1968). *Report of the National Advisory Commission on Civil Disorders*. (Report No. 1968 O-291-729). Washington, DC: US Government Printing Office.

Kimmel, A. J., & Keefer, R. (1991). Psychological correlates of the transmission and acceptance of rumors about AIDS. *Journal of Applied Social Psychology, 21*, 1608–1628.

Knapp, R. H. (1944). A psychology of rumor. *Public Opinion Quarterly, 8*, 22–27.

Latané, B. (1981). The psychology of social impact. *American Psychologist, 36*, 343–356.

Latané, B. (1996). Dynamic social impact: The creation of culture by communication. *Journal of Communication, 46*, 13–25.

Latané, B. (1997). Dynamic social impact: The societal consequences of human interaction. In C. McGarty & S. A. Haslam (Eds.), *The message of social psychology: Perspectives on mind in society* (pp. 200–220). Malden, MA: Blackwell.

Latané, B. & Bourgeois, M. J. (1996). Experimental evidence for dynamic social impact: The formations of subcultures in electronic groups. *Journal of Communication, 46*, 35–47.

Latané, B., & Bourgeois, M. J. (2001). Dynamic social impact and the consolidation, clustering, correlation, and continuing diversity of culture. In R. S. Tindale & M. Hogg (Eds.), *Handbook of social psychology, Vol. 4: Group Processes*. London: Blackwell.

Latané, B., & L'Herrou, T. (1996). Spatial clustering in the conformity game: Dynamic social impact in electronic groups. *Journal of Personality and Social Psychology, 70*, 1218–1230.

Leary, M. R. (1995). *Self-presentation: Impression management and interpersonal behavior*. Boulder, CO: Westview.

Lynch, R. D. (1989). Psychological impact of AIDS on individual, family, community, nation, and world in a historical perspective. *Family Community Health, 12*(2), 52–59.

Lynn, M. (1991). Scarcity effects on desirability: A quantitative review of the commodity theory literature. *Psychology and Marketing, 8*, 43–57.

Mikkelson, B. (2004, July 8). *Deja 'roo*. Retrieved November 9, 2004, from http://www.snopes.com/critters/malice/kangaroo.htm

Mikkelson, B., & Mikkelson, D. (2004, February 11). *Lead by the nose*. Retrieved March 2, 2005, from http://www.snopes.com/college/exam/pencils.asp

Milgram, S. (1969). Inter-disciplinary thinking and the small world problem. In M. Sherif & C. W. Sherif (Eds.), *Interdisciplinary relationships in the social sciences* (pp. 103–120). Chicago: Aldine.

Nisbett, R. E., & Ross, L. (1980). *Human inference: Strategies and shortcomings of social judgment*. Englewood Cliffs, NJ: Prentice-Hall.

Peterson, W. A., & Gist, N. P. (1951). Rumor and public opinion. *American Journal of Sociology, 57*, 159–167.

Pezzo, M., & Yost, J. (2003, February). *Too much of a bad thing: The curvilinear relationship between anxiety and rumor transmission*. Paper presented at the 4th Annual Meeting of the Society for Personality and Social Psychologists, Los Angeles.

Polidoro, M. (2005). Facts and fiction in the Kennedy assassination. *The Skeptical Inquirer, 29*(1), 22–24.

Porter, E. G. (1984). Birth control discontinuance as a diffusion process. *Studies in Family Planning, 15,* 20–29.

Prasad, J. (1950). A comparative study of rumours and reports in earthquakes. *British Journal of Psychology, 41,* 129–144.

Pratkanis, A. R., & Aronson, E. (1991). *Age of propaganda: The everyday use and abuse of persuasion.* New York: W. H. Freeman.

Rogers, E. M. (1995). *Diffusion of innovations* (4th ed.). New York: The Free Press.

Rogers, E. M., & Agarwala-Rogers, R. (1976). *Communication in organizations.* New York: Free Press.

Rosenthal, M. (1971). Where rumor raged. *Trans-Action, 8*(4), 34–43.

Rosnow, R. L. (1980). Psychology of rumor reconsidered. *Psychological Bulletin, 87*(3), 578–591.

Rosnow, R. L. (1991). Inside rumor: A personal journey. *American Psychologist, 46*(5), 484–496.

Rosnow, R. L. (2001). Rumor and gossip in interpersonal interaction and beyond: A social exchange perspective. In R. M. Kowalski (Ed.), *Behaving badly: Aversive behaviors in interpersonal relationships* (pp. 203–232). Washington, DC: American Psychological Association.

Rosnow, R. L., Esposito, J. L., & Gibney, L. (1988). Factors influencing rumor spreading: Replication and extension. *Language and Communication, 8*(1), 29–42.

Rosnow, R. L., & Fine, G. A. (1976). *Rumor and gossip: The social psychology of hearsay.* New York: Elsevier.

Rosnow, R. L., Yost, J. H., & Esposito, J. L. (1986). Belief in rumor and likelihood of rumor transmission. *Language and Communication, 6*(3), 189–194.

Rucker, D. D., & Pratkanis, A. R. (2001). Projection as an interpersonal influence tactic: The effects of the pot calling the kettle black. *Personality and Social Psychology Bulletin, 27*(11), 1494–1507.

Sabini, J., & Silver, M. (1982). *Moralities of everyday life.* Oxford: Oxford University Press.

Sarkar, S. (2005, February 17). *Tsunami rumors from Sri Lanka.* Retrieved February 18, 2005, from http://webapp.utexas.edu/blogs/sarkarlab

Schachter, S., & Burdick, H. (1955). A field experiment on rumor transmission and distortion. *Journal of Abnormal and Social Psychology, 50,* 363–371.

Schelling, T. C. (1978). *Micromotives and macrobehavior.* New York: Norton.

Shibutani, T. (1966). *Improvised news: A sociological study of rumor.* Indianapolis, IN: Bobbs-Merrill.

Sinha, D. (1952). Behaviour in a catastrophic situation: A psychological study of reports and rumours. *British Journal of Psychology, 43,* 200–209.

Smith, L. C., Lucas, K. C., & Latkin, C. (1999). Rumor and gossip: Social discourse on HIV and AIDS. *Anthropology and Medicine, 6*(1), 121–131.

Strogatz, S. (2003). *Sync: How order emerges from chaos in the universe, nature, and daily life.* New York: Hyperion.

Suls, J. M., & Goodkin, F. (1994). Medical gossip and rumor: Their role in the lay referral system. In R. F. Goodman & A. Ben-Ze'ev, *Good gossip* (pp. 169–179). Lawrence: University Press of Kansas.

Turner, P. A. (1993). *I heard it through the grapevine: Rumor in African-American culture.* Berkeley: University of California Press.

Turner, P. A., & Fine, G. A. (2001). *Whispers on the color line: Rumor and race in America.* Berkeley: University of California Press.

Turner, R. H. (1964). Collective behavior. In R. E. L. Faris (Ed.), *Handbook of modern sociology* (pp. 382–425). Chicago: Rand McNally.

Turner, R. H. (1994). Rumor as intensified information seeking: Earthquake rumors in China and the United States. In R. R. Dynes & K. J. Tierney (Eds.), *Disasters, collective behavior, and social organization* (pp. 244–256). Newark, DE: University of Delaware Press.

Turner, R. H., & Killian, L. M. (1972). *Collective behavior* (2nd ed.). Englewood Cliffs, NJ: Prentice Hall.

Tybout, A. M., Calder, B. J., & Sternthal, B. (1981). Using information processing theory to design marketing strategies. *Journal of Marketing Research, 18*(1), 73–79.

Unger, H. (1979). Psst – heard about Pop Rocks? Business rumors and how to counteract them. *Canadian Business*, June, 39.

Verma, S. K. (2003, February 21). I would rather die than eat beef, says PM. *The Statesman* (India).

Walker, C. J., & Beckerle, C. A. (1987). The effect of anxiety on rumor transmission. *Journal of Social Behavior and Personality, 2*, 353–360.

Walker, C. J., & Blaine, B. E. (1991). The virulence of dread rumors: A field experiment. *Language and Communication, 11*, 291–297.

Watts, D. J. (2003). *Six degrees: The science of a connected age*. New York: W. W. Norton.

Wegner, D. M., Wenzlaff, R., Kerker, R. M., & Beattie, A. E. (1981). Incrimination through innuendo: Can media questions become public answers? *Journal of Personality and Social Psychology, 40*(5), 822–832.

Weinberg, S. B., Regan, E. A., Weiman, L., Thon, L. J., Kuehn, B., Mond, C. J., et al. (1980). Anatomy of a rumor: A field study of rumor dissemination in a university setting. *Journal of Applied Communication Research, 8*(2), 156–160.

Wheelan, S. A. (1994). *Group processes: A developmental perspective*. Boston: Allyn & Bacon.

Wood, W. (1999). Motives and modes of processing in the social influence of groups. In S. Chaiken & Y. Trope (Eds.), *Dual process theories in social psychology* (pp. 547–570). New York: Guilford Press.

Wood, W. (2000). Attitude change: Persuasion and social influence. *Annual Review of Psychology, 51*, 539–570.

12

Self-Defeating Leader Behavior: Why Leaders Misuse Their Power and Influence

RODERICK M. KRAMER

Yet have I something in me dangerous, which let thy wiseness fear
Hamlet, *Hamlet, Prince of Denmark* (V, I)

*F*ew concepts in the social sciences are evoked with the same ease or employed so readily to explain so many social and institutional outcomes as power. The concept of power has been used to explain, for example, how organizational resources are allocated (Pfeffer, 1992), how decisions are made (Neustadt, 1990), the control of attention (Fiske, 1993), behavioral disinhibition (Galinsky, Gruenfeld, & Magee, 2003; Keltner, Gruenfeld, & Anderson, 2003), and the resolution of conflict (Boulding, 1966, 1989), to name just a few important processes and outcomes. The concept of power is routinely invoked, moreover, not only to explain why such outcomes do happen, but also why they don't. Russell's (1938) observation that power is a "fundamental concept" in the social sciences remains as true today as it was when he first uttered it.

As March (1994) noted, most conceptions of power reflect "the intuitive notion of struggle, with outcomes determined by the relative strength of contending forces" (p. 140). Wrong's (1979) definition is representative of this tradition, characterizing power as the "capacity of some persons to produce intended and foreseen effects on others" (p. 2). Along similar lines, Blau (1964) proposed that actors possess power when they can "induce others to accede to wishes by rewarding them for doing so" (p. 115). As these definitions make clear, social scientists have long presumed an intimate relationship between power and influence (French & Raven, 1959; McClelland, 1975): The effective use of social influence helps individuals obtain power; power, in turn, facilitates social influence because powerful social actors possess more resources that can be brought to bear on solving their problems (Pfeffer, 1992).

Drawing on these distinctions, effective social influence can be defined as the process of successfully inducing change in other people's attitudes, beliefs, perceptions, feelings, values, and behaviors by means of one's own behavioral tactics (see also Pratkanis, Chapter 2, this volume for a fuller elaboration). Thus defined, the use of effective influence tactics has been the subject of considerable prior theory and research (see, e.g., Cialdini, 1988; Kramer & Neale, 1998; Levine, 2003; Pratkanis & Aronson, 1992; Zimbardo, Ebbesen, & Maslach, 1977 for more comprehensive treatments of the social psychological literature on effective influence).

Given these presumed linkages between power and effective influence, it is hardly surprising that leadership theorists have afforded considerable attention to the study of how leaders use their power and social influence when trying to achieve their goals. Most prominently, perhaps, the distinguished presidential scholar Richard Neustadt (1990) characterized power in terms of "personal influence of an effective sort" (p. ix). Subsequent studies have only served to reinforce this view and to deepen our understanding of this important relationship between power and influence (see, e.g., Caro, 2002; Gergen, 2000; Kellerman, 1994). These case studies document, in particular, the intimate relationship between the skillful use of social influence by leaders and the accomplishment of difficult institutional goals.

From the standpoint of such accounts, the phenomenon of self-defeating influence behavior by leaders – influence behavior that proves counterproductive or self-destructive – represents a rather provocative and puzzling phenomenon. If "self-preservation and the pursuit of self-interest are essential features of rational behavior," as Baumeister and Scher (1988) proposed, then self-defeating influence behaviors must be counted among the hallmarks of leader irrationality.

Self-defeating influence behavior by experienced and successful leaders is particularly puzzling because, on *prima facie* grounds, one might argue that such behavior should be rather unlikely. After all, when political novices use influence processes ineptly, it is easy to discount their mistakes as reflecting simply lack of sophistication or requisite experience. Their mistakes can be attributed, for example, to naive misperceptions or miscalculations that taint their influence attempts. When experienced and politically savvy leaders make such mistakes, however, there is often a more perplexing and paradoxical quality to their actions. Because they are seasoned and proven influence professionals, we might expect, powerful leaders should be fairly discriminating when it comes to sizing up influence situations and equally adept at finding the "right" (i.e., most effective) influence strategies to use in that situation.

As recent social, corporate, and political scandals have amply documented, however, even the most savvy and experienced leaders are capable of shooting themselves in the proverbial foot (Kramer, 2003a). Indeed, when we examine the recurrent and persistent self-defeating behavior of a political virtuoso such as President Clinton – to use just one recent example – who has not asked, "What was he thinking? How could he have been so stupid?" (see Maraniss, 1998 for a particularly compelling analysis). What accounts for the stunning ability of some leaders to snatch defeat from the jaws of victory?

Despite the obvious importance of this topic, the study of self-defeating influence behavior by leaders has received relatively little systematic attention from social psychologists. A primary aim of the present chapter, accordingly, is to address this gap in our understanding. In particular, I examine some of the possible determinants and dynamics of self-defeating influence behaviors by leaders. The chapter is organized as follows. First, I offer a definition of self-defeating influence behavior. Second, I identify some of the different forms that self-defeating influence behaviors take. I then present a social cognitive model of self-defeating influence behavior. According to this model, leaders can be conceptualized as strategic actors who monitor or "audit" their influence transactions with the aim of realizing their aims or objectives. I then examine some social cognitive processes that lead this auditing process astray, fostering misperception and miscalculation. I next consider some of the psychological and social dynamics that contribute to the persistence of self-defeating influence behaviors. Again, the persistence of such behavior seems puzzling: If experienced leaders receive feedback that their influence attempts are failing, why do they not change their course of action? Why do they persist in their path to folly? I close the chapter by discussing briefly some of the implications of the framework for our understanding of self-defeating influence behavior.

CONCEPTUALIZING SELF-DEFEATING INFLUENCE BEHAVIOR

Historically, the scholarly study of self-defeating behavior has stood at the intersection of social psychology and clinical psychology (e.g., Berglas & Baumeister, 1993). Baumeister and Scher (1988) provided one of the first comprehensive literature reviews. They defined self-defeating behavior as "any deliberate or intentional behavior that has clear, definitely or probably negative effects on the self or on the self's projects" (p. 3). They go on to posit that the behavior "must be intentional, although harm to self did not have to be the intended or primary goal of the action" (p. 3).

Much of the initial research in this area focused on motivated forms of self-defeating behavior. Baumeister and Scher characterized these as deliberate or primary self-destructive behaviors. An assumption behind this early emphasis was that decision-makers' willingness to engage in, and persist with, obviously self-destructive behaviors suggests that they must have some sort of psychological investment or stake in the negative outcomes or failure those behaviors were producing (see, e.g., Berglas & Baumeister, 1993, 1996). As Baumeister and Scher (1988) noted in their careful assessment of such research, however, the evidence that people deliberately engage in behavior that harms the self in a foreseeable and desired way is actually quite thin. Consequently, they concluded, the range of normal adult self-defeating behaviors they examined simply "does not conform to the pattern of deliberate self-destruction" (p. 7).

It seemed a more fruitful approach, therefore, to pursue psychological and social processes that might impel even normal, ordinary decision-makers to unintentionally engage in, and persist with, self-defeating modes of judgment and action. Thus, the second category of self-defeating behavior Baumeister and Scher addressed involves situations where decision-makers do not desire, intend, or foresee the harmful or self-destructive consequences of their acts. This category includes situations where a decision-maker "seeks some positive goal, but uses a technique or strategy that impairs the chances of success . . . The focus is neither on normal behaviors that occasionally turn out badly, nor on isolated accidents or mishaps. Rather, it is on *systematic behavior patterns that . . . lead reliably to self-harmful outcomes*" (Baumeister & Scher, 1988, p. 12, emphasis added). It is this category of self-defeating leader behavior that this chapter is particularly concerned with.

FORMS OF SELF-DEFEATING INFLUENCE BEHAVIORS

In their review of the literature, Baumeister and Scher (1988) identified several forms of self-defeating behaviors that might adversely affect leaders' social influence behaviors. The first is irrational persistence or perseveration. As Baumeister and Scher (1988) noted, "Although persistence is often regarded as a virtue, misguided persistence can waste time and resources and therefore defeat one's chance of success at superordinate goals" (p. 12). One classic example of such counterproductive perseverance in the leadership realm was Lyndon Johnson's persistence in simultaneously pursuing the prosecution of the Vietnam War and the attainment of his Great Society goals. His unwillingness to make the necessary, albeit difficult, trade-offs between "guns and butter" ultimately compromised the successful pursuit of both programs. Equally importantly, it defeated his often-stated goal of being remembered as one of the greatest and most beloved US Presidents (Kearns-Goodwin, 1976).

A second category of self-defeating behavior identified by Baumeister and Scher (1988) that might adversely affect a leader's effectiveness as an influence agent is choking under pressure. Individuals choke under pressure when they select a coping strategy that they are unable to carry out successfully in a situation where performing well is vitally important. Many journalists and political commentators have noted the recurrent and almost uncanny ability of Dan Quayle to choke under pressure when confronted with difficult or embarrassing questions – his speech slows and his gaze freezes, giving the impression of a "deer caught in the high beams of an onrushing pick-up truck."

Counterproductive bargaining strategies constitute another important category of self-defeating behaviors and one directly related to ineffective influence in leadership contexts. Leaders use bargaining as a way of dealing with the diverse preferences of their opponents and constituents. Counterproductive bargaining strategies arise when leaders' strategic choices about how to influence those opponents or constituents are based on various misperceptions of the bargaining situation and/or the nature of one's opponent. For example, bargainers can misperceive the payoff structure or bargaining range in a situation. A classic example is the tendency to perceive the situation as more "zero sum" than it really is, resulting in an inability to find integrative or "win–win" solutions (Thompson, 1998). Alternatively, bargainers can underestimate the cooperativeness or trustworthiness of their opponents, resulting in adoption of overly harsh influence strategies that produce reactance and retaliation from their opponents or resistance from their constituents (Bendor, Kramer, & Stout, 1991).

A final category of self-defeating behavior discussed by Baumeister and Scher (1988) consists of ineffective ingratiation strategies. Such behaviors entail "misjudging how the target of an influence attempt will interpret and respond to one's behavior. The person overestimates the likelihood of positive response to flattery or doing a favor" (p. 15). For example, an influence agent might attempt to use ingratiation to curry favor, only to discover that the target of his or her influence attempt devalues the effort, attributing not positive but negative qualities to the agent. A famous instance in the leadership realm occurred when President Richard Nixon decided to surprise some protestors, encamped in Washington to oppose the Vietnam War, in the middle of the night. Nixon wandered among the group of protestors, trying to engage them in friendly banter about surfing and football. Rather than winning them over, however, he only caused them to feel more estranged from his leadership and policies.

Self-handicapping behavior is another form of behavior that, while effective from the standpoint of promoting short-term goals (e.g., protection of the individual's self-esteem), can prove self-defeating in the long run. Self-handicapping involves arranging the circumstances surrounding one's performance so as to provide a plausible attribution for lack of success. Classic examples include drinking heavily before an important presentation or failing to get enough sleep before an important exam (see Jones & Berglas, 1999 for a fuller exposition).

Another provocative form of self-defeating behavior can arise when group members – finding their group under external threat – take steps to protect and maintain a shared sense of the group's positive social identity (Turner, Pratkanis, Probasco, & Leve, 1992). In so doing, group members may find themselves able to collectively justify actions that individually they might hesitate to endorse. The extreme, illegal behaviors of numerous members of Richard Nixon's inner circle proved enormously costly to his presidency and to themselves in retrospect. Yet at the time they felt justified in doing everything necessary to defend what they perceived as an unjustly beleaguered presidency (Dean, 1972; Raven, 1974).

As such examples make clear, a leader's influence behaviors can be self-defeating or counterproductive in several different ways. First, influence behaviors that are intended to advance a chosen goal can unintentionally backfire, undermining achievement of that goal. Relatedly, leaders may try to employ a variety of impression management attempts that can fail to produce their intended effects (Elsbach & Kramer, 2003; Ginzel, Kramer, & Sutton, 1993; Sutton & Kramer, 1986). Third, influence behaviors aimed at reducing or resolving identified problems can make them worse rather than better. For example, conflict resolution attempts can lead to escalation rather than reduction of conflict (Pruitt & Rubin, 1986). Finally, influence attempts intended to generate constructive change can instead produce reactance, hardening rather than softening resistance to a chosen course of action (Kramer, Pradhan-Shah, & Woerner, 1995).

To summarize, extant research on self-defeating behavior has identified numerous forms that such behavior takes. Given the obvious undesirability of such outcomes, it behooves us to have a better understanding of why it is that self-defeating influence behaviors by leaders seem to be both common and persistent. In the next section, I present one framework for beginning to think about this issue.

LEADER JUDGMENT AND DECISION-MAKING IN INFLUENCE SITUATIONS: THE INTUITIVE SOCIAL AUDITOR MODEL

As noted above, one of the primary aims of the present chapter is to isolate some of the prominent forms of self-defeating influence behavior in which leaders engage. A second aim is to identify some of the determinants and dynamics that contribute to the emergence and persistence of such behaviors. To achieve these aims, it might be useful to begin by describing a framework that I have found helpful for organizing theory and research on these two questions. I characterize this framework as the intuitive social auditor model because it assumes that leaders (and other influence agents) are social information processors who pay close attention to their environments in an effort to monitor the causes and consequences of their actions. In much the same way that a vigilant bookkeeper might keep track of his or her economic transactions, so, the model posits, do leaders keep track of or "audit" their influence experiences in the hope of becoming more effective in pursuing their objectives.

The essential features of the intuitive social auditor model are as follows. First, the model assumes that leaders, as influence agents, are intendedly rational social actors. In other words, it is assumed that leaders' strategic choices regarding which influence behaviors to use in a given situation are driven, in part, by what are – from their perspective – reasonable assessments and prudent calculative considerations. In particular, they reflect leaders' *a priori* beliefs regarding the efficacy of different influence strategies and tactics. These beliefs, it is assumed, are based on their prior experience in such situations. Thus, if they use "hard" influence tactics such as ultimatums when trying to achieve their goals it is because they believe that such tactics are necessary or sufficient; conversely, if they use "soft power" forms of influence, such as ingratiation and conciliation, it is because they believe that the effects of such soft influence attempts will be positive (Nye, 2004).

The intuitive social auditor framework emphasizes further that leaders' strategic choices about influence tactics also reflect a variety of social and relational considerations. In particular, it is assumed that leaders care about not only the efficacy of a given influence strategy or tactic with respect to obtaining a specific material outcome (e.g., a better payoff in a contentious negotiation), but also its self-relevant implications. Leaders often care, for example, not only about whether they get what they want in a negotiation, but also about their personal identities and images (i.e., "how they come across" or look). Thus, their strategic choices in influence situations serve the purpose of advancing their material goals, but also of enabling them to affirm central and cherished personal identities. A leader's personal identity, from this perspective, encompasses the "sense of continuity, integration, identification, and differentiation constructed by the person not in relation to a community and its culture, but in relation to the self and its projects" (Hitlin, 2003, p. 121).

The model assumes further that leaders are highly motivated in most situations to affirm not only their actual positive personal identities – identities they have already established and articulated to themselves – but also those ideal identities they hope to develop and are still striving to achieve (Elsbach & Kramer, 1996). Leader identities, like other forms of social identity, are socially constructed or negotiated (Swann, 1987).

The model assumes also that leaders' strategic choices are social decisions in another important way. If strategic choices have important implications for how leaders perceive themselves, they also have important self-presentational implications in terms of how various audiences view them (Ginzel et al., 1993; Sutton & Kramer, 1986). Some choices have identity-enhancing implications for leaders; others pose identity threats. For example, the failure to be perceived as having acted decisively when constituents expect resolute action can be enormously distressing to a leader who is trying to impress, please, or placate those audiences (e.g., Bush and the "wimp factor"). Consequently, leaders are assumed to pay close attention to the self-presentational implications of their influence behaviors and, relatedly, to use their influence behaviors to advance their self-presentational goals. Thus, leaders can use their strategic choices not only to advance their endogenous goals in a given situation (e.g., improving their power or bargaining position in a negotiation), but also for exogenous social gains (e.g., to improve their social standing or reputation within a group as a tough negotiator) (Kramer & Carnevale, 2001). It is assumed also that strategic choices are socially expressive acts in that they enable leaders to affirm, for example, their loyalty or commitment to a group. In short, strategic choices about social influence constitute complex, multipurpose social decisions.

The social auditor model assumes that, having made a cognitive choice as to which influence tactic to use, leaders then try to successfully enact that tactic through their actual behaviors. It is important to note that strategic choice (the cognitive selection of an intended influence tactic) is different from the effective enactment of that choice. Strategic choices reflect leaders' goals, intentions, aspirations, hopes, and expectations (Greenhalgh & Kramer, 1986). Enactments reflect the often harsher realities of skillful or flawed execution. For example, a leader can decide (and intend) to use a given tactic, but can be incompetent in the implementation of that tactic. Indeed, many of the more interesting examples of self-defeating influence behavior arise when leaders' cognitive assessments of the situation seem to be perfectly accurate and their strategic choice for that situation valid, yet their execution or implementation clumsy or inept. For instance, former US President Richard Nixon often expressed privately the desire to inspire the American people: He claimed in private that he wanted to "to lift the spirit" of the American people, and to set an inspiring tone of public service. At one point, he even proclaimed to himself that the "major goal" of his administration was to provide "moral leadership" (Reeves, 2001, p. 25). His ability to successfully implement that goal, however, was obviously limited. Similarly, a leader can render an astute political assessment of a situation, but fail to pull the right (behavioral) rabbit out of the hat. The journalist Theodore White once quipped that, "Teddy [Kennedy] had all the correct instincts, but he lived by very few of them" (Hoffman, 1995, p. 6).

Regardless of their *a priori* aims or intentions, leaders' influence behaviors produce consequences. From the standpoint of understanding how leaders perceive (and misperceive) influence situations, it is, of course, the perceived consequences of their actions that carry the freight when it comes to leaders' attempts to make sense of what's going on. Thus, leaders' interpretations or construals (and misconstruals) of their influence behaviors and their effects are presumably most important in terms of driving their subsequent behavior.

Along these lines, the intuitive auditor model assumes that leaders, like all social perceivers, are serial social information processors whose attention is captured by, among other things, those outcomes they expect, find salient, feel comfortable seeing, etc. (Gilovich, 1991). However, attention can be claimed also by those outcomes that violate expectancies or are seen as particularly novel or unexpected (Weick, 1993). Moreover, leaders often pay as much attention to things that don't happen as to things that do happen – and draw inferences from them (Kramer, 1995, 2004). Moreover, the model assumes differences in leaders' social intelligence (Gardner, 1995): Some leaders are assumed to be fairly mindful and discerning; others are assumed to be less discriminating in their assessments of situations or others. Interpretations may be accurate or inaccurate. Some interpretations may reflect considerable cognitive complexity as decision-makers appreciate the role nuance and chance played in outcomes; others may be quite simplistic. Thus, vigilance is a complex state.

Regardless of their veridicality or complexity, leaders' interpretations inform their assessments of subsequent attempts to exert influence in the same situation or in similar-seeming situations.

To summarize, the intuitive social auditor model posits a set of generic cognitive processes that guide leaders' perceptions, judgments, and actions in influence situations. It portrays a leader's sensemaking process as one of moving through cycles of anticipation, action, and interpretation. As such, the intuitive social auditor framework represents one variant of a more general class of experiential learning cycle models described by March (1994). Such models posit a dynamic interplay between decision-makers' psychological states (expectations, interpretative categories, etc.), the behaviors those states support (exploration, inhibition, etc.), and the vagaries of the contexts in which their learning occurs (their richness, stability, etc.).

RESEARCH IMPLICATIONS OF THE INTUITIVE SOCIAL AUDITOR MODEL

From the pragmatic standpoint of helping us assess the state of our current knowledge about self-defeating influence processes, such a model is useful in several ways. First, it suggests several points of special vulnerability in the sensemaking and learning process that leaders confront. For example, it is clear that leaders can misperceive and misjudge influence situations, based on erroneous assumptions and interpretations. These misperceptions and misjudgments are obviously important because they directly affect leaders' strategic choices regarding which influence behaviors to use in a given situation. Thus, strategic choices can backfire badly, as when a leader opts to use a conciliatory or "soft" influence tactic when the target disparages weakness and timidity. When President Kennedy first encountered Premier Nikita Khrushchev in Vienna early in his presidency, he felt that a reasonable dialogue about political realities would help establish common ground between them and the beginning of a constructive working relationship. He tried to engage Khrushchev in an intellectual debate regarding the respective political philosophies of their countries and their merits. By all accounts, that intent backfired badly as Khrushchev lectured Kennedy on the historical roots and justification for Marxism and, in the end, concluded that Kennedy was a young, inexperienced, tentative, and unsteady leader (Reeves, 1993; Dallek, 2003).

Second, even if predicated on a prudent and circumspect assessment of a given situation, leaders' influence behaviors can be poorly executed. Thus, leaders can intend to employ an influence tactic with a constructive aim in mind, only to see it backfire or fail. Based on his decades of experience influencing Washington politicians, Lyndon Johnson believed that the most effective way to influence Ho Chi Minh was to treat the conflict in Vietnam as essentially a bargaining problem, the solution to which required simply locating the right mixture of "carrots and sticks" that would bring Ho to the bargaining table. Unfortunately, Johnson completely misread Ho's own construal of the situation and his resolve not to negotiate with his enemies.

Third, in any influence situation, there is considerable room for misconstrual of the efficacy of an influence attempt. Leaders can draw erroneous inferences regarding the efficacy of their actions. They can believe they were effective when they were not. And even if the actions were efficacious, leaders can be mistaken about the reasons for their effectiveness. They may, for example, attribute their success to their social perceptiveness or political skill when, in fact, non-self relevant causes played a major, determining role. Most famously, perhaps, British Prime Minister Neville Chamberlain returned from his personal meeting with Adolf Hitler having concluded that a genuine rapport and constructive relationship between the two leaders had been established.

METHODOLOGICAL PERSPECTIVES ON THE STUDY OF SELF-DEFEATING INFLUENCE BEHAVIOR BY LEADERS

Having discussed the theoretical issues at some length, it might be fitting at this point to provide an overview of some of the methodological considerations that social scientists have taken to the study of self-defeating influence behavior.

One major approach has been the laboratory experiment. Experimental studies of self-defeating behavior present a number of obvious advantages. First, researchers can create convincing laboratory analogs that preserve the essential features of real-world situations, and yet allow them to remove extraneous causal influences that might otherwise inject unwanted "noise" into the interpretation process. For example, Rothbart and Hallmark (1988) developed a compelling laboratory paradigm for studying counterproductive influence behavior in inter-group contexts. In particular, they developed a procedure for evaluating differences in decision-makers' perceptions of the efficacy of coercive versus conciliatory acts as a function of the ingroup versus outgroup status of the intended target. Along related lines, Pradhan-Shah, Woerner, and I developed a laboratory paradigm for studying the relationship between the salience of negotiators' social identities and their use of self-defeating ultimatum behaviors in a mixed-motive conflict (Kramer, Pradhan-Shah, & Woerner, 1995).

Computer simulation is yet another approach that has been employed to study ineffective influence behaviors. In computer simulations, researchers create artificial social actors or agents who employ precisely specified influence strategies. These agents can then be paired against other agents using other strategies. By systematically pitting strategies against each other, and examining the joint outcomes they produce, the comparative efficacy of different influence strategies can be precisely evaluated and calibrated. Perhaps the best-known studies in this vein are simulations comparing the efficacy of different influence tactics for eliciting cooperative responses from other social actors (Axelrod, 1997). Using a computer simulation approach, for example, Bendor, Stout, and I examined the comparative efficacy of variations on a tactic known as tit-for-tat for eliciting and sustaining cooperative exchanges in a noisy n-person prisoner's dilemma game (Bendor, Kramer, & Stout, 1991). Using this methodology, we were able to document some counterintuitive trade-offs between generosity (giving others the benefit of the doubt) and defense competitiveness (assuming the worst about one's opponents).

A third methodological approach is to examine self-defeating influence behaviors in the context of real-world situations. This approach includes the use of archival case materials to trace the antecedents and consequences of self-defeating influence behaviors. Caro's idiographic studies of the uses and misuses of influence by Lyndon Johnson (Caro, 2002) are perhaps the prototypic example of such studies. Other studies have used archival case studies comparatively, examining how different US Presidents use and misuse influence when pursuing their politics (e.g., Gergen, 2000; Kellerman, 1984; Kramer, 1995, 1998; Neustadt, 1990).

A fourth method for studying both effective and ineffective influence behavior is more ethnographic and entails the direct observation of influence situations in field settings. As numerous studies have shown (Cialdini, 1988; Levine, 2003), researchers can learn a great deal about the efficacy and lack of efficacy of influence tactics by observing their use and misuse in real-world situations in real time. Using such an approach, Elsbach and I investigated some of the determinants of effective and ineffective influence attempts by Hollywood screenwriters and agents as they attempt to "pitch" screenplay ideas to studio executives and producers (Elsbach & Kramer, 2003). In particular, we examined the mistakes novice pitchers made when trying to "win over" or persuade executives to whom they were pitching that they themselves or their ideas were creative.

Each of these methodologies provides one avenue for learning more about the antecedents and consequences of self-defeating influence behavior. No one methodology, it should be noted, is perfect. Each has familiar advantages and disadvantages, manifested as trade-offs with respect to the internal versus external validity of the results they produce (Campbell & Fiske, 1959). Accordingly, a multimethod approach that provides convergent validity for propositions is essential. As Webb, Campbell, Schwartz, and Sechrest (1966) suggested, "If a [theoretical] proposition can survive the onslaught of a series of imperfect measures, with all their irrelevant error, confidence should be placed in it" (p. 3).

Up to this point in this chapter, I have described a social cognitive model for thinking about the processes associated with self-defeating influence behaviors. I have also summarized some of the methodologies that have been used to investigate such processes. I turn next to reviewing some evidence regarding the determinants of self-defeating influence that has emerged from research employing those methods.

SOME DETERMINANTS OF SELF-DEFEATING INFLUENCE BEHAVIORS

A large body of social cognitive (Gilovich, 1991) and decision-making (Dawes, 2001) research has illustrated how various forms of misperception and judgmental bias can contribute to the misconstrual and misevaluation of social situations. Research on the social cognitive determinants of self-defeating influence behavior has followed this lead, focusing on how our intuitive social auditor sometimes gets into trouble in influence situations. Although a complete and exhaustive review of this empirical evidence is beyond the scope of the present chapter, some illustrative examples help provide a flavor of the kinds of variables that recent research has examined.

The Shadow of the Past: How History Sometimes Hurts

When leaders are trying to decide which strategy or tactic to use when endeavoring to influence another party, they are likely to search for past situations and experiences for guidance. In other words, they may try to compare their current situation with prior examples that might be informative or salient. Thus, they are likely to search for previous examples of effective influence that might be successfully applied once again. Conversely, in order to avoid repeating the mistakes of the past, they are likely to look for mistakes that they and other leaders have made.

In their systematic examination of the role such historical analogies have played in leader judgment and decision-making, Neustadt and May (1986) argued along such lines that contemporary leaders often compare their current situation with situations faced by earlier leaders in similar-seeming circumstances. For example, when President Kennedy was trying to decide how much toughness and resolve to display to the Soviets in dealing with the Berlin crisis, he compared the situation he faced with Khrushchev to British decisions with respect to Hitler's increasingly bold gestures in Europe. (The British analogy, it should be noted, may have been especially salient to President Kennedy because he himself had written at length about the dangers of complacency and inaction in his best-selling book, *Why England Slept.*)

Although analogies can be informative in terms of providing useful points of comparison and raising important caveats, they can also mislead a leader by providing false assurance or fueling unrealistic optimism. An archival study of President Lyndon Johnson's decisions about how much toughness to display towards Ho Chi Minh in dealing with the escalating conflict in Vietnam revealed more than a dozen specific references made by the President to analogies between his situation and situations faced by previous Presidents, including allusions to Abraham Lincoln, Franklin D. Roosevelt, Harry Truman, Dwight Eisenhower, and John F. Kennedy (Kramer, 1995, 1998). For example, when not only his critics but even his advisors and friends suggested that Lyndon Johnson might be perceived as a greater president if he were to bring an end to what had become an enormously unpopular conflict, Johnson retorted, "Everything I know about history proves this absolutely wrong. It was our lack of strength and our failure to show stamina, our hesitancy and vacillation . . . that caused all our problems before World War I, World War II, and Korea . . . You see, I deeply believe we are quarantining aggressors over there . . . just like FDR [did] with Hitler, just like Wilson [did] with the Kaiser. You've simply got to see this thing in historical perspective" (cited in Kearns-Goodwin, 1976, p. 313). He said on another occasion, "I read all about Lincoln and his problems, yet Lincoln persevered and history rewarded him for his perseverance" (Kearns-Goodwin, 1976, p. 314). Interestingly, in pondering his own more recent political difficulties, Secretary of Defense Rumsfeld sought reassurance in the past as well: "I've been reading a book about the Civil War and Ulysses Grant – and I'm not going to compare the two, don't get me wrong, and don't anybody rush off and say he doesn't get the difference between Iraq and the Civil War . . . [but] the fact of the matter is, the casualties were high, the same kinds of concerns that we're expressing here were expressed then . . . [the people then] were despairing, they were hopeful, they were concerned, they were combative . . . the carnage was horrendous, *and it was worth it*" (Bumiller, 2004, emphasis added).

Leader Identity and Self-Presentational Concerns

As noted earlier, the use of influence strategies can have significant identity-relevant implications. Specifically, influence attempts that are perceived as successful constitute important identity-enhancing opportunities for leaders, especially when they enable leaders to project valued or desired identities through their decisions. Kennedy's conduct during the Cuban Missile Crisis was widely perceived as an enormous success at the time. Kennedy had deftly navigated through the crisis and seemingly without blinking or backing down. He had displayed, in short, precisely the sort of resolve that he had been accused of lacking during the earlier Bay of Pigs fiasco. Ironically, we now know that the actual influence behaviors that characterized Kennedy's actions – many of which were "offstage" and unknown to the American people for several decades – were quite different. While the public posture was one of toughness and resolve, the private actions were more flexible, accommodative, and reciprocative: Kennedy evinced a willingness to bargain so that both US and Soviet objectives were furthered and interests protected. Our reassessment of the true "lessons" of the Cuban Missile Crisis illustrates, moreover, how easy it is for leaders with incomplete information to draw erroneous or misleading conclusions from past crises and conflicts: They can be seriously off with respect to inferring what worked and why.

Influence attempts can also pose significant identity-threatening predicaments for leaders, especially when they seem to violate leader or audience expectations. For example, Ronald Reagan's initial attempts to influence Gorbachev during the Iceland Arms Control talks were widely viewed initially as a dramatic failure. Interestingly, however, through skillful impression management, Reagan and his team of advisors and aides were able to transform this seeming failure of influence into a stunning diplomatic triumph (see Sutton & Kramer, 1986 for a fuller account and analysis).

In emphasizing the psychological importance of such consequences, March (1994) noted that: "Decision makers can violate a logic of consequences and be considered stupid or naïve, *but if they violate the moral obligations of identity, they will be condemned as lacking in elementary virtue*" (p. 65, emphasis added). Violating the perceived obligations of identity creates an identity-threatening predicament.

Self-enhancing Cognitive Illusions in Influence Situations

When leaders select a given influence strategy, it is reasonable to assume that they believe the use of that strategy will, more likely than not, move them closer to achieving their aims. The definition of self-defeating influence presented earlier, in fact, presupposes that leaders' behaviors are intendedly adaptive, and emphasizes the unintended and unforeseen consequences of one's influence behaviors. This raises the question, "What psychological factors might inadvertently affect leaders' judgments regarding the efficacy or probability of success of a given influence strategy?" Certainly near the top of our list should be those various well-documented cognitive illusions that influence individuals' risk assessment and risk-taking behavior. Many studies have shown, for example, that decision-makers maintain a variety of positive illusions about themselves and their behaviors. These include overly positive self-evaluations, unrealistic optimism, exaggerated perceptions of control, and illusions of personal invulnerability (Taylor & Brown, 1988). In an experimental investigation of the role positive illusions played in negotiation situations, Newton, Pommerenke, and I showed that negotiators in a good mood tended to overestimate how well they had done in extracting value from the other party (Kramer, Newton, & Pommerenke, 1993).

SOCIAL CONTEXTUAL FACTORS THAT CONTRIBUTE TO SELF-DEFEATING INFLUENCE BEHAVIORS

Although the primary focus of this analysis is on social cognitive factors that contribute to leaders' self-defeating influence behaviors, it is important to note that there are many social contextual and organizational factors that can contribute to such behaviors. For example, role-embeddedness can constrain leaders' strategic choices. Leaders are expected, after all, to enact the role they've assumed. Such perceived role requirements can make it difficult for leaders to change their behavior, even when that behavior is recognized as counterproductive (Kahn, Wolfe, Quinn, Snoek, & Rosenthal, 1964). Leaders' interpretations of what their role requires, for example, can force them to draw a distinction between what they would like to do personally (e.g., end a costly conflict) amd what they believe fulfilling the obligations of role dictates (e.g., a US President can never afford to show weakness or vacillation). Lyndon Johnson repeatedly voiced a strong antipathy toward the war in Vietnam and a deep personal anguish over the loss of American lives in that conflict. Yet, in the role of President, he felt he had a moral obligation to fulfill US treaty commitments around the globe. Perceived role-constraints of this sort can be reinforced also by historical, institutional imperatives that dictate compliance with past traditions and requirements.

The structure and organization of advice that surrounds a leader can also influence the options he or she perceives as available. The key role that presidential advisors play in helping presidents select their influence strategies is amply documented (Barrett, 1993; Berman, 1982; George, 1980). To the extent that advisors help broaden the panoply of considerations to which leaders attend and provide richer data for decision, such advisors can play a critical role in improving the quality of the decision-making process. However, to the extent that leaders engage in homosocial reproduction when selecting advisors – selecting those who think and act like them – the range and quality of inputs can be sharply curtailed (Janis, 1983, 1989; Kramer, 1998). Advisors often shave their views to placate or please leaders. A nice illustration of this tendency emerges in one of the early Nixon tapes. When Richard Nixon was discussing the likely reaction of the public to the Watergate break-in, he predicted, "My view is . . . that in terms of the reaction of people . . . I think the country doesn't give much of a shit about it other than the ones we've already bugged . . . most people around the country think that this is routine, that everybody's trying to bug everybody else . . . Look, breaking and entering and so forth, without accomplishing it, is not a hell of a lot of crime" (reported in Kutler, 1997, pp. 54–55). Nixon's aides were more than willing to aid and abet such misperception. In a meeting with aide Charles Colson, Nixon speculated, "They [the public] don't give a shit about repression and bugging and all the rest." To which Colson replied helpfully, "I think they expect it. As I've said to you, they think political parties do this all the time." "They do, they certainly do," chimes in Nixon. Colson embellishes, "They think that companies do this. You know, there have been marvelous stories written about industrial espionage." Nixon adds eagerly, "Sure, sure, sure. Well, they do." Colson then adds, "How Henry J. Ford sends agents into General Motors to get the designs. People just sort of expect this . . ." "Governments do it. We all know that," agrees Nixon (reported in Kutler, 1997, p. 59).

OFTEN WRONG, NEVER IN DOUBT: PSYCHOLOGICAL DYNAMICS THAT SUSTAIN SELF-DEFEATING INFLUENCE BEHAVIOR

Up to this point, I have described a variety of ways in which leaders are prone to use self-defeating forms of social influence when trying to achieve their objectives. As shown above, the decision by a leader to use a form of influence likely to prove self-defeating is often predicated on an initial misperception of a situation or miscalculation of the efficacy of an influence tactic selected for it. Such misperceptions and miscalculations are understandable. However, even if we can understand the initial reasons why leaders might adopt a self-defeating influence strategy, it's harder to comprehend why they sometimes persist in the use of such counter-productive or ineffective strategies. All else being equal, it might seem that the various judgmental distortions and sources of misperception and miscalculation described thus far would be rather difficult for experienced and savvy leaders to sustain. After all, we might expect leaders, as highly motivated influence agents, to remain vigilant regarding the consequences of their actions, and attentive to any indications that their efforts are not succeeding. Similarly, we might expect them to change to a new influence tactic when presented with feedback that the old one isn't succeeding. Yet, if anything, the evidence suggests that leaders sometimes persist on a chosen course of action, upping the ante and sometimes digging themselves into even deeper difficulties. The persistence of such self-defeating behavioral propensities invites consideration of some of the dynamics that create and sustain self-defeating influence behaviors.

Difficulties in Generating Diagnostic Experience

As with any form of learning, learning about the efficacy of one's influence behaviors requires amassing relevant evidence and extracting reasonable infer-ences from that evidence. Obviously, any systematic bias in the generation of such data creates the possibility of errors in calibrating the efficacy of one's action.

Consider, for example, the difficulty someone might have in discerning the efficacy of particularly tough-minded, coercive influence tactics. To the extent that individuals possess *a priori* beliefs that such actions are necessary (and sufficient), they are likely to pre-emptively invoke those tactics whenever the situation seems to call for them. Moreover, if they produce any discernible benefit in such situ-ations, leaders are likely to note the evidence of their efficacy and conclude that the pre-emptive actions were entirely justified. An instructive parallel that sup-ports this logic can be found in research on the dynamics of the development and persistence of hostile behavior among aggressive children (Dodge, 1980). Such children, research has shown, tend to approach their social interactions "pre-offended." In other words, they enter social transactions already expecting the worst from other people they encounter. Therefore they are pre-emptively pre-pared to defend themselves against the assaults they expect – and even believe are inevitable, given others' presumed hostility. Ironically, however, because they assume others' hostility, they end up eliciting it through their own defensive behaviors. In much the same fashion as these overly aggressive boys, the overly competitive or aggressive leader is primed for the prospect of resistance or con-flict, and is therefore perceptually vigilant to detecting signs of it. Because the leader's behavior is grounded in presumptive competitiveness or hostility, it ends up eliciting the very sort of unproductive social interactions that reinforce mutual hostility and wariness. Thus, the competitive leader's pessimistic expect-ations – predicated on dubious assumptions – serve as a foundation for an equally questionable set of influence strategies for dealing with them.

Gilovich (1991) has suggested another reason why people may be able to sustain beliefs in questionable assumptions about the world, which has relevance to understanding why leaders might sustain untenable beliefs in the effectiveness of their ineffective influence behaviors. Because a given orientation toward others is initially thought to be valid or effective, he notes, only that orientation is likely to be employed when similar-seeming situations are encountered. As a consequence, a person never learns what would have happened had a different orientation toward the situation been afforded or approach taken. In other words, the individual cannot (or, more accurately, simply does not) assess the true appropriateness of the orientation, or the efficacy of the approach it seems to dictate. This pattern of dysfunctional social interaction can be aided and abetted, Gilovich goes on to argue, by a self-fulfilling prophecy. Like someone who believes that the only way to get ahead is to be competitive or to come on strong when dealing with other people, such individuals will consistently push too aggressively for what they want. "The occasional success," Gilovich notes, "will 'prove' the wisdom of the rule, and *the individual will never learn how effective he might have been had a different strategy been employed*" (p. 153, emphasis added). Because of their focus on influencing the other, moreover, leaders may fail to appreciate fully or discern accurately the extent to which their own behavior, ironically, elicits reac-tions from others that justify their dubious presumptions about human nature in the first place.

We might draw an instructive analogy, in this regard, with the experience of freeway drivers who are either much faster than or much slower than other drivers around them. Consider first the case of the extremely fast, impatient, and time-urgent driver. For such individuals, the daily experience on the freeway is one of persistent annoyance and frustration as seemingly countless slow, incompetent drivers are continually found to be in their way. Each press of the pedal and each lane change generates yet another interaction with yet another foolishly slow driver, hindering them from reaching their destination in a more timely fashion. Over time, such fast and time-urgent drivers are likely to develop a view of the world as populated by incompetent and inconsiderate drivers. On average, after all, their experience is that people around them are overly cautious and stupid – from the reference point they adopt regarding efficient and prudent driving speeds, it is the other drivers who are out of touch and in the way.

Consider, on the other hand, the experience of the very slow and extremely cautious driver navigating on the same freeways. From the standpoint of these drivers, other people on the freeway seems always to be in a hurry – aggressively honking and rudely passing around the slow driver. The world of the slow driver is a world populated by reckless, angry, and impatient people – people who don't understand the laws of physics when it comes to safe braking distances, the limits of human reflexes, and so forth. Their experience is also one of comparative friction and frustration, as they experience the rude gestures and annoying looks from passing cars.

In both instances, however, it is only the very simple fact that these social actors remain "out of synch" with others in their world that leads to their self-generated and self-sustaining theories regarding others' basic hostility, unreliability and incompetence or stupidity. Note also that, because of the positive illusions that social perceivers sustain about themselves as better than average drivers, they are unlikely to realize fully how their own behavior might be responsible for eliciting some of the behavior from other drivers that they find so annoying. Thus, the fast and reckless driver may, without intending it, actually end up eliciting greater caution and slowing down of cars around them, while the slow driver may actually cause people to speed up in order to get around them.

Difficulties in Learning From Influence Experiences

Leaders not only might encounter substantial difficulties when it comes to generating diagnostic, representative samples of experience from which to learn, but also face formidable difficulties when trying to draw appropriate inferences from the data they do generate. Self-serving construals of influence situations, for example, can seriously impede learning the efficacy of one's social influence attempts. Numerous case studies and experiments have demonstrated, for example, how biased construals of social interactions lead to self-serving interpretations that justify one's own harsh or punitive actions (Jervis, 1976; Lord, Ross, & Lepper, 1979; Plous, 1985). These studies demonstrate that people tend to fit incoming information, especially when it is ambiguous or inconclusive, into their pre-existing stereotypes and categories.

One particularly interesting form of biased construal is the self-serving punctuation of social interactions. There is evidence that the parties involved in social interactions don't perceive their interactions as smooth, continuous causal streams. Instead, they punctuate causal episodes into discriminable "chunks" that help them make sense of what is happening (Swann, Pelham, & Roberts, 1987). Thus, two actors engaged in an acrimonious mutual influence attempt are likely to punctuate the conflict differently, making each seem virtuous and simply responding to the offensive or objectionable acts of the other. Consider the case, for example, of the leader who suspects others around him or her are untrustworthy in terms of being likely to respond to positive forms of social influence, yet clever at feigning cooperativeness and trustworthiness. Because of their presumption that others around them lack trustworthiness or the willingness to cooperate, the perceived diagnostic value of any particular social cue or bit of observed behavior is, from the outset, suspect. As Weick (1993) noted in this regard, when a perceiver recognizes that social cues are potentially corruptible, it is easy to assume that they are actually corrupted. To illustrate this point, he cites an interesting historical example. The day before the Japanese attack on Pearl Harbor, an American naval attaché had informed Washington that he did not believe a surprise attack by the Japanese was imminent. To justify his prediction, he cited the "fact" that the Japanese fleet was still stationed at its home base. The clear and compelling evidence for this conclusion, he noted, was that large crowds of sailors could be observed happily and casually strolling the streets of Tokyo. Without sailors, the fleet obviously could not have sailed. If the sailors were still in port, so was the fleet. What the attaché did not know – and, more importantly, failed to even imagine – was that these "sailors" were actually Japanese soldiers disguised as sailors. They had been ordered to pose as sailors and stroll the streets to conceal the fact that the Japanese fleet had, in fact, left port and was already on its way to Pearl Harbor. From the perspective of the suspicious, wary, skeptical and pessimistic social perceiver, of course, the attaché's experience provides dramatic proof of what happens when individuals allow themselves to relax their assumptions. In a world presumed to be sinister, innocence regarding others' trustworthiness can have fatal consequences. In such a world, social cues are always corrupted and always in a predictably dangerous direction.

In elaborating on the implications of this incident, Weick noted that the very desire of the attaché to find a "foolproof" cue regarding Japanese intentions made him more vulnerable, ironically, to manipulation regarding the nature of those intentions. Weick reasoned that, "The very fact that the observer finds himself looking to a particular bit of evidence as an incorruptible check on what is or might be corruptible, is the very reason he should be suspicious of this evidence" (p. 172). After all, the best evidence for him is also the best evidence for the deceiver to tamper with or manipulate. As a consequence, Weick observes, "when the situation seems to be exactly what it appears to be" a likely alternative is that "the situation has been completely faked" (p. 173).

Ironically, for the skeptical social perceiver even the complete absence of any evidence or cues at all can be construed as a portent that something is amiss. Dawes (1988) provided a nice illustration of this possibility in his discussion of the debate over the necessity of internment of Japanese-Americans at the beginning of the Second World War. The question, of course, was the danger posed to national security by the presence of a sizable contingent of Japanese-Americans. Where would their loyalties lie? Could they be trusted? When the late Supreme Court Chief Justice Earl Warren (then Governor of California) testified before a congressional hearing regarding the wisdom of internment, one of his interrogators noted that absolutely no evidence of espionage or sabotage on the part of any Japanese-Americans had been presented or was available to the committee. Thus, there was absolutely no objective evidence of danger at all. Warren's response as to how best to interpret this absence of evidence is revealing. "I take the view that this lack [of evidence] is the *most ominous sign* in our whole situation. It convinces me *more than perhaps any other factor* that the sabotage we are to get, the Fifth Column activities we are to get, are timed just like Pearl Harbor was timed"

(p. 251, emphasis added). He went on: "I believe we are just being lulled into a false sense of security" (p. 251).

SUMMARY AND CONCLUSION

A primary purpose of this chapter was to identify an important area of influence research where further theory and empirical evidence are greatly needed. As the examples provided throughout this chapter hopefully make clear, the costs of misguided or ineffective influence attempts can be substantial. In that spirit, this chapter laid some theoretical grounds and conceptual foundations for further research on self-defeating social influence. The intuitive social auditor model was intended to provide a descriptive platform that might stimulate further research in this area. As noted earlier, one distinct advantage of the framework is that it identifies points of special weakness or vulnerability to misdirected influence. In that respect, it helps us understand how and why even politically savvy, experienced, and otherwise intelligent leaders might embark on self-destructive courses of action.

Additionally, the chapter has identified a variety of methodological approaches that might be used in the further study of self-defeating influence behaviors, ranging from traditional experimental techniques favored by social psychologists to more ethnographic and comparative approaches. A comprehensive understanding of failed social influence behavior obviously benefits from a multiple methods approach.

Given the enormously serious consequences that arise when powerful leaders embark on and persist with self-defeating influence behaviors in pursuing their objectives, it is imperative that we develop a better understanding of the forms, dynamics, and remedies for such behaviors. At the moment of greatest tension during the Cuban Missile Crisis, Chairman Khrushchev sent President Kennedy a message in which he worried, "The harder you and I pull, the tighter this knot [of war] will become. And a time may come when this knot is tied so tight that the person who tied it is no longer capable of untying it." A more thorough understanding of the causes and dynamics of self-defeating influence behaviors may help leaders untie such knots – and thereby avoid catastrophic error.

ACKNOWLEDGMENTS

This chapter was written while the author was a Visiting Professor of Public Policy at the John F. Kennedy School of Government. I am grateful to the Kennedy School and its staff for their generous support of this project. I am also extremely grateful to Anthony Pratkanis for his thoughtful reading of this chapter and keen-eyed editorial inputs. Both enormously improved the theoretical argument and its flow. I am grateful also to Richard Hackman, Barbara Kellerman, Dutch Leonard, and David Messick for their insightful informal comments during early discussions about this research.

REFERENCES

Axelrod, R. (1997). *The complexity of cooperation: Agent-based models of competition and collaboration*. Princeton, NJ: Princeton University Press.

Barrett, D. M. (1993) *Uncertain warriors: Lyndon Johnson and his Vietnam advisors*. Lawrence: Kansas University Press.

Baumeister, R. F., & Scher, S. J. (1988). Self-defeating behavior patterns among normal individuals: Review and analysis of common self-destructive tendencies. *Psychological Bulletin, 104*, 3–22.

Bendor, J., Kramer, R. M., & Stout, S. (1991). When in doubt: Cooperation in the noisy prisoner's dilemma. *Journal of Conflict Resolution, 35*, 691–719.

Berglas, S., & Baumeister, R. F. (1993). *Your own worst enemy: Understanding the paradox of self-defeating behavior*. New York: Basic Books.

Berman, L. (1982). *Planning a tragedy: The Americanization of the war in Vietnam*. New York: Norton.

Blau, P. M. (1964). *Exchange and power in social life*. New York: Wiley.

Boulding, K. B. (1966). *Conflict and defense*. New York: Harper & Row.

Boulding, K. B. (1989). *Three faces of power*. Thousand Oaks, CA: Sage.

Brockner, J., & Rubin, J. (1985). *Entrapment in escalating conflicts*. New York: Springer-Verlag.

Bumiller, E. (2004, May 12). Stolid Rumsfeld soldiers on, but weighs ability to serve. *New York Times*, p. A12.

Burns, J. M. (1978). *Leadership*. New York: Harper & Row.

Campbell, D. T., & Fiske, D. W. (1959). Convergent and discriminant validation by the multitrait–multimethod matrix. *Psychological Bulletin, 56*, 81–105.

Caro, R. (2002). *Master of the Senate: The years of Lyndon Johnson*. New York: Alfred Knopf.

Caro, R. A. (1982). *The path to power: The years of Lyndon Johnson*. New York: Vintage Books.

Cialdini, R. B. (1988). *Influence: Science and practice* (2nd ed.). Glenview, IL: Scott, Foresman.

Dallek, R. (2003). *An unfinished life: John F. Kennedy, 1917–1963*. New York: Little, Brown.

Dawes, R. M. (1988). *Rational choice in an uncertain world*. New York: Wiley.

Dawes, R. M. (2001). *Everyday irrationality: How pseudo-scientists, lunatics, and the rest of us systematically fail to think rationally*. Boulder, CO: Westview.

Dean, J. (1972). *Blind ambition*. New York: Scribners.

Dodge, K. (1980). Social cognition and children's aggressive behavior. *Child Development, 51*, 162–170.

Elsbach, K. D., & Kramer, R. M. (1996). Members' responses to organizational identity threats: Encountering and countering the *Business Week* rankings. *Administrative Science Quarterly, 41*, 442–476.

Elsbach, K. D., & Kramer, R. M. (2003). Assessing creativity in Hollywood pitch meetings: A dual process model of creativity judgment. *Academy of Management Journal, 46*(3), 283–301.

Emerson, R. M. (1962). Power–dependence relations. *American Sociological Review, 27*, 31–40.

Fiske, S. T. (1993). Controlling other people: The impact of power on stereotyping. *American Psychologist, 48*, 621–628.

French, J. R. P., Jr., & Raven, B. (1959). The bases of social power. In D. Cartwright (Ed.), *Studies in social power* (pp. 150–167). Ann Arbor: University of Michigan.

Galinsky, A., Gruenfeld, D. H., & Magee, J. (2003). From power to action. *Journal of Personality and Social Psychology, 85*, 453–466.

Gardner, H. (1995). *Leading minds: An anatomy of leadership*. New York: Basic Books.

George, A. (1980). *Presidential decisionmaking in foreign policy: The effective use of information and advice*. Boulder, CO: Westview.

Gergen, D. (2000). *Eyewitness to power: The essence of leadership from Nixon to Clinton*. New York: Simon & Schuster.

Gilovich, T. (1991). *How we know what isn't so: The fallibility of human reason in everyday life*. New York: Free Press.

Ginzel, L. E., Kramer, R. M., & Sutton, R. I. (1993). Organizational impression management as a reciprocal influence process: The neglected role of the organizational audience. In L. L. Cummings and B. M. Staw (Eds.), *Research in organizational behavior* (Vol. 15, pp. 227–266). Greenwich, CT: JAI Press.

Greenhalgh, L., & Kramer, R. M. (1986). Strategic choice in conflicts: The importance of relationships. In R. L. Kahn & M. N. Zald (Eds.), *Organizations and nation-states: New perspectives on conflict and cooperation* (pp.181–220). San Francisco: Jossey-Bass.

Herring, G. C. (1993). The reluctant warrior: Lyndon Johnson as Commander in Chief. In D. L. Anderson (Ed.), *Shadow on the white house: Presidents and the Vietnam War, 1945–1975* (pp. 87–112). Lawrence: University of Kansas Press.

Hitlin, S. (2003). Values as the core of personal identity: Drawing links between two theories of the self. *Social Psychology Quarterly, 66*, 118–137.

Hoffman, J. (1995). *Theodore H. White and journalism as illusion*. Columbia: University of Missouri Press.

Janis, I. L. (1983). *Groupthink* (2nd ed.). Boston: Houghton-Mifflin.

Janis, I. L. (1989). *Crucial decisions*. New York: Free Press.

Jervis, R. (1976). *Perception and misperception in international politics*. Princeton, NJ: Princeton University Press.

Jones, E. E., & Berglas, S. (1999). Control of the attributions about the self through self-handicapping strategies: The appeal of alcohol and the role of underachievement. In R. Baumeister (Ed.), *The self in social psychology* (pp. 430–435). New York: Psychology Press.

Kahn, R. L., & Kramer, R. M. (1986). Untying the knot: De-escalatory processes in international conflict. In R. L. Kahn & M. N. Zald (Eds.), *Organizations and nation-states: New perspectives on conflict and cooperation* (pp. 139–180). San Francisco: Jossey-Bass.

Kahn, R. L., Wolfe, D. M., Quinn, R. P., Snoek, J. D., & Rosenthal, R. A. (1964). *Organizational stress: Studies in role conflict and ambiguity*. New York: Wiley.

Kearns-Goodwin, D. (1976). *Lyndon Johnson and the American dream*. New York: New American Library.

Kellerman, B. (1984). *The political presidency: Practice of leadership from Kennedy through Reagan*. Oxford: Oxford University Press.

Keltner, D., Gruenfeld, D. H., & Anderson, C. (2003). Power, approach, and inhibition. *Psychological Review, 110*, 265–284.

Kramer, R. M. (1995). In dubious battle: Heightened accountability, dysphoric cognition, and self-defeating bargaining behavior. In R. M. Kramer & D. M. Messick (Eds.), *Negotiation as a social process* (pp. 95–120). Thousand Oaks, CA: Sage.

Kramer, R. M. (1998). Revisiting the Bay of Pigs and Vietnam decisions 25 years later: How well has the groupthink hypothesis stood the test of time? *Organizational Behavior and Human Decision Processes, 73*, 236–271.

Kramer, R. M. (2003a). The harder they fall. *Harvard Business Review*, *81*, 58–68.

Kramer, R. M. (2003b). The imperatives of identity: The role of identity in leader judgment and decision making. In D. van Knippenberg & M. A. Hogg (Eds.), *Leadership and power: Identity processes in groups and organizations* (pp. 184–196). London: Sage.

Kramer, R. M. (2004). Perceptions of conspiracy. In D. M. Messick & R. M. Kramer (Eds.), *The psychology of leadership*. Mahwah, NJ: Lawrence Erlbaum Associates, Inc.

Kramer, R. M., & Carnevale, P. G. (2001). Trust and distrust in intergroup negotiations. In R. Brown & S. Gaertner (Eds.), *Blackwell handbook in social psychology*, Vol. 4: *Intergroup processes* (pp. 431–450). Malden, MA: Blackwell.

Kramer, R. M., & Hanna, B. A. (1998). Under the influence. In R. M. Kramer & M. A. Neale (Eds.), *Power and influence in organizations* (pp. 145–180). Thousand Oaks, CA: Sage.

Kramer, R. M., & Neale, M. A. (Eds.). (1998). *Power and influence in organizations*. Thousand Oaks, CA: Sage.

Kramer, R., Newton, E., & Pommerenke, P. (1993). Self-enhancement biases and negotiator judgment: Effects of self-esteem and mood. *Organizational Behavior and Human Decision Processes*, *56*, 110–133.

Kramer, R., Pommerenke, P., & Newton, E. (1993). The social context of negotiation: Effects of social identity and accountability on negotiator judgment and decision making. *Journal of Conflict Resolution*, *37*, 633–654.

Kramer, R. M., Pradhan-Shah, P., & Woerner, S. L. (1995). Why ultimatums fail: Social identity and moralistic aggression in coercive bargaining. In R. M. Kramer & D. M. Messick (Eds.), *Negotiation as a social process* (pp. 285–308). Thousand Oaks, CA: Sage.

Kutler, S. I. (1997). *Abuse of power: The new Nixon tapes*. New York: Free Press.

Levine, R. (2003). *The power of persuasion: How we're bought and sold*. New York: Wiley.

Lord, C. G., Ross, L., & Lepper, M. R. (1979). Biased assimilation and attitude polarization: The effects of prior theories on subsequent considered evidence. *Journal of Personality and Social Psychology*, *55*, 396–409.

Maraniss, D. (1998). *The Clinton enigma*. New York: Simon & Schuster.

March, J. G. (1994). *A primer on decision making: How decisions happen*. New York: Free Press.

McClelland, D. C. (1975). *Power: The inner experience*. New York: Irvington.

Pfeffer, J. (1992). *Managing with power: Politics and influence in organizations*. Boston, MA: Harvard Business School Press.

Neustadt, R. E. (1990). *Presidential power and the modern presidents: The politics of leadership from Roosevelt to Reagan*. New York: Free Press.

Neustadt, R. E., & May, E. R. (1986). *Thinking in time: The uses of history for decision makers*. New York: Free Press.

Nye, J. (2004). *Soft power*. New York: Oxford University Press.

Pfeffer, J. (1981). Management as symbolic action. In L. L. Cummings and B. M. Staw (Eds.), *Research in organizational behavior* (Vol. 3, pp. 1–52). Greenwich, CT: JAI Press.

Pfeffer, J. (1992). *Managing with power*. Cambridge, MA: Harvard Business School Press.

Plous, S. (1985). Perceptual illusions and military realities: the nuclear arms race. *Journal of Conflict Resolution*, *29*, 363–389.

Pratkanis, A., & Aronson, E. (1992). *The age of propaganda: The everyday use and abuse of persuasion*. New York: W. H. Freeman.

Pruitt, D. G., & Rubin, J. Z. (1986). *Social conflict: Escalation, stalemate, and settlement.* New York: Random House.

Raven, B. (1974). The Nixon group. *Journal of Social Issues, 30,* 297–320.

Reeves, R. (1993). *President Kennedy: Profile of power.* New York: Simon & Schuster.

Reeves, R. (2001). *President Nixon: Alone in the White House.* New York: Simon & Schuster.

Rothbart, M., & Hallmark, W. (1988). Ingroup–outgroup differences in the perceived efficacy of coercion and conciliation in resolving social conflict. *Journal of Personality and Social Psychology, 55*(2), 248–257.

Russell, B. (1938). *Power: A new social analysis.* London: Allen & Unwin.

Sutton, R. I., & Kramer, R. M. (1986). Transforming failure into success: Spin control in the Iceland Arms Control Talks. In R. L. Kahn & M. Zald (Eds.), *Organizations and nation-states* (pp. 221–248). San Francisco: Jossey-Bass.

Swann, W. B. (1987). Identity negotiation: Where two roads meet. *Journal of Personality and Social Psychology, 53,* 1038–1051.

Swann, W. B. (1996). *Self-traps: The elusive quest for higher self-esteem.* San Francisco: Freeman.

Swann, W. B., Pelham, B. W., & Roberts, D. C. (1987). Causal chunking: Memory and inference in ongoing interaction. *Journal of Personality and Social Psychology, 53,* 858–865.

Taylor, S., & Brown, J. (1988). Positive illusions and well-being: A social psychological perspective. *Psychological Bulletin, 103,* 193–210.

Thompson, L. (1998). *The mind and heart of the negotiator.* Upper Saddle River, NJ: Prentice Hall.

Turner, M. E., Pratkanis, A. R., Probasco, P., & Leve, C. (1992). Threat, cohesion, and group effectiveness: Testing a social identity maintenance perspective on groupthink. *Journal of Personality and Social Psychology, 63,* 781–796.

Webb, E. J., Campbell, D. T., Schwartz, R. D., & Sechrest, L. (1966). *Unobtrusive measures: Nonreactive research in the social sciences.* New York: Rand McNally.

Weick, K. E. (1993). Sensemaking in organizations. In J. K. Murnighan (Ed.), *Social psychology in organizations: Advances in theory and practice.* Englewood Cliffs, NJ: Prentice-Hall.

Wrong, D. H. (1979). *Power: Its forms, bases, and uses.* Oxford: Basil Blackwell.

Zimbardo, P. G., Ebbesen, E. B., & Maslach, C. (1977). *Influencing attitudes and changing behavior.* Reading, MA: Addison-Wesley.

13

Resistance to Influence

BRAD J. SAGARIN and SARAH E. WOOD

> Resistance is futile.
> The Borg

W elcome to the last chapter of the book. The preceding twelve chapters focused on the many psychological processes and persuasive techniques that advertisers and other influence professionals can use to change our attitudes or elicit our compliance. Given the power of conformity pressures (Nail & MacDonald, Chapter 8, this volume), social norms (Goldstein & Cialdini, Chapter 7, this volume), cognitive inconsistency (Aronson, Chapter 4, this volume), and emotional appeals (Dolinski, Chapter 5, this volume), as well as the myriad tactics designed to increase influence (Pratkanis, Chapter 2, this volume) and reduce resistance (Knowles & Riner, Chapter 3, this volume), we might be tempted to throw up our hands and admit defeat. Why try to defend ourselves from the overwhelming power of what Cialdini (2001) calls the "weapons of influence"? Perhaps resistance is futile.

Fortunately, we need not surrender our attitudes (and wallets) just yet. We're armed with a number of psychological defenses that quite effectively fend off persuasive attacks. Knowles and Riner (this volume) present three of these defenses: reactance (our tendency to resist attempts to take away our freedoms or choices), skepticism (our tendency to counterargue against persuasive messages), and inertia (our tendency to resist change). This chapter expands the discussion of psychological defense to include the processes that protect our current attitudes and the methods of increasing our resistance to influence.

In this chapter, we ask several questions at the heart of research on resistance to influence. We begin with the question of attitude strength. Why are strong attitudes so resistant to change? Next, we consider the question of forewarning. What do we do when we're warned of an impending persuasive attack? We then turn to the question of individual differences in persuasiveness. What makes some people more resistant than others? Finally, we ask what we can do to protect ourselves from the weapons of influence. How do we increase our resistance to persuasion?

ATTITUDE STRENGTH: WHY ARE STRONG ATTITUDES SO RESISTANT TO CHANGE?

Have you ever tried to change someone's attitude on abortion? Ever tried to convince a New York Mets fan to root for the Yankees? If so, you probably ran headlong into the wall of resistance that protects strong attitudes. Strong attitudes (attitudes about abortion, beloved sports teams, etc.) differ from weak attitudes (attitudes about toilet paper, the incumbent county clerk, etc.) on a number of motivational and cognitive dimensions (Eagly & Chaiken, 1993). The motivational dimensions include the importance of the attitude, the certainty with which the attitude is held, and the public commitment to the attitude. The cognitive dimensions include the embeddedness of the attitude within a web of other attitudes, the degree to which beliefs support or oppose the attitude, and the accessibility of the attitude (the ease with which the attitude can be brought to mind). The end result is that important, embedded, accessible attitudes that are held with certainty, expressed publicly, and supported by beliefs are highly resistant to influence. We should note that although these are all characteristics of strong attitudes, not all strong attitudes have all these characteristics. For example, an attitude that is highly important to a person's sense of self may be quite strong even if the attitude has never been expressed publicly. Furthermore, not all these characteristics of attitude strength have been tested to determine whether they enhance resistance; much work remains to be done.

Importance

How do we react when our important attitudes are threatened? To examine this question Zuwerink and Devine (1996) recruited students who were in favor of allowing gays in the military and measured their reactions to a speech arguing against this position. Half of the participants were high in attitude importance (they agreed with statements like, "My attitude towards gays in the military is very important to me personally"; p. 933). The other half were low in attitude importance (they agreed with statements like, "I don't have very intense feelings about this issue"; p. 933). The speech contained five arguments, including, "Gays in the military undermine unit cohesion and therefore combat performance" and "It is uncomfortable to shower, dress and so on, in front of others who view one as a sex object" (p. 934). Participants listened to the speech and reported their emotional reactions (anger, confusion, happiness, etc.), their cognitive reactions (counter-arguments and other thoughts), and their post-essay attitudes about gays in the military.

Although all participants began the study in favor of gays in the military, participants low in attitude importance were significantly less successful in defending their attitudes than participants high in attitude importance. Participants high in attitude importance resisted the essay through both affective and cognitive means; they felt greater anger and irritation, and they responded with more counterarguments. It appears that when our important attitudes are threatened, we react cognitively and emotionally with both skepticism and anger. One limitation of Zuwerink and Devine (1996) stems from their operationalization of attitude importance. Because Zuwerink and Devine measured attitude importance rather than manipulating it, importance in their study could represent a variety of things – strong beliefs, importance to self, importance for other beliefs, and so on. Future studies could reduce this ambiguity by manipulating attitude importance and then examining the causal effects of attitude importance on resistance.

Public Commitment

Like attitude importance, public commitment to an attitude is likely to strengthen the attitude and make the attitude more resistant to influence. Often, this resistance to influence is beneficial. For example, public commitments to weight loss or smoking cessation can help people resist the temptation to break the diet or sneak a cigarette (Cialdini, 2001). But in one particular situation – in the jury room – this resistance can be highly detrimental. In American criminal cases, the jury must reach a unanimous decision to convict or to acquit. If a jury cannot reach a unanimous decision, the case ends in a mistrial. This is referred to as a hung jury. Given the social and economic costs of mistrials, researchers have focused great effort on identifying the causes of hung juries.

Based on the effects of public commitment, Kerr and MacCoun (1985) predicted that juries that used open show-of-hands voting during their deliberations would be less likely to reach a unanimous verdict than juries that used secret ballots. They reasoned that once a juror has committed publicly to a verdict, he or she will resist efforts to change that verdict. The researchers created 89 mock juries, some with twelve members, some with six members, and some with three members. Each jury read nine short case summaries and tried to reach a unanimous verdict for each case. Approximately half of the juries were instructed to use only open voting during deliberations. The other half were instructed to use only secret ballots.

For relatively clear cases in which most jurors agreed on the verdict initially, open voting and secret ballots produced equivalent numbers of hung juries. But for close cases decided by six- or twelve-person juries, open voting caused significantly more hung juries than secret ballots. As Kerr and MacCoun (1985) explain, "Being publicly identified with a position may force early commitment to that position and make it difficult to change one's position without appearing inconsistent or irresolute" (p. 361). More generally, public commitment to an attitude can increase the attitude's resistance to change.

Embedded and Self-Related Attitudes

The cognitive features of strong attitudes also increase their resistance to change. Attitudes about abortion, for example, are often connected to attitudes about religion, morality, freedom, personal liberty, women's rights, and so on. Such deeply embedded attitudes are resistant to change because a change in one attitude threatens to cause an uncomfortable state of imbalance (see Aronson, Chapter 4, this volume) or a cascade of changes to other attitudes. In addition, the greater accessibility of strong attitudes increases the ability of a person to muster counterarguments against a persuasive message.

In a vivid demonstration of the lengths people will go to defend their strong attitudes, Ahluwalia (2000) polled Clinton supporters and other voters at key moments in 1998 during the Clinton–Lewinsky scandal. Participants were recruited in late January, a week after the scandal first broke. Participants were contacted next in late August after Clinton's public admission of an "inappropriate relationship" with Lewinsky. According to Ahluwalia, at this point in the scandal, Clinton supporters defended their pro-Clinton attitudes primarily by rejecting the validity of the negative information being released – a process Ahluwalia termed *biased assimilation*. Biased assimilation was measured by asking participants, "Do you think President Clinton lied under oath?" (p. 221). Significantly more Clinton supporters than other voters answered "no."

Alas, with the release of the Starr Report, biased assimilation no longer worked. By mid-October, dedicated Clinton supporters could no longer defend their pro-Clinton attitudes by denying that Clinton had lied under oath. Instead, they switched to a new strategy: *relative weighting of attributes*. They perceived Clinton as less honest, but they decided that honesty was not as important as his other positive attributes. In other words, Clinton supporters placed less weight on the attribute that had been negatively impacted by the scandal and greater weight on the attributes that had been left unscathed. Both before and after the release of the Starr Report, Clinton supporters practiced *minimization of spillover*. Whereas other voters generalized the implications of Clinton's reduced honesty to a number of other, related attributes, Clinton supporters allowed the negative implications regarding Clinton's honesty to affect only one other attribute: morality.

Elaboration

Persuasion research has shown that one reliable way to create strong attitudes is by getting people to think carefully about a message. The elaboration likelihood model (ELM) of persuasion suggests that "The strength of an attitude is based on the amount of issue-relevant thinking (elaboration)" (Petty, Haugtvedt, & Smith, 1995, p. 94). Two important factors make people more or less likely to think carefully about an issue: ability and motivation. Ability generally refers to situational constraints on message processing such as distractions and time pressure. If you only have 30 seconds to think about a message it's likely that you won't elaborate much. Motivation generally refers to an individual's desire to think carefully about an issue. We are most likely to think carefully about a message when it is personally relevant to us, when it violates our expectations, or when it is delivered via multiple sources (individual differences such as need for cognition and mood can also affect elaboration; Petty et al., 1995). If we think carefully about one message and form a strong attitude based on this message, what happens when we're faced with an opposing message? Is our strong attitude resistant to this second persuasion attempt? The elaboration–resistance hypothesis suggests that when we think carefully about an initial message, we will be more resistant to an opposing message than when we haven't thought carefully about the initial message (Petty et al., 1995).

In one study (Haugtvedt & Wegener, 1994), participants read a message in favor of and a message opposing a new comprehensive exam that college seniors had to pass before graduating. Some participants were told that the exam would be instituted at their own university (high relevance) and others were told the exam would be instituted at a distant university (low relevance). Participants in the high-relevance condition were expected to think more carefully about the issue than participants in the low-relevance condition. Additionally, some participants read arguments in favor of the comprehensive exams first and others read arguments opposing the comprehensive exams first. Results demonstrated that participants in the high-relevance conditions were more resistant to the second message than participants in the low-relevance conditions, regardless of whether they read the pro or con arguments first. In other words, participants who thought carefully about the first message were more resistant to the second message, even if they disagreed with the first message.

When Resistance Causes Attitude Strength

Historically, researchers examining the relationship between attitude strength and resistance to influence have focused on whether greater attitude strength causes resistance. Recently, Rich Petty and his colleagues have begun to examine the relationship in the other direction – whether resistance causes greater attitude strength. Tormala and Petty (2002) reasoned that, "When people perceive that they have resisted persuasion successfully, they might infer that their attitude is correct, or valid, and thus feel more certain about it" (p. 1298). They predicted that this effect would occur only when people perceive that they have successfully resisted a strong persuasive message. Successfully resisting a weak persuasive message offers no evidence that the attitude is strong – even a weak attitude might have withstood a weak onslaught.

Tormala and Petty (2002) tested their theory with a series of experiments that cleverly manipulated the perceived strength of the attacking message without manipulating the actual strength of the attacking message. In the first study, participants were told that their university was considering implementing senior comprehensive exams that students would need to pass before receiving their degrees. Participants were then told that they would read a series of arguments in favor of comprehensive exams. Some participants were told that the arguments would be strong; others were told that the arguments would be weak. In actuality, all participants received the same persuasive message that contained a mix of strong arguments ("The average starting salary of graduates would increase," p. 1301) and weak arguments ("Implementing the exams would allow students to compare their scores with those of students at other universities," p. 1301).

Regardless of the perceived strength of the arguments, participants successfully resisted the persuasive message; their attitudes about senior comprehensive exams were unchanged. For some participants, however, the strength of their attitudes had changed. Participants who perceived that they had fended off a strong attack reported attitudes that were significantly stronger than participants who had brushed aside a weak attack (they reported greater certainty in response to the question "How certain are you of your opinion toward the comprehensive exam policy?", p. 1301). Tormala and Petty's (2002) second study demonstrated that only successful resistance increases attitude strength; participants who were given false feedback that they had failed to resist the persuasive message did not show a change in attitude strength. Finally, Tormala and Petty's third and fourth studies demonstrated that participants who perceived that they had successfully resisted a strong persuasive message showed greater resistance to a subsequent persuasive attack and a stronger relationship between attitudes and behavioral intentions. These results suggest that the strongest attitudes might not be those attitudes that have never been challenged but rather those attitudes that have withstood worthy attacks.

In an interesting twist on Tormala and Petty's (2002) findings, Rucker and Petty (2004) demonstrated that a failed attempt to resist a strong attack increases the strength of the new attitude. Rucker and Petty gave participants very strong persuasive messages and instructed them either to counterargue or to just think about the message. Regardless of instructions, the persuasive message successfully changed participants' attitudes. But the strength of the changed attitude and the strength of the association between the changed attitude and behavioral intentions were significantly higher for participants who had tried unsuccessfully to resist. According to Rucker and Petty, "Having attempted, but failed, to find fault in a message allows people to infer that they have few reasons against accepting the message" (p. 231). A useful extension of Rucker and Petty's work would be to examine whether failed attempts to resist strong attacks produce new attitudes that are resistant to subsequent attacks.

FOREWARNING: WHAT DO WE DO WHEN WE'RE WARNED OF AN IMPENDING PERSUASIVE ATTACK?

What do we do when we're warned of an impending persuasive attack? If you predicted that we would resist the attack, you'd be right. On the other hand, if you predicted that we would appear to be more receptive to the attack, you'd also be right. In 1965, Freedman and Sears published a study that found support for the first prediction – that forewarning causes resistance. The researchers surveyed high-school students about their attitudes toward teenage driving. Not surprisingly, nearly everyone was opposed to limits on teen driving. A few weeks later, everyone heard "a noted expert on automobiles, highway administration and driving in general" (p. 263) give a speech against teen driving. Some participants were warned ahead of time of the title ("Why Teen-Agers Should Not Drive") and the nature of the talk. Others were simply told they were about to hear a talk from this expert. After hearing the speech, participants reported their attitudes about teenage driving. The results showed that participants who were warned about the nature of the upcoming speech were significantly less persuaded by the speech than participants who were not warned.

A few months later, McGuire and Millman (1965) published a study in the same journal that found support for the second prediction. The researchers predicted that "forewarning a person that he is about to receive strong persuasive attacks on specified beliefs which he holds will result, under our experimental conditions, in an anticipatory lowering of these beliefs" (p. 471). Students in an educational methods course read four persuasive messages, two on controversial, emotional issues (e.g., "the growing likelihood of a third world war," p. 473) and two on non-controversial, technical issues (e.g., "the continuing need for propeller planes in commercial aviation," p. 473). After reading the messages, participants reported their attitudes on these four issues as well as four additional issues unrelated to the persuasive messages. Participants were warned ahead of time about two of the emotional issues (one related to a persuasive message, one unrelated) and two of the technical issues (again, one related to a persuasive message, one unrelated). The issues were prescreened to ensure that participants would disagree with all of them.

In contrast to the resistance-enhancing effect of forewarning found in Freedman and Sears (1965), forewarning had no effect whatsoever on participants' responses to the persuasive messages. Participants were just as persuaded by messages they had been warned about as messages they had not been warned about. Forewarning did have an effect, however, on the emotional issues unrelated to the persuasive messages. On these issues, participants reported attitudes that were significantly more in favor of the issues they had been warned about compared to issues they had not been warned about. In other words, forewarning caused an anticipatory shift toward the topic and away from participants' actual attitudes.

In the years that followed, researchers attempted to determine under what circumstances forewarning causes resistance (as found in Freedman & Sears, 1965) and under what circumstances forewarning seemingly causes less resistance (as found in McGuire & Millman, 1965). Then, in 1981, Robert Cialdini and Richard Petty published a review of the first 15–20 years of research on forewarning. The review attempted to resolve the seemingly incompatible findings and to summarize the empirical evidence. Cialdini and Petty described the state of affairs as follows:

> One aspect of anticipatory opinion effects that was puzzling during the initial years of research on the phenomenon was the seemingly unpredictable direction that the effects would take . . . some studies indicated that forewarning of the onset of a persuasive communication produced *less* change in the direction of the message than no such warning, but others indicated that forewarning produced *more* change in the direction of the expected communication.
>
> (pp. 220–221; emphasis in original)

According to Cialdini and Petty (1981), the critical difference between Freedman and Sears (1965) and McGuire and Millman (1965) was the importance of the issue. Moreover, the critical factor was the "direct, *personal* importance" (p. 222) of the issue. For example, the teenage participants in Freedman and Sears (1965) heard a persuasive message arguing for a ban on teen driving. For these participants, the issue was indeed of direct, personal importance. As a result, forewarning caused resistance. In contrast, participants in McGuire and Millman (1965) read about a series of issues including "the growing likelihood of a third world war." The possibility of a third world war is certainly an important issue, but for McGuire and Millman's participants, it was probably not of direct, personal importance. As a result, forewarning caused an anticipatory shift toward the persuasive message.

In 1979, Petty and Cacioppo published a study that nicely illustrated the effects of personal issue importance on forewarning. In their study, college students heard a tape-recorded persuasive message arguing for the institution of senior comprehensive examinations that students would be required to pass before graduation. Some participants were warned of the persuasive intent of the upcoming message ("the tape was designed specifically to try to persuade you and other college students of the desirability of changing certain college regulations," p. 174). Others did not receive this warning. In addition, some participants were told that their university was considering implementing the exams before they had graduated, thus creating a high level of personal involvement in the issue. Others were told that their university was considering implementing the exams 11 years later or that the exams were being considered at a different university, thus creating a low level of personal involvement. All participants then listened to the persuasive message. Overall, forewarned participants were less persuaded than unwarned participants, but the resistance was significantly greater for participants who would be personally affected by the exams.

Across the studies they reviewed, Cialdini and Petty (1981) showed that personal issue importance explains the otherwise discrepant findings. For personally important issues, participants generated counterarguments before and during the persuasive message, and these counterarguments caused greater resistance. For less personally important issues, participants tended to shift their attitudes toward a more moderate position (often toward the anticipated message). Cialdini and Petty described these shifts as strategic and elastic: strategic in that the shifts represent an attempt to "seize the middle of the opinion scale and thereby afford subjects a safe, defensible position in the expected discussion" (p. 230; see Cialdini, Levy, Herman, & Evenbeck, 1973), and elastic in that the shifts disappeared and the attitudes reverted to their original state when the anticipated discussion was cancelled (Cialdini et al., 1973).

In 2003, Wendy Wood and Jeffrey Quinn published a meta-analysis of the forewarning literature. In a meta-analysis, researchers statistically combine the results of a set of studies. Wood and Quinn's meta-analysis confirmed a number of the conclusions reached by Cialdini and Petty (1981). Consistent with Cialdini and Petty, Wood and Quinn found that studies that used personally relevant issues produced significantly more resistance than studies that used less personally relevant issues. Furthermore, consistent with Cialdini and Petty's conclusion that when forewarning causes resistance, this resistance occurs as a result of increased counterarguments, Wood and Quinn found that factors that disrupt counterargumentation (such as distraction) eliminate resistance and factors that increase counterargumentation (such as thought listing) increase resistance.

Wood and Quinn (2003) also examined the factors that lead to a shift toward the message. According to Wood and Quinn, before receiving a persuasive message people shift their stated opinion toward the message in an effort to protect the self-image from the threat of gullibility – you can't be persuaded if you already agree with the message. Factors that increase this threat (such as the anticipation that the message comes from an expert) tend to increase these shifts. However, when the topic is highly personally involving, the threat to an important attitude outweighs the threat to the self-image, and forewarning causes resistance even before the message is received.

So, in answer to our original question, warning about an imminent persuasive attack causes resistance to that attack once the attack has taken place, if the target has the time and ability to counterargue. However, before the attack takes place, forewarning causes resistance for personally involving issues but anticipatory agreement for less involving issues.

INDIVIDUAL DIFFERENCES: WHAT MAKES SOME PEOPLE MORE RESISTANT THAN OTHERS?

Psychologists have also examined how a number of individual difference variables impact resistance to influence, including self-esteem, intelligence, need for closure (i.e., the desire to reach or have a definite opinion about a topic; Kruglanski, Webster, & Klem, 1993), need for cognition (i.e., the extent to which a person enjoys thinking, Cacioppo & Petty, 1982), argumentativeness, and gender.

Self-Esteem and Intelligence

A meta-analysis by Rhodes and Wood (1992) examined the relationships between self-esteem and resistance to influence and between intelligence and resistance. The meta-analysis revealed a strong tendency for individuals with moderate self-esteem to be more easily persuaded than individuals with high or low self-esteem. According to Rhodes and Wood, individuals with high self-esteem resist influence more effectively because they are more confident about their opinions. In contrast, individuals with low self-esteem are more resistant to influence because they may be less likely to pay attention to the message. The relationship between intelligence and resistance was somewhat simpler. Like individuals high in self-esteem, highly intelligent individuals are likely to be confident in their own opinions. As a result, highly intelligent individuals are more resistant to influence than low-intelligence individuals.

Need for Closure

According to Kruglanski et al. (1993), individuals high in need for closure have a strong preference for having a definite opinion. As a result, they're much less likely to want to change an already-formed opinion than individuals low in need for closure. In a series of studies, Kruglanski et al. asked participants to deliberate a legal case (a negligence lawsuit against an airline) in a mock-jury situation. Participants were given case summaries and a legal analysis (which was either pro-plaintiff or pro-defendant). All deliberations were done in pairs. Sometimes one of the pair was a confederate who argued against the participant's pre-deliberation attitude. Across three studies, participants high in need for closure were less easily persuaded than participants low in need for closure.

Need for Cognition

Need for cognition refers to "individual differences in intrinsic motivation to engage in effortful cognitive endeavors" (Haugtvedt & Petty, 1992, p. 309). People high in need for cognition like to think about things. As a result, they are likely to think deeply about persuasive messages they encounter. According to Haugtvedt and Petty, one implication of this tendency is that people high in need for cognition are likely to have attitudes that are resistant to change. They tested this by exposing participants to a persuasive message that advocated a ban on a food additive. The message was attributed to a highly credible source: "Dr. James Dobbs, Professor of Food Sciences at Princeton University." Then, after rating the safety of the food additive, participants read a second persuasive message that disagreed with the first message. The second message was also attributed to a highly credible source: "Dr. William C. Manchester, Professor of Nutrition at Cornell University" (p. 315).

The first persuasive message was equally effective for participants high in need for cognition and low in need for cognition. All participants were persuaded that the additive was unsafe. But the second message was only effective for participants low in need for cognition. These participants changed their opinions back to believing the additive was safe. Participants high in need for cognition, on the other hand, resisted the second message. Haugtvedt and Petty (1992) explained that participants low in need for cognition had been persuaded initially by the expertise of the source. Then, when presented with an equally expert source, they changed their opinions back. Participants high in need for cognition, on the other hand, were persuaded by the arguments presented in the first message. When they encountered the second message, they recalled these arguments and successfully counterargued against the second message.

Argumentativeness

Another variable that impacts resistance to influence is argumentativeness. Argumentativeness can be described as a tendency to enjoy arguing and attacking other people's positions, particularly on controversial issues (Kazoleas, 1993; Levine & Badger, 1993). In one study participants watched a television commercial and read two printed messages. The commercial was from Anheuser-Busch in which an LA Laker advocated drinking in moderation and not driving drunk (Kazoleas, 1993). The first printed message argued against the Clean Air Act, and the second printed message was from the American Cancer Association arguing against sunbathing and going to tanning booths. Despite the fact that participants may have agreed with some of these messages, participants higher in argumentativeness showed less attitude change than participants lower in argumentativeness. Kazoleas explains: "In situations where the argumentative individual agrees with the position advocated, low and moderate argumentatives may be less interested in arguing. However, highly argumentative individuals might argue against positions they initially agree with, thus playing the role of 'devil's advocate' " (p. 121).

Gender

Finally, one of the most widely researched questions regarding individual differences in resistance is whether men are more resistant to influence than women. As Pfau and Burgoon (1990) point out, it has been a relatively longstanding belief that women are more easily persuaded than men. In a meta-analysis of persuasion studies, Eagly and Carli (1981) found that though the differences aren't huge, women do appear to be more easily persuaded. However, Eagly and Carli's meta-analysis uncovered an important qualification to this conclusion: The gender difference in persuasion is affected by the gender of the researcher! As Eagly and Carli explain:

> In general, male researchers have found men to be relatively independent in social influence experiments and not as inaccurate in decoding nonverbal cues as female researchers have. Female researchers have not found women to be especially conforming or persuasible, but they have found that women are highly accurate in decoding nonverbal cues. (p. 17)

INOCULATION AND OTHER METHODS: HOW DO WE INCREASE OUR RESISTANCE TO INFLUENCE?

So far we've explored the factors that make some attitudes and some people particularly resistant to influence. We've also talked about the situations in which forewarning of a persuasive attack leads to greater resistance (and the situations in which forewarning leads to greater persuasion). In this section, we discuss the techniques that psychologists have developed to increase resistance to influence.

Given the numerous techniques that psychologists have developed to increase influence, you'd think they would have developed a similar number to increase resistance. Alas, there are very few. Although this might seem disheartening from the perspective of a persuasive target trying to fend off attacks, for a researcher, resistance to influence represents a wide-open territory. Below, we review McGuire's inoculation theory, the most famous and well-researched resistance technique developed by psychologists. We then discuss a recent program of research on a method to instill resistance to illegitimate persuasive techniques. Thereafter, we present the ideas, suggestions, guidelines, and speculations offered by some of the foremost researchers on influence: Robert Cialdini, Anthony

Pratkanis, and Elliot Aronson. These suggestions – few of which have been empirically tested so far – offer guidance to influence targets and a treasure trove of ideas for psychological researchers.

McGuire's (1964) inoculation theory posits that individuals can be made resistant to persuasive attack by pre-exposing them to weakened forms of the attack. McGuire based this on the biological immunization process, in which individuals are made resistant to viral attack by being exposed to a weakened form of the virus. This allows the body to prepare defenses against subsequent attack. McGuire reasoned that, as with viral inoculation, those who have been exposed to weak persuasive attacks will develop defenses (in the form of counterarguments) to subsequent persuasive attack. McGuire's original research focused on attacks on cultural truisms – widely held beliefs that are seldom challenged, such as, "It's a good idea to brush your teeth after every meal if at all possible" (p. 201). McGuire chose cultural truisms because they exist in a "germ free" environment – they are relatively free from previous attack. For example, most people probably have never heard an argument against frequent tooth brushing. As a result, most people probably haven't bothered to create defenses for this belief. Inoculation motivates people to create defenses by threatening the belief with a weak attack.

McGuire's (1964) original experiments typically presented participants with either a nonthreatening supportive defense (presentation of arguments that support the initial belief; for example, brushing your teeth after meals prevents cavities) or a threatening refutational defense (presentation of arguments that oppose the initial belief; for example, brushing your teeth too often could damage the enamel). In a series of experiments McGuire demonstrated that, in general, the refutational defense was substantially more effective than the supportive defense in repelling subsequent persuasive attacks. According to McGuire, the refutational defense provided two critical components of resistance to persuasion: motivation and ability. By demonstrating that the belief can be attacked, inoculation motivates people to build resistance. Furthermore, by providing people with the opportunity to counterargue against weak arguments, inoculation gives people the ability to counterargue against subsequent stronger arguments.

In the years since McGuire introduced inoculation theory, other researchers have extended the theory well beyond the defense of cultural truisms. One important application of the inoculation paradigm has been to promote resistance to smoking (Killen, 1985; Pfau & Van Bockern, 1994; Pfau, Van Bockern, & Kang, 1992) and other risky health behaviors (Duryea, Ransom, & English, 1990). One study followed over 1,000 seventh grade students over the course of one school year to determine the effectiveness of different inoculation procedures in preventing smoking. Pfau et al. (1992) point out that prior to middle school, children typically have strong antismoking attitudes but as they advance through middle school these attitudes diminish as students are faced with increased peer pressure. Thus, the timing of an inoculation intervention is critical. For the program to succeed, it must be implemented while the students still have strong antismoking attitudes (i.e., before they have heard arguments in favor of smoking). The focus of the inoculation was to build defenses against the social pressure students would face in middle school (e.g., "smoking is cool"). Students were randomly assigned to one of three treatment conditions: inoculation, inoculation plus reinforcement (to help preserve the inoculation effects), or control. Students were shown a series of videos, which included threat and refutational defense. The videos warned students that despite their current negative views toward smoking, many would likely change their opinions as a result of peer pressure. The videos also presented attacks such as "smoking is socially cool" and then refuted these attacks (Pfau et al., 1992, p. 219). Not surprisingly, attitudes toward smoking and smokers became more positive over the course of the year for all students. But the inoculation intervention increased resistance to smoking behavior, particularly for individuals low in self-esteem. This finding is important because, as the researchers note, individuals with low self-esteem are the most vulnerable to smoking initiation (Pfau et al., 1992). A follow-up study was conducted to gauge the long-term effectiveness of the inoculation program (Pfau & Van Bockern, 1994). The results showed that antismoking attitudes continued to diminish during eighth grade but that the inoculation treatment seemed to provide some residual resistance. Though the effects were small, the researchers point out that any remaining effects of inoculation on attitudes measured one year after treatment is promising (Pfau & Van Bockern, 1994).

Pfau, Kenski, Nitz, and Sorenson (1990) applied inoculation to political communications via direct mail during the 1988 US Presidential campaign. As political attack ads have become increasingly popular, campaigns face the challenge of how to overcome the negative information typically represented in these advertisements. One option is to attempt to refute negative claims after the fact (a "post-hoc refutation"). Another option is to use inoculation. Instead of trying to repair the damage after the attack, inoculation attempts to warn people of impending attack so they may resist the negative persuasive messages.

To test the effectiveness of inoculation in defending against attack ads, a group of potential voters were surveyed as to party affiliation and then randomly assigned to an inoculation, inoculation-plus-reinforcement, post-hoc refutation, or control condition (Pfau et al., 1990). Inoculation and attack messages were created using actual campaign materials available at the time. For example, "The Bush messages attacked Dukakis for being weak on crime and for deception involving his record as Governor of Massachusetts. The Dukakis messages attacked Bush for his support for agricultural and development policies that have hurt rural America and for insensitivity to the plight of the average working person" (Pfau et al., p. 31). Participants in the inoculation conditions received pieces of direct mail that contained the inoculation message, and half of these participants later received reinforcement messages. Participants in the post-hoc refutation condition received the attack message via direct mail and then, several days later, they received a message refuting the attack. Finally, interviewers administered attack message and post-treatment questionnaires to all the inoculated participants and control participants. Refutation condition participants (who had received the attack message via direct mail) simply completed post-treatment questionnaires.

Overall, the inoculation strategy appeared to provide the strongest resistance to the attack ad (although the reinforcement of the inoculation did not increase this resistance). Inoculation was somewhat superior to the post-hoc refutation, particularly regarding attitudes toward the candidate. Furthermore, despite the fact that many people say they ignore direct mail (a.k.a. junk mail), this seemed to be an effective method for distributing the inoculation messages.

Although inoculation has been shown to build resistance in a number of contexts (e.g., cultural truisms, antismoking interventions, political campaigns), inoculation theory has its limits. For example, successful inoculation requires anticipating a specific persuasive message. In an attempt to transcend this limitation, Sagarin, Cialdini, Rice, and Serna (2002) developed a method of instilling resistance to a full persuasive technique – the use of illegitimate authorities in advertisements – rather than to a specific persuasive message.

Sagarin et al. (2002) set out to teach participants to distinguish legitimate authorities (i.e., experts speaking within their areas of expertise) from illegitimate authorities (i.e., experts speaking outside their areas of expertise or actors merely dressed up to look like experts). Participants readily learned this distinction, but they developed very little resistance against ads containing illegitimate authorities. Sagarin et al. speculated that participants didn't bother to develop resistance because they didn't believe they needed to. Participants may have recognized that their fellow students could be fooled by illegitimate authorities, but they believed that they were personally invulnerable to such manipulation.

To remedy this, Sagarin et al. (2002) attempted to dispel participants' illusions of invulnerability. Before learning the distinction between legitimate and illegitimate authorities, participants examined an ad containing an illegitimate authority. Some participants were then instructed to write down how convincing they had found the ad (most found it at least somewhat convincing). Others just examined the ad without recording their reactions. Participants were then shown how, if they had found the ad even somewhat convincing, they had been fooled. The results showed that participants who had written down their reactions to the ad developed significant resistance to subsequent ads containing illegitimate authorities. Participants who had not recorded their reactions retained their illusions of invulnerability and failed to develop resistance. These results suggest that one method of motivating people to develop resistance is to demonstrate that they are personally vulnerable to being manipulated. More recently, a number of researchers have used this technique to dispel participants' illusions of invulnerability to sexually transmitted diseases (Patock-Peckham, Cialdini, Sagarin, Gerend, & Aiken, 2003) and urban legends (Sovern, 2004), although the technique was less successful against illusions of invulnerability to illegitimate social proof (i.e., manufactured consensus information; Phelps, 2004).

Although the research described above represents a good start, much work remains in the development of methods to instill resistance to influence. Below, we explore the recommendations made by some of the foremost experts on social influence on how to resist a wider range of influence tactics. Most of these recommendations have not been tested empirically, and we believe they provide exciting opportunities for researchers interested in resistance to influence.

In *Age of Propaganda* (2001), Pratkanis and Aronson offer a series of recommendations for building resistance that range from the psychological (e.g., "Monitor your emotions," p. 342) to the pragmatic (e.g., "If the deal looks too good to be true, it probably is," p. 344) to the political (e.g., "Support efforts to protect vulnerable groups such as children from exploitative persuasion," p. 344). But their #1 recommendation, without which the rest of the recommendations are likely to be meaningless, is to realize that we're vulnerable. As Sagarin et al. (2002) discovered, without this realization, attempts to instill resistance are likely to fail.

Pratkanis and Aronson's (2001) other recommendations fall roughly into four categories. They recommend that we try to think more rationally and less emotionally, that we approach persuasive messages with a healthy level of skepticism, that we learn about influence techniques, and that we advocate for consumer-oriented action and legislation.

With respect to rational thought, Pratkanis and Aronson (2001) begin by recommending that we "Monitor [our] emotions . . . If you feel that your emotions are being played on, get out of the situation and then analyze what is going on" (p. 342). Along these lines, Cialdini (2001) recommends that we defend ourselves against scarcity (i.e., the persuasive principle, often fueled by reactance, that causes us to desire things more as they become less available) by being alert to the "rush of arousal" (p. 231) characteristic of situations involving scarcity. Then, "once alerted, we can take steps to calm the arousal and assess the merits of the opportunity in terms of why we want it" (p. 231).

Pratkanis and Aronson (2001) also make the following recommendations: "Think rationally about any proposal or issue" (p. 342), "Attempt to understand the full range of options before making a decision" (p. 342), and "Always ask yourself: 'What are the arguments for the other side?' "(p. 344). All of these recommendations are likely to lead to better decisions based on logic rather than emotion. Or, in the terminology of the heuristic–systematic model of persuasion (Chaiken, 1980, 1987), these recommendations are likely to increase systematic processing (i.e., the use of thoughtful, effortful thinking to process a persuasive message) and decrease heuristic processing (i.e., the use of simple decision rules to process a persuasive message). Unfortunately, switching from heuristic processing to systematic processing may be easier said than done, particularly because many influence tactics seem designed to decrease our ability to think rationally. One particularly important area for future research is to develop methods of (a) enabling people to determine when heuristic processing is dangerous to good decision-making, and (b) empowering people to switch to systematic processing in these situations.

With respect to skepticism, Pratkanis and Aronson (2001) recommend: "Explore the motivations and credibility of the source of the communication" (p. 342), "Stop to consider the possibility that any information you receive may be a factoid [unverified information]" (p. 343), and "Avoid being dependent on a single source of information" (p. 345), and they warn that "If the deal looks too good to be true, it probably is" (p. 344). As with rational thought, skepticism requires the ability to think clearly and carefully. We hope that future researchers will focus their efforts on developing methods of increasing healthy skepticism without increasing cynicism.

One suggestion that highlights both the importance and the challenge of maintaining skepticism is Pratkanis and Aronson's (2001) recommendation: "Think of the news as the news and try to separate it in your own mind from entertainment" (p. 345). The challenge lies in the increasing attempt by marketers to blur the lines between news, entertainment, and advertising. Many magazines now contain multi-page advertising sections that are designed to look like news stories. Alert readers may notice the word "advertisement" in tiny type at the top of each page, but are all readers paying sufficiently close attention? Similarly, on many radio stations, the news anchors transition seamlessly from reporting a news story to reciting an advertisement. Once again, listeners not paying attention may give the ad the same level of credibility that they gave the preceding news story.

A particularly troubling example of the attempt to blur the line between news and advertising was recently reported in the *New York Times* (Pear, 2004). According to the article, "the Bush administration had violated federal law by producing and disseminating television news segments that portray the new Medicare law as a boon to the elderly. [Congress' General Accounting Office] said the videos were a form of 'covert propaganda' because the government was not identified as the source of the materials." (¶s 1, 2). The General Accounting Office said, "The government . . . served up a 'purported news story' using 'alleged reporters' to read scripts prepared by the government, but 'nothing in the story packages permits the viewer to know that Karen Ryan and Alberto Garcia [the ostensible reporters] were paid with federal funds' "(¶ 12). This story highlights the importance of maintaining a firm line between journalism and marketing. Blurring the line might provide a short-term benefit for unscrupulous marketers, but it will damage the reputation and credibility of a critical social institution.

With respect to education, Pratkanis and Aronson (2001) recommend that we educate ourselves and teach our children about the techniques of influence and propaganda. As children are exposed to more advertisements at younger and younger ages, as marketing increasingly infiltrates schools and other domains previously free from advertising, as new media, such as the Internet, provide additional avenues of marketing to children (and to all of us), educational programs designed to teach media literacy, critical thinking, and resistance to influence are sorely needed.

With respect to consumer advocacy, Pratkanis and Aronson (2001) recommend that we "Support efforts to protect vulnerable groups such as children from exploitative persuasion" (p. 344), "Support campaign spending reform" (p. 345), "Demand consumer affairs shows" (p. 347), "Write companies asking for proof of advertised claims" (p. 347), "Support and extend efforts to squelch deceptive advertisements" (p. 347), and "Support and extend efforts to eliminate misleading labels and other deceptive practices" (p. 347). We concur with these recommendations and suggest that social psychologists support these efforts through research. Studies that examine the effects of misleading labels on consumer perceptions and purchase decisions, for example, could provide critical evidence regarding the need for legislation to curb these practices.

Cialdini (2001) organizes his resistance recommendations around his six principles of influence: reciprocity, commitment and consistency, social proof, liking, authority, and scarcity. His suggestion for authority – that we ask ourselves whether the authority is truly an impartial expert – forms the basis of the resistance method developed by Sagarin et al. (2002). His suggestions for the other principles of influence similarly recommend that we try to distinguish situations in which the principle occurs legitimately from other situations in which the principle is artificially manufactured. With respect to social proof, for example, Cialdini recommends that we remain receptive to the important information that the opinions and actions of others can provide, but that we reject obviously faked evidence such as laugh tracks and staged "person on the street" testimonials. Similarly, with respect to liking, Cialdini recommends that we should be open to requests from people we know and like, but we should be wary if we find ourselves liking a salesperson surprisingly quickly.

With respect to reciprocity (i.e., our feeling of obligation when someone does us a favor to respond with a favor in return, Cialdini, 2001), Cialdini recommends that we be wary of compliance tactics masquerading as favors. This does not mean that we should ignore reciprocal obligations. Such a stance would damage important relationships with friends, romantic partners, coworkers, etc. Instead, we should be alert to favors that are merely attempts gain compliance. For example, charitable requests often arrive with a free gift such as a page of address labels or a calendar. Cialdini recommends that the recipient of such a request redefine the gift "as a compliance device instead of a favor" (p. 47). This redefinition defuses the reciprocal obligation, and without the reciprocal obligation, the recipient is empowered to resist or accept the request on its own merits.

Commitment and consistency refer to our desire to act in a way that is consistent with our prior commitments (Cialdini, 2001). As with reciprocity, acting with consistency is usually beneficial to us. But also as with reciprocity, this tendency can get us into trouble. One all too common technique that exploits this principle is the low ball. A typical low ball works like this: A customer enters a car dealership. He has a trade-in that he knows is worth about $2500. The dealership's appraiser values the car at $3000. The customer smiles to himself; he's already $500 ahead on the deal. As a result, he might not bargain quite as hard during negotiations. Perhaps he buys an expensive option or two that he wouldn't have purchased otherwise. Then, just as the contract is about to be signed, the sales manager notices that the appraiser overvalued the trade-in. With the trade-in now worth only $2500, the deal isn't nearly as good. But many customers, grumbling to themselves, buy the car anyway. According to Cialdini, we can avoid getting tricked by the low ball if we pay attention to a certain signal: "It occurs right in the pit of our stomachs when we realize we are trapped into complying with a request we *know* we don't want to perform" (p. 91, emphasis in original). Once we notice that feeling, we should take a step back and decide whether we really want to go through with the deal.

Commitment and consistency can also get us stuck in unhealthy relationships, poor jobs, or bad investments. Having committed so much time and effort, it's hard to know when to get out. Cialdini (2001) recommends that we ask ourselves, "Knowing what I now know, if I could go back in time, would I make the same choice?" (p. 93) and that we pay attention to the first feeling we get in response to the question. The feeling that occurs before all the rationalizations kick in may tell us when it's time to re-evaluate our commitment.

CONCLUSIONS

This chapter has reviewed four of the major areas of research on resistance to influence: the resistance-enhancing properties of strong attitudes, the situations in which forewarning causes resistance, the personality characteristics associated with resistance, and the methods of increasing resistance to influence. Although these lines of research represent the efforts of a substantial number of researchers, a quick search of PsycINFO (or, indeed, a glance through the table of contents of this book) reveals that psychologists have spent considerably more effort studying social influence than studying resistance to influence. We believe that this imbalance represents an exciting opportunity for social psychological researchers. The results of this research will provide psychologists with important insights into the processes of social influence and resistance to persuasion and consumers with much-needed methods of defending against the weapons of influence.

REFERENCES

Ahluwalia, R. (2000). Examination of psychological processes underlying resistance to persuasion. *Journal of Consumer Research*, 27, 217–232.

Cacioppo, J. T., & Petty, R. E. (1982). The need for cognition. *Journal of Personality and Social Psychology*, 42, 116–131.

Chaiken, S. (1980). Heuristic versus systematic information processing and the use of source versus message cues in persuasion. *Journal of Personality and Social Psychology*, 39, 752–766.

Chaiken, S. (1987). The heuristic model of persuasion. In M. P. Zanna, J. M. Olson, & C. P. Herman (Eds.), *Social influence: The Ontario symposium* (Vol. 5, pp. 3–39). Hillsdale, NJ: Lawrence Erlbaum Associates, Inc.

Cialdini, R. B. (2001). *Influence: Science and practice* (4th ed.). Boston: Allyn & Bacon.

Cialdini, R. B., Levy, A. Herman, C. P., & Evenbeck, S. (1973). Attitudinal politics: The strategy of moderation. *Journal of Personality and Social Psychology*, 25, 100–108.

Cialdini, R. B., & Petty, R. E. (1981). Anticipatory opinion effects. In R. E. Petty, T. M. Ostrom, & T. C. Brock (Eds.), *Cognitive responses in persuasion* (pp. 217–235). Hillsdale, NJ: Lawrence Erlbaum Associates, Inc.

Duryea, E. J., Ransom, M. V., & English, G. (1990). Psychological immunization: Theory, research, and current health behavior applications. *Health Education Quarterly*, 17, 169–178.

Eagly, A. H., & Carli, L. L. (1981). Sex of researchers and sex-typed communications as determinants of sex differences in influenceability: A meta-analysis of social influence studies. *Psychological Bulletin*, 90, 1–20.

Eagly, A. H. & Chaiken, S. (1993). *The psychology of attitudes*. San Diego, CA: Harcourt Brace.

Freedman, J. L., & Sears, D. O. (1965). Warning, distraction, and resistance to influence. *Journal of Personality and Social Psychology*, 1, 262–266.

Haugtvedt, C. P., & Petty, R. E. (1992). Personality and persuasion: Need for cognition moderates the persistence and resistance of attitude changes. *Journal of Personality and Social Psychology*, 63, 308–319.

Haugtvedt, C. P., & Wegener, D. T. (1994). Message order effects in persuasion: An attitude strength perspective. *Journal of Consumer Research*, *21*, 205–218.

Kazoleas, D. (1993). The impact of argumentativeness and resistance to persuasion. *Human Communication Research*, *20*, 118–137.

Kerr, N. L., & MacCoun, R. J. (1985). The effects of jury size and polling method on the process and product of jury deliberation. *Journal of Personality and Social Psychology*, *48*, 349–363.

Killen, J. D. (1985). Prevention of adolescent tobacco smoking: The social pressure resistance training approach. *Journal of Child Psychology and Psychiatry and Allied Disciplines*, *26*, 7–15.

Kruglanski, A. W., Webster, D. M., & Klem, A. (1993). Motivated resistance and openness to persuasion in the presence or absence of prior information. *Journal of Personality and Social Psychology*, *65*, 861–876.

Levine, T. R., & Badger, E. E. (1993). Argumentativeness and resistance to persuasion. *Communication Reports*, *6*, 71–78.

McGuire, W. J. (1964). Inducing resistance to persuasion: Some contemporary approaches. In L. Berkowitz (Ed.), *Advances in experimental social psychology* (Vol. 1, pp. 191–229). New York: Academic Press.

McGuire, W. J., & Millman, S. (1965). Anticipatory belief lowering following forewarning of a persuasive attack. *Journal of Personality and Social Psychology*, *2*, 471–479.

Patock-Peckham, J. A., Cialdini, R. B., Sagarin, B. J., Gerend, M., & Aiken, L. S. (2003, May). *Piercing the illusion of invulnerability to STD risk*. Paper presented at the 2003 meeting of the Western Psychological Association, Vancouver, BC.

Pear, R. (2004, May 20). Ruling says White House's Medicare videos were illegal [Electronic version]. *New York Times*.

Petty, R. E., & Cacioppo, J. T. (1979). Effects of forewarning of persuasive intent and involvement on cognitive responses and persuasion. *Personality and Social Psychology Bulletin*, *5*, 173–176.

Petty, R. E., Haugtvedt, C., & Smith, S. M. (1995). Elaboration as a determinant of attitude strength: Creating attitudes that are persistent, resistant, and predictive of behavior. In R. E. Petty & J. A. Krosnick (Eds.), *Attitude strength: Antecedents and consequences* (pp. 93–130). Mahwah, NJ: Lawrence Erlbaum Associates, Inc.

Pfau, M., & Burgoon, M. (1990). Inoculation in political campaigns and gender. *Women's Studies in Communication*, *13*, 1–21.

Pfau, M., Kenski, H. C., Nitz, M., & Sorenson, J. (1990). Efficacy of inoculation strategies in promoting resistance to political attack messages: Application to direct mail. *Communication Monographs*, *57*, 25–43.

Pfau, M. & Van Bockern, S. (1994). The persistence of inoculation in conferring resistance to smoking initiation among adolescents: The second year. *Human Communication Quarterly*, *20*, 413–430.

Pfau, M., Van Bockern, S., & Kang, J. G. (1992). Use of inoculation to promote resistance to smoking initiation among adolescents. *Communication Monographs*, *59*, 213–230.

Phelps, J. M. (2004). *Instilling resistance to persuasion: Legitimate vs. illegitimate use of the principle of social proof*. Unpublished master's thesis, University of Central Lancashire, Preston, UK.

Pratkanis, A. R., & Aronson, E. (2001). *Age of propaganda: The everyday use and abuse of persuasion*. New York: W. H. Freeman.

Rhodes, N., & Wood, W. (1992). Self-esteem and intelligence affect influenceability: The mediating role of message reception. *Psychological Bulletin*, *111*, 156–171.

Rucker, D. D., & Petty, R. E. (2004). When resistance is futile: Consequences of failed counterarguing for attitude certainty. *Journal of Personality and Social Psychology, 86,* 219–235.

Sagarin, B. J., Cialdini, R. B., Rice, W. E., & Serna, S. B. (2002). Dispelling the illusion of invulnerability: The motivations and mechanisms of resistance to persuasion. *Journal of Personality and Social Psychology, 83,* 526–541.

Sovern, H. (2004, May). *A social enigma: Investigating the pervasiveness of urban legends.* Poster presented at the Midwestern Psychological Association's annual meeting, Chicago.

Tormala, Z. L., & Petty, R. E. (2002). What doesn't kill me makes me stronger: The effects of resisting persuasion on attitude certainty. *Journal of Personality and Social Psychology, 83,* 1298–1313.

Wood, W., & Quinn, J. M. (2003). Forewarned and forearmed? Two meta-analytic syntheses of forewarnings of influence appeals. *Psychological Bulletin, 129,* 119–138.

Zuwerink, J. R., & Devine, P. G. (1996). Attitude importance and resistance to persuasion: It's not just the thought that counts. *Journal of Personality and Social Psychology, 70,* 931–944.

Author Index

Subject Index